THE WAY WE WERE

First published
in the United Kingdom in 2018 by

Dewi Lewis Publishing
8, Broomfield Road, Heaton Moor
Stockport SK4 4ND, England
www.dewilewis.com

ISBN: 978-1-911306-40-5

Design: Dewi Lewis Publishing
Print: EBS, Verona, Italy

MY BRITISH ARCHIVE

The Way We Were: 1968-1983

Homer Sykes

Dewi Lewis Publishing

For my birth father, Homer Warwick Sykes (1909-1948); a keen and serious amateur photographer, who died tragically in an accident in Shanghai, China before I was born. He left no possessions. However, in the mid 1950s two trunks of his belongings, including three photo albums, turned up at a garage sale in California. They were bought and some of the contents returned to my mother, who had, by then, remarried and was living in Birmingham, England. The photo albums covered his travels in the Middle East, India and North Africa.

My stepfather, J.J. Sykes (1896-1970) who gave me his Ihagee Parvola camera that fitted neatly into a leather tobacco pouch and let me build a darkroom in my bathroom in our family home.

My mother, Helen Elsie Sykes (1916-1974) who bought me my first copy of *Creative Camera Owner*. She also saved copies of *Life, Look, Town* and *The Sunday Times* magazines for me to read when I got home from boarding school. And, in 1968, she gave me *Photographs by Henri Cartier-Bresson*.

INTRODUCTION

I have been documenting Britain for fifty years, it's where I grew up, it's the country I know and love. This book is not supposed to be a chronicle or a comprehensive visual account of the social history of the period, but it is a personal view of 'life' that I encountered. Some may consider the content London-centric; it is, but that's where I've lived.

In 1968 I took my first serious photographs. I was a first year photography student at LCP – the London College of Printing and Graphic Arts. Reading copies of *Creative Camera* magazine, edited by Bill Jay, I came across the work of the young American street photographers, Garry Winogrand, Bruce Davidson and the Swiss-American Robert Frank. And, of course, the great humanist Magnum photographers.

I had moved to London. I was surprised and excited by what I saw. I became aware of a social reality and of the political landscape, and I decided to document those aspects that interested me. It was the tail end of the swinging Sixties, the turbulent Seventies were awaiting. My photographs became narrative led as I began to understand the many contradictions that permeate British life; 'the have and have nots', the 'top hat, cloth cap' characteristics of society that were still very present at the time. I was intrigued by the way people interrelated or didn't, what they wore – their dress code marking them out as belonging to a certain class or aspiring to belong to an alternative tribe. I was a flâneur, I hung around on street corners, and made friends with strangers and tried to get myself invited back into their homes, clubs and workplaces to make more intimate photographs that revealed their lives.

Throughout this period I covered numerous weekend demonstrations that pitted one political class, one section of society against another and the government. But always I attempted to get behind the more obvious news image; I was looking for other moments, spontaneous juxtapositions that gave depth and understanding to the demonstrator's predicaments.

This was the midpoint in Prime Minister Harold Wilson's 1966 Labour Party's term in government. Over the next fifteen years the country was led by Edward Heath, Wilson once more and James Callaghan. In 1979 Margaret Thatcher, a Tory, became Britain's first woman Prime Minister, she was to usher in another, entirely different era; Thatcherism.

Homer Sykes
London, 2018

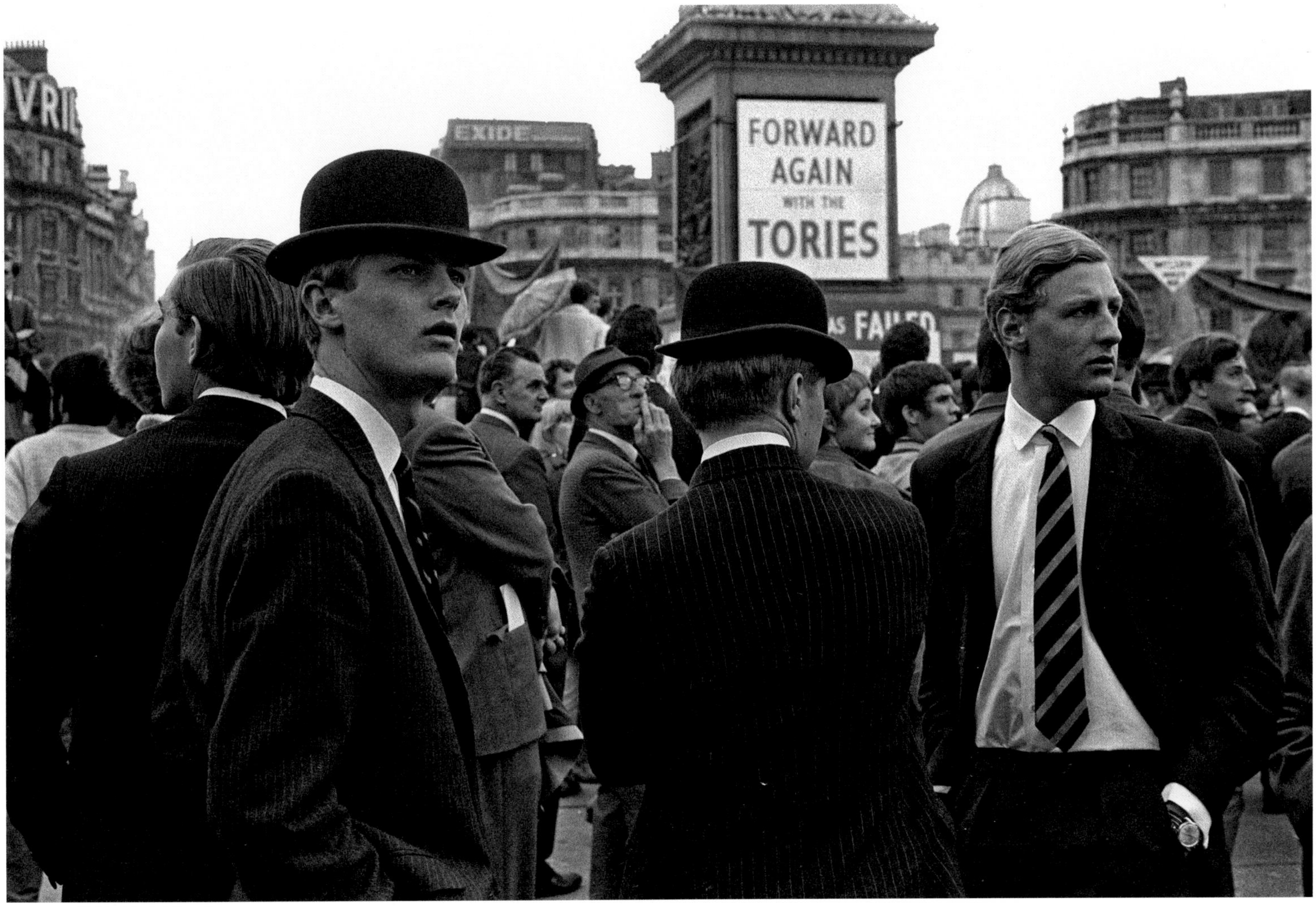

Westminster, London. 1969

Bowler hatted, suited and wearing their old school ties, four young city gents attend a Conservative Party 'Forward Again with the Tories' rally in Trafalgar Square in preparation for the 1970 General Election. Edward Heath went on to win for the Tories with a surprise, but small, majority.

The bowler hat had once been popular with the working classes; it was their hat of choice. During the 20th century it became synonymous with upper middle class men working in the City of London. By the mid 1980s it had all but disappeared.

Whitechapel, London. 1975

Great Eastern Buildings, Peabody Housing Estate. A resident in her living room covers her eyes, head in hand, exhausted after a hard day's work. She is wearing a typical 1970's housecoat, an overall that covered her best clothes and was often worn rather than an apron for housework. Yesterday's empty glass pint milk bottle and today's fresh pinta stand on the crowded table while the tea brews. On the walls are photographs of her daughter's wedding and a large heart-shaped decoration. These crumbling blocks of flats began to be torn down during the mid 1970s.

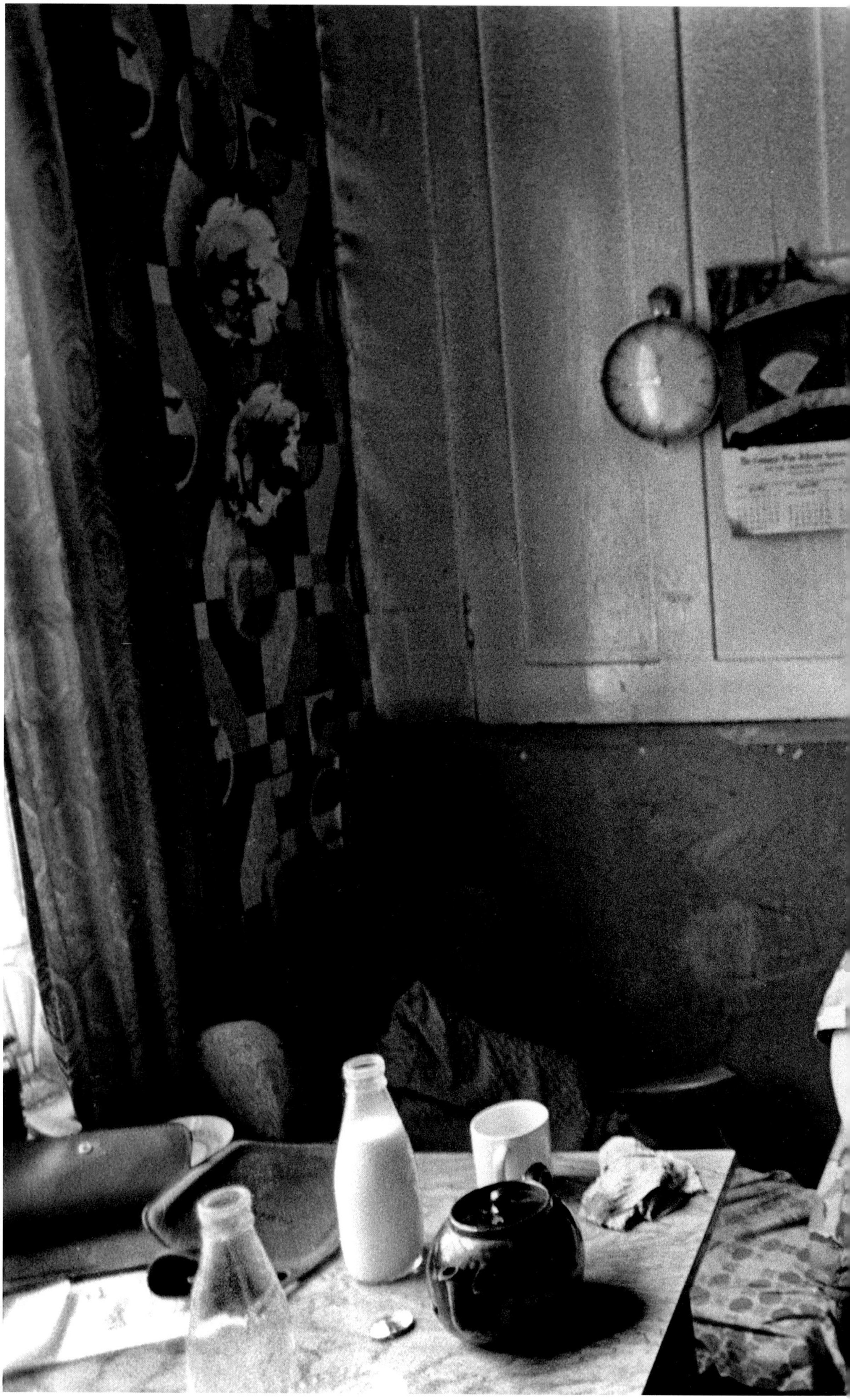

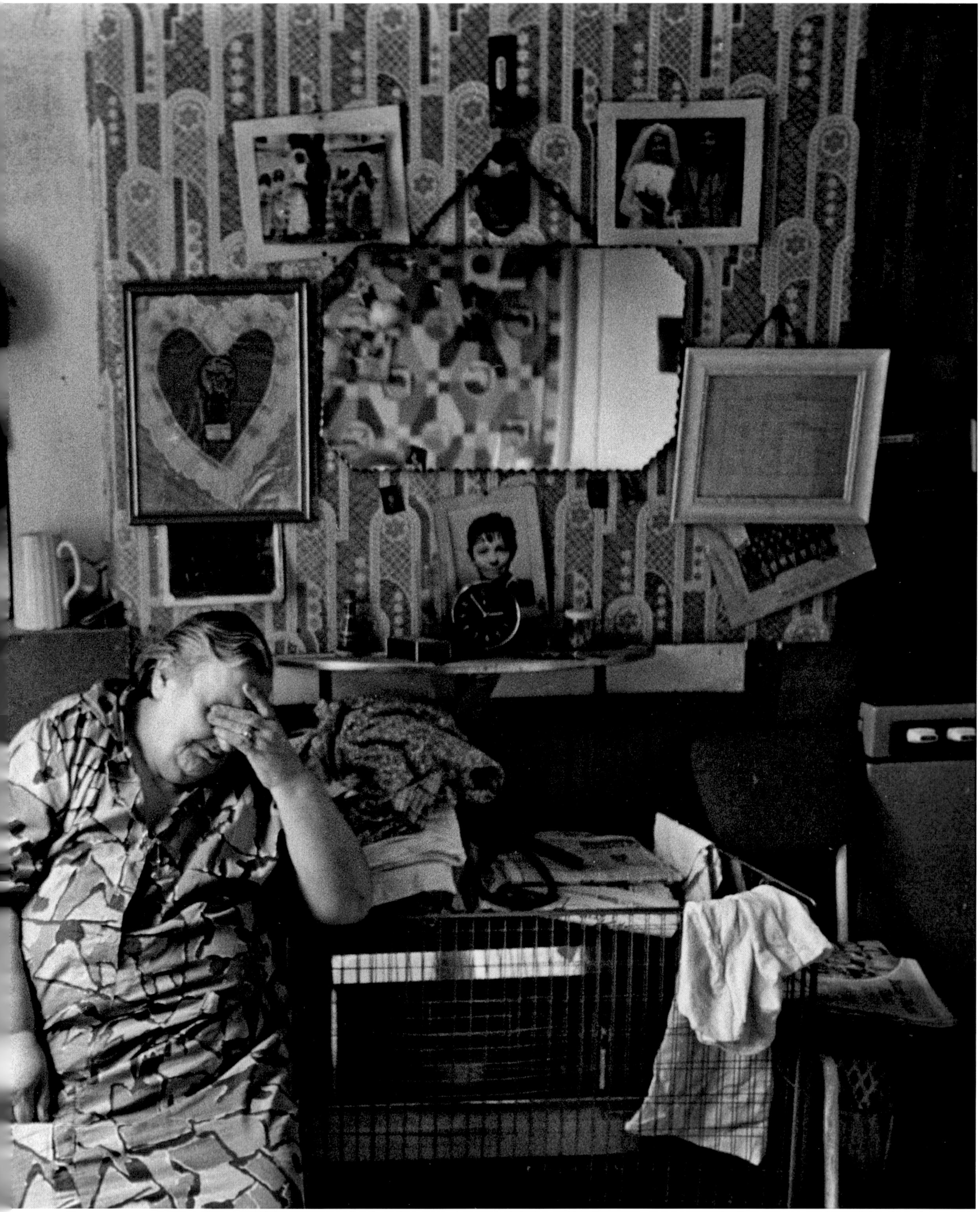

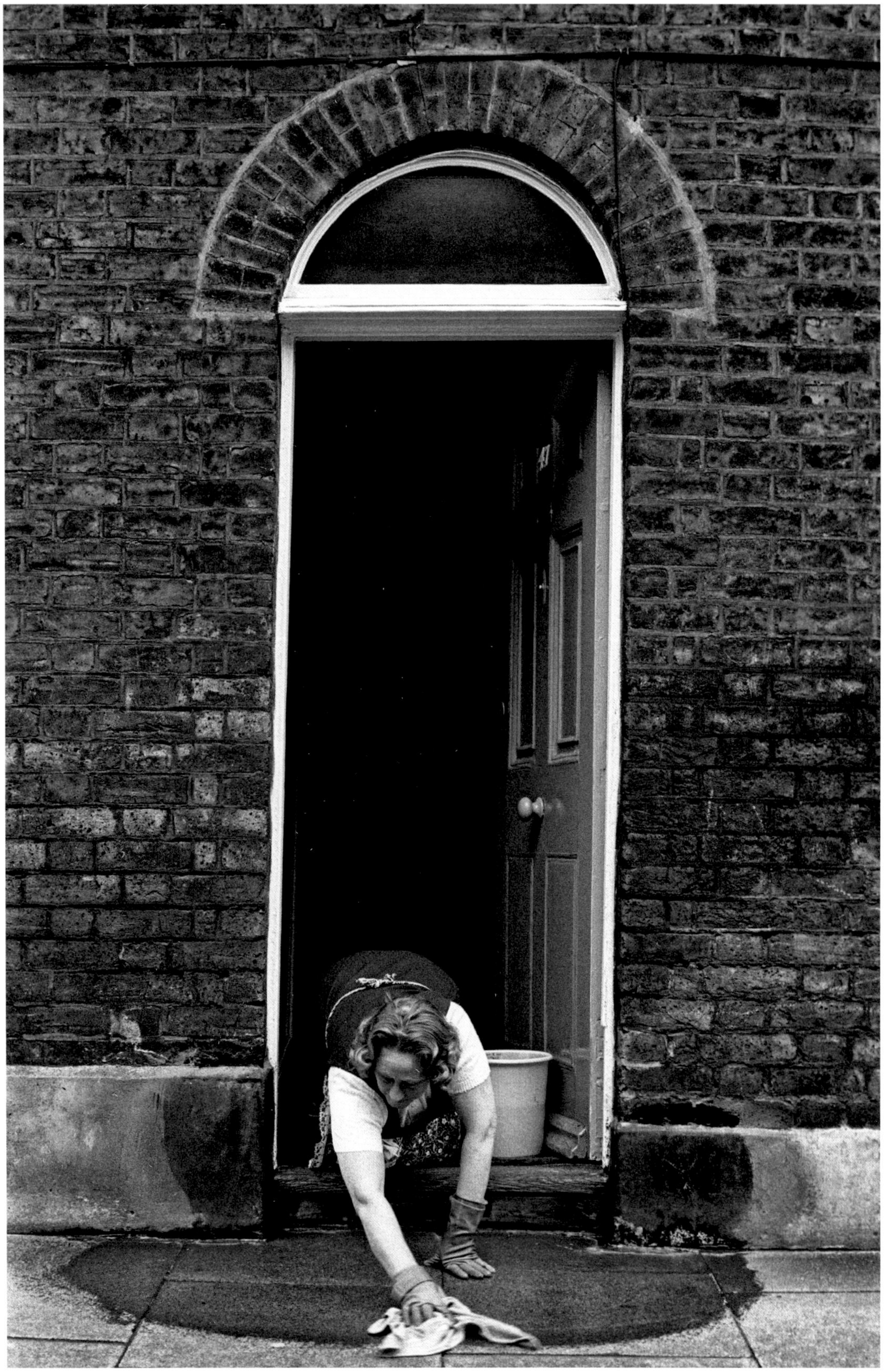

Waterloo, London. 1975

A house-proud resident washes her front door step and pavement, creating a separation from the everyday grime and the virtuous cleanliness of the inside. Roupell Street was first developed by John Roupell in the 1820s. Artisans and skilled workers originally occupied this Georgian terrace of nineteenth century cottages in the heart of Southwark. It was one of several streets developed by the Roupell family who had made their money from lead-smelting and scrap metal. The properties in their Lambeth estate passed into private ownership in 1976.

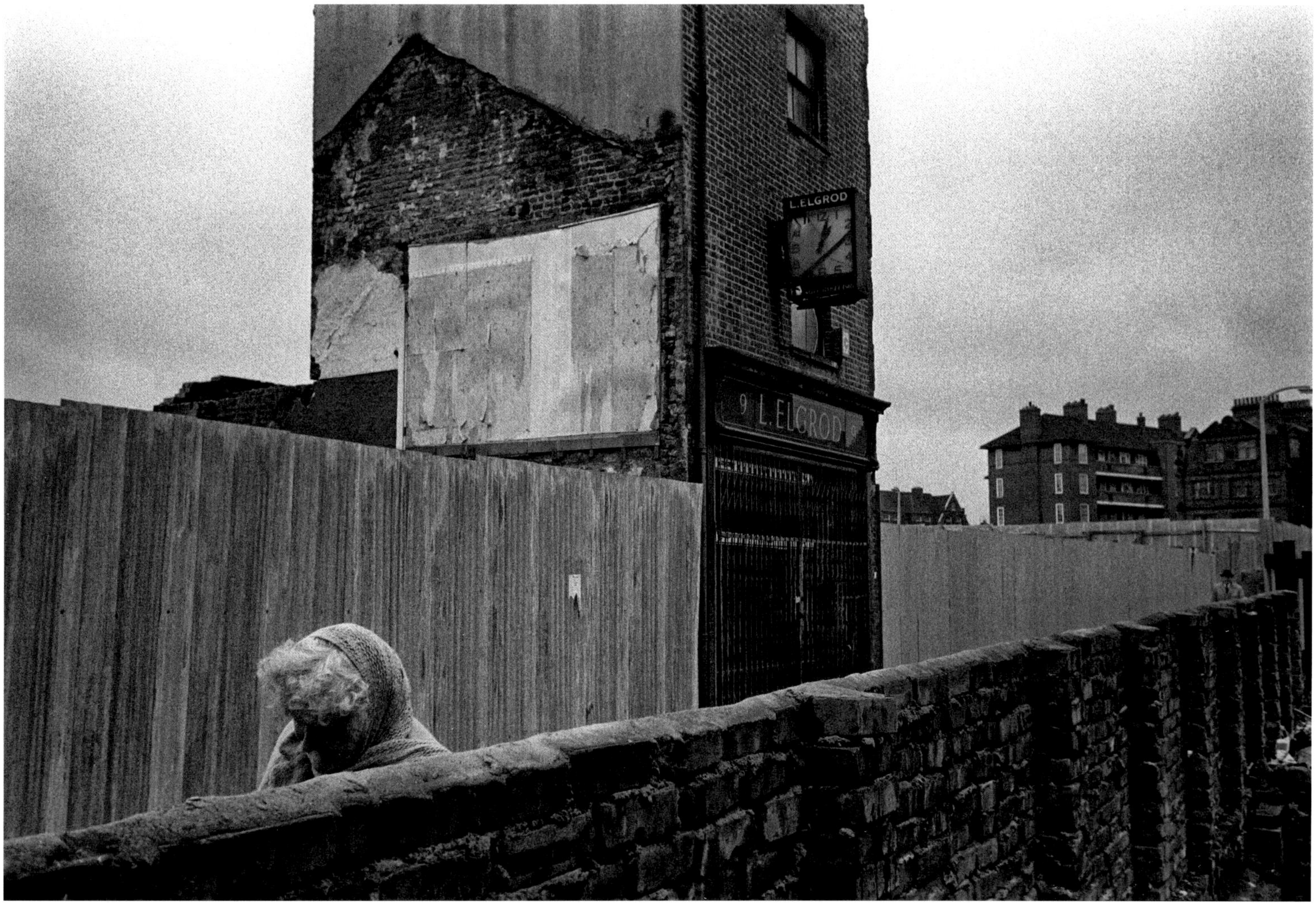

Whitechapel, London. 1975

In an alley off Whitechapel High Street, head bowed against the cold, an elderly resident passes the shop of L. Elgrod watchmaker and jeweller, which now stands alone defying the property developer and his demolition team.

Fulham, London. 1972

A working class family have just finished breakfast; this is their kitchen. The boy is having his face washed in the butler kitchen sink. They don't have their own bathroom but share one with other families in the multi-occupancy house. The kitchen table is not big enough for everyone to sit around. Mother uses the small pull down sideboard on the extreme right when they all eat together. Both parents are in work, the father is a jobbing builder and the mother a charlady for wealthy Chelsea familes.

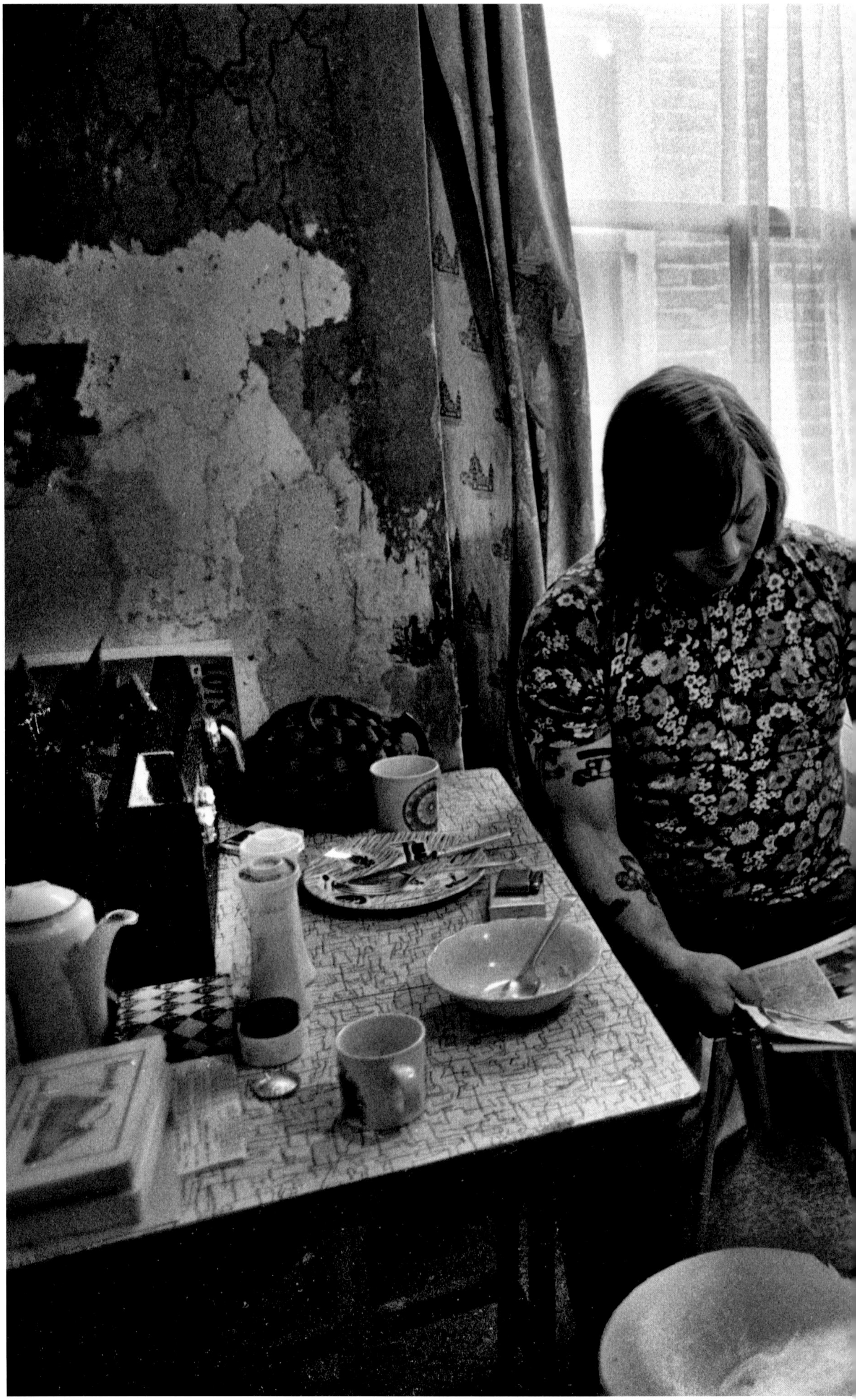

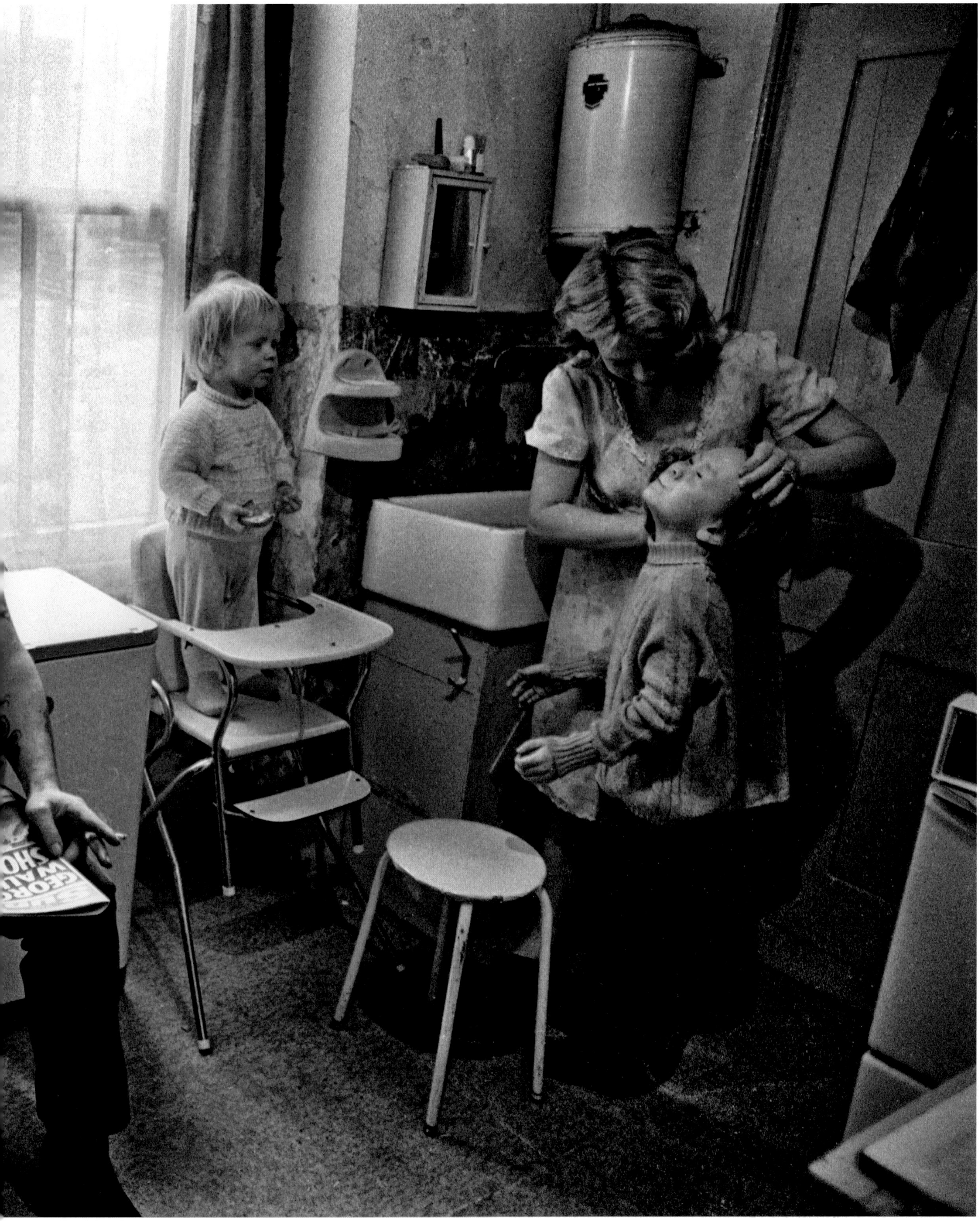

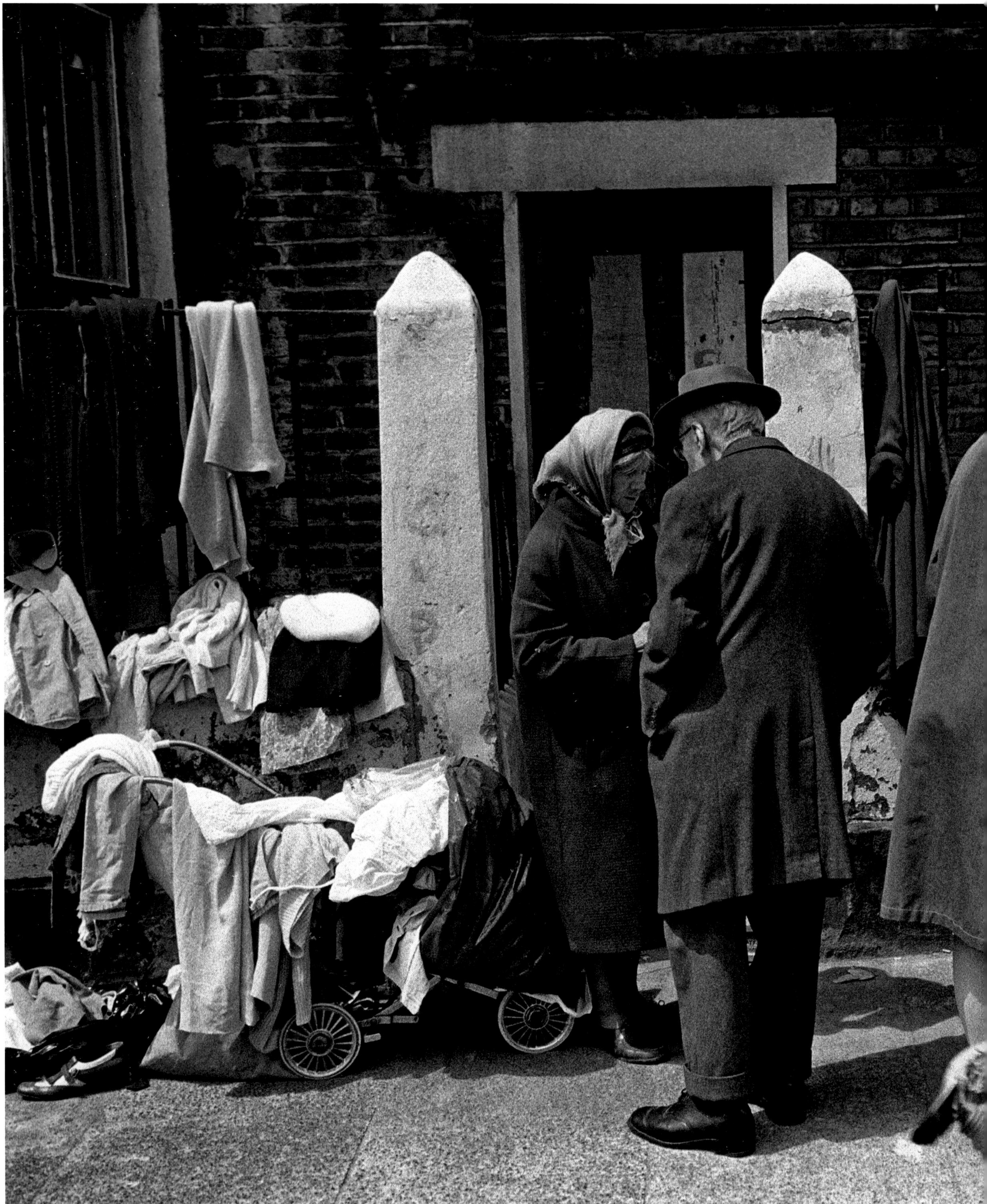

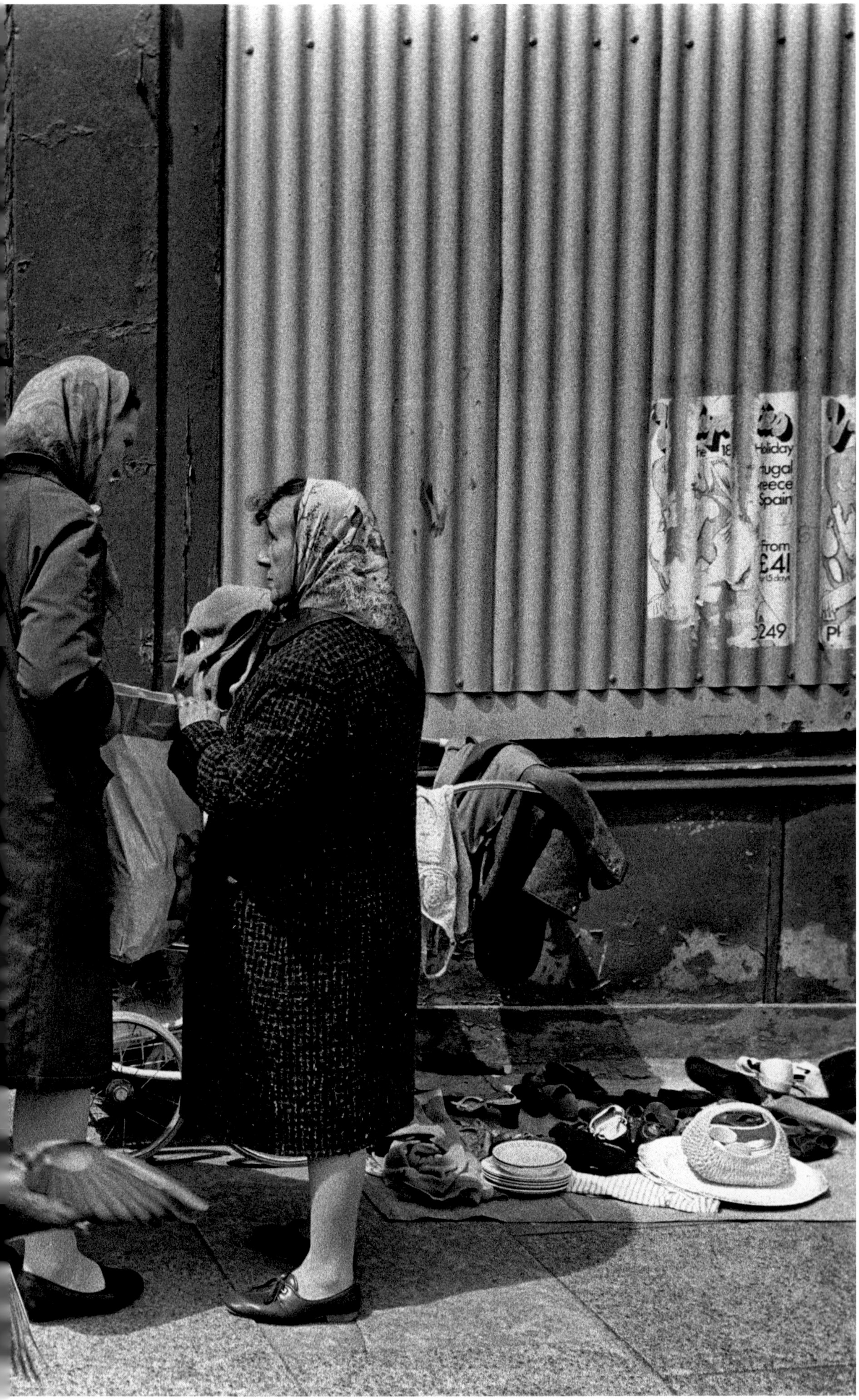

Whitechapel, London. 1972

Unemployed women sell old clothes and bric-a-brac from prams to supplement their meagre living. One wears her headscarf over her hat to keep out the cold.

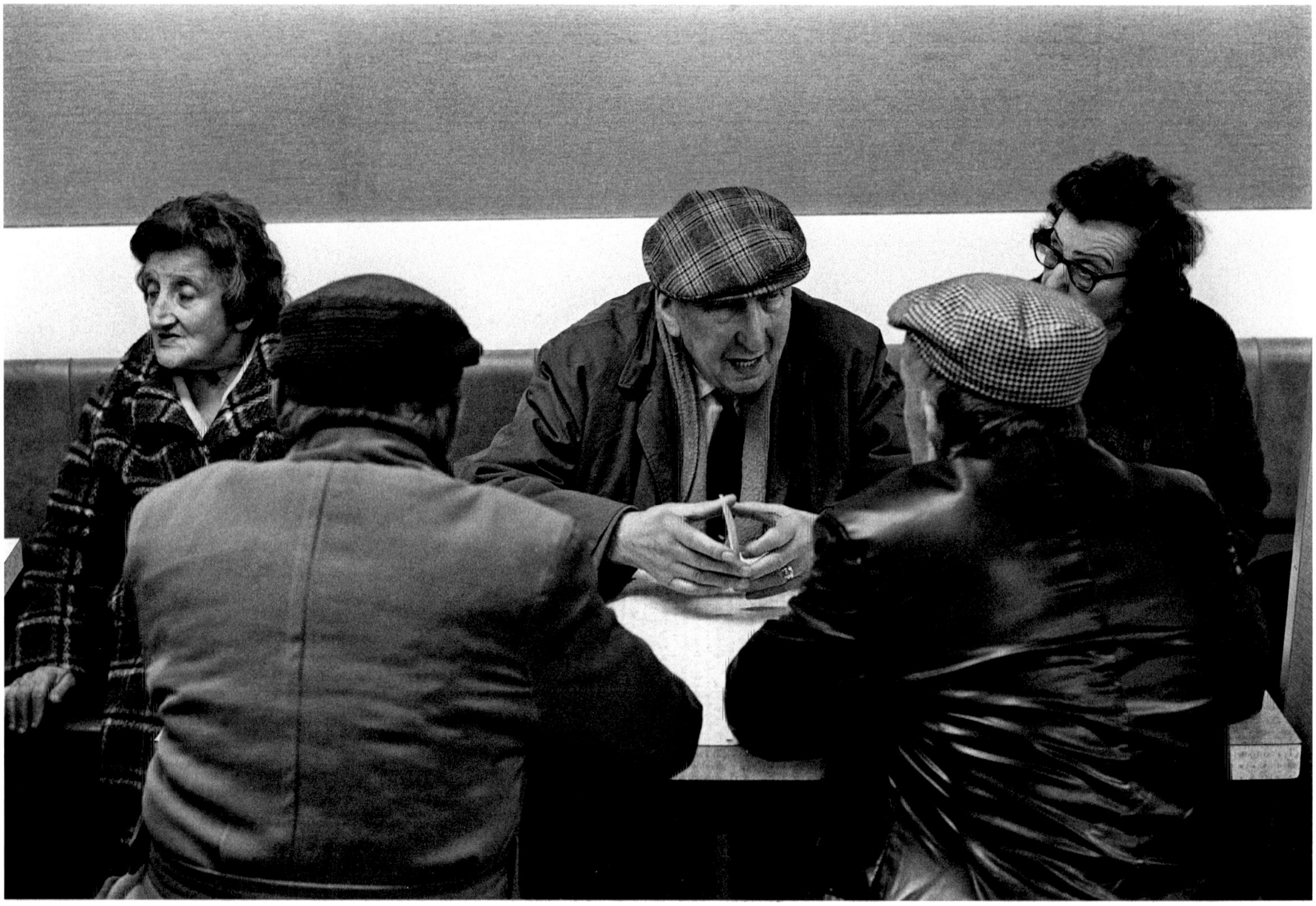

Whitechapel, London. 1974

In a café on Whitechapel High Street, a group of friends discuss life. Whitechapel has always been a melting pot. Since the 18th century these streets have been home to Huguenots, Jews, Asian and African communities, all fleeing religious persecution, war and famine in their own homelands.

Whitechapel, London. 1974

The proprietor in chef's hat and apron, buttoned up to his jacket, stands outside his greasy spoon Dinners café in Brick Lane waiting for lunchtime customers. Chalked up on the blackboard is the menu: almost everything is with chips. Fish & chips 27p, Liver & chips 30p, Vienna steak & chips 28p, Egg & chips 18p, Hamburger steak & 2 veg 28p, Sausage egg & chips 26p, 2 egg & chips 26p, 2 sausage & chips 26p, Pork chop & chips 45p, Stewed lamb & 2 veg 30p, Steak pie & 2 veg 30p, and finally, for dessert, Semolina Pudding 6p.

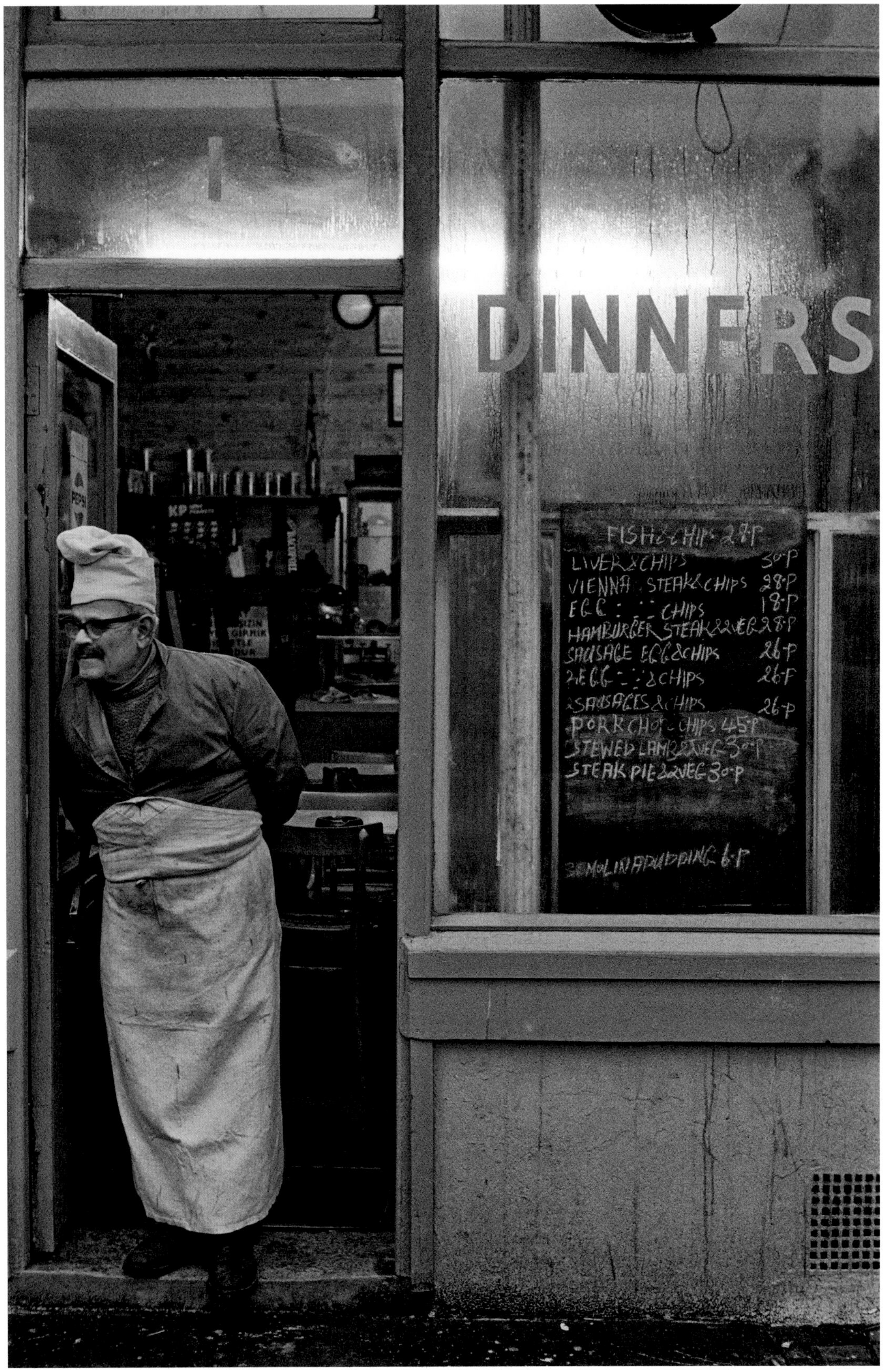

Hackney, London. 1978

Sister Patricia hands out cups of tea from St Saviour's Priory annex, at the time a disused vicarage on the Kingsland Road, while the Priory was being refurbished. St Saviour's Priory is part of the Society of St Margaret founded by John Mason Neale in 1855. The Sisters explore contemporary ways of living the religious life in the community through a balance of prayer and ministry amongst marginalised groups who are in need.

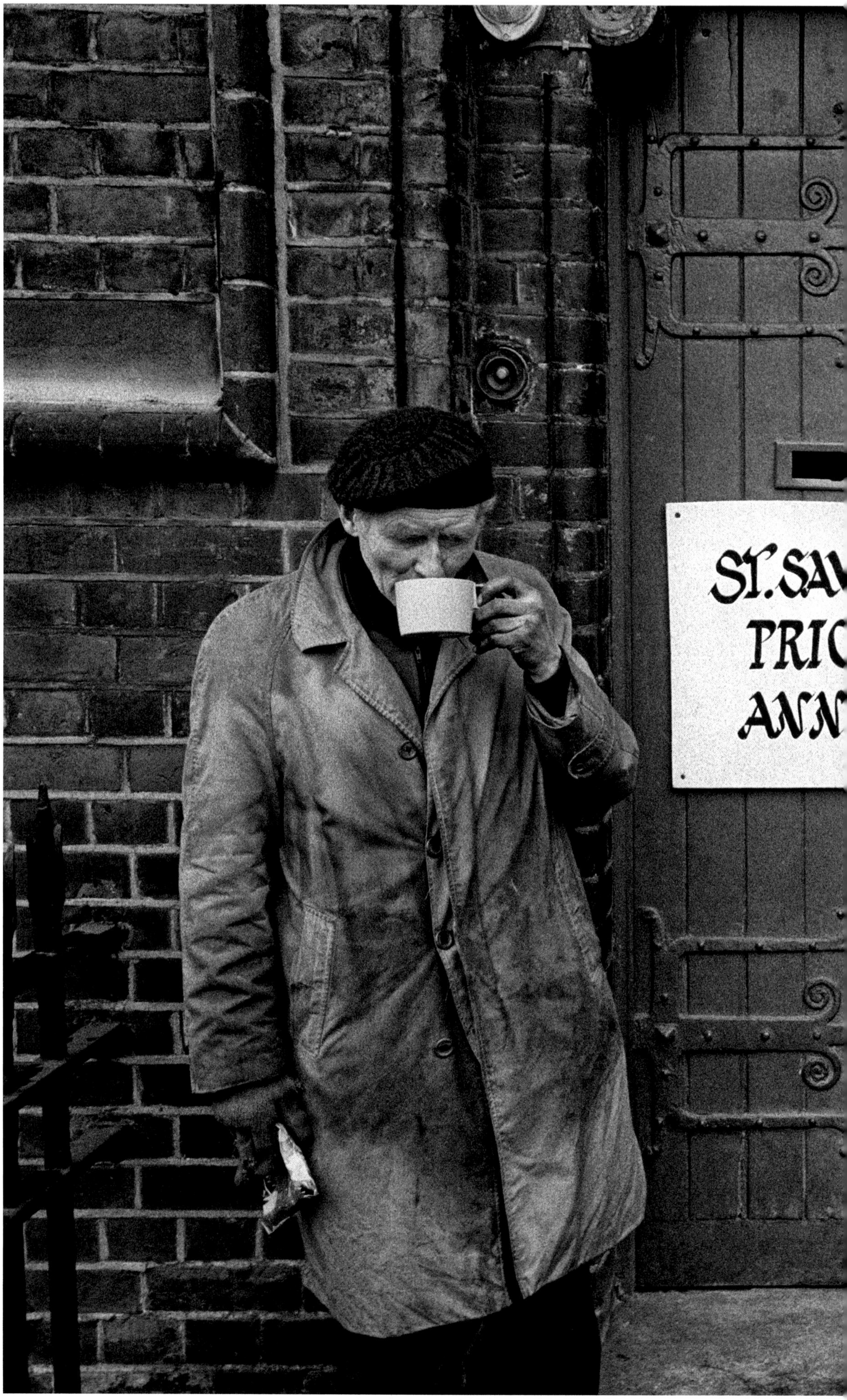

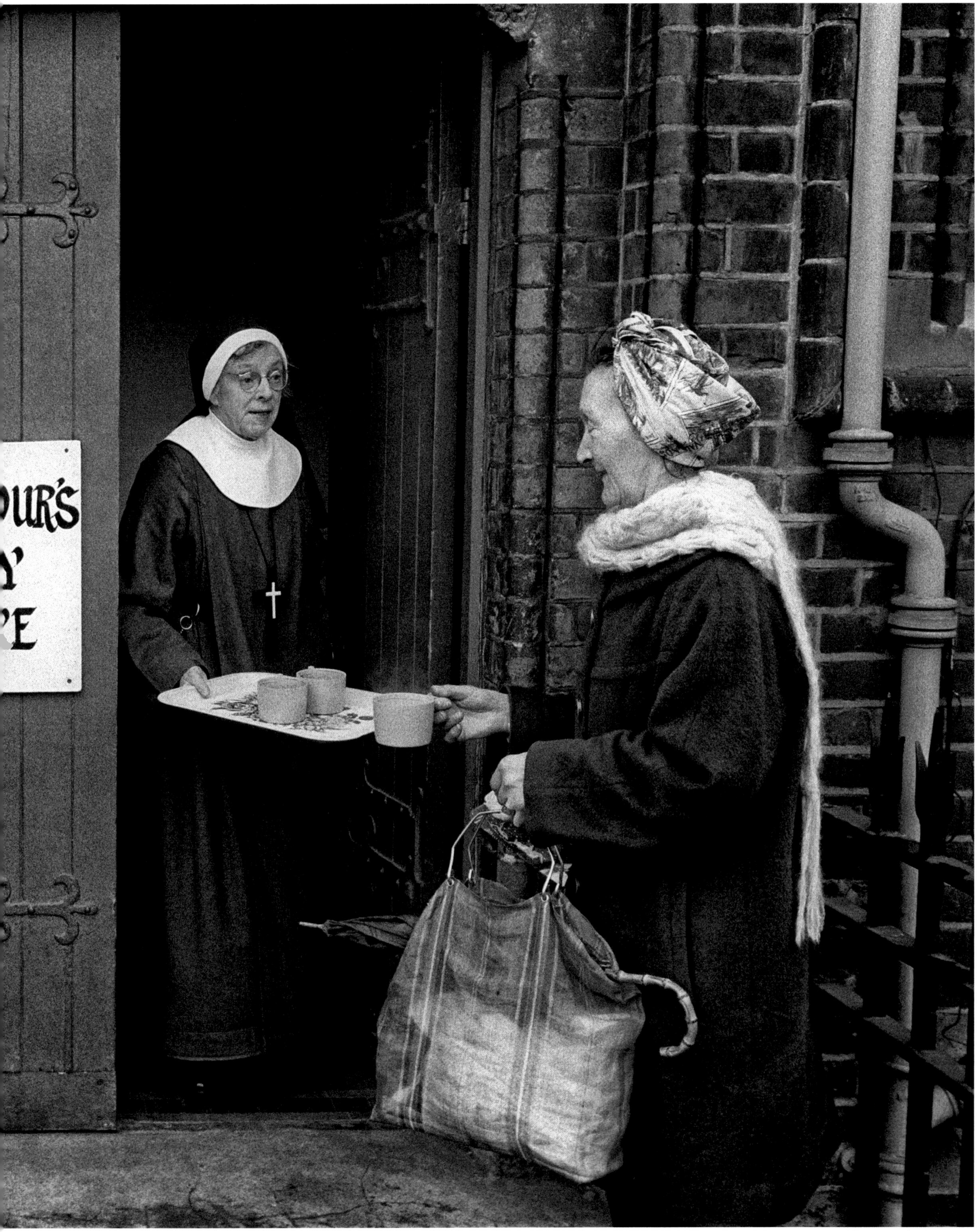

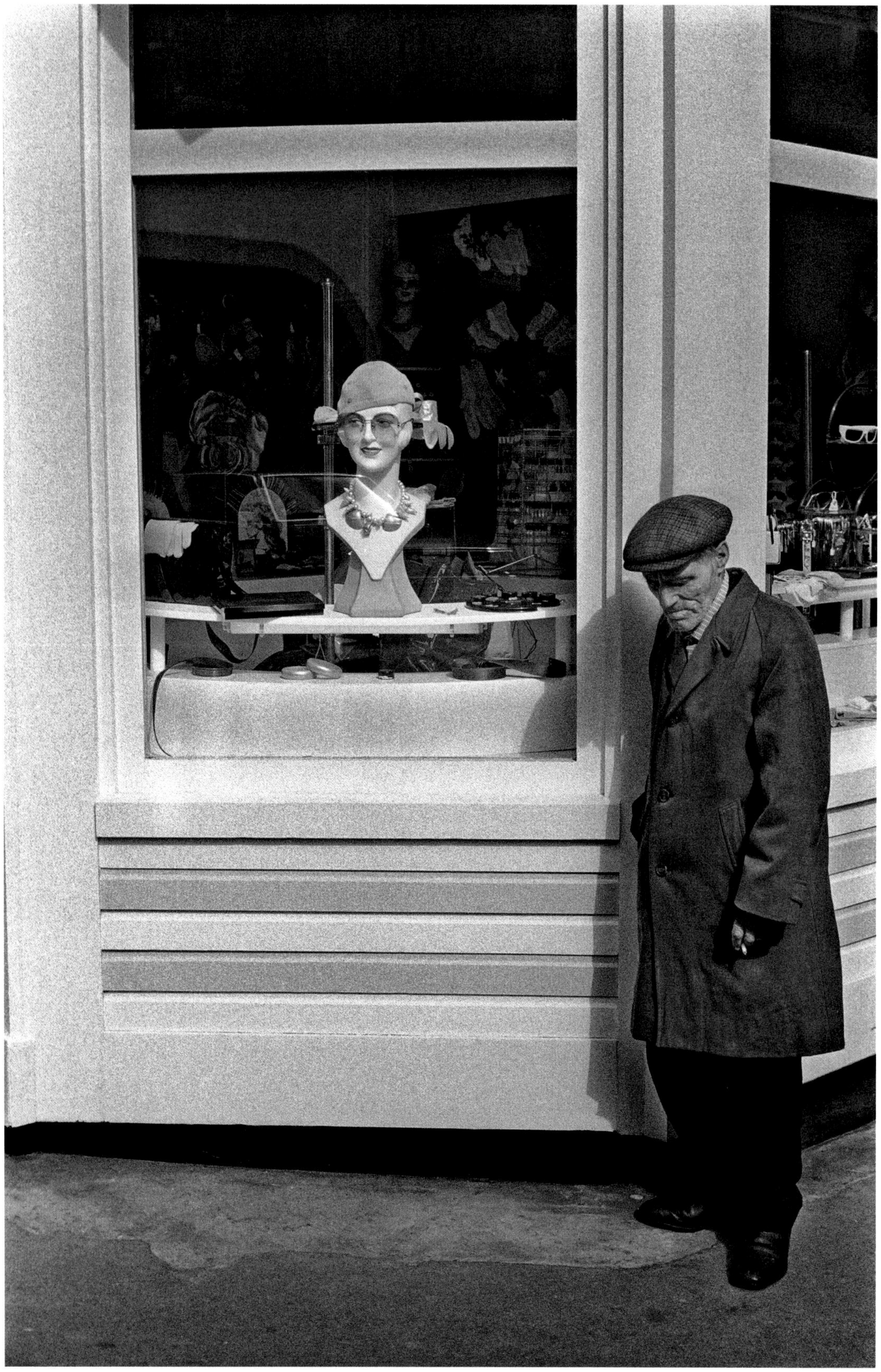

Westminster, London. 1980

A gentleman of the road leans against a newly opened fashion boutique in the recently developed Covent Garden Piazza. This had been London's fruit and vegetable market which was first developed in the 1650s. 330 years later it was transformed into a modern tourist shopping experience.

Whitechapel, London. 1976

Nightfall in Brick Lane at the junction with Sheba Street.

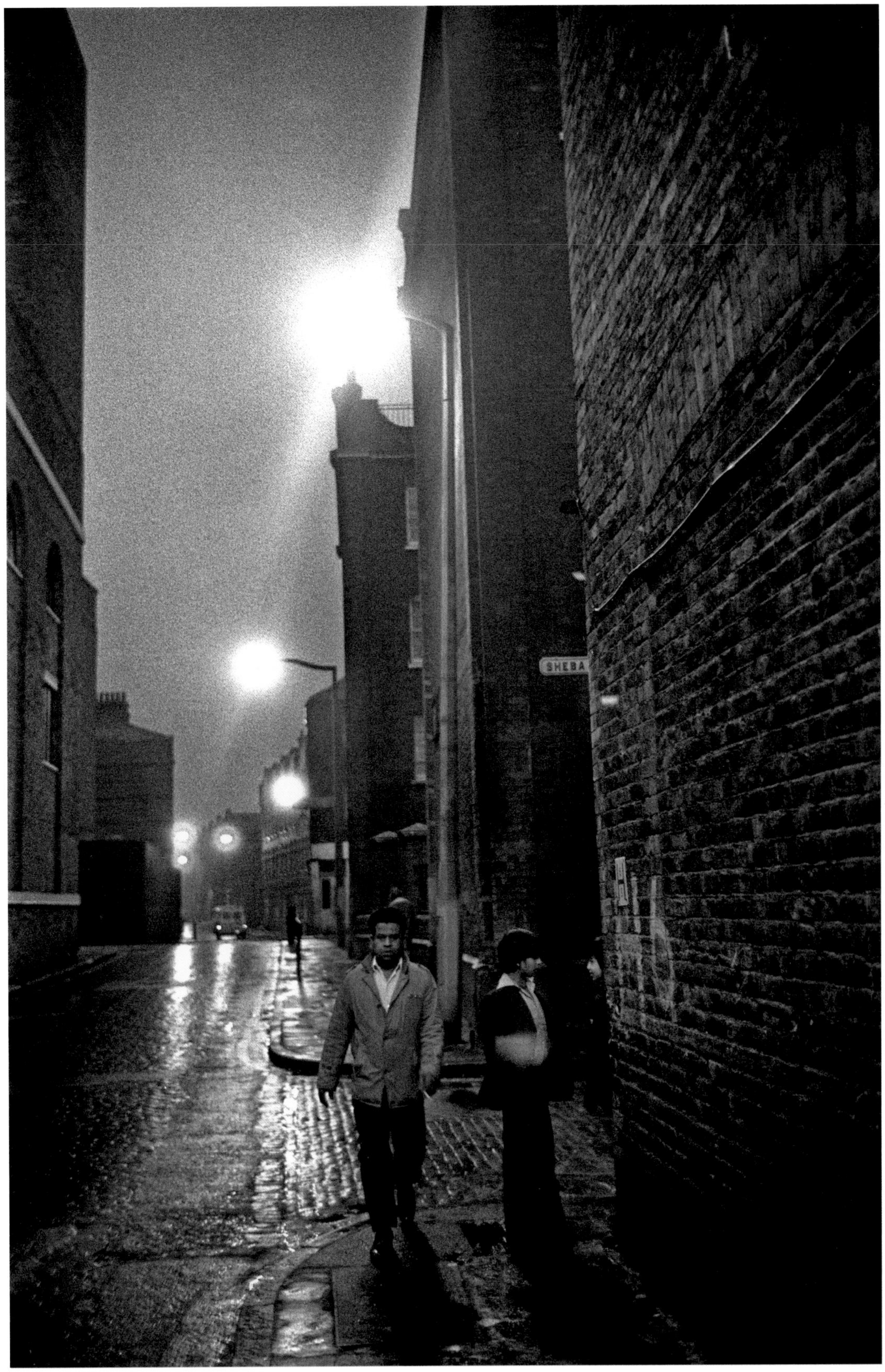

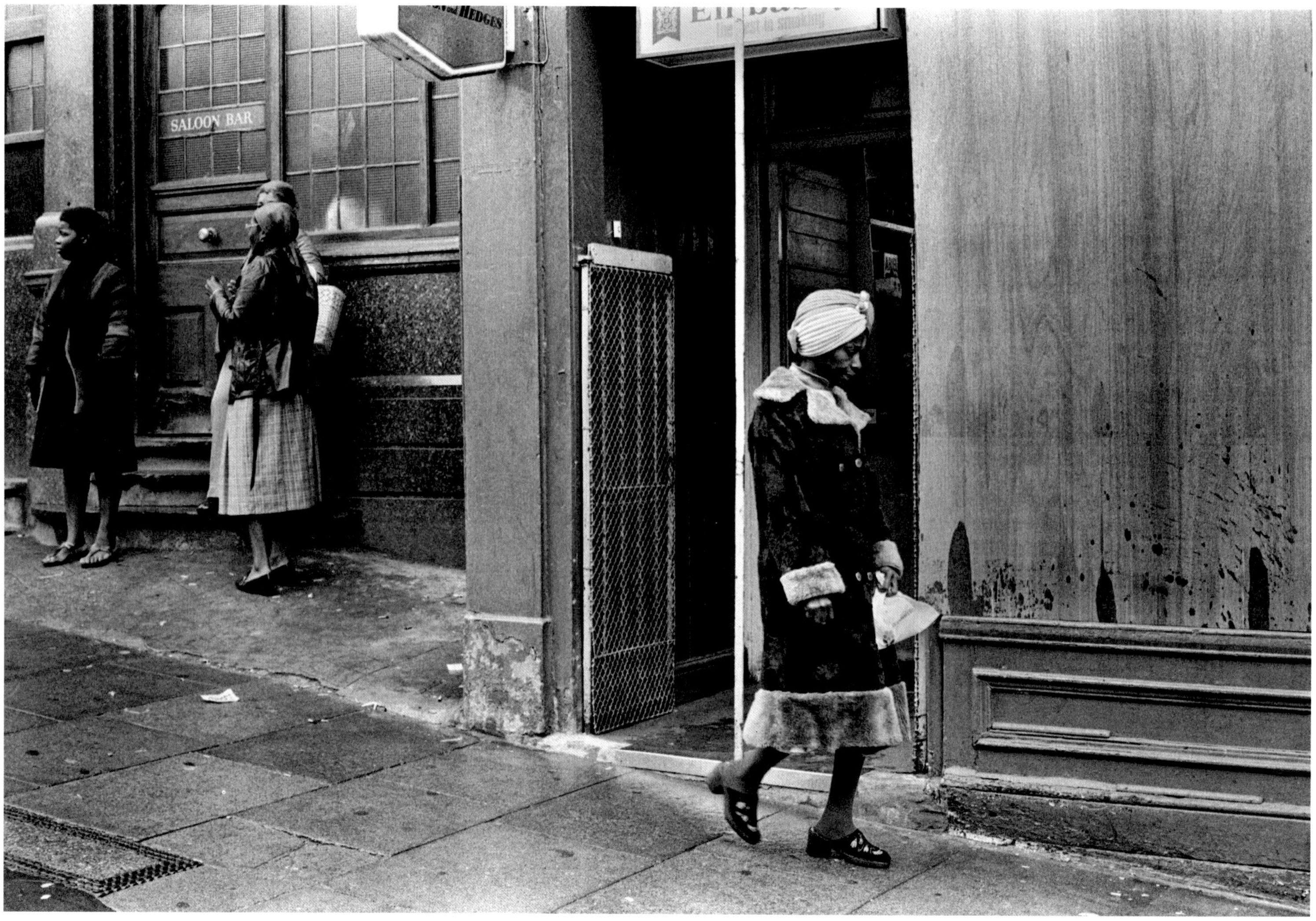

New Cross, London. 1977

A dejected turban-wearing local resident in her fur-trimmed overcoat wanders past boarded up shop windows in New Cross. The Lewisham riots took place on 13th August. 500 members of the National Front had marched from New Cross to Lewisham. Various counter-demonstrations led to violent clashes between the two main groups and between the anti-NF demonstrators and police. 214 people were arrested for obstructing the police, threatening behaviour, assault, possession of an offensive weapon and throwing missiles.

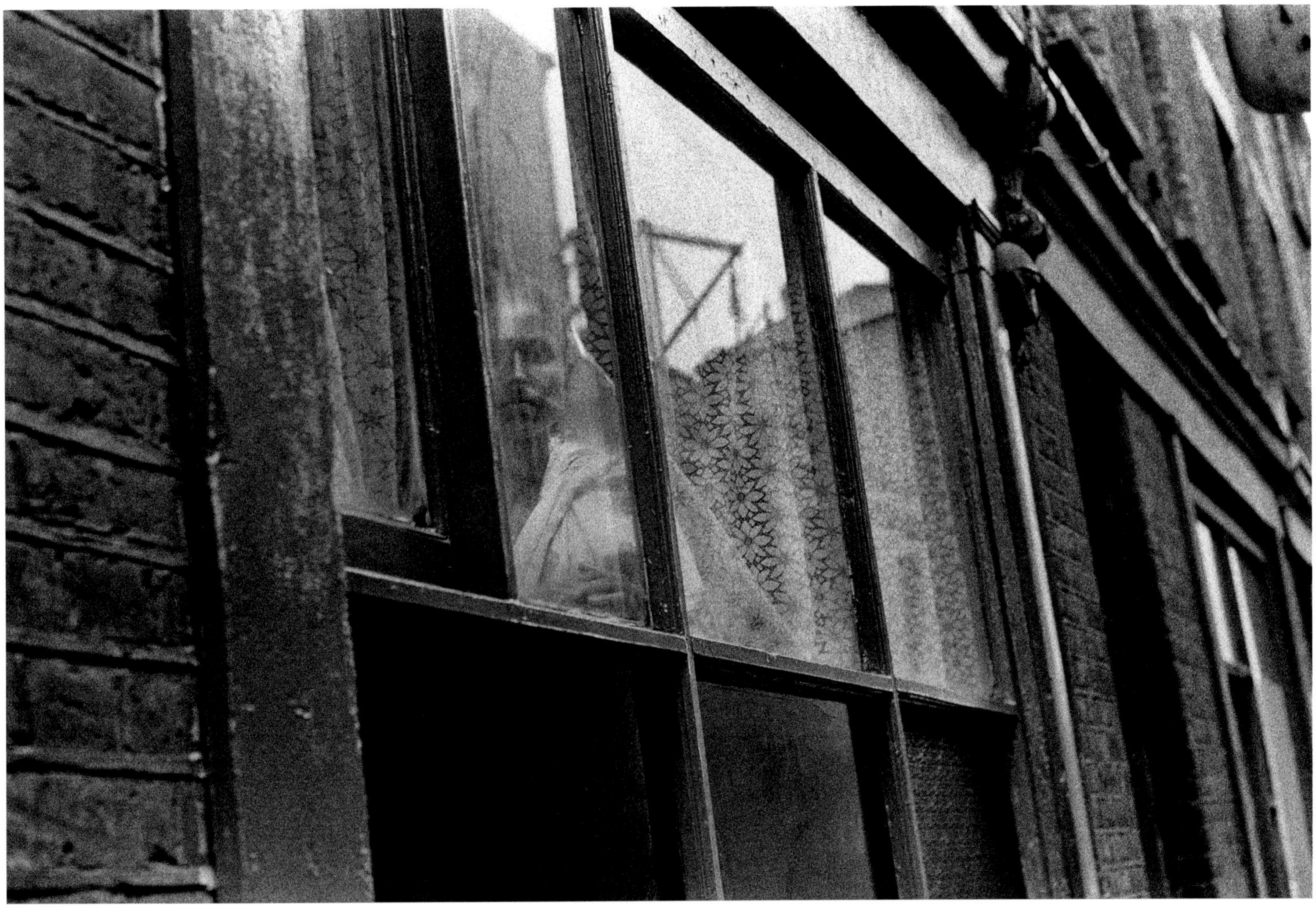

Whitechapel, London. 1978

In a road just off Brick Lane, a lone Asian woman stares out of her flat window. There had been reports in the press that many new immigrants to Britain, and in particular Bangladeshi women who didn't speak English, were being kept under lock and key by their menfolk and rarely allowed out of their homes.

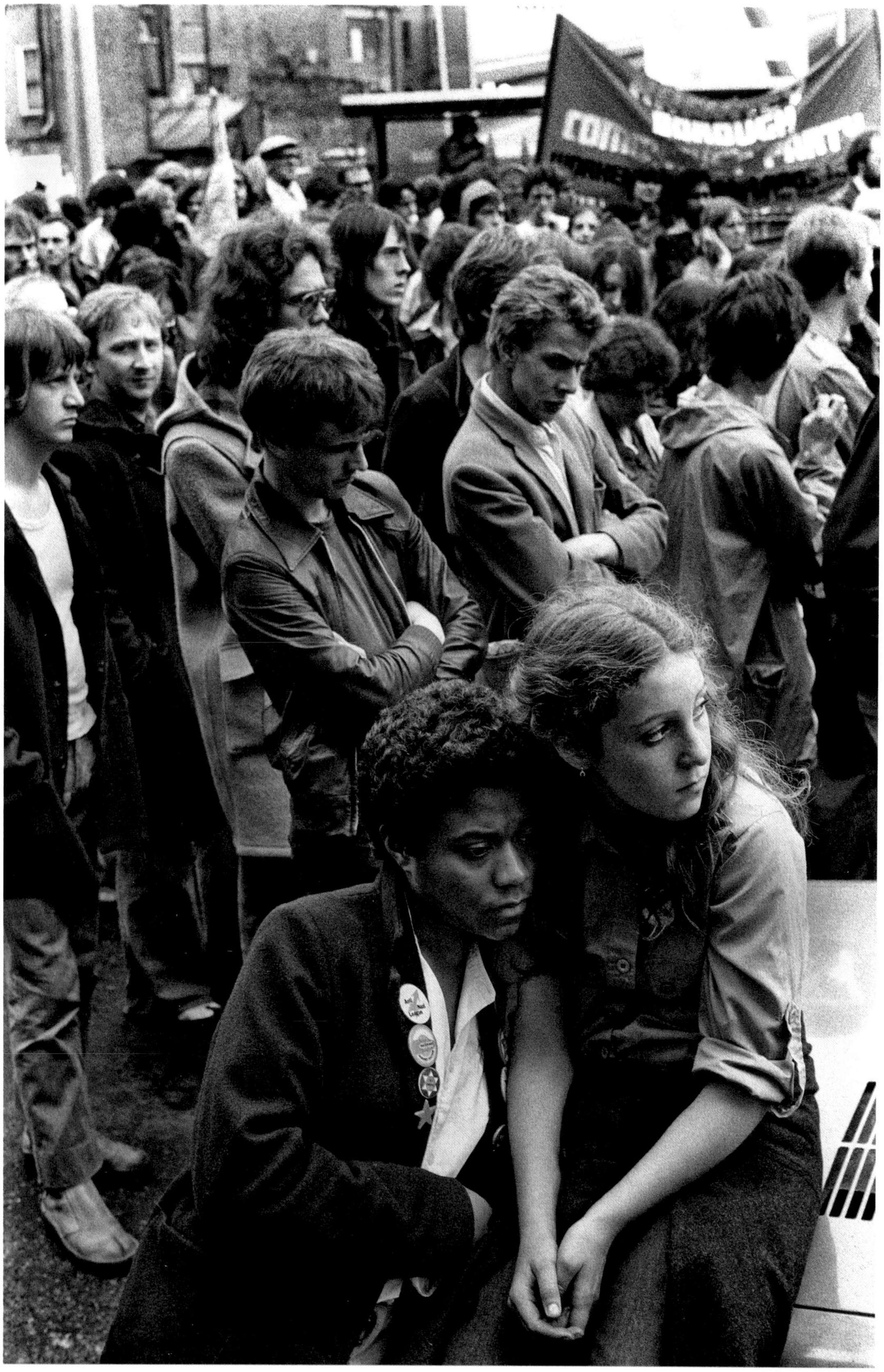

Whitechapel, London. 1978

During the summer, at the junction of Brick Lane and Bethnal Green Road, the Socialist Workers Party organised regular Saturday Anti Nazi League demonstrations against the National Front who, in turn, held their meetings and distributed their newspapers from the same place each Sunday. A young woman wears pin button badges proclaiming, 'Gays Against the Nazis', 'Right to Work', 'Anti Nazi League', 'Skateboard Against Racism', and the Star of David.

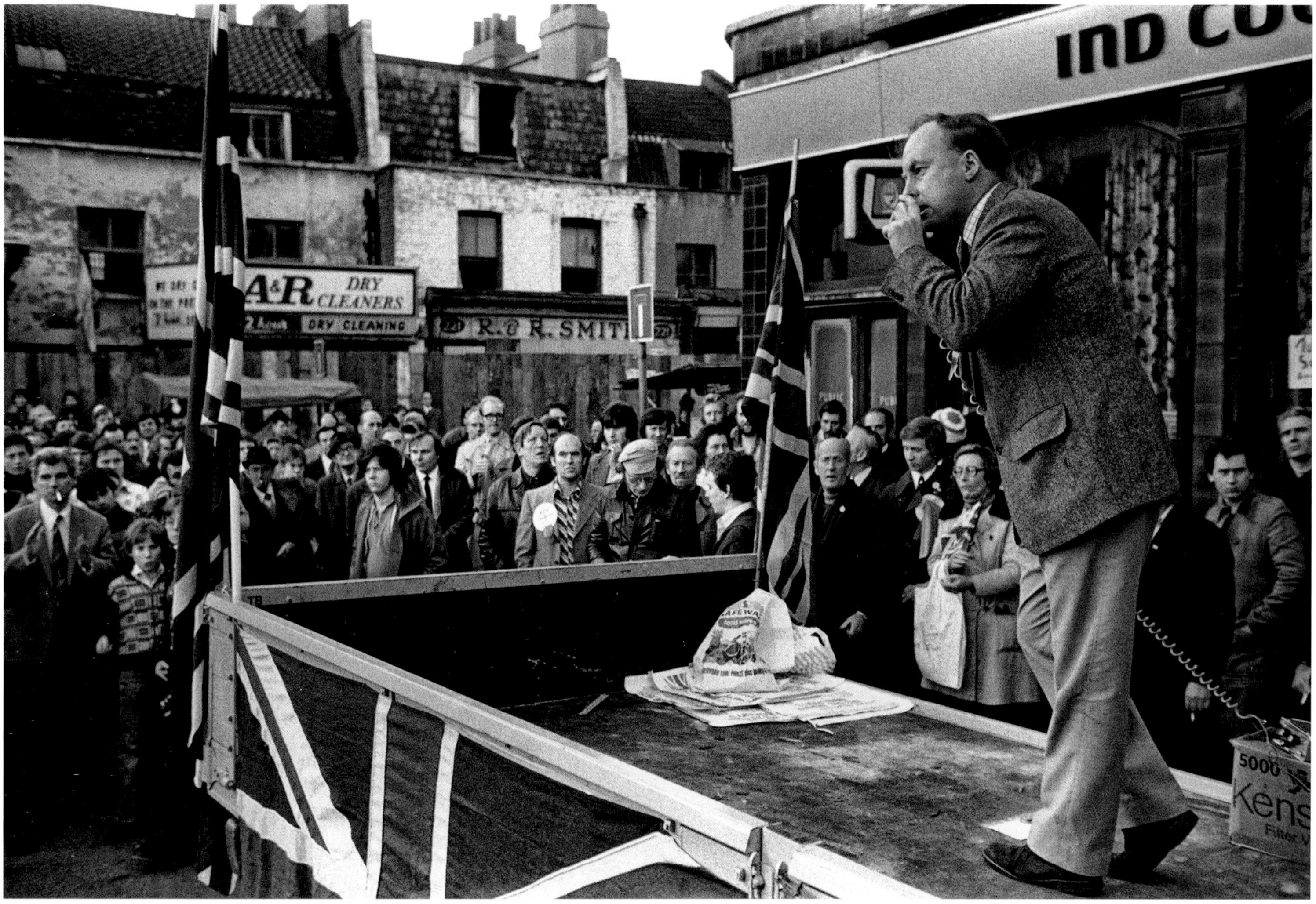

Hoxton, London. 1976

John Tyndall leader of the National Front, a racist anti-immigration party, drums up support from the back of a lorry decked in Union Jack flags at the Saturday Hoxton Street market. His audience is almost exclusive male. By the 1979 General Election, the NF was able to field 303 candidates, polling over 191,000 votes, though it failed to win a single seat in parliament.

Lewisham, London. 1977

Police protect defiant National Front supporters, during the so-called Battle of Lewisham. Some carry printed placards, 'National Front is a Racialist Front. Join the National Front.'

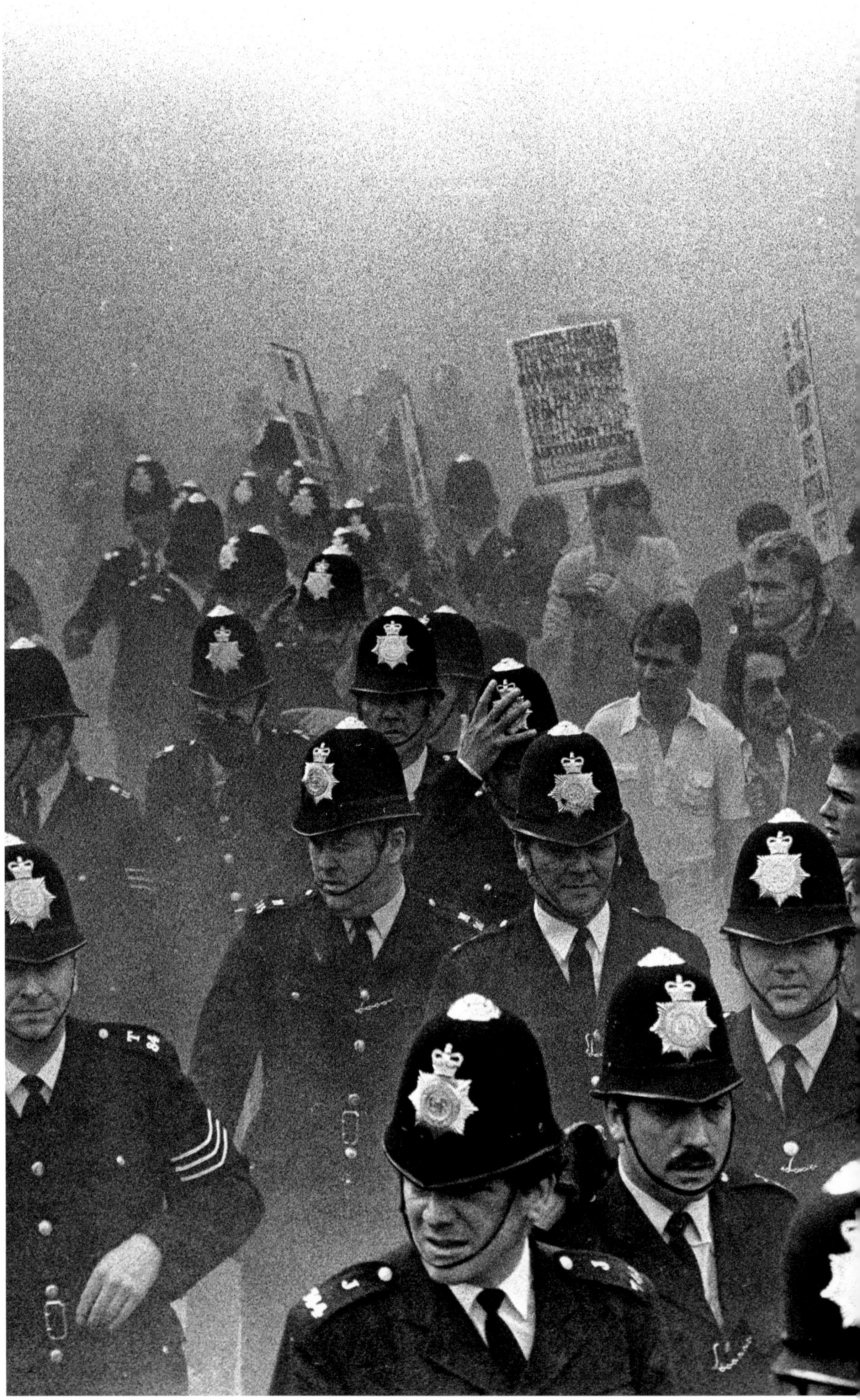

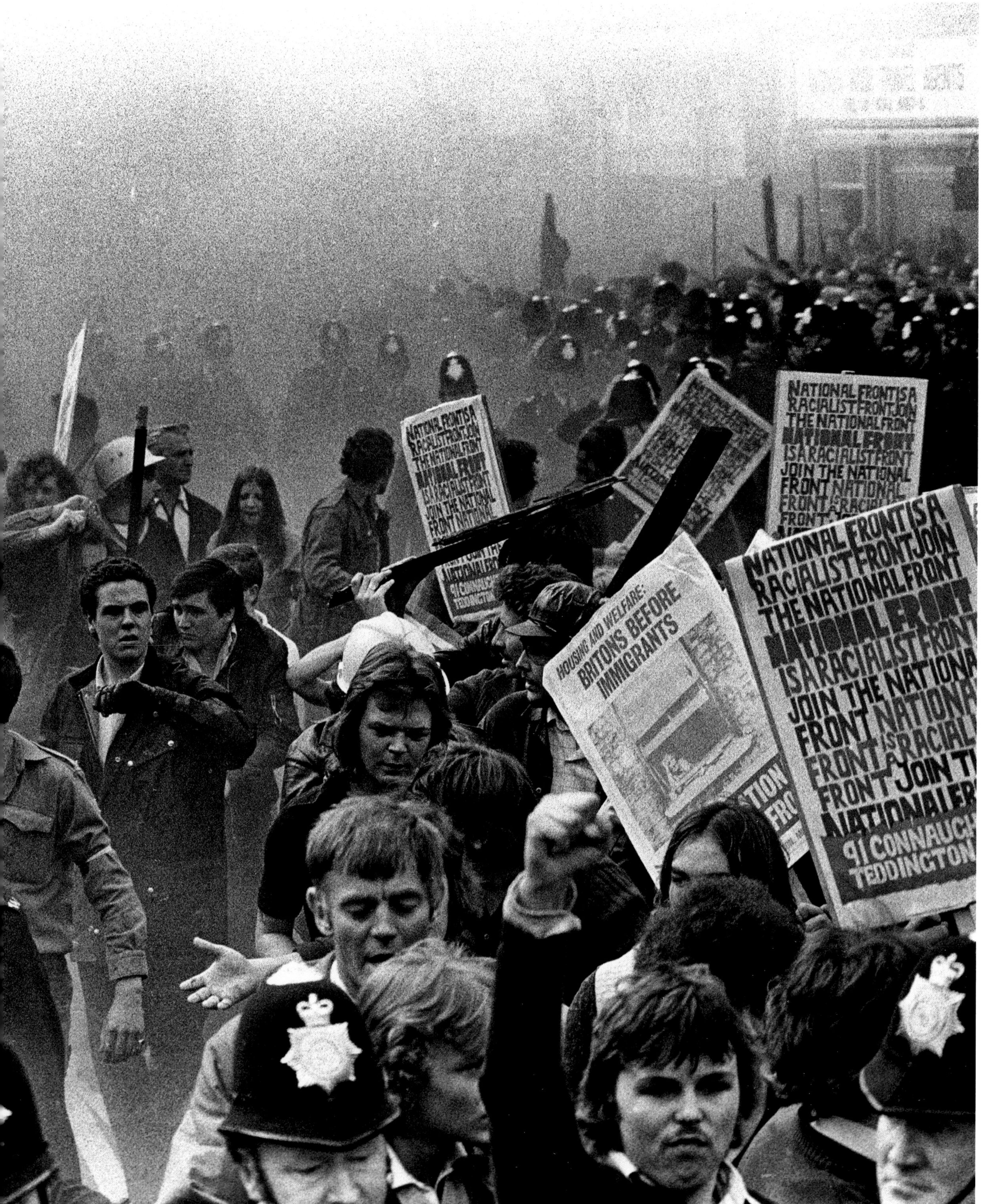
NATIONAL FRONT IS A
RACIALIST FRONT JOIN
THE NATIONAL FRONT
NATIONAL FRONT
IS A RACIALIST FRONT
JOIN THE NATIONAL
HOUSING AND WELFARE:
BRITONS BEFORE
IMMIGRANTS
TEDDINGTON

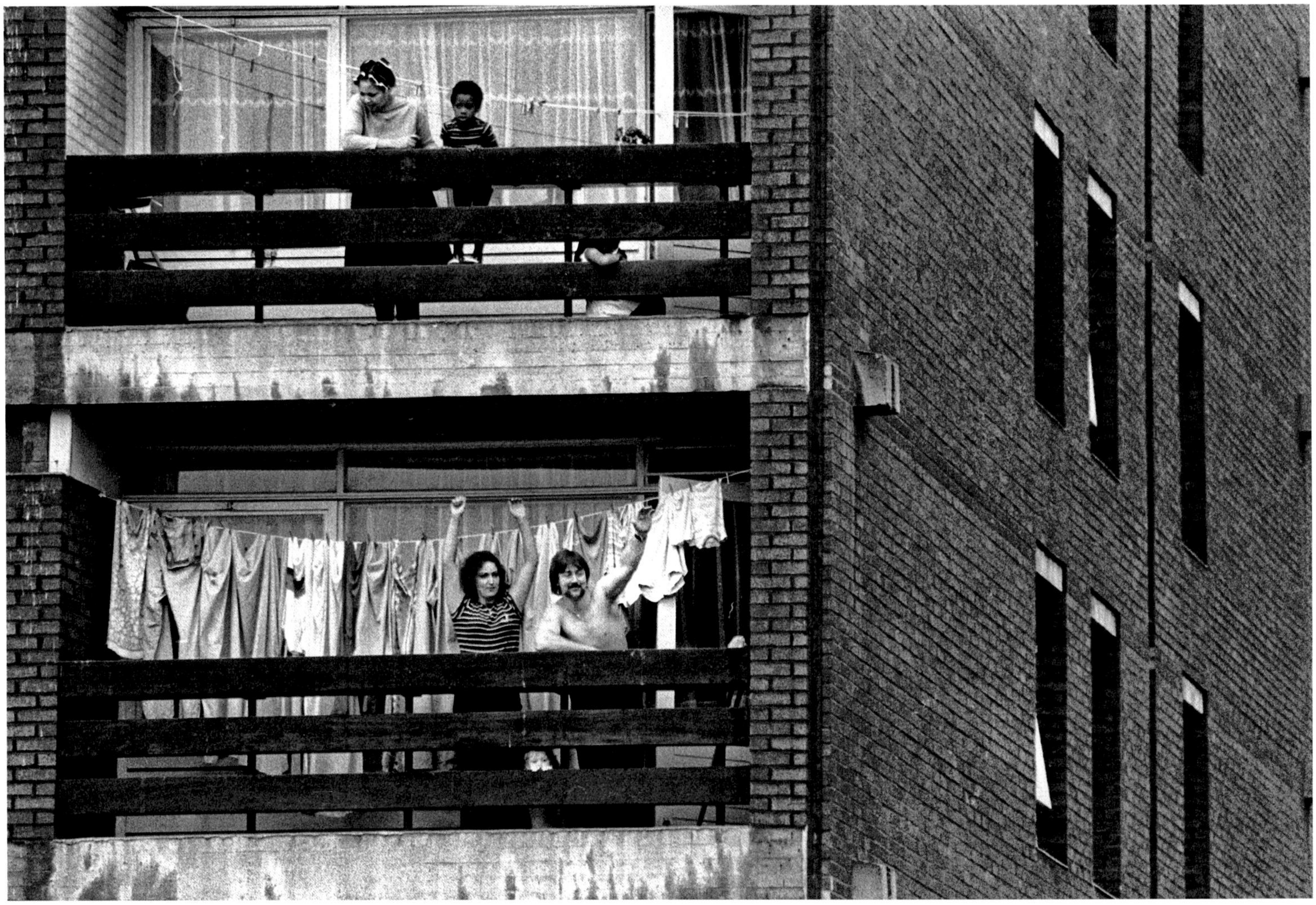

Lewisham, London.1977

A National Front supporting family cheer from the balcony of their tower block flat, while their upstairs neighbour and her two children are not so ecstatic.

Lewisham, London. 1977

A National Front supporter carries wooden weapons. Behind him, a placard declares, 'Housing and Welfare: Britons Before Immigrants.'

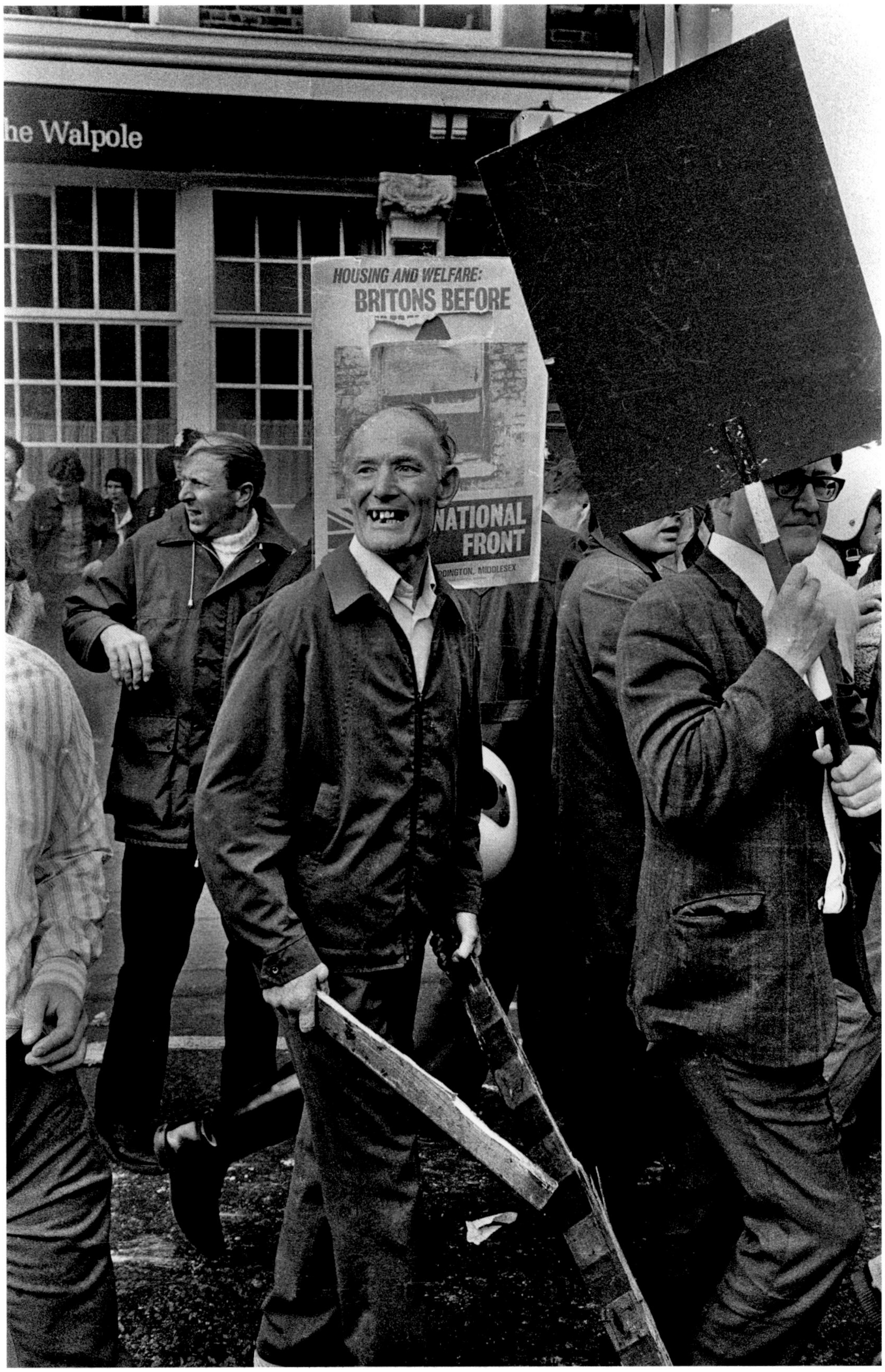

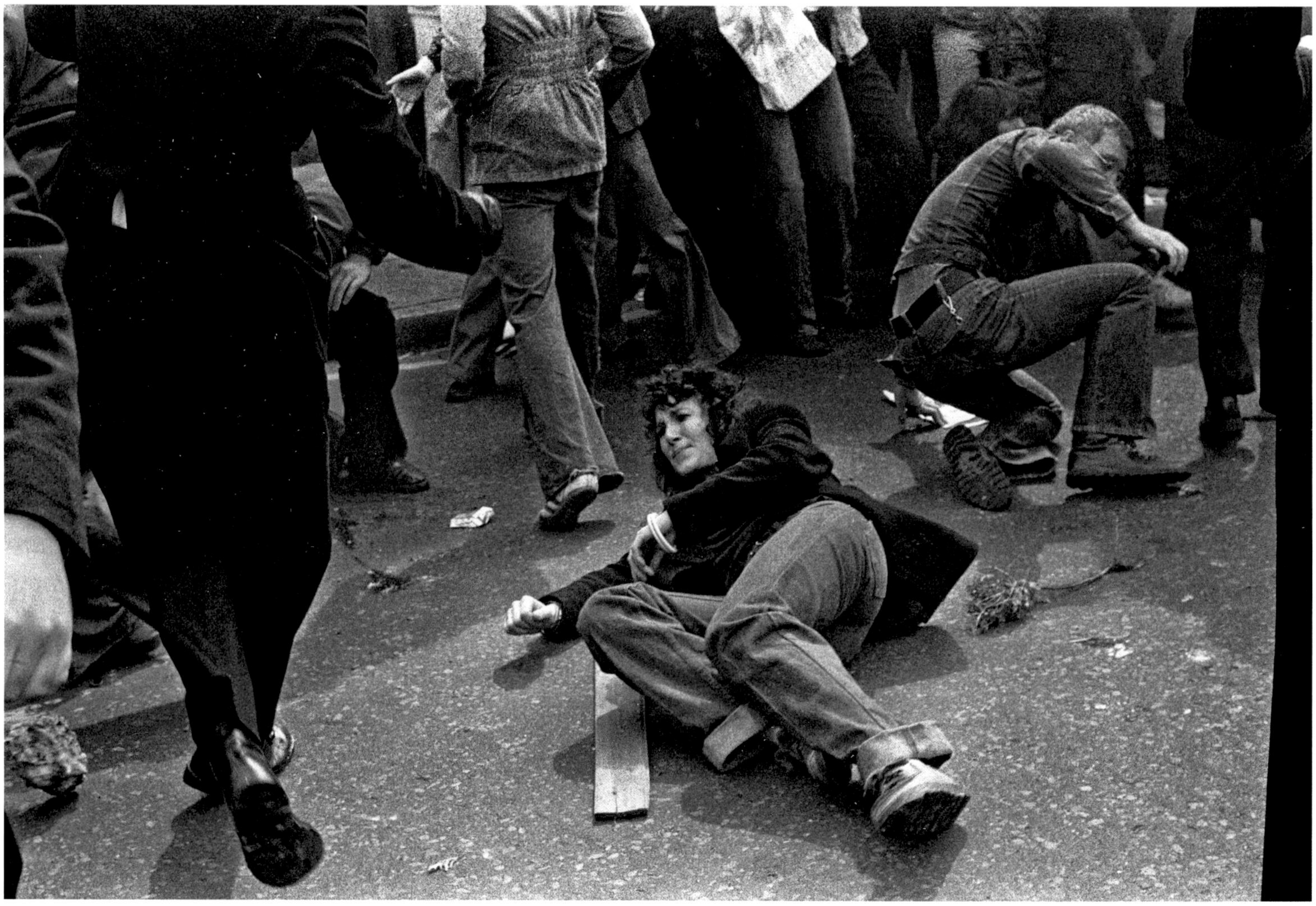

Lewisham, London. 1977

Demonstrators fall to the ground as mounted police charge into the crowds that block the road.

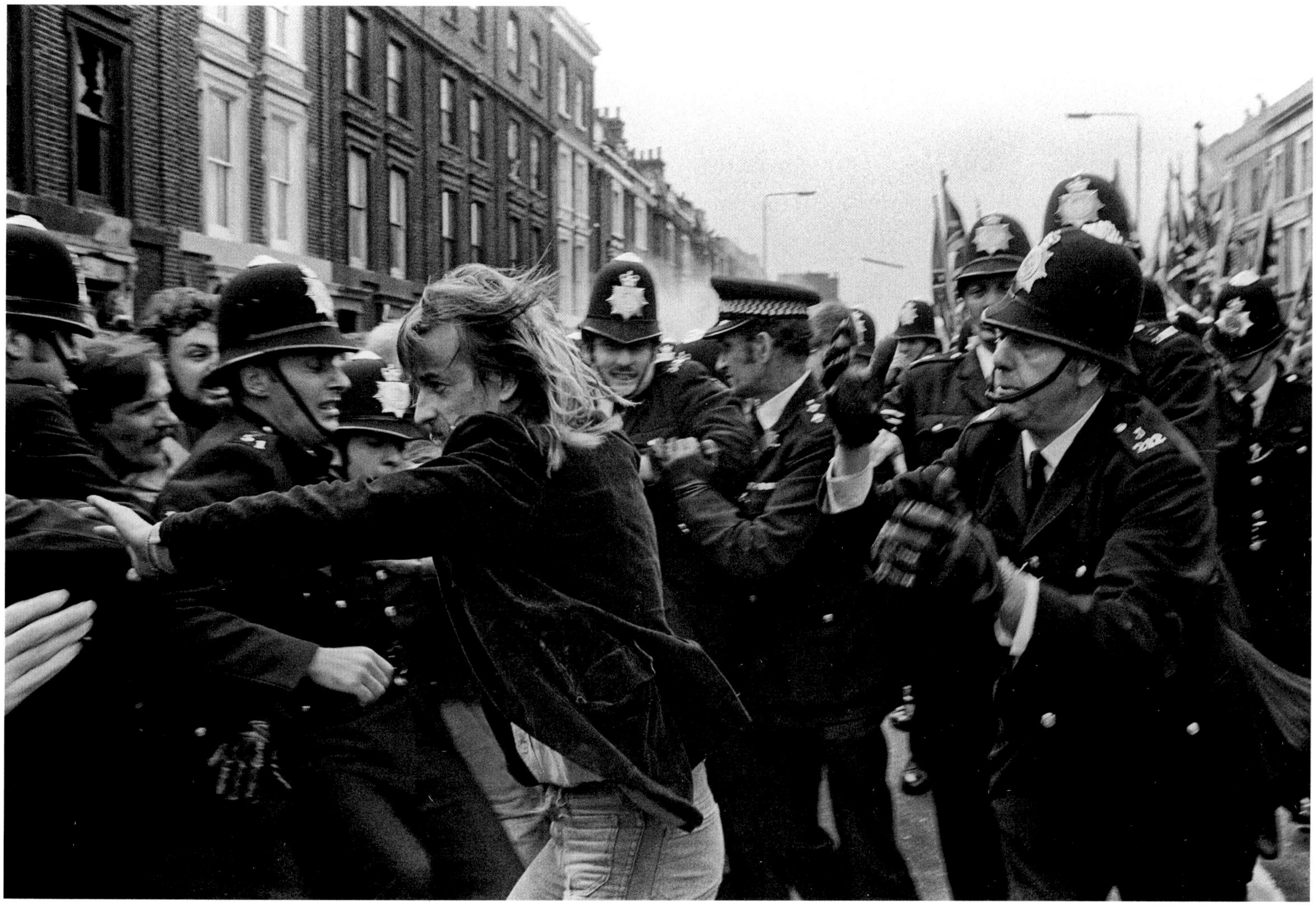

Lewisham, London. 1977

Robert Johnson from Sydenham, southeast London, bursts through a police cordon to confront National Front supporters protected behind police lines. Moments earlier he had been pinned down by four policemen. In the confusion he managed to escape their grip, knocking one policeman's helmet askew. The crowd moved in behind him and he escaped arrest.

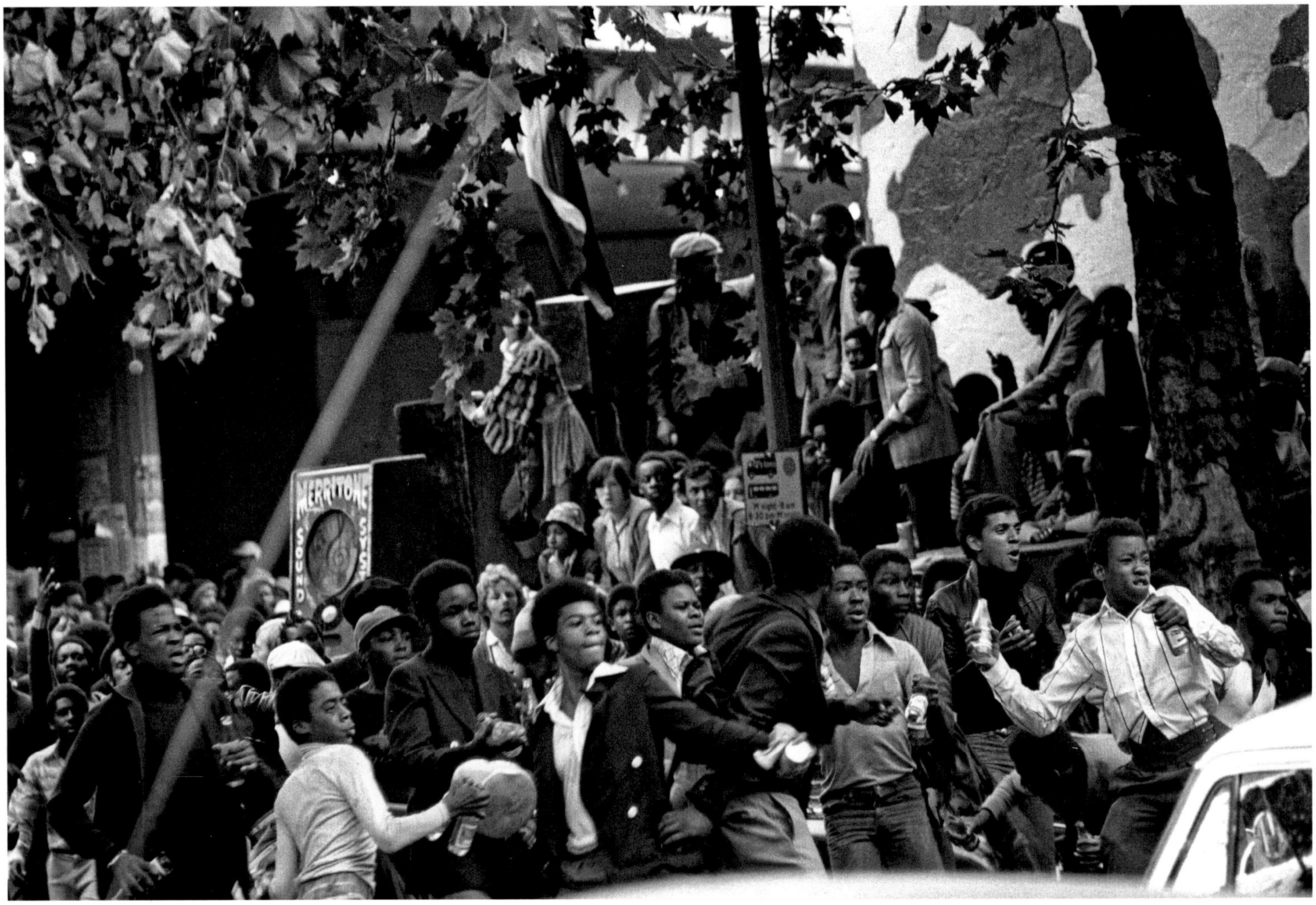

Notting Hill, London. 1976

Notting Hill Carnival began in 1966 and was a low-key local Caribbean community event. By 1976 as many as 150,000 people were attending. In the late afternoon, at the north end of Portobello Road near the Westway flyover, violence erupted after police officers attempted to arrest a group of pickpockets working the crowd. Running skirmishes developed and led to a full-scale riot. Bricks and bottles were thrown, by both black and white youths. Woefully unprepared the police defended themselves with amongst other things dustbin lids. 160 people were hospitalised, there were over 60 arrests.

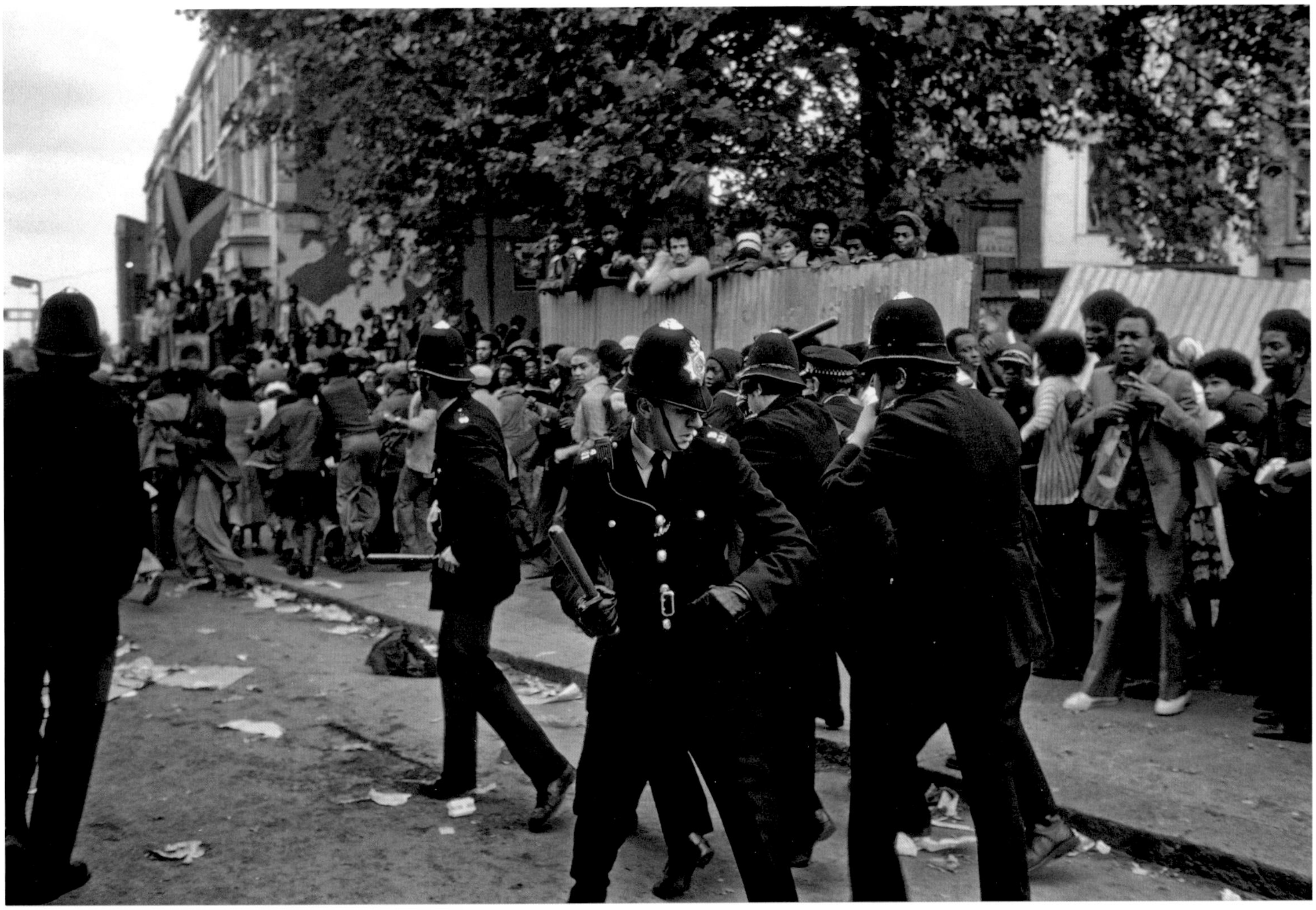

Notting Hill, London. 1976

A small group of police, with truncheons drawn, come under attack as a hail of bricks and bottles are thrown at them.

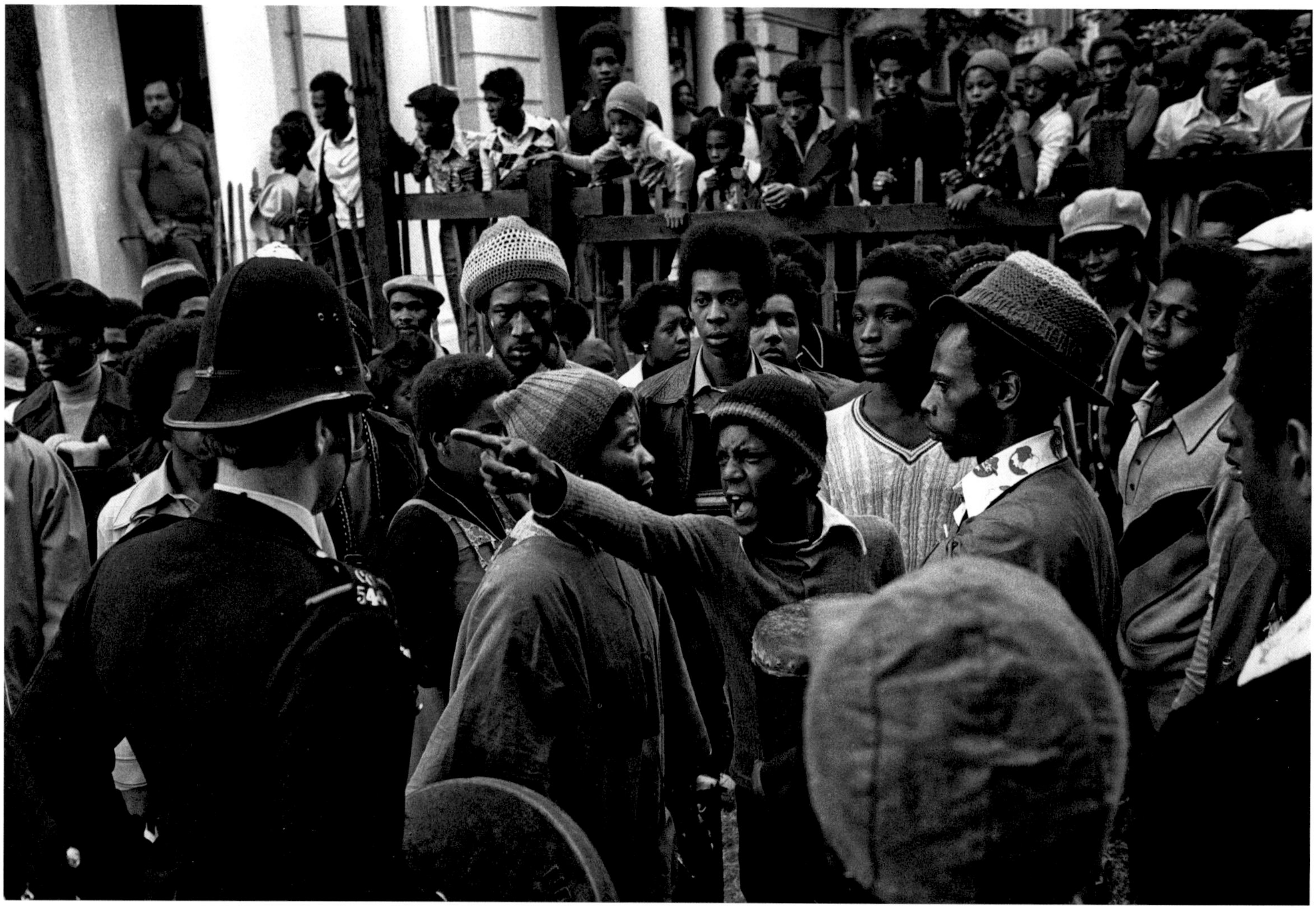

Notting Hill, London. 1976

At the Notting Hill Carnival a peaceful group of Rastafarians drumming and chanting were broken up and moved on by the police. A furious young Rastafarian lets the police know what he thinks, as an Elder wills him to calm down.

Notting Hill, London. 1977

A distraught couple; the older man had been attacked and his wallet stolen. Gay bashing or queer rolling were terms used at the time and gay men were often seen as an easy target by homophobic youths.

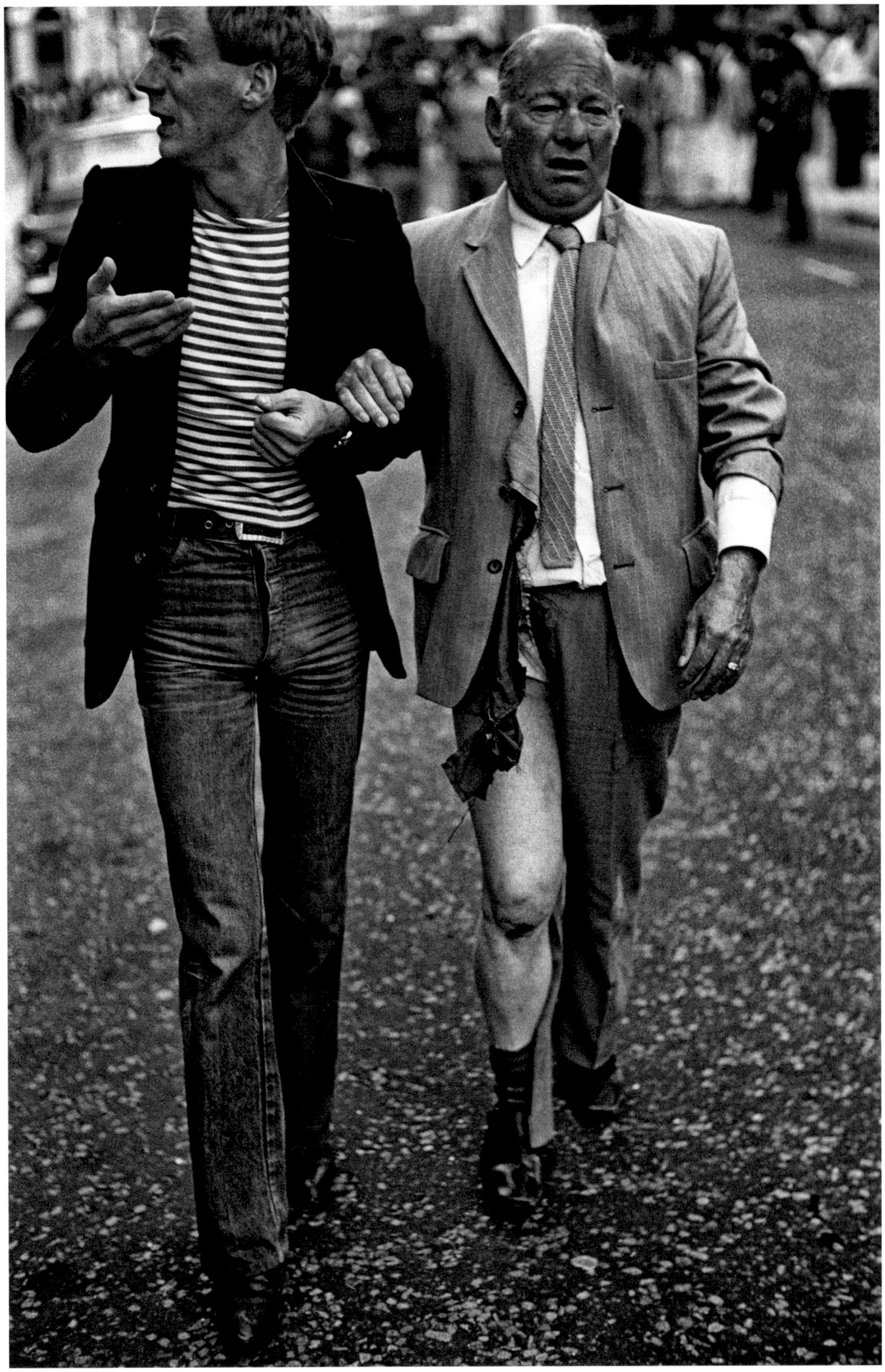

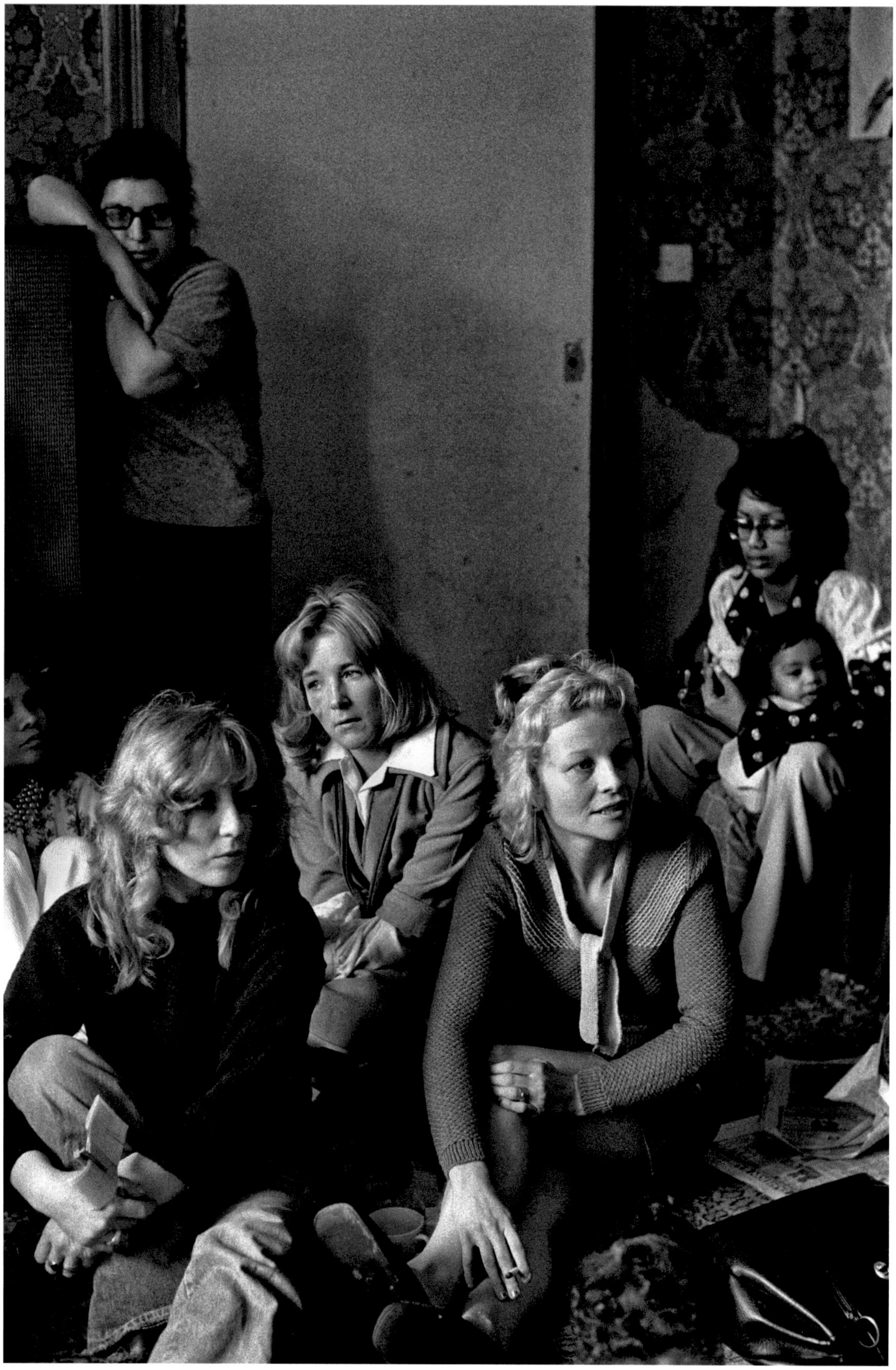

Richmond, London. 1975

Chiswick Women's Aid, a refuge for women suffering domestic violence was founded in 1971 by Erin Pizzey with Anne Ashby. In 1975 they had moved into the Palm Court Hotel, Richmond, a derelict, unoccupied former four-star hotel. Each morning house meetings were held to discuss mutual problems.

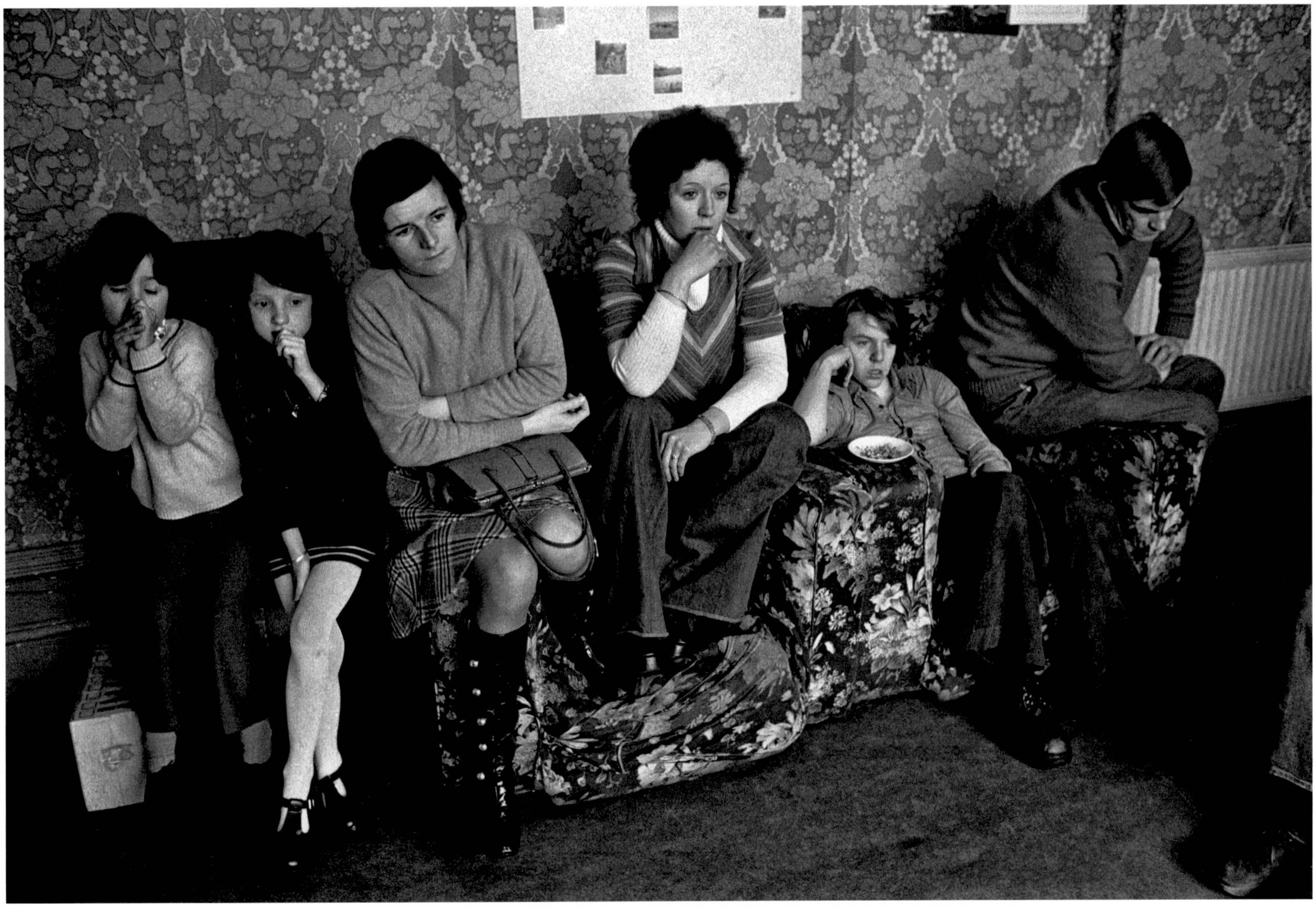

Richmond, London. 1975

In the 1970s it was unofficially estimated that as many as 25,000 families in Britain were subject to violence. No one talked about domestic abuse. What went on behind closed doors was considered private and no-one else's business.

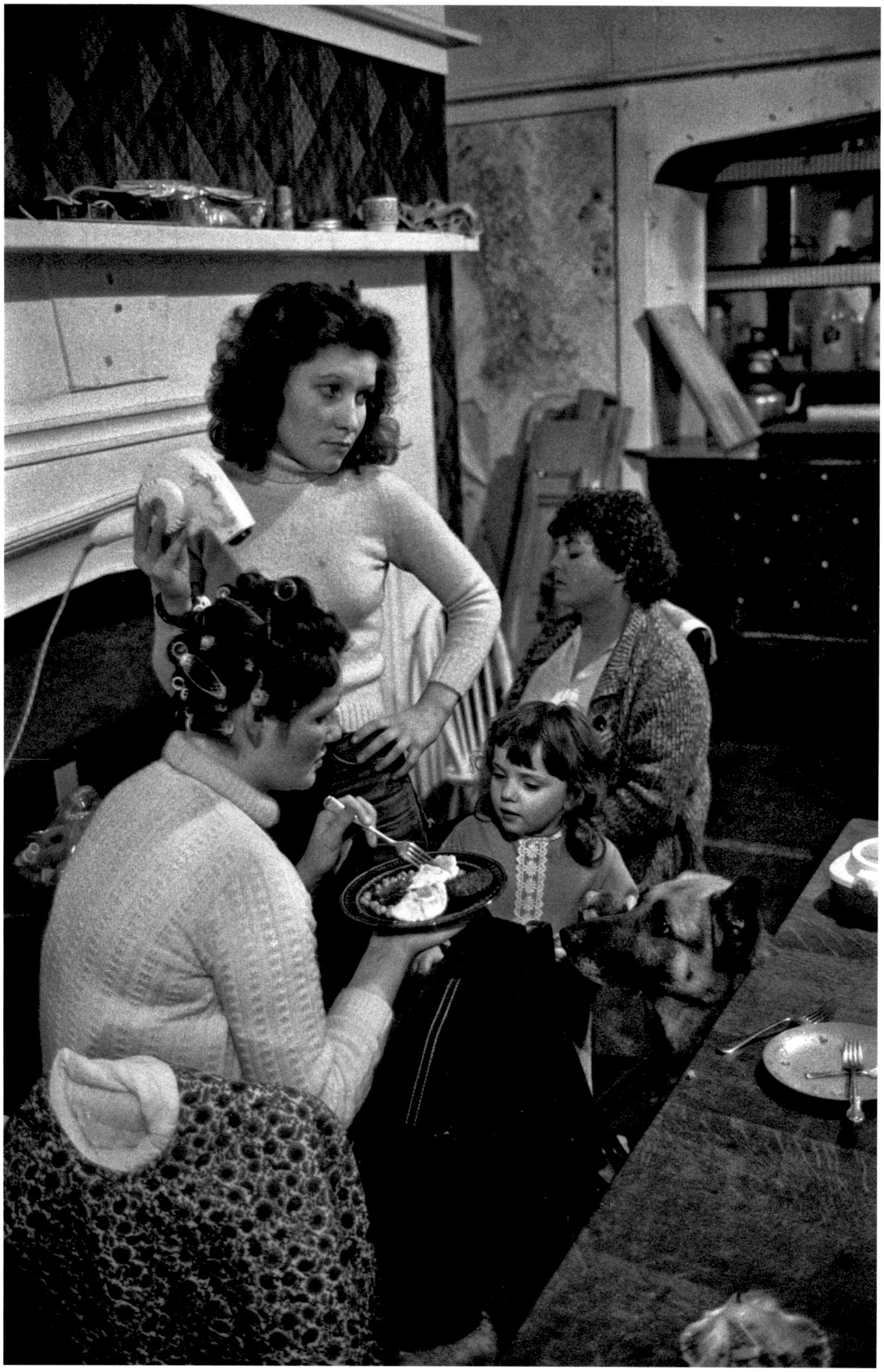

Richmond, London. 1975

Chiswick Women's Aid operated an open door policy; women suffering abuse could just turn up. They came with their often disturbed children and were sometimes mentally damaged themselves. The community offered an environment in which women in similar circumstances could provide each other with emotional and moral support as well as friendship.

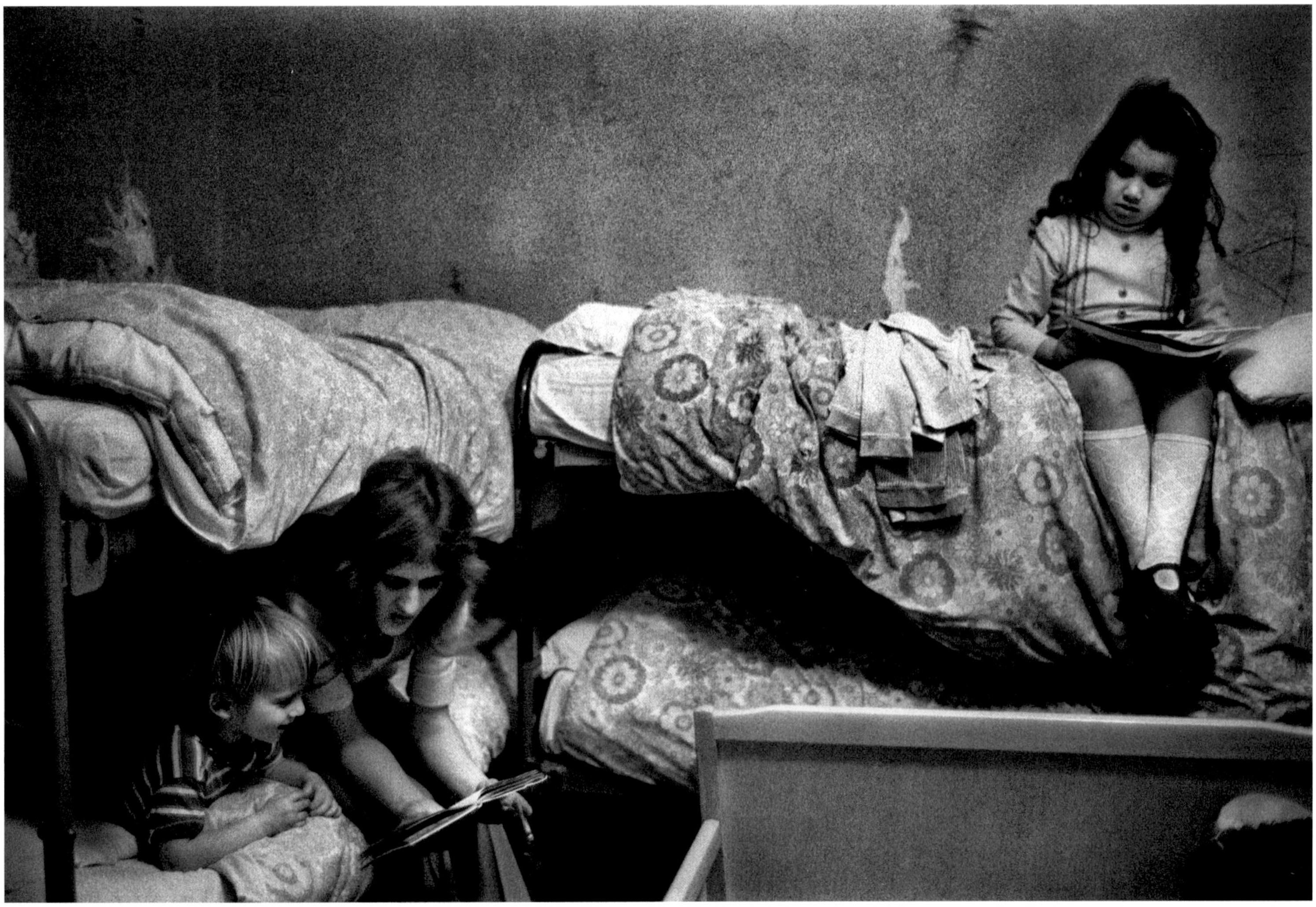

Richmond, London. 1975

A mother reads a bedtime story; it was their first Christmas away from the family home. Chiswick Women's Aid also worked with fathers who were non-violent, in order to try and resolve matters. Sadly many mothers and children often remained in the refuge for up to three or four years before being rehoused by the authorities.

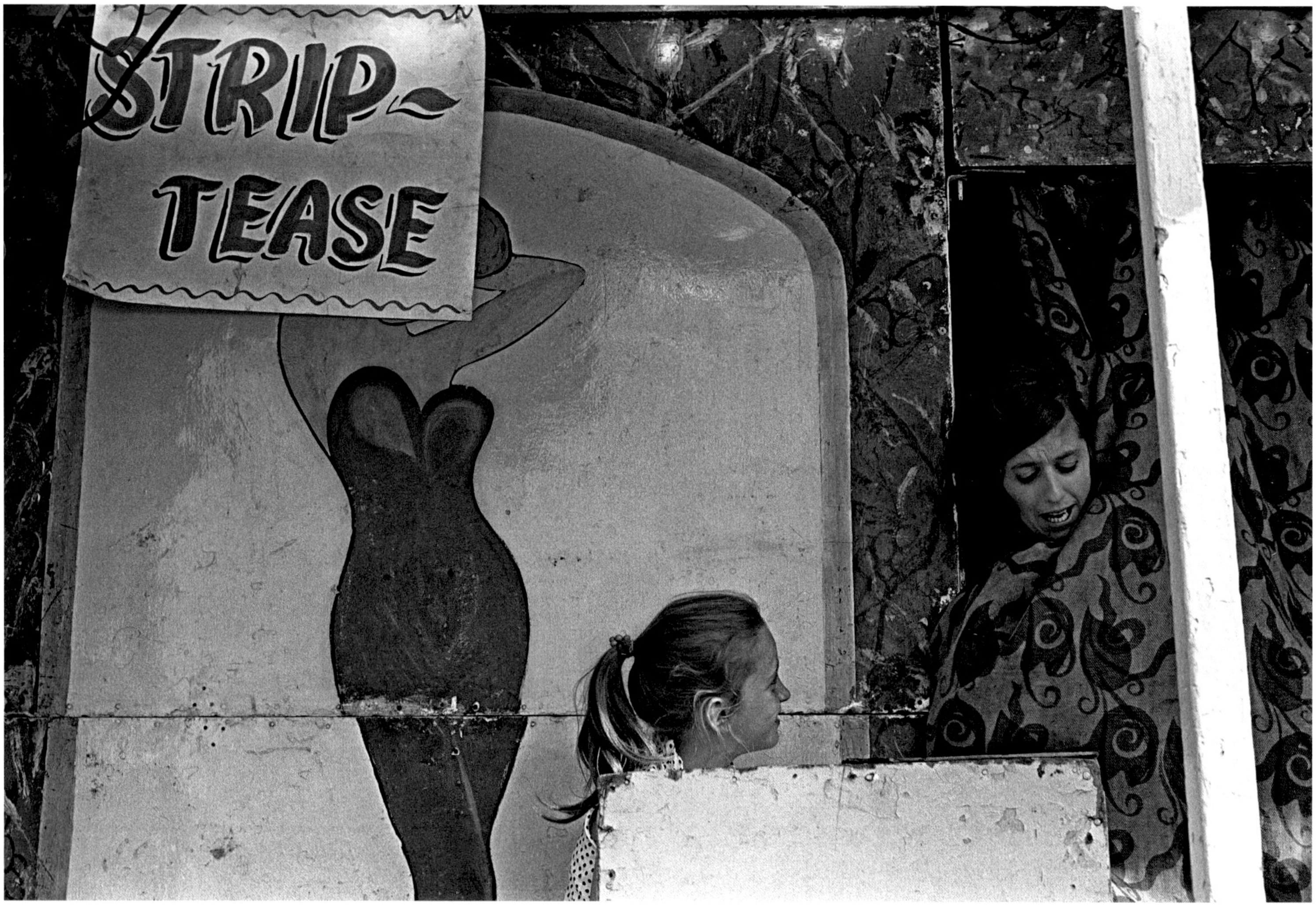

Epsom Downs, Surrey. 1969

While tens of thousands of racegoers chance their luck with a wager on the runners at The Derby, on 'The Hill' more discreet punters enjoy the annual funfair and sideshows.

Epsom Downs, Surrey. 1969

Wally Shufflebottom's knife throwing striptease fairground act, was billed as the 'Texans', and 'Greater than Strip Tease', it was a family affair. While Wally juggled his throwing knives, his wife Cissy Rosaire called in the audience by banging a large drum, and a young woman held up a sign, 'Nude Lady as Target'. The Shufflebottom family had been showmen since the 1850s and Wally was one of the last to present a live Wild West Show at British fairgrounds; he died in 1998 age 89.

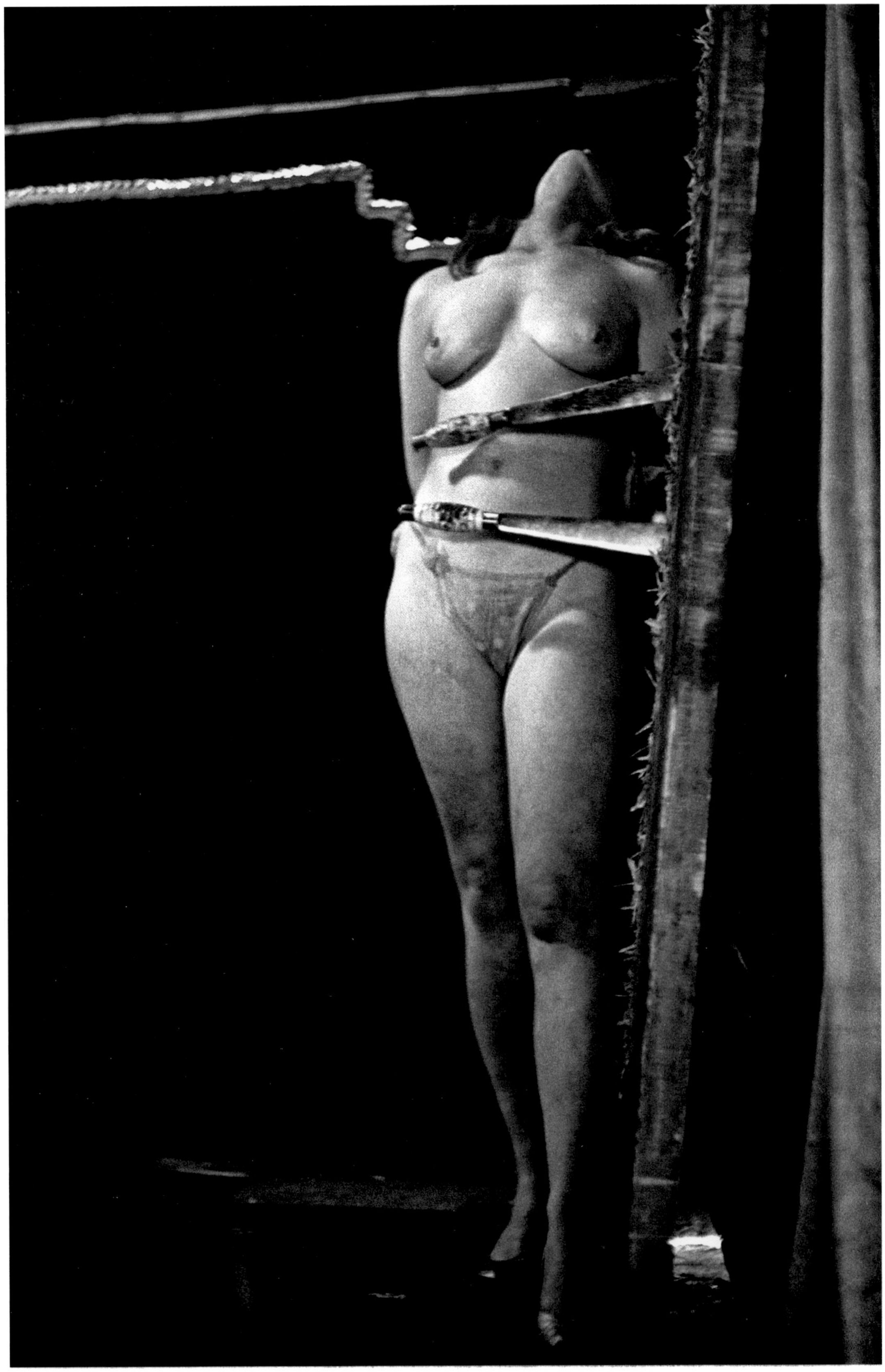

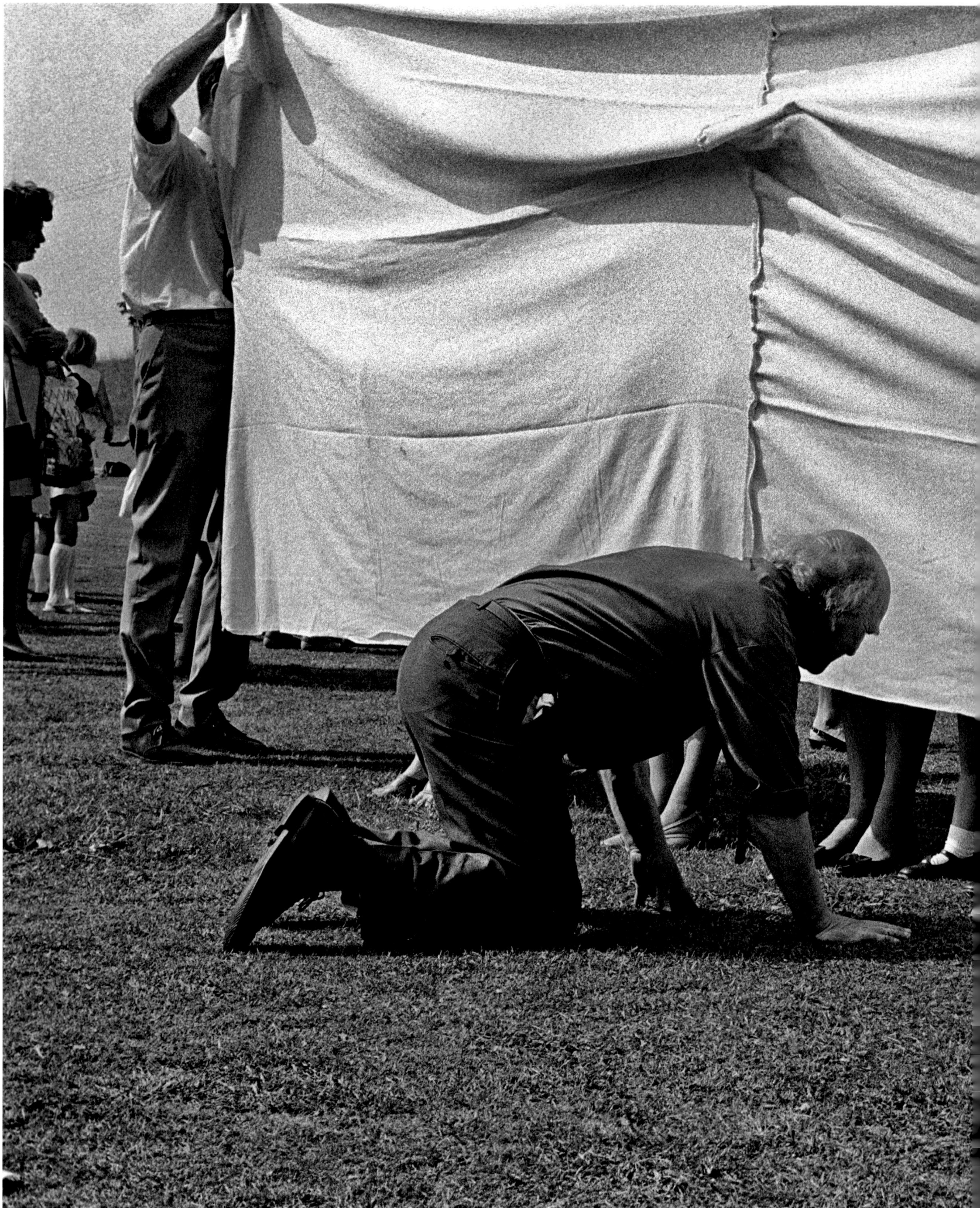

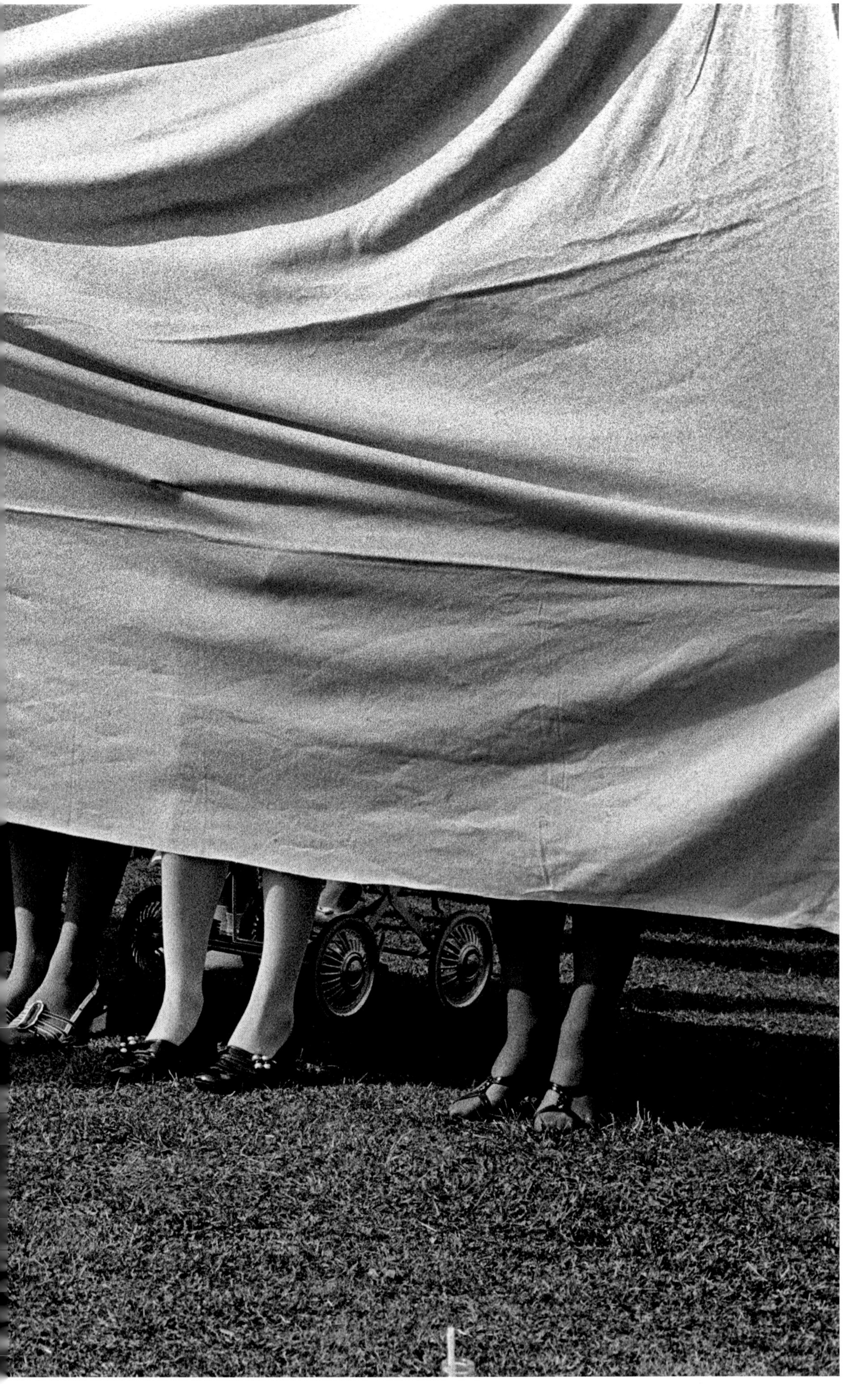

Marhamchurch, Cornwall. 1970

The village revel is held annually on the Monday following 12th of August. The Queen of the Revel is chosen from the village schoolgirls and crowned by Father Time in front of the church where St. Morwenna is thought to have founded her hermitage at the end of the fifth century. Led by the local band and the newly crowned Revel Queen, a procession moves through the village to the Revel Ground, where the prettiest ankles competition takes place.

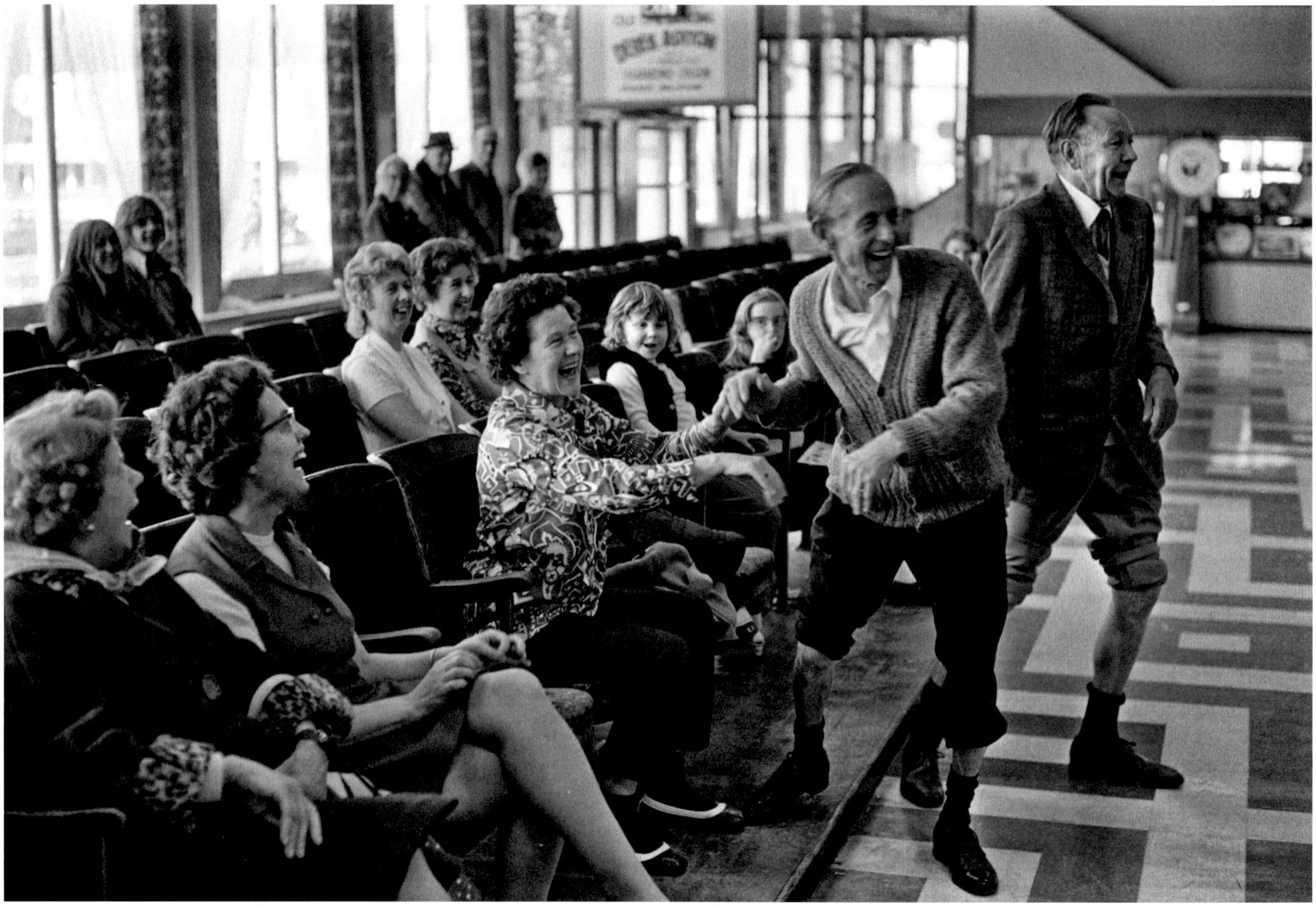

Bognor Regis, West Sussex. 1972

At Butlins holiday camp, two holidaymakers with their trouser legs rolled up take part in the best looking and firmest calf muscle competition, causing great hilarity for their watching wives.

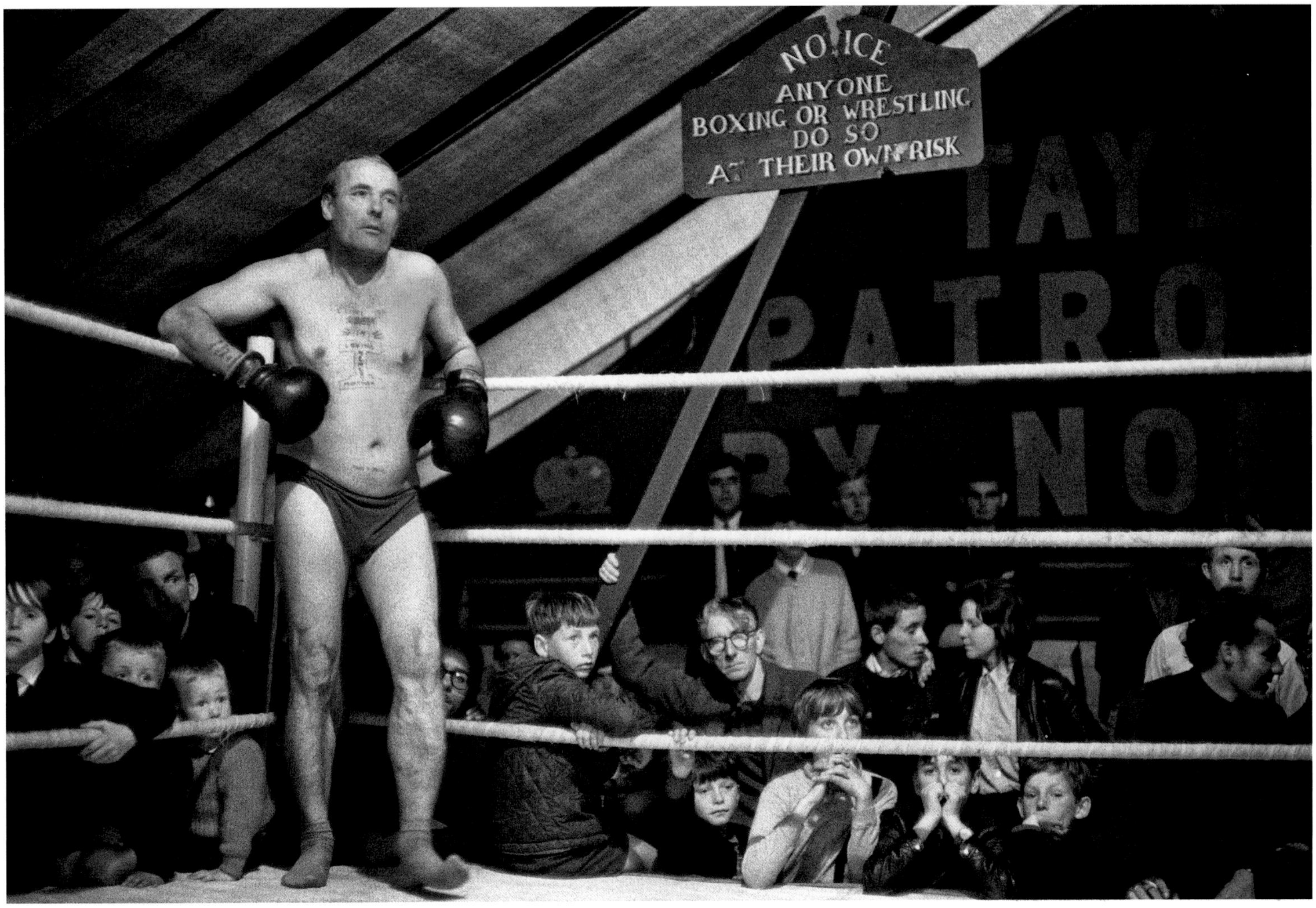

Gloucestershire. 1970

At a village annual summer fête, a man from the audience wearing only his underpants chances his luck, though as the sign says 'Anyone Boxing Or Wrestling Do So At Their Own Risk'.

Brighton, Sussex. 1970

A group of men are 'blacksanding' under the pier. William Henry Smallman (left) known as Harry by most, or Sailor by close friends, searches for coins that may have tumbled out of a one-armed bandit, been dropped, or perhaps fallen from a pocket, through the pier's slatted wooden flooring to be washed up with that Sunday morning's incoming tide.

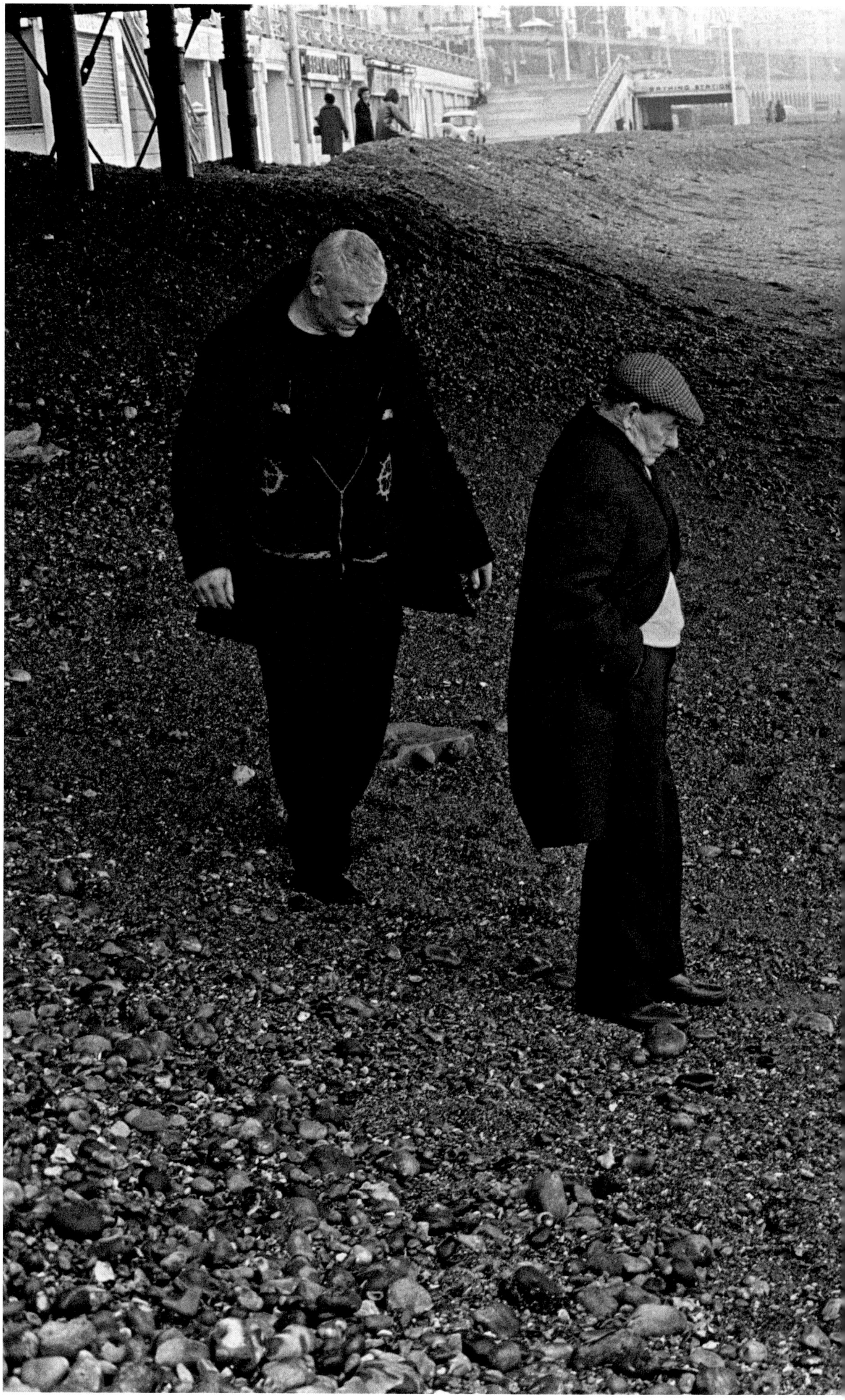

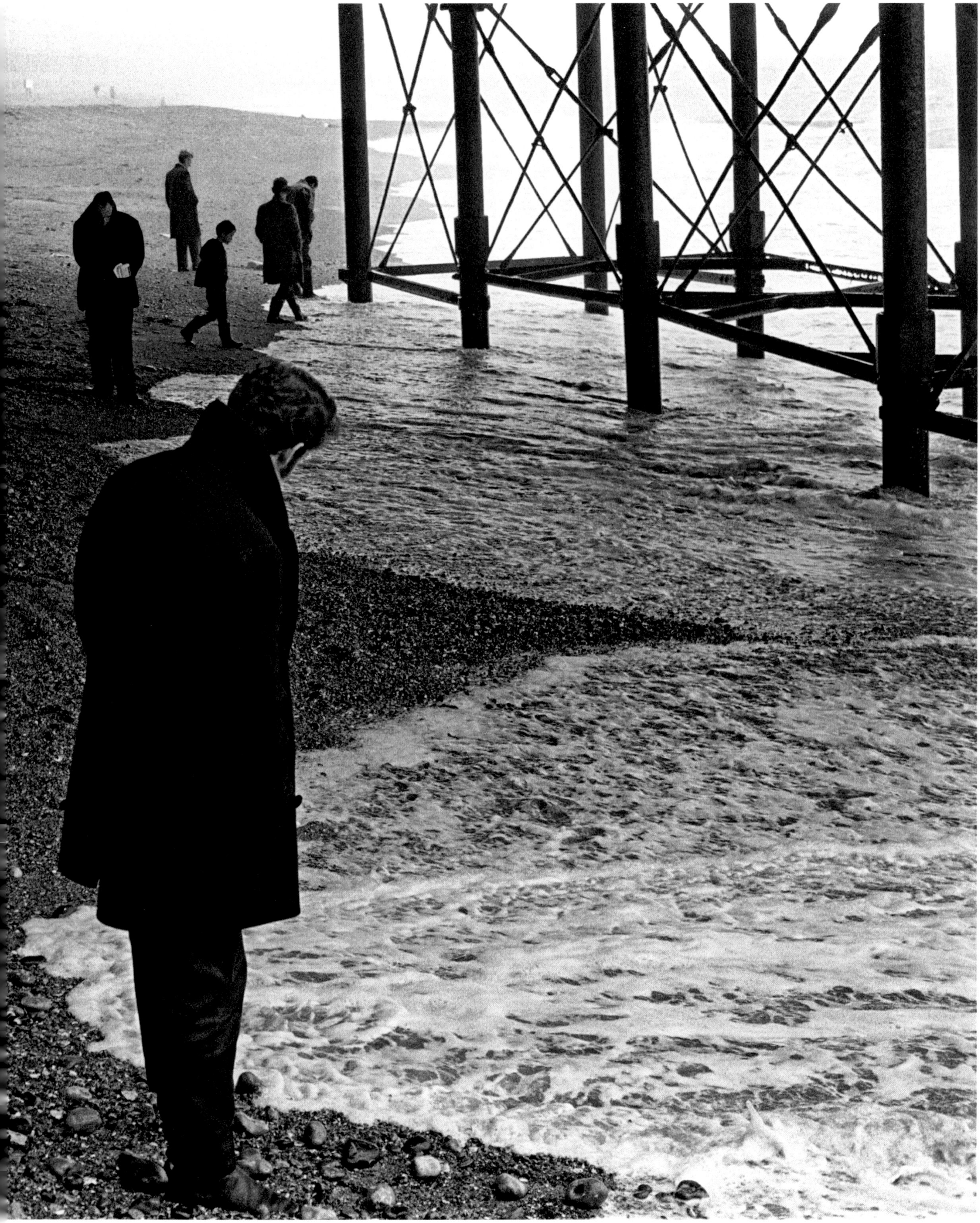

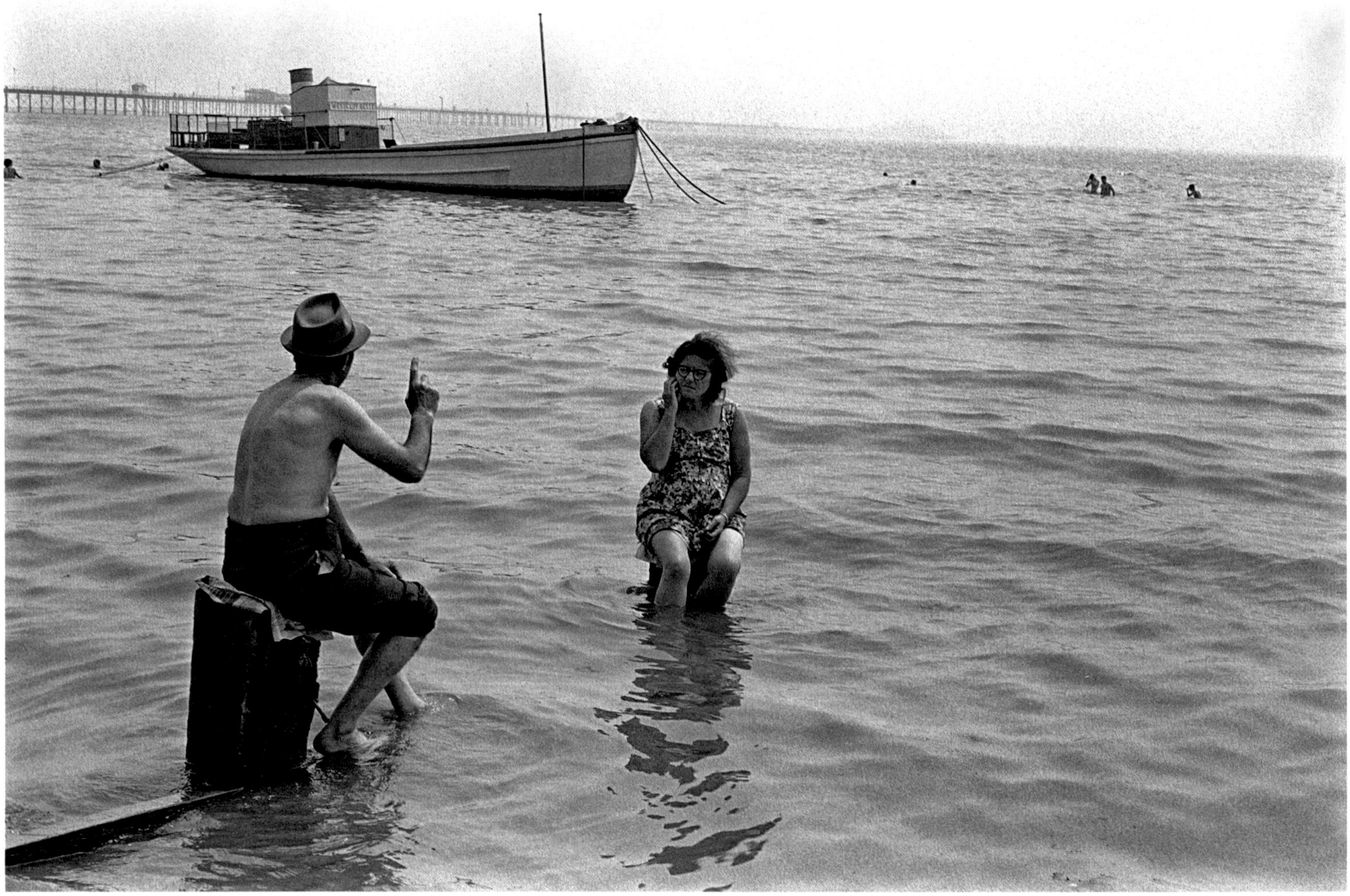

Southend-on-Sea, Essex. 1969

Sir John Betjeman once said, 'The Pier is Southend, Southend is the Pier.' The longest pier in the world it extends 1.34 miles into the Thames Estuary.

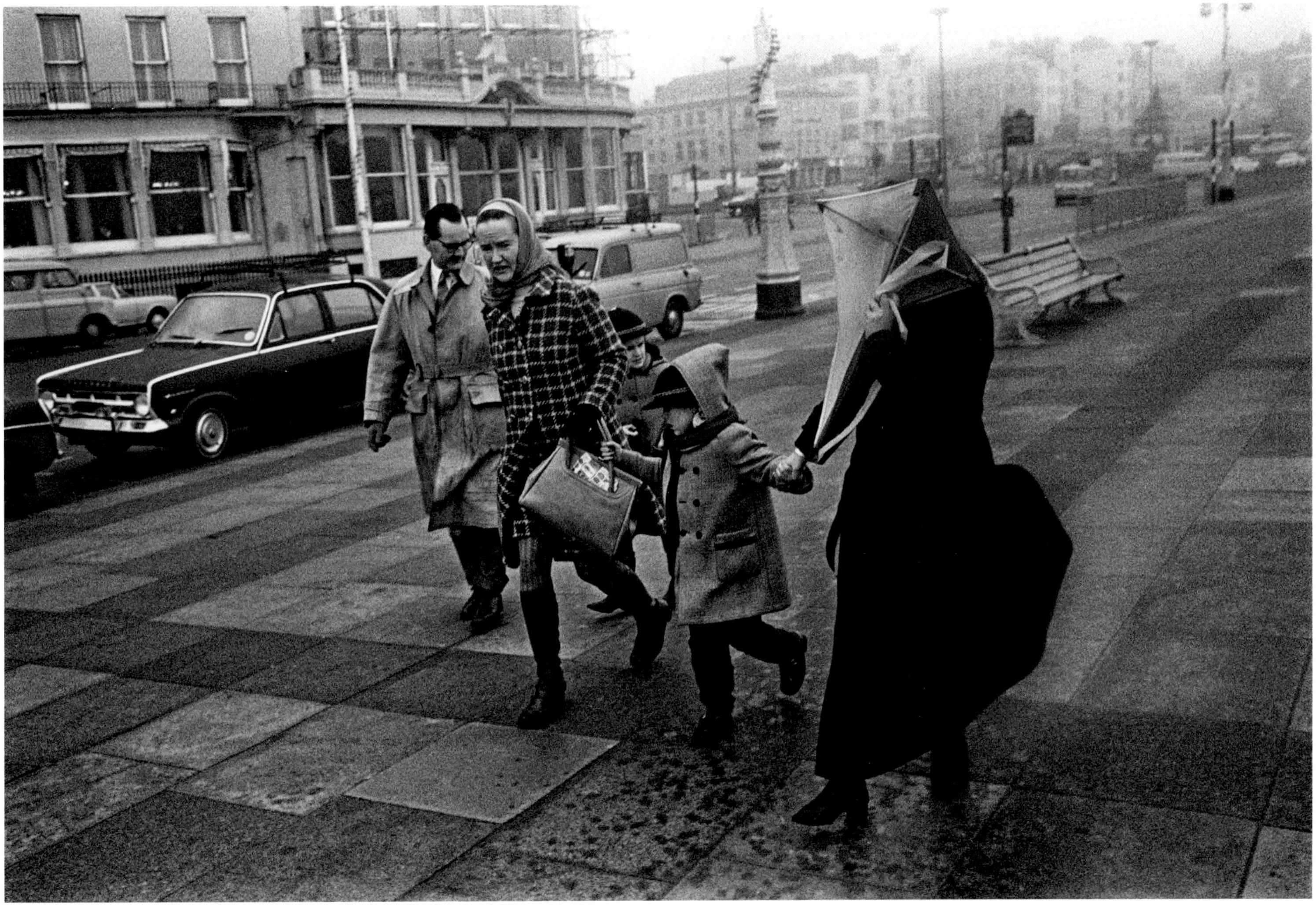

Brighton, Sussex. 1968

Rain and a blustering wind lash a Sunday morning family walk along the seafront.

Cirencester, Gloucestershire. 1974

At the Church of St. John the Baptist annual summer fête, women shelter from the rain.

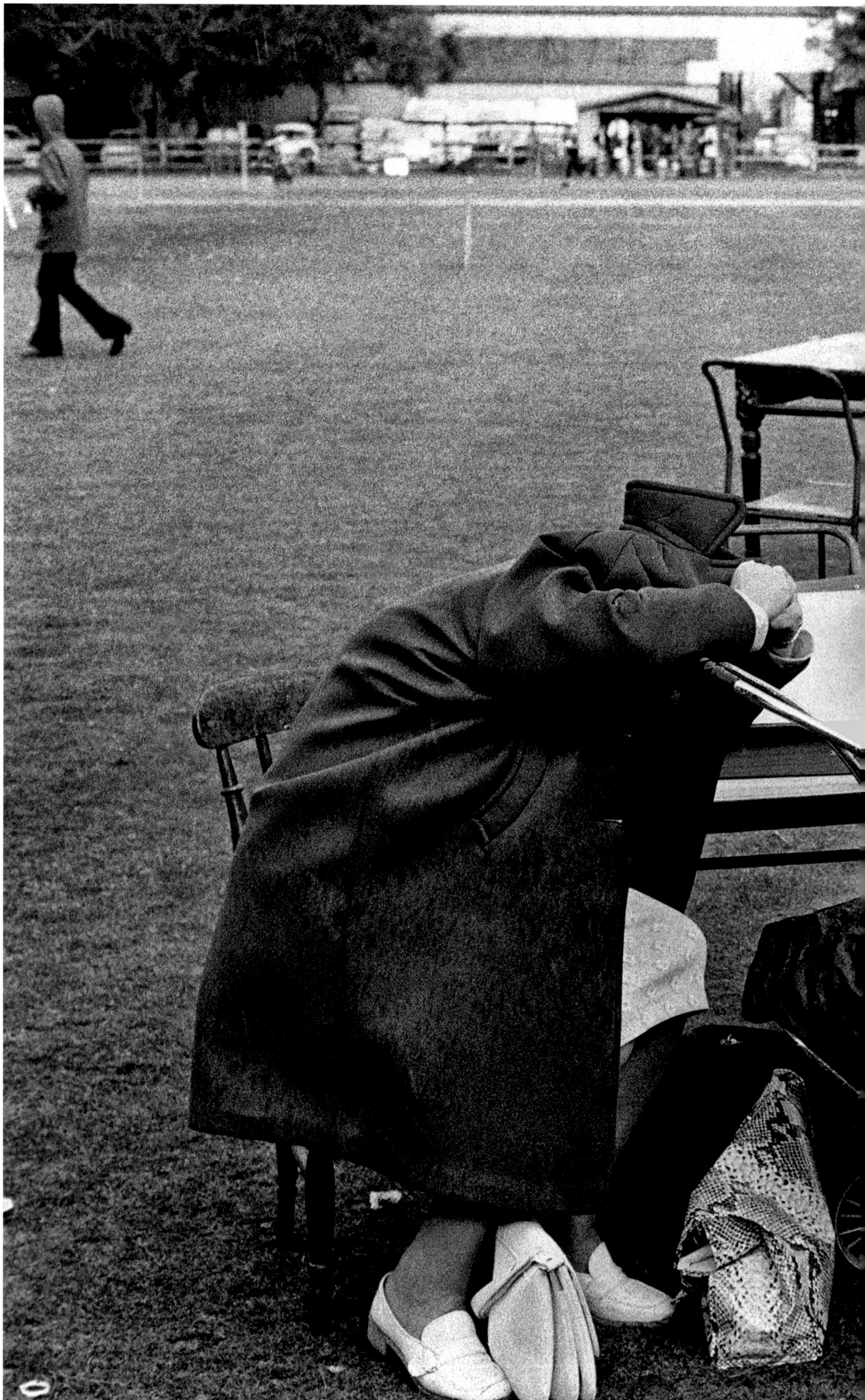

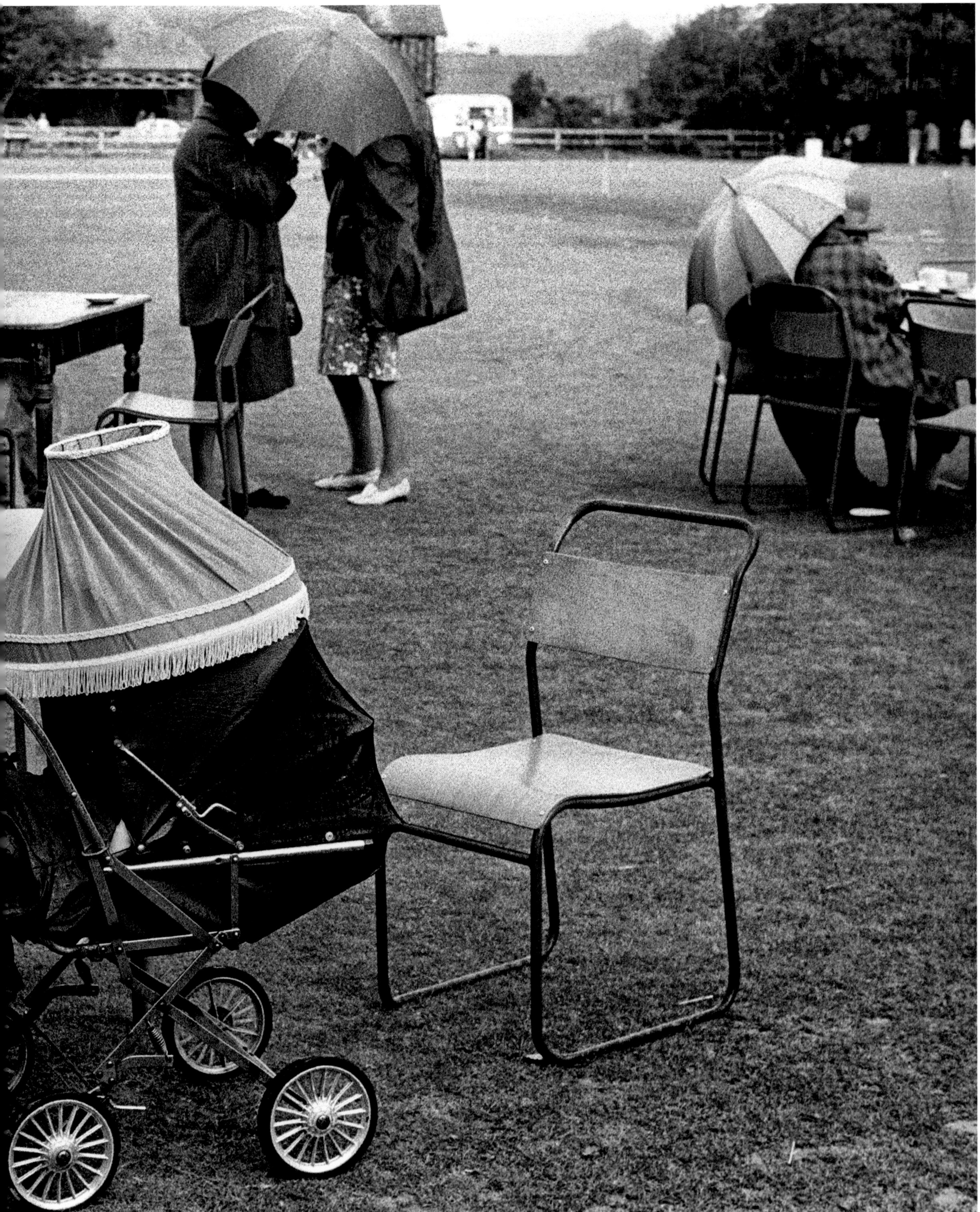

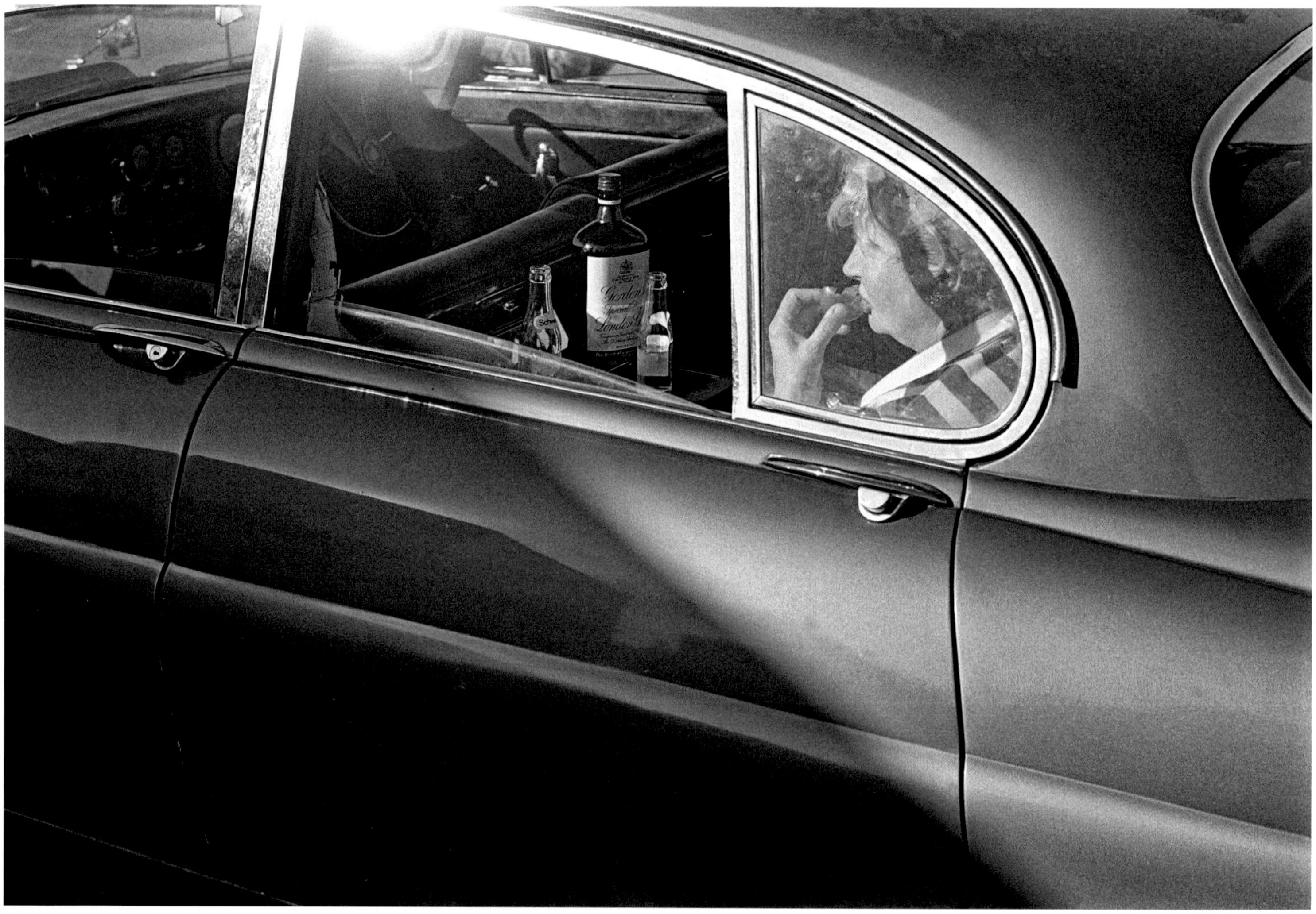

Epsom Downs, Surrey. 1970

Derby Day, in the car park and before 'The Off', a racegoer enjoys a Gordon's Special Dry London Gin and tonic and a cup cake in the back of the Jaguar.

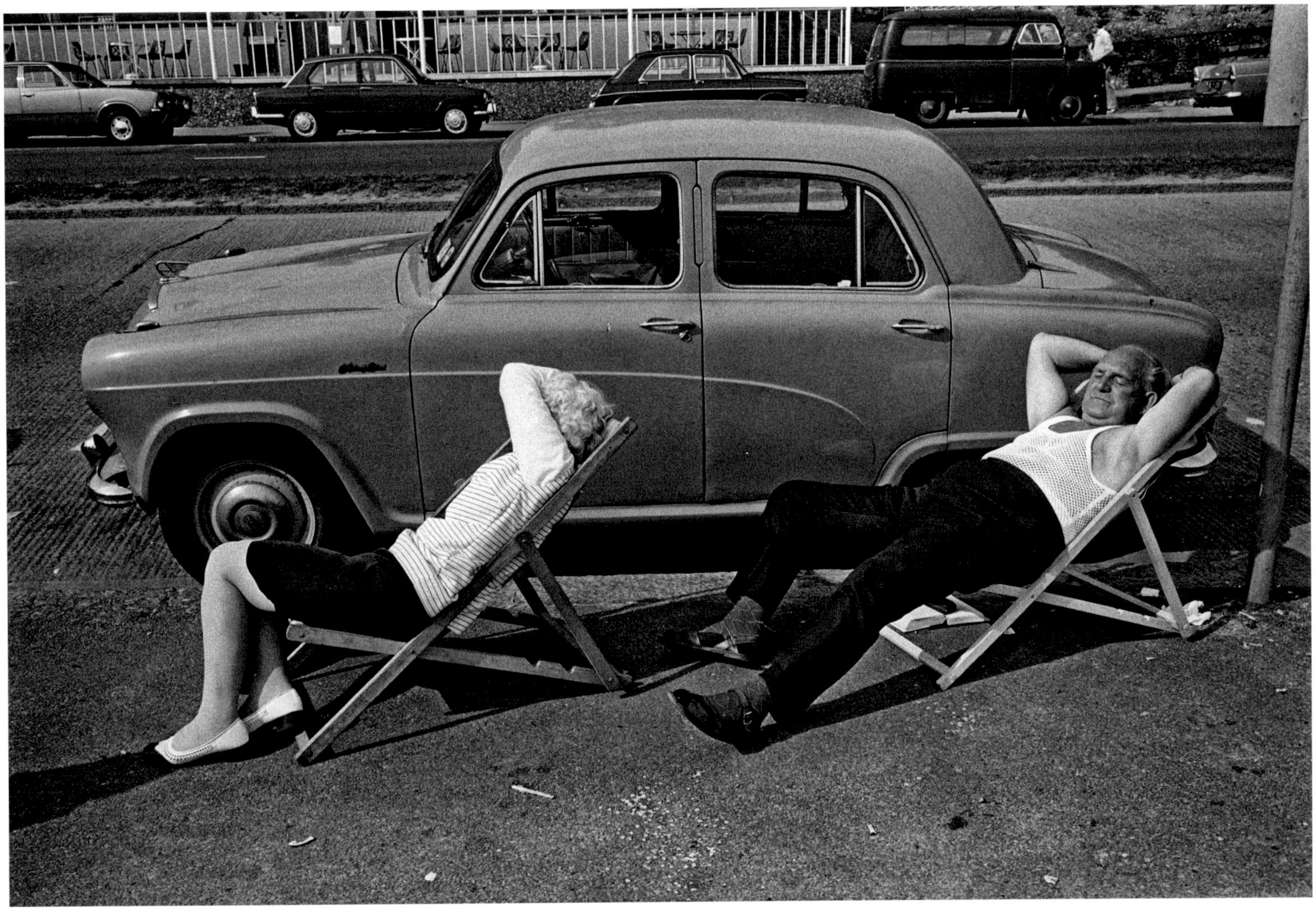

Southend-on-Sea, Essex. 1974

A middle-aged couple with their Austin Cambridge A50 and own deckchairs enjoy a sleepy Saturday afternoon in sun.

Epsom Downs, Surrey. 1970

Top hat and tails, cloth cap and pipe, it's Derby Day. Londoners down for a day at the races enjoy an alfresco picnic in the car park, sheltered from the breeze and warm in the summer sun as they lean up against a returning racegoer's Jaguar.

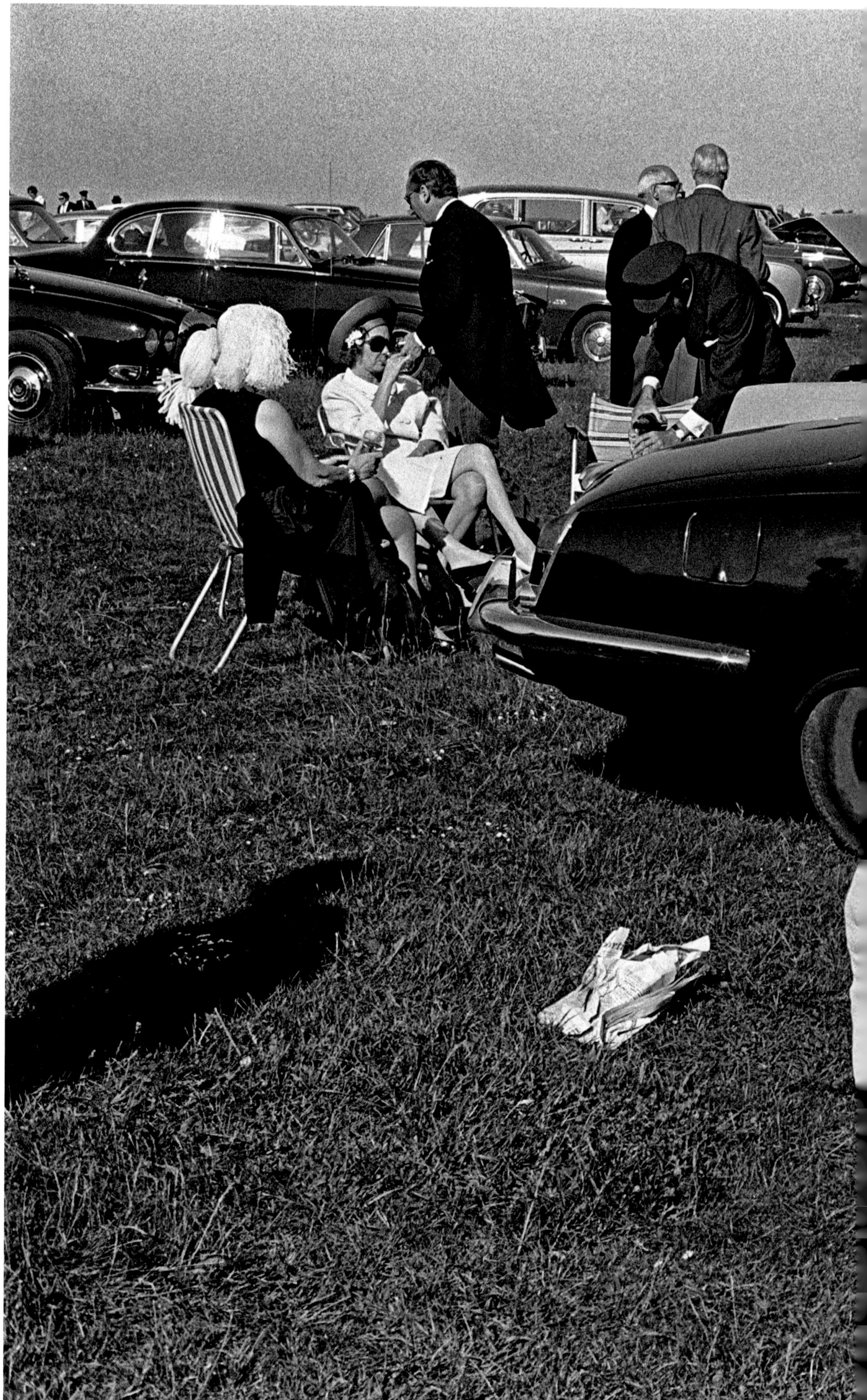

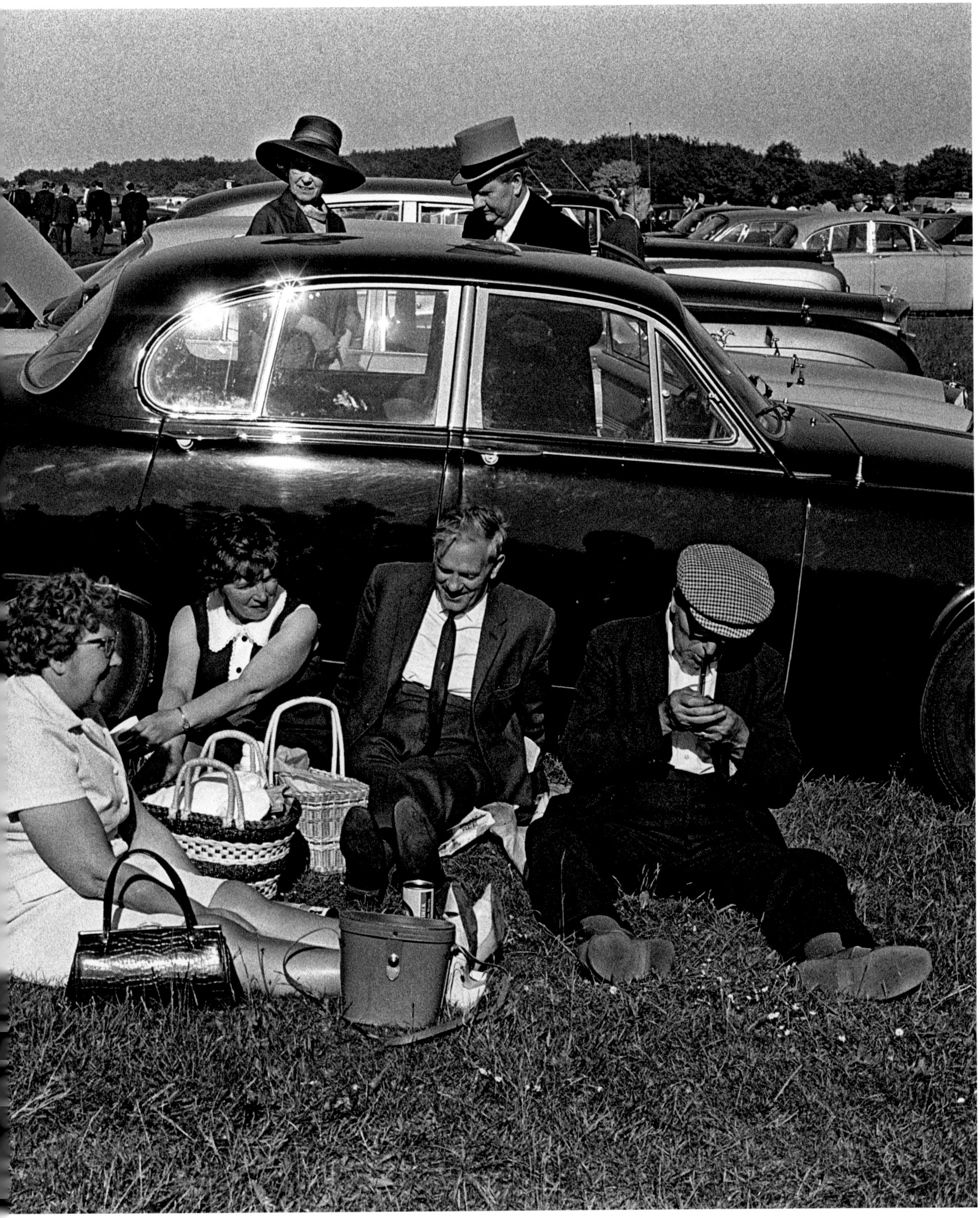

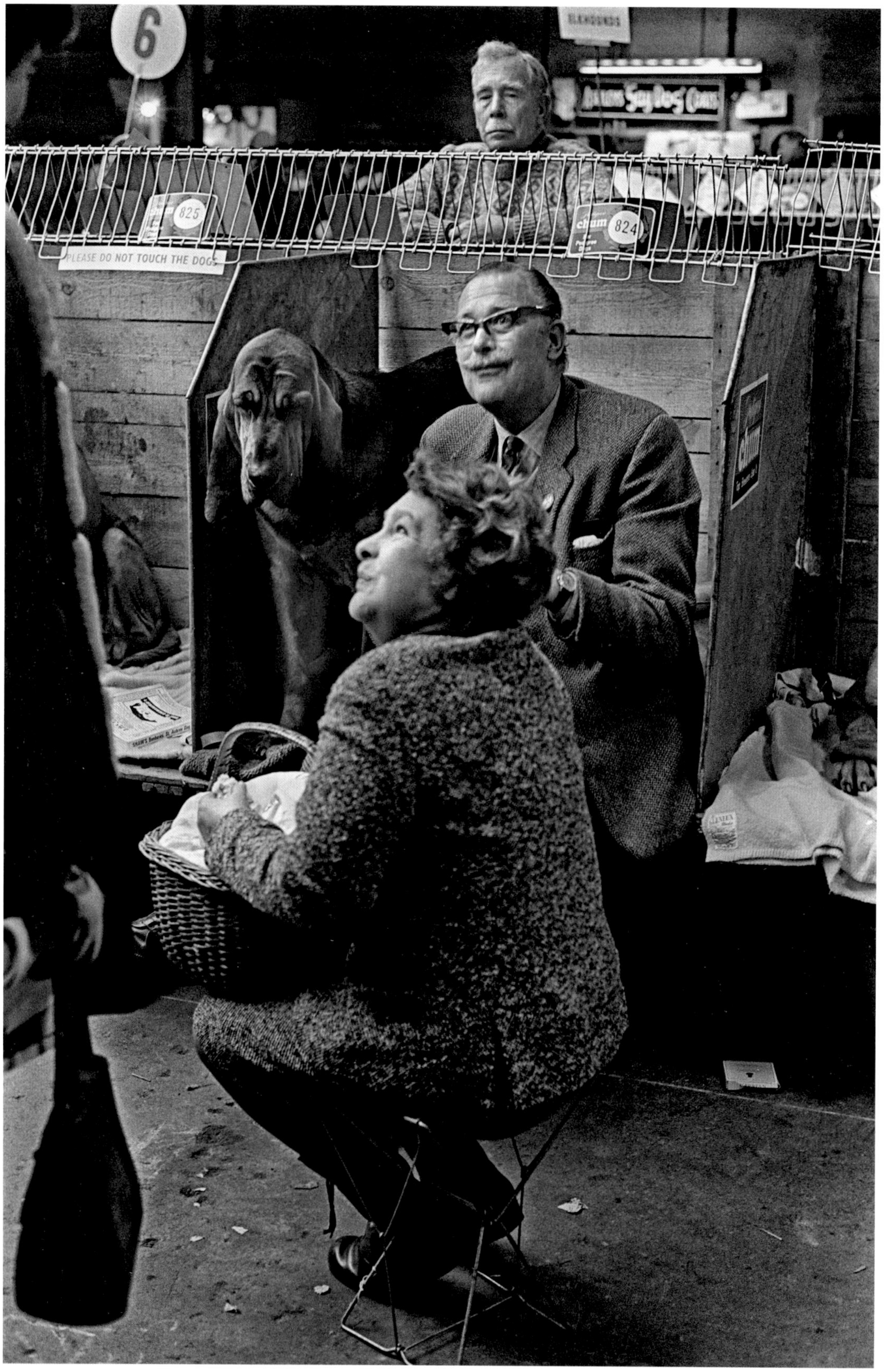

Earls Court, London. 1968

A prize bloodhound sizes up his owners' picnic basket at Crufts Dog Show at the Earls Court Exhibition Centre.

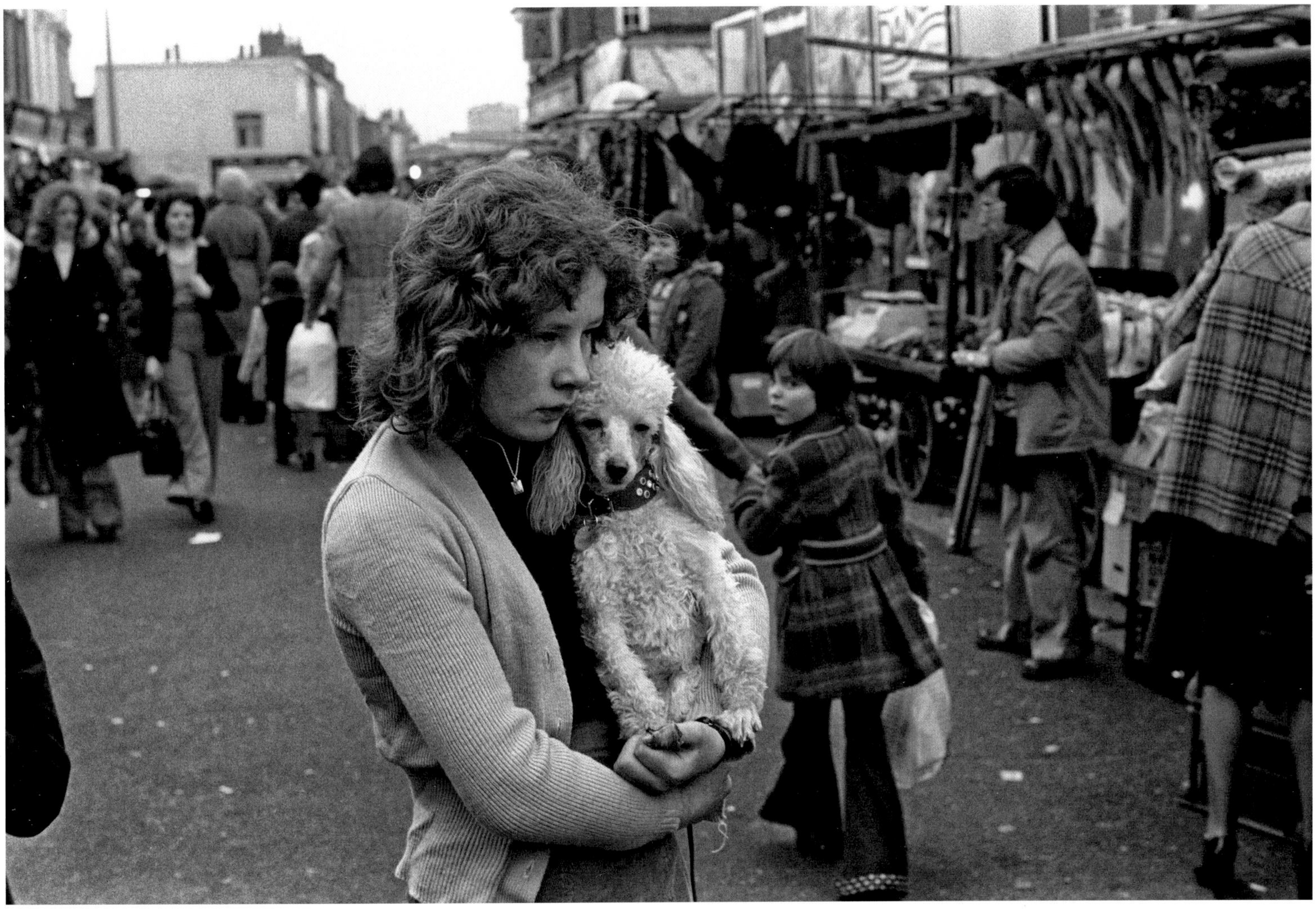

Tower Hamlets, London. 1975

A young girl and her much-loved poodle in the Roman Road Market. The market is the heart of Bow, and 'going down the Roman' has been a tradition for generations.

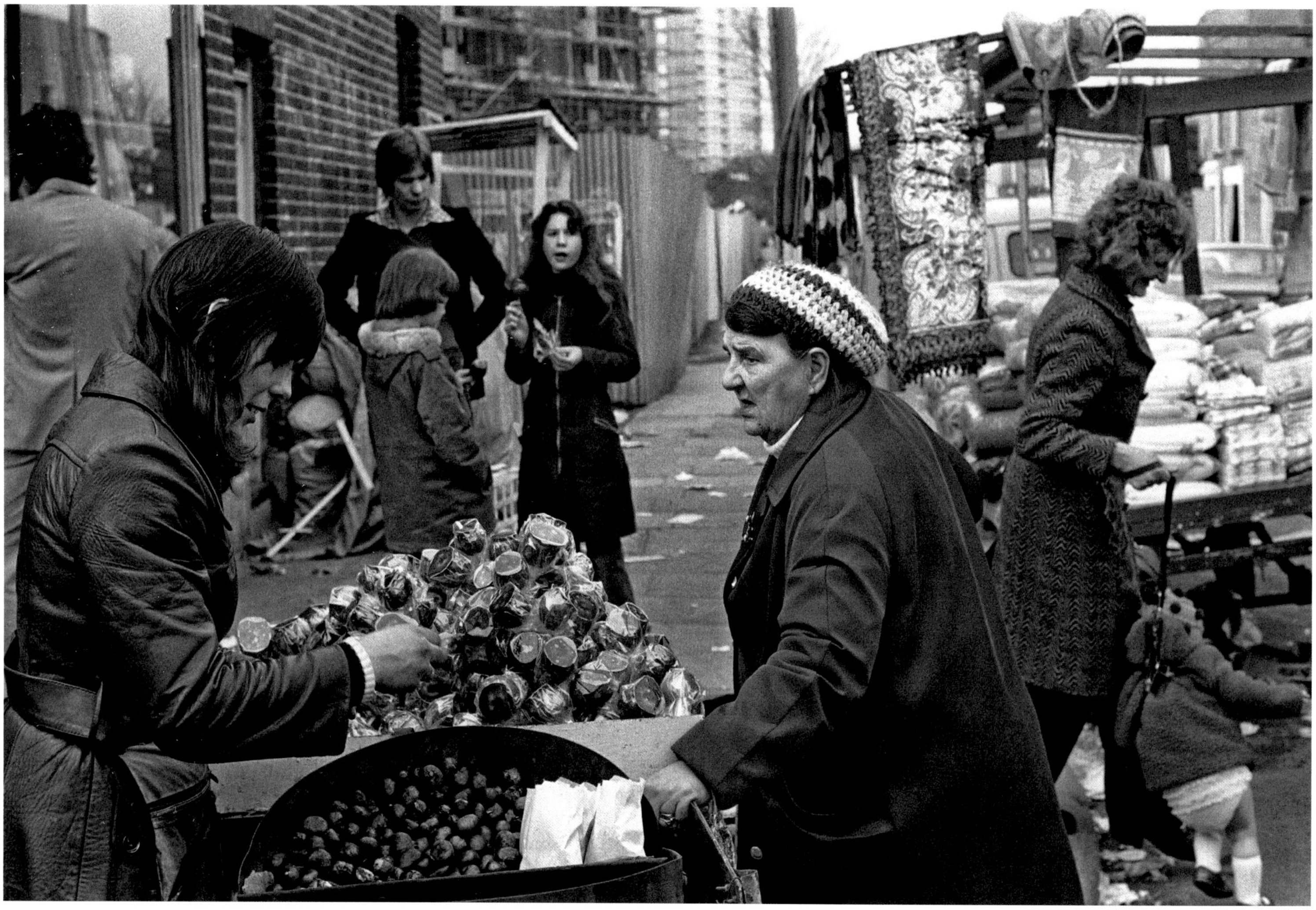

Tower Hamlets, London. 1975

A market trader in Roman Road sells hot roasted chestnuts and toffee apples with a hard brittle toffee exterior. They are protected by heavy duty, clear cellophane wrapping.

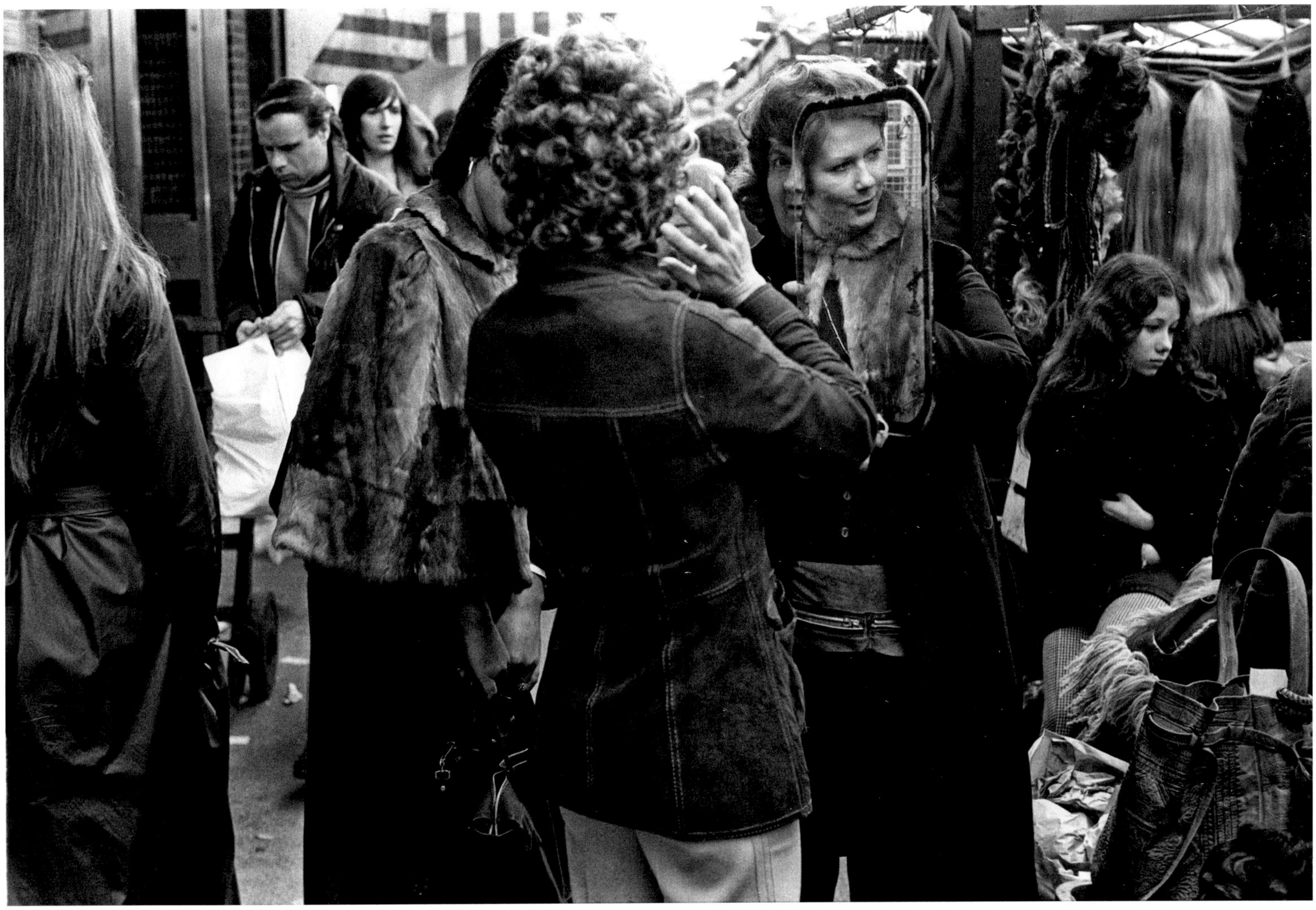

Tower Hamlets, London. 1975

Down the Roman, a chic East Ender
tries on a fashionable curly wig.

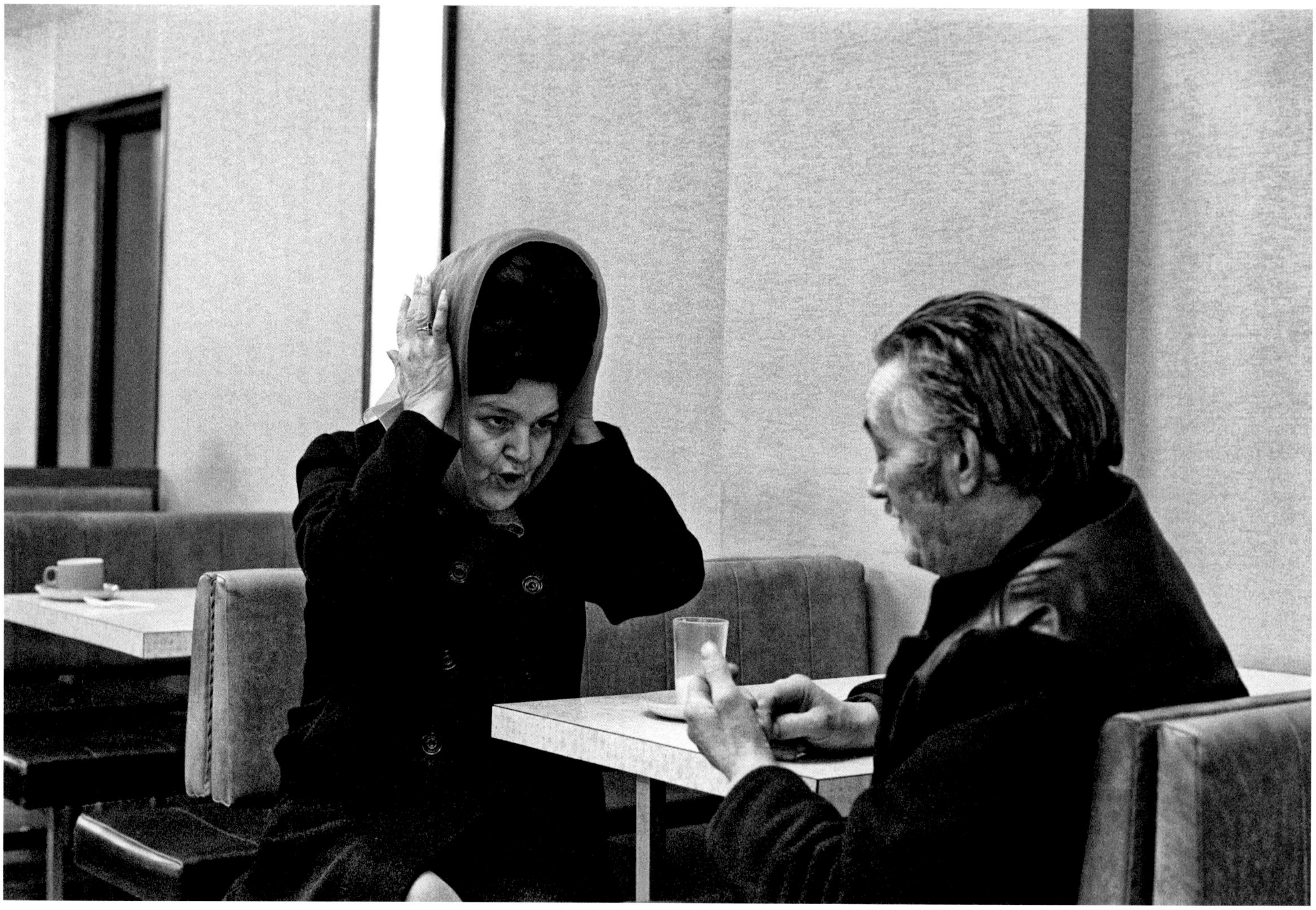

Whitechapel, London. 1974

Straight out of the hairdressers, and into a café, her fashionable beehive hairdo protected by a chiffon headscarf. Originally created in the 1960s in downtown Chicago, the beehive involves backcombing or teasing the hair with a comb, creating a tangled pile, which is lightly combed over to make a smooth outer surface. The longer the hair, the higher the beehive. Soap opera star Bet Lynch wore one in *Coronation Street* during the 1970s.

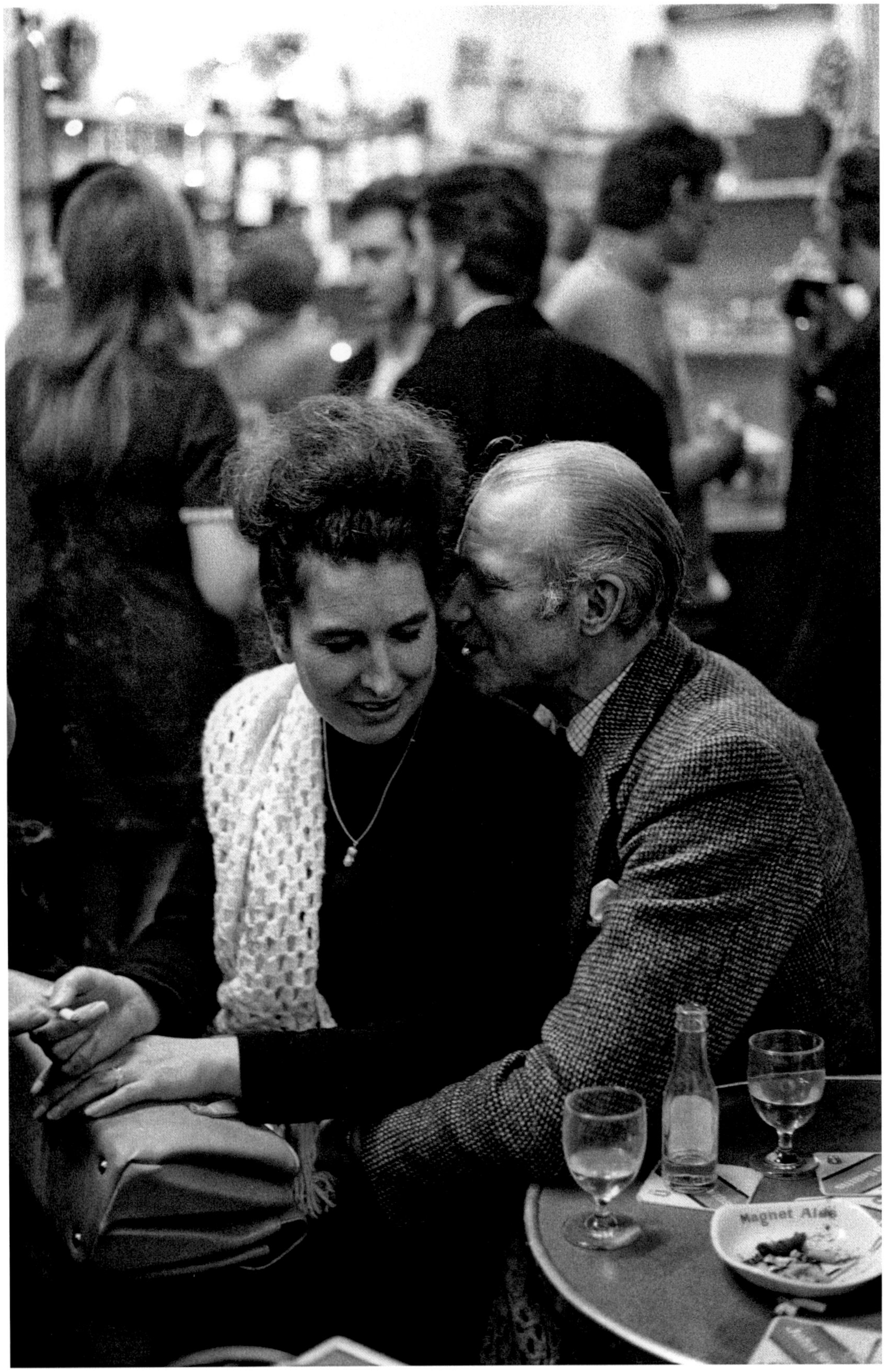

Haxey, Lincolnshire. 1972

Oblivious to the Kings Arms pub regulars crowded all around, a tweed-jacketed, middle-aged lothario with his hair brylcreemed straight back, places his hand on his lover's crotch, discreetly hidden by her handbag.

Chelsea, London. 1969

An anthophile in a floral hat admires a stand of narcissi at the Chelsea Flower Show.

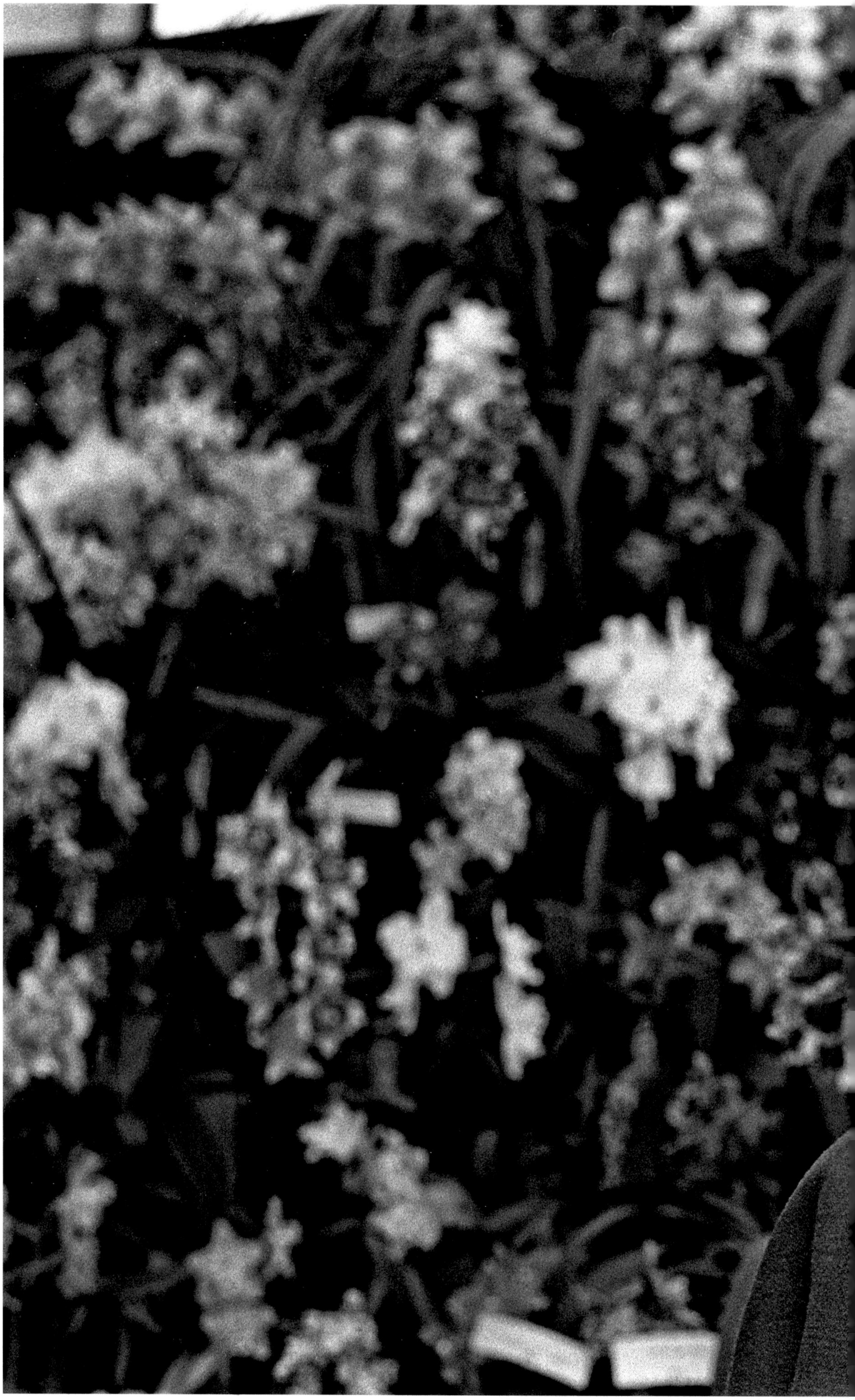

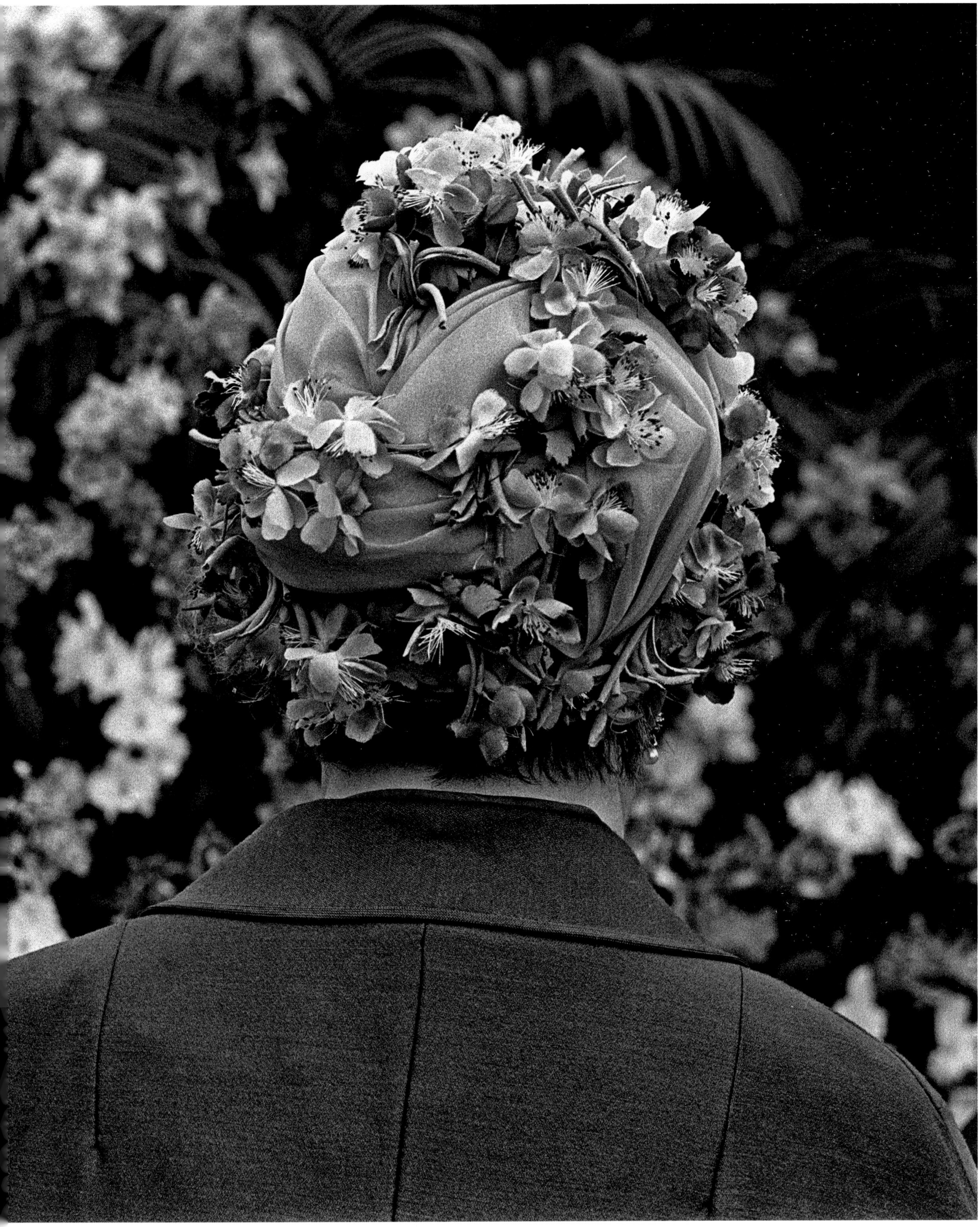

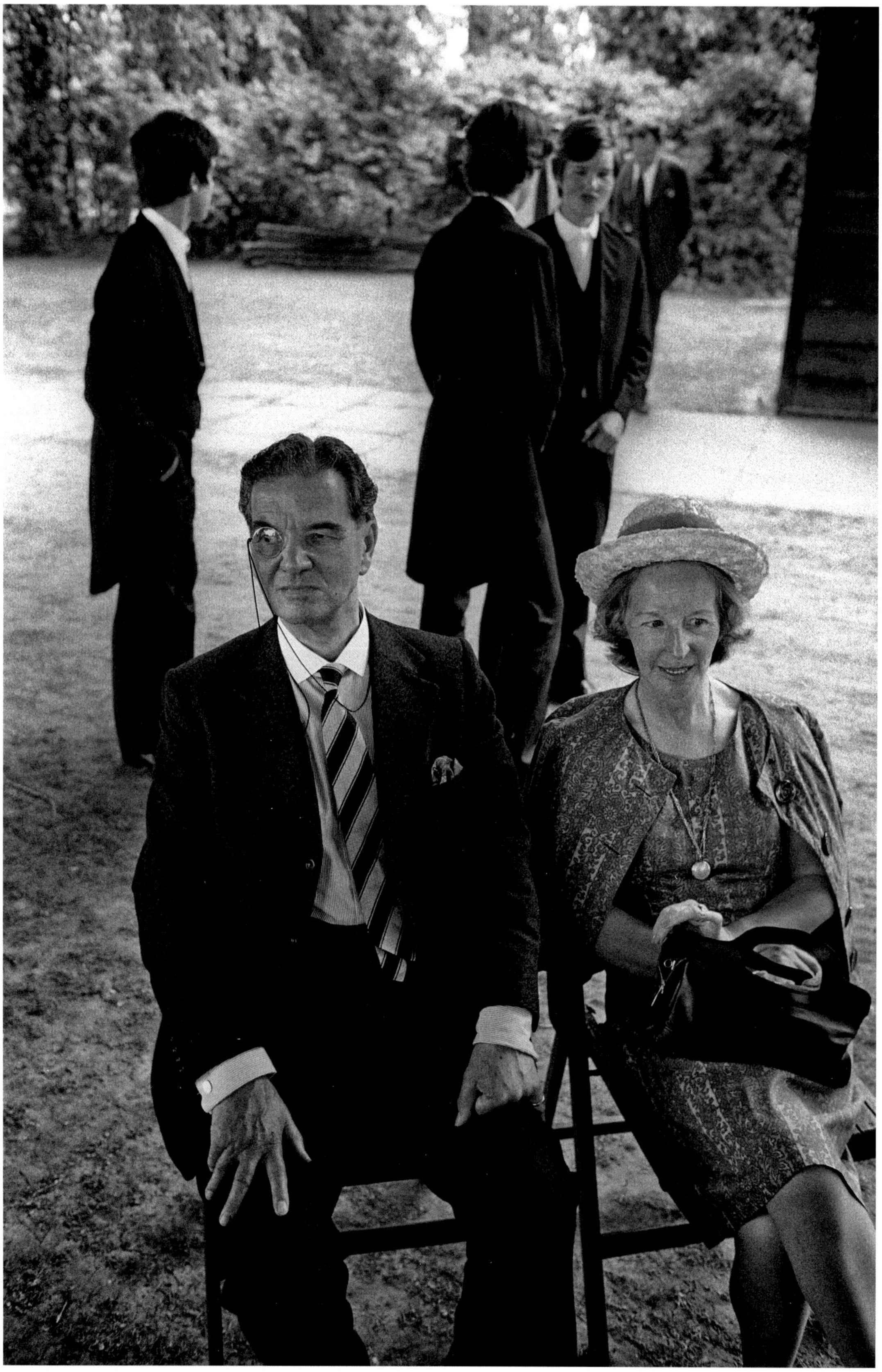

Eton, Berkshire. 1978

The Fourth of June, Eton College; proud parents watch an inter-house cricket match. The monocle-wearing gent sports what was fashionable before the First World War. Thereafter monocles became a PR disaster, as they were closely associated with the German High Command.

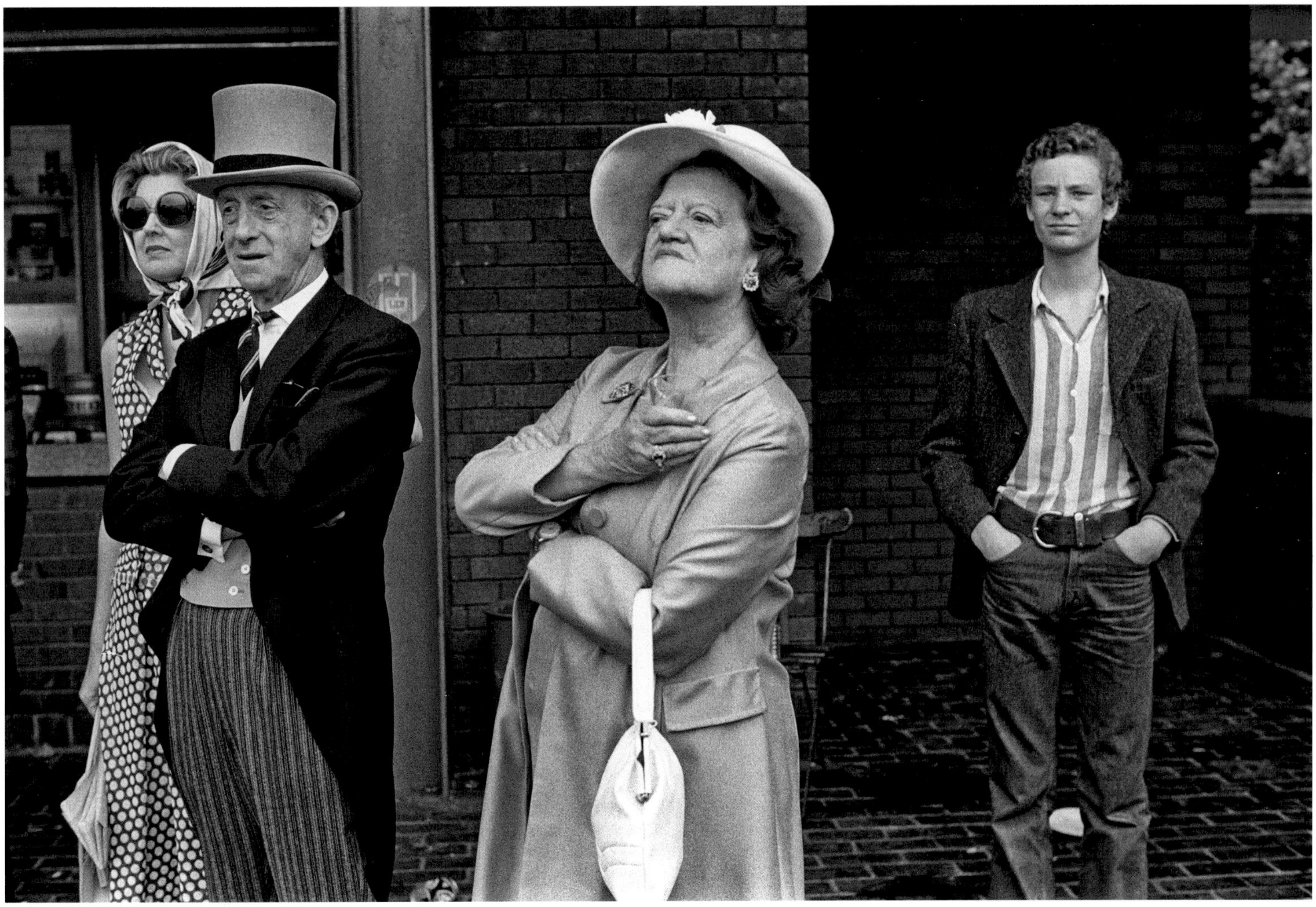

St Johns Wood, London. 1975

The Eton v Harrow cricket match played at Lords Cricket Ground is one of the longest running annual sporting fixtures in the world. The dress code; fathers wear morning dress, comprising of top hats and tails, whilst mothers may dress less formally; headscarves and dark glasses. Scholars, both old and new, smart casual, please.

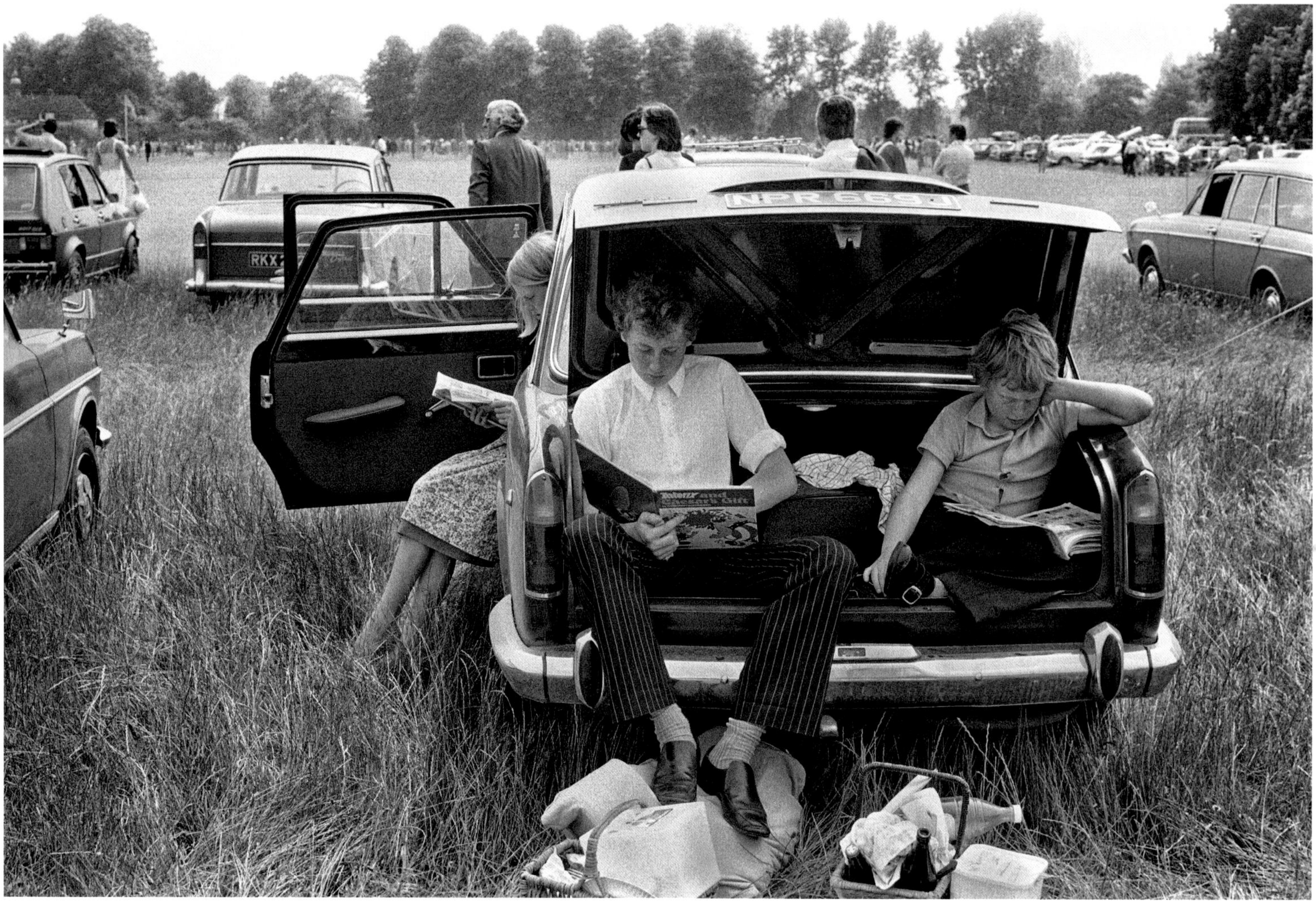

Eton, Berkshire. 1978

The remains from a family picnic lie scattered on the ground, and the inter-house cricket match on Agar's Plough has resumed. A young Etonian could not care less, he's engrossed in a copy of *Asterix and Caesar's Gift*, the 21st volume in the series.

Eton, Berkshire. 1978

The Fourth of June at Eton College, a day of celebrations, rowing on the river, inter-house cricket matches and a chance for old scholars to turn up sporting new girlfriends.

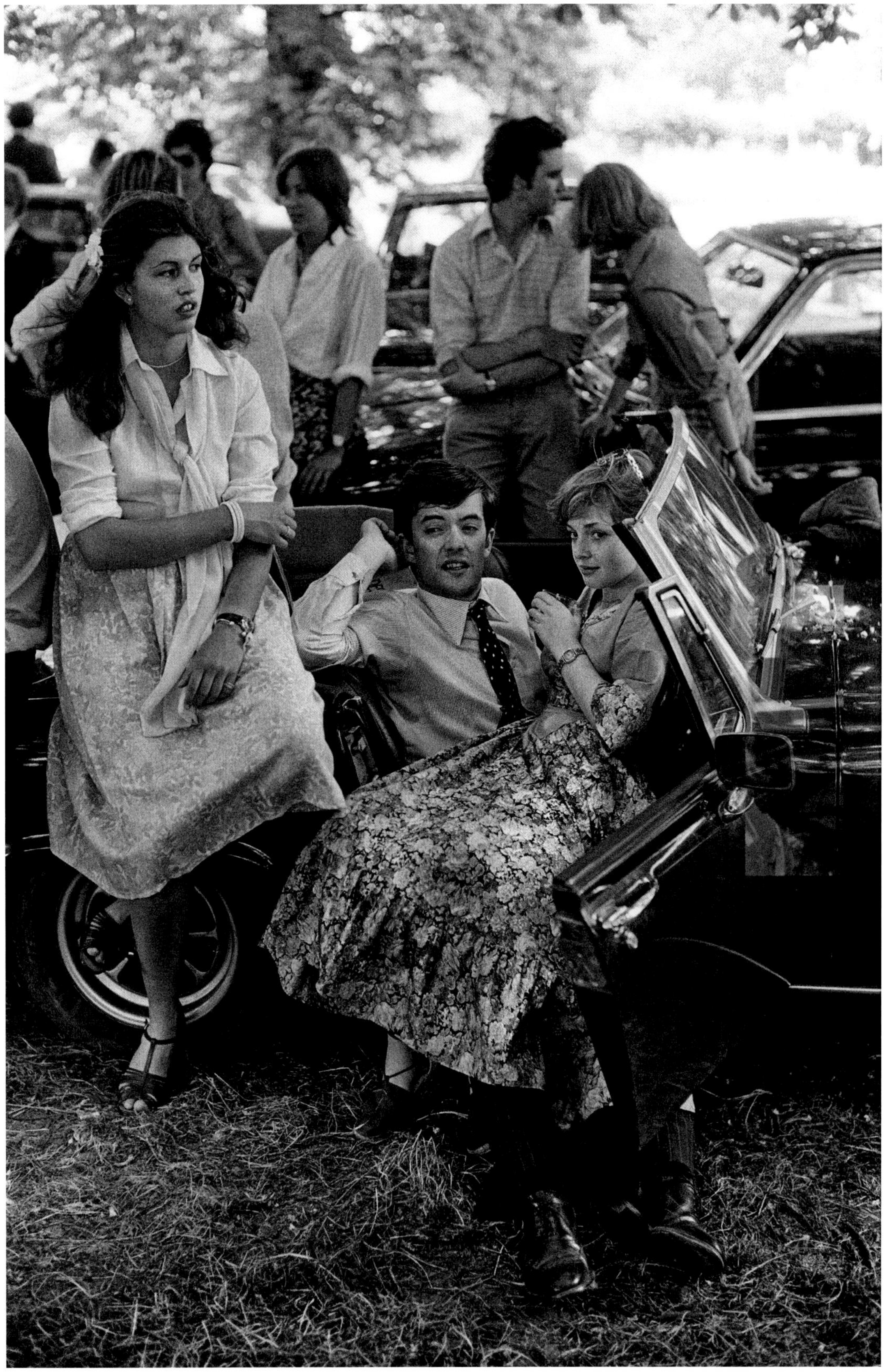

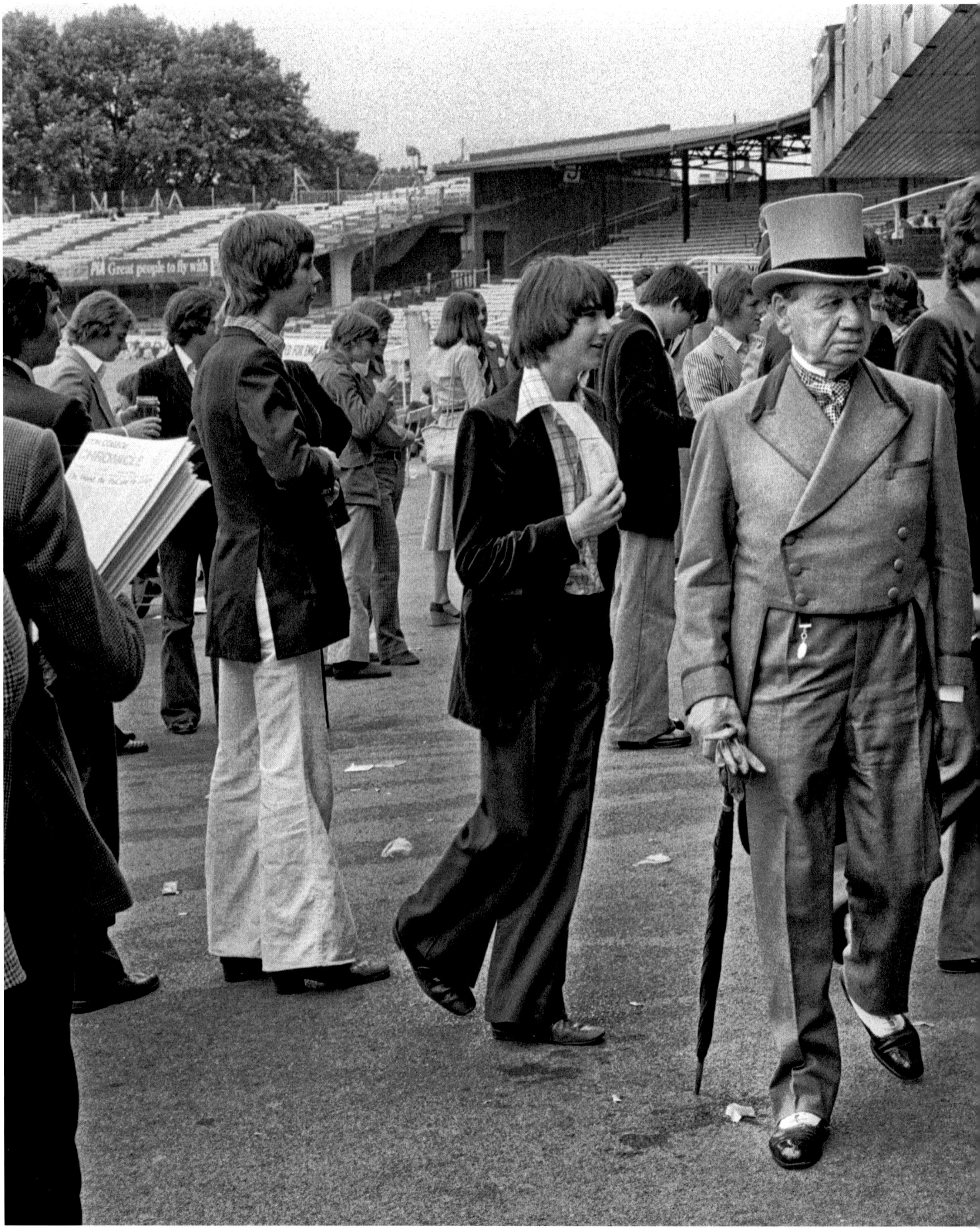
PIA Great people to fly with
CHRONICLE

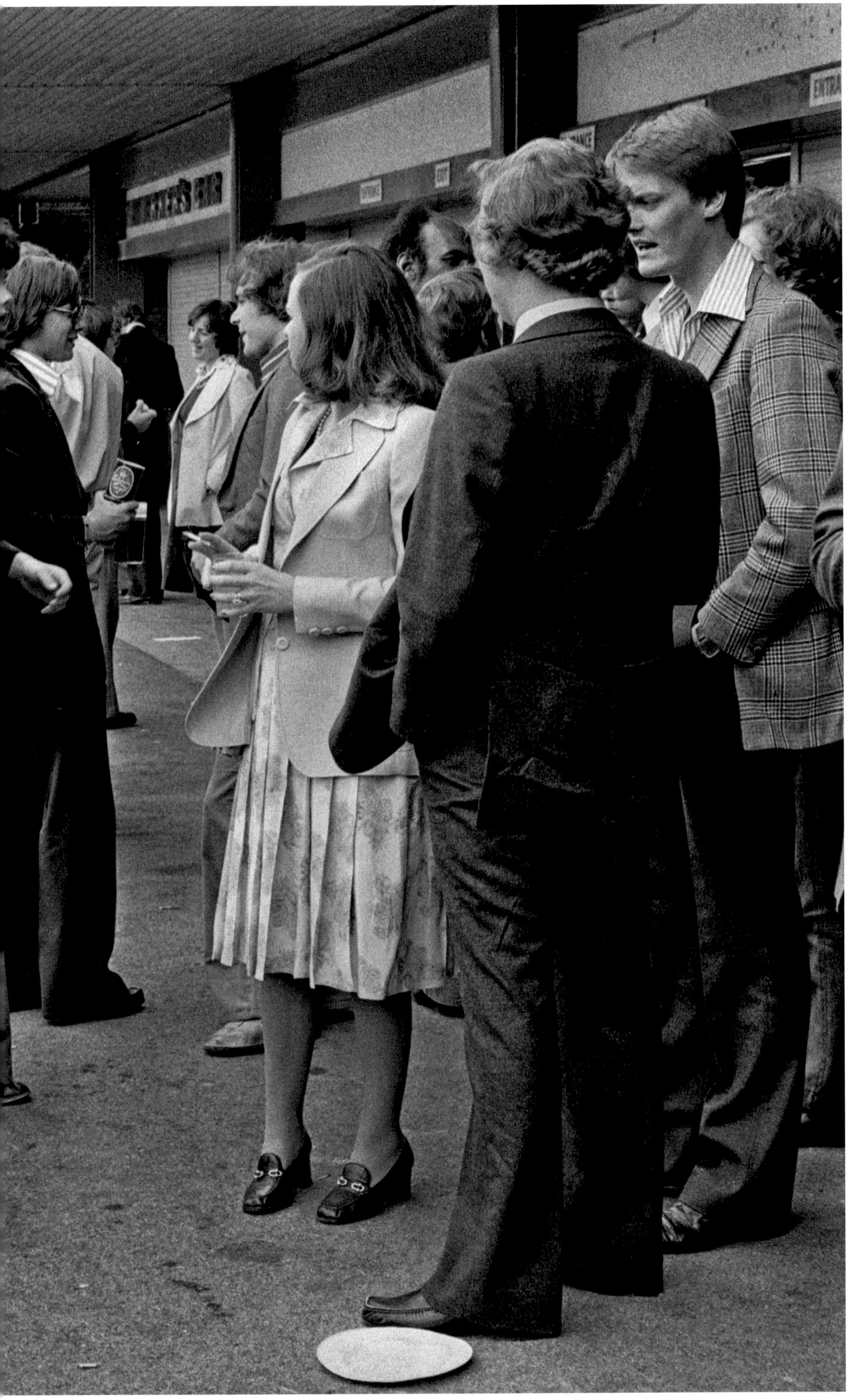

St Johns Wood, London. 1975

At the Eton v Harrow annual cricket match at Lords. An old Etonian wears a grey top hat and velvet trimmed double-breasted Regency style cutaway tail coat, with a wing collared shirt and cravat. Buckskin grey gloves and black and white two-tone shoes complete his ensemble. Surely the height of sartorial elegance?

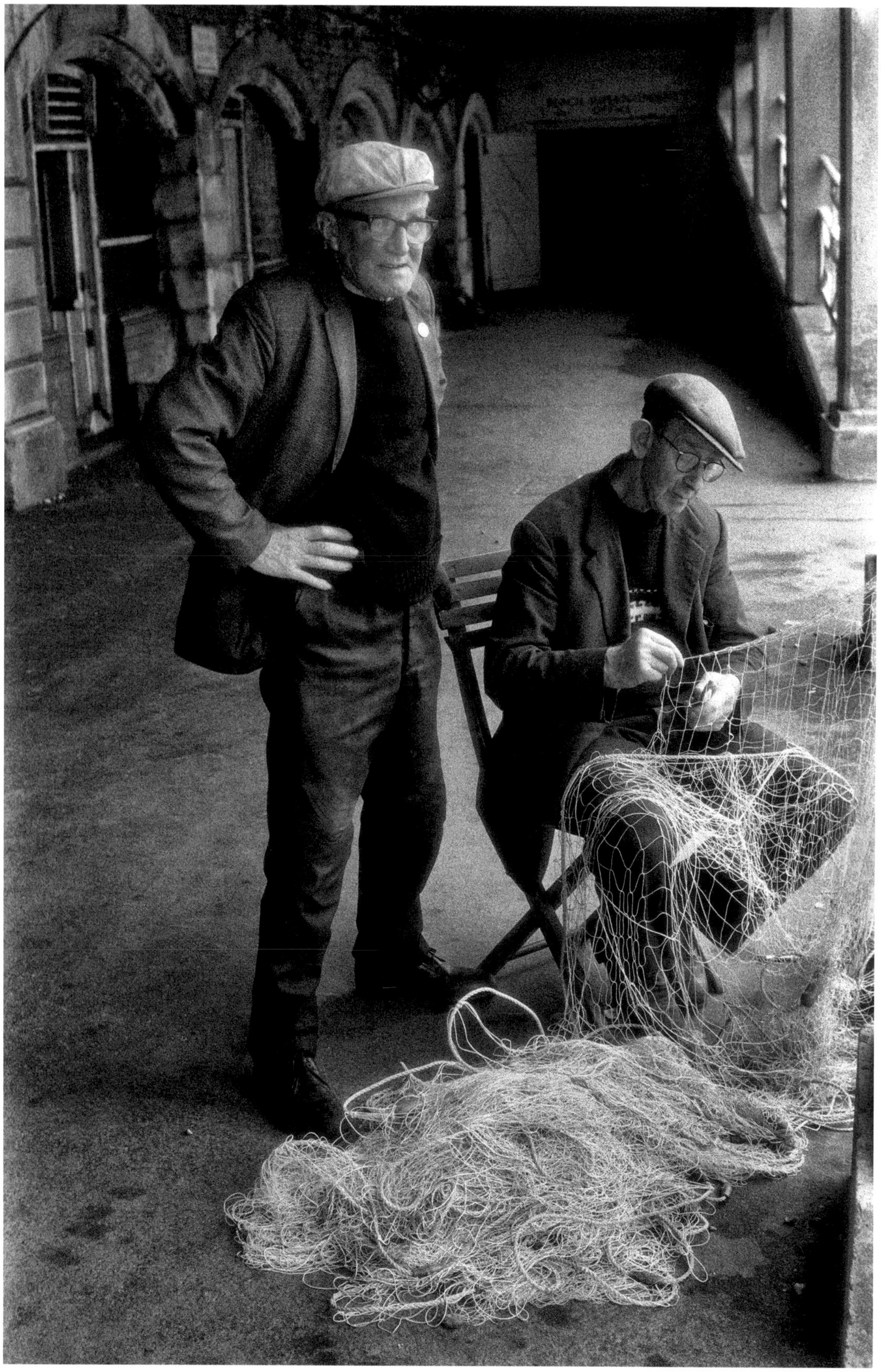

Brighton, Sussex. 1971

The Deep Sea Anglers Club; George Hillman mending the nets outside the club house and bar at the King's Road Arches on Brighton beach.

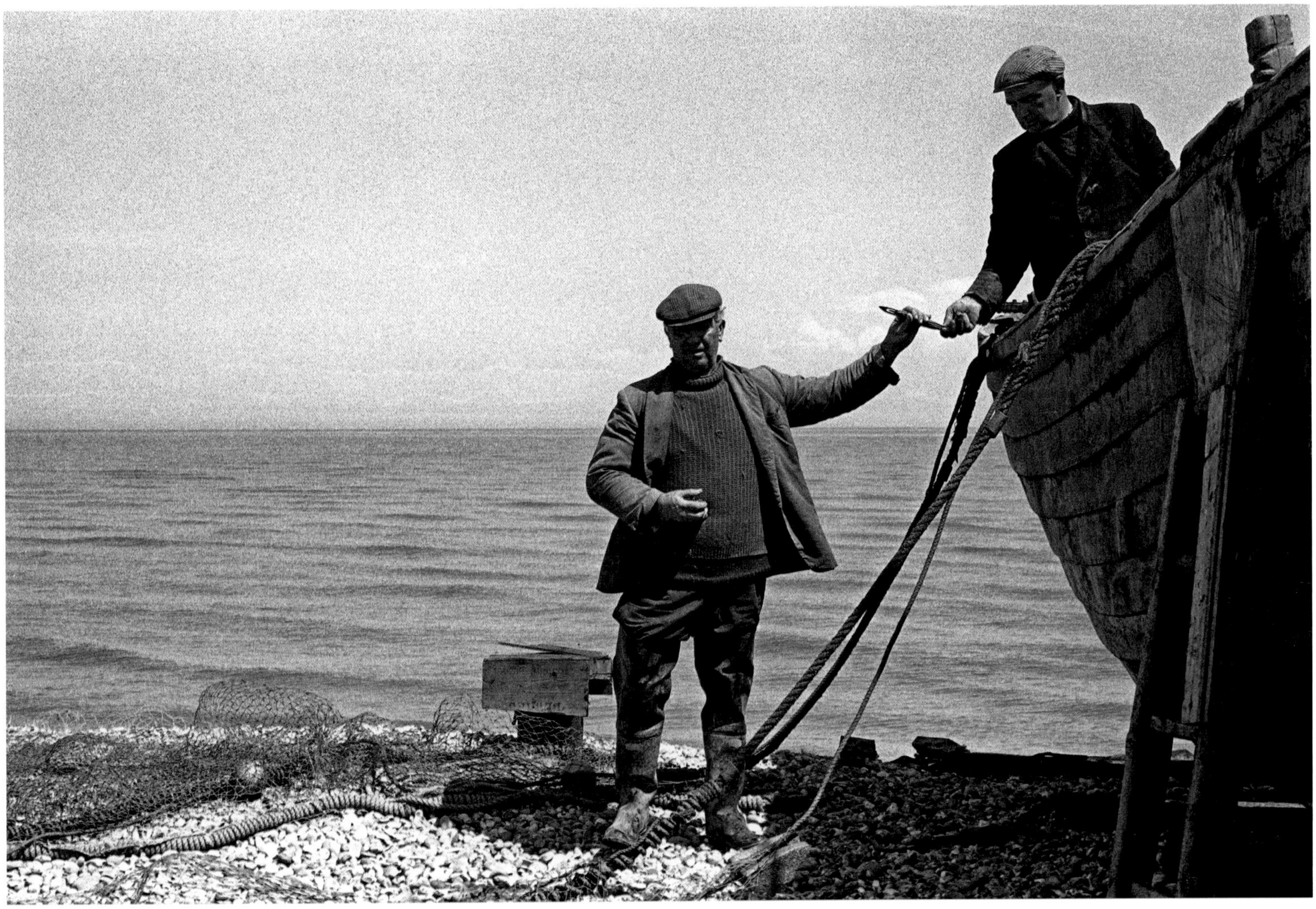

Dungeness, Kent. 1969

Fisherman Charlie Tart working on light repairs to his boat. The Tart family, along with the Oliers, are the two most prominent fishing families in Dungeness and have lived and fished off the flint shingle beach since the early 20th century.

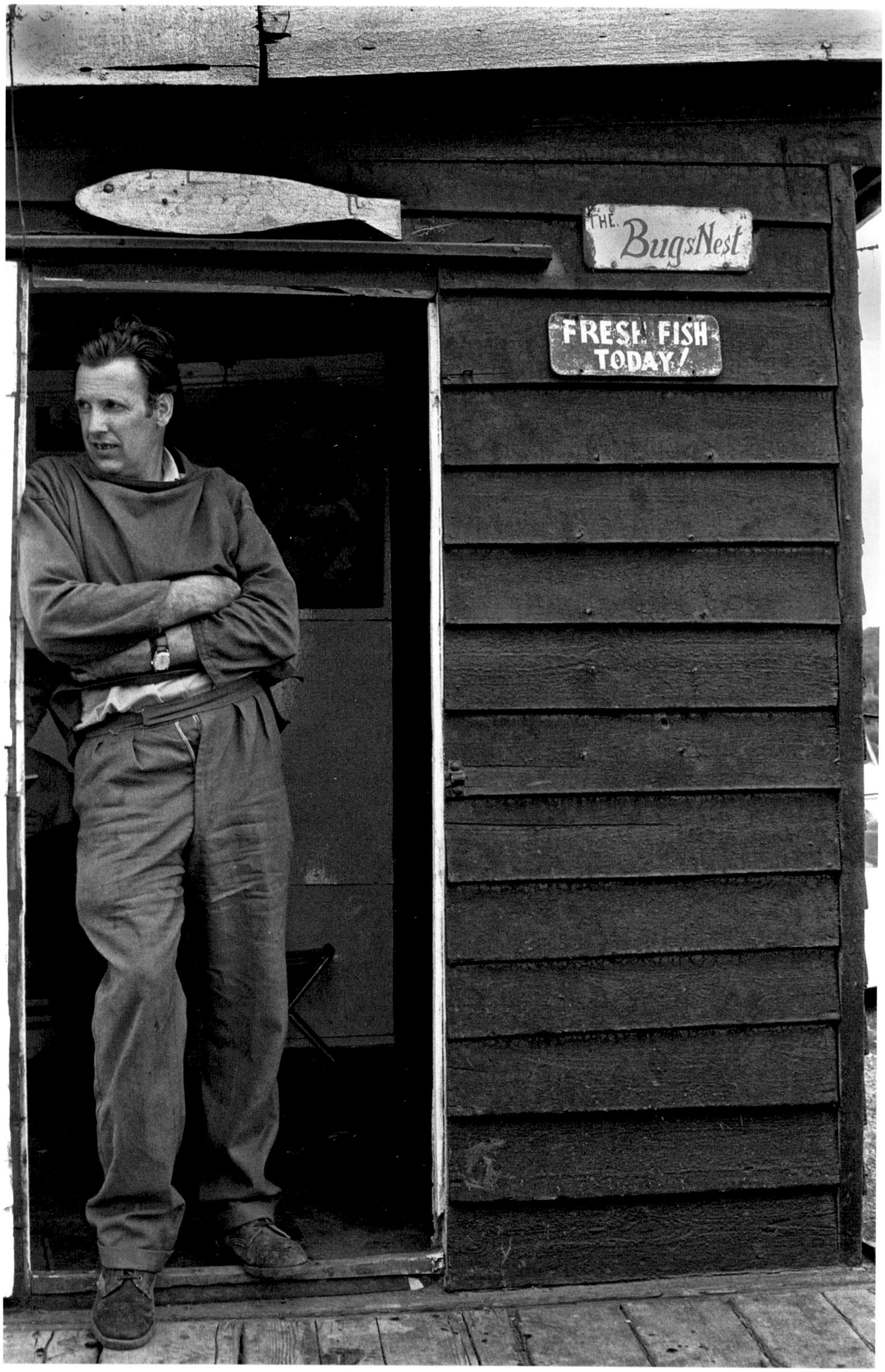

Dunwich, Suffolk. 1973

A fisherman sells today's fresh fish from The Bugs Nest. In Anglo Saxon times Dunwich was the capital of the Kingdom of East Angles, and was a port the size of 14th century London. Almost nothing remains now except The Ship public house and a scattering of cottages.

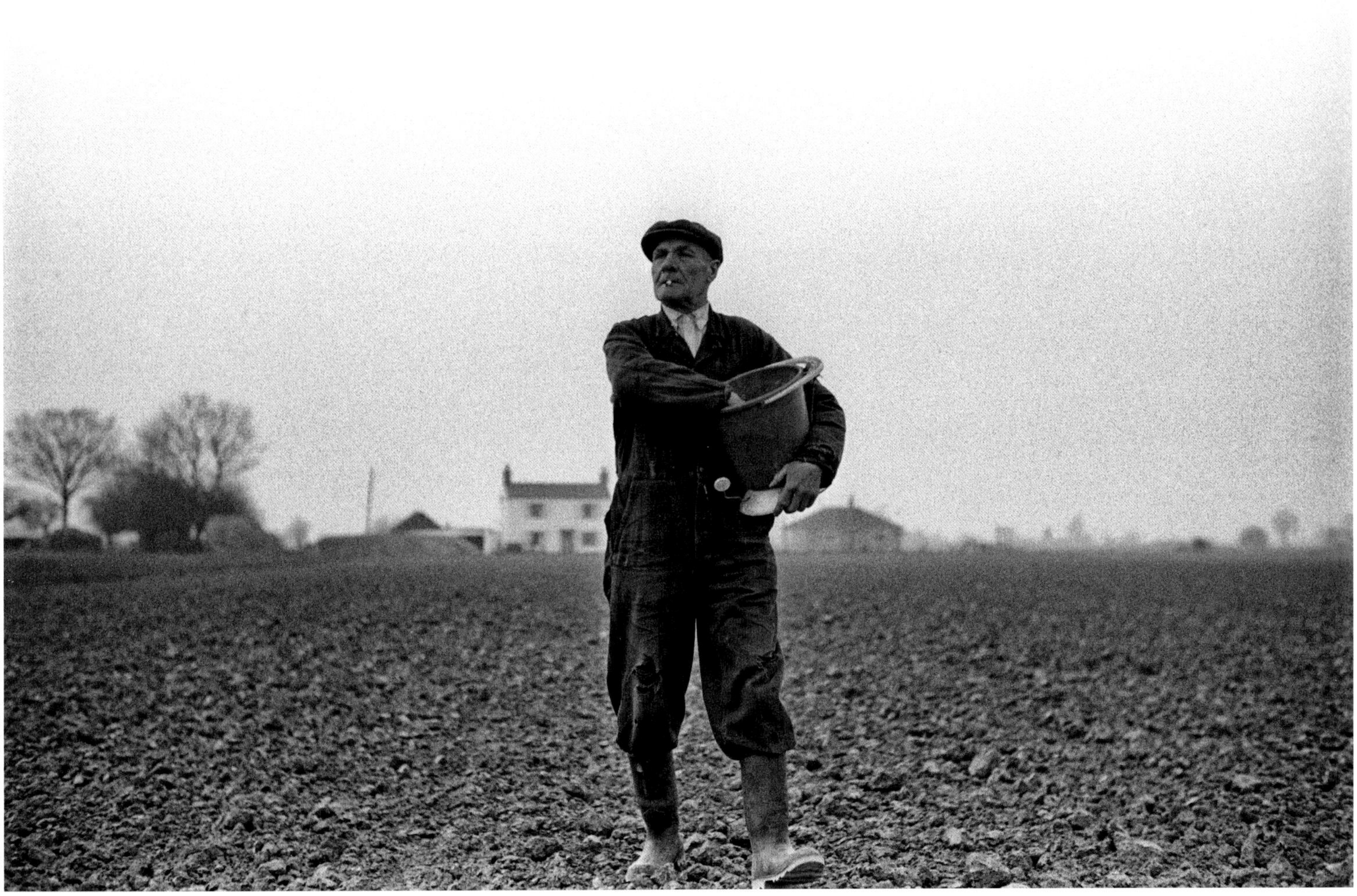

Norfolk. 1974

In his patched-at-the-knee overalls, and shirt buttoned tight, a farmer strides out across his recently ploughed field. He is sowing seed by hand, as men have done since the beginning of time.

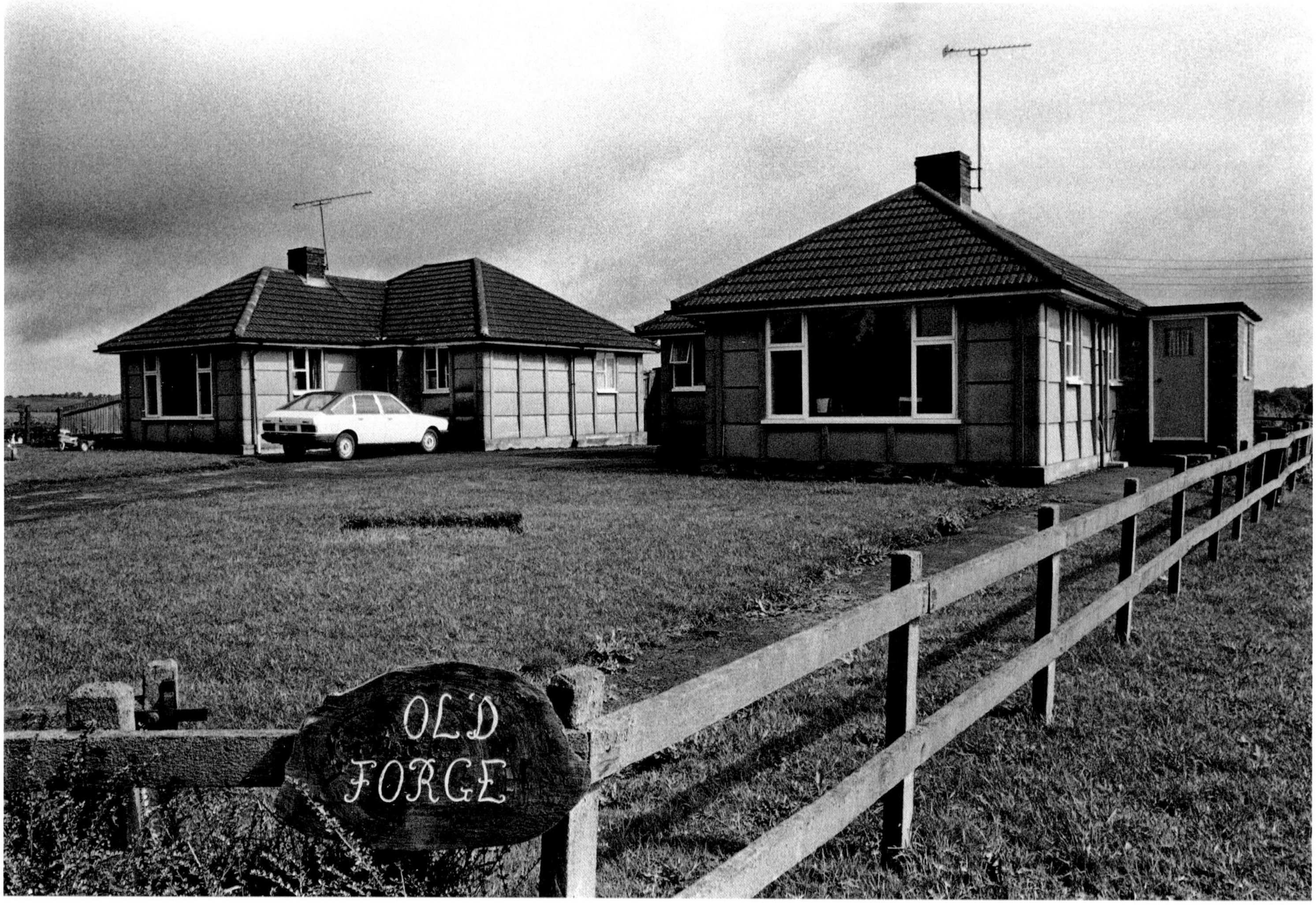

Upper Basildon, Berkshire. 1983

The Old Forge. Twin post war prefabricated bungalows now stand on the site of the old blacksmith's forge.

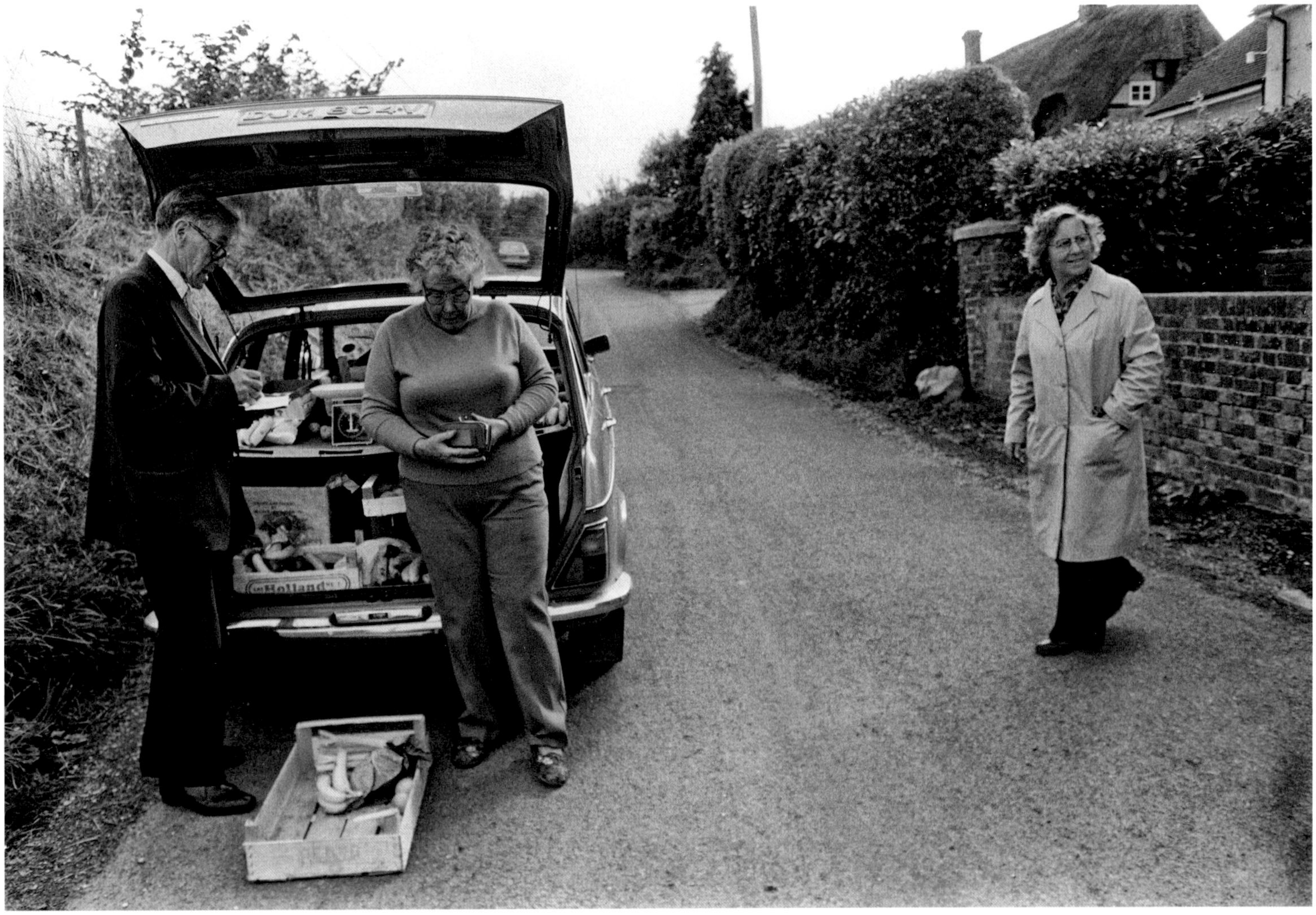

Upper Basildon, Berkshire. 1983

The local Methodist lay preacher delivers pre-ordered groceries once a week from the back of his car. The village shop had recently closed down.

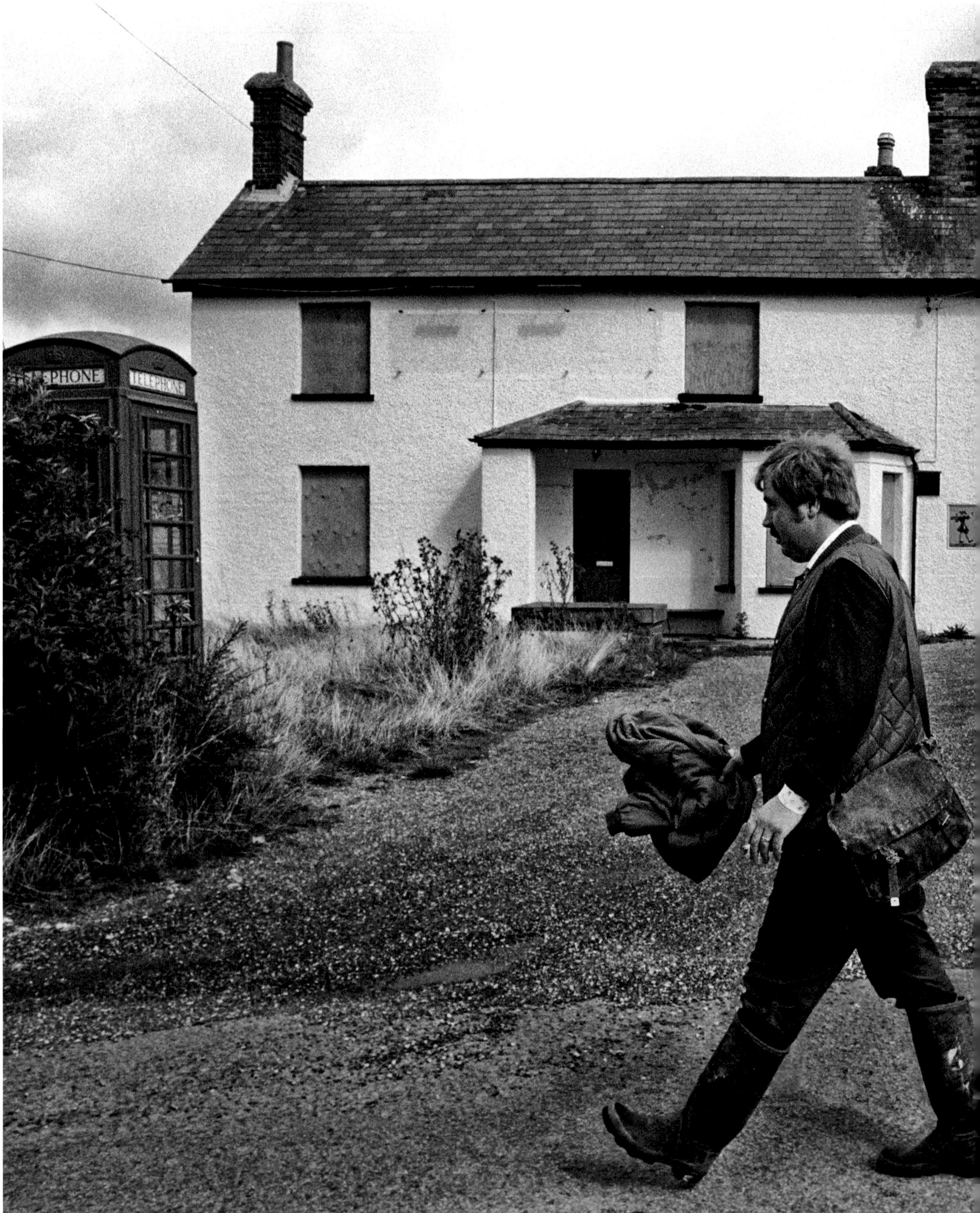
TELEPHONE

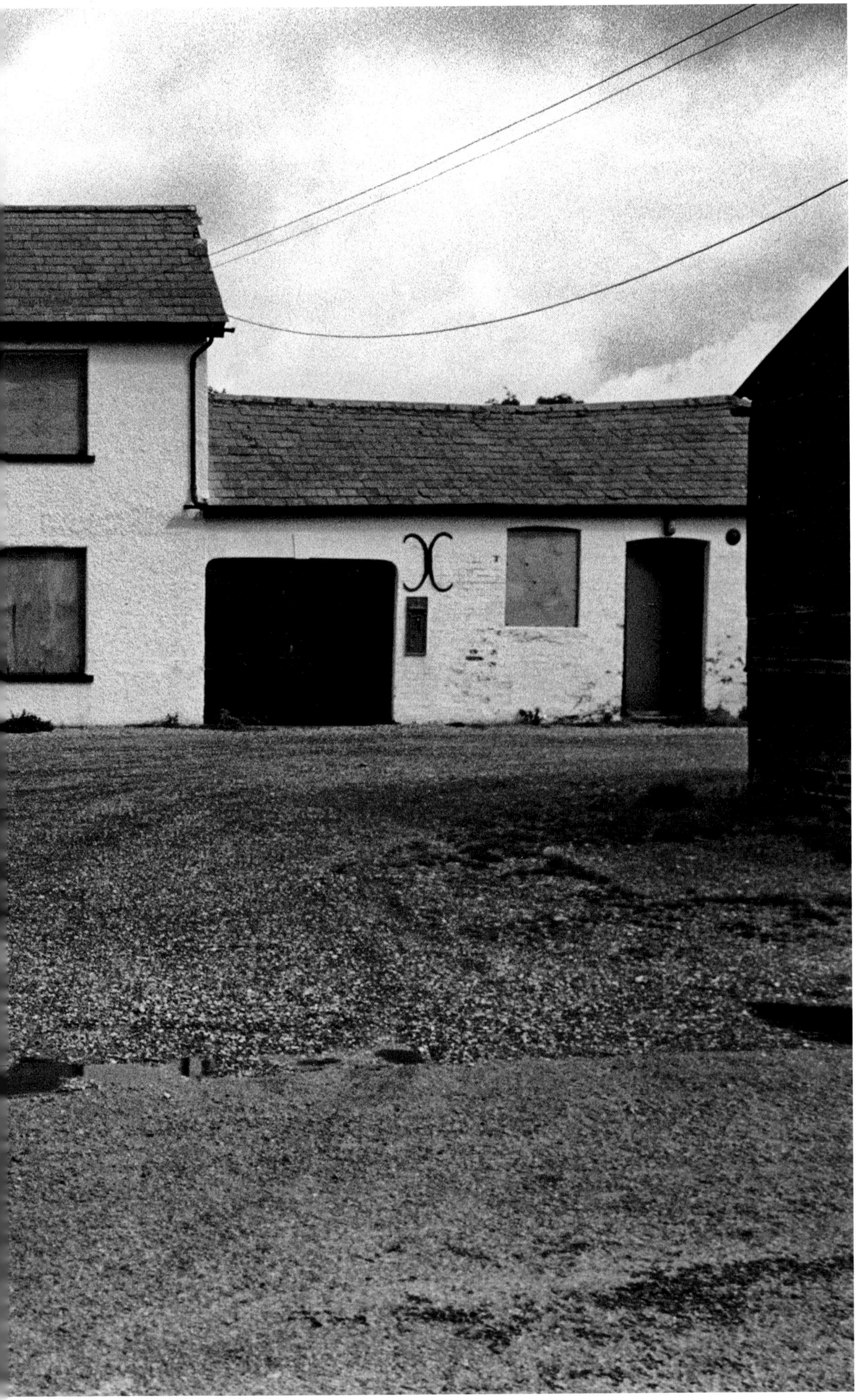

Upper Basildon, Berkshire. 1983

A farm labourer on his way home after a day's work, walks past what was once his local pub, The Fox and Cubs.

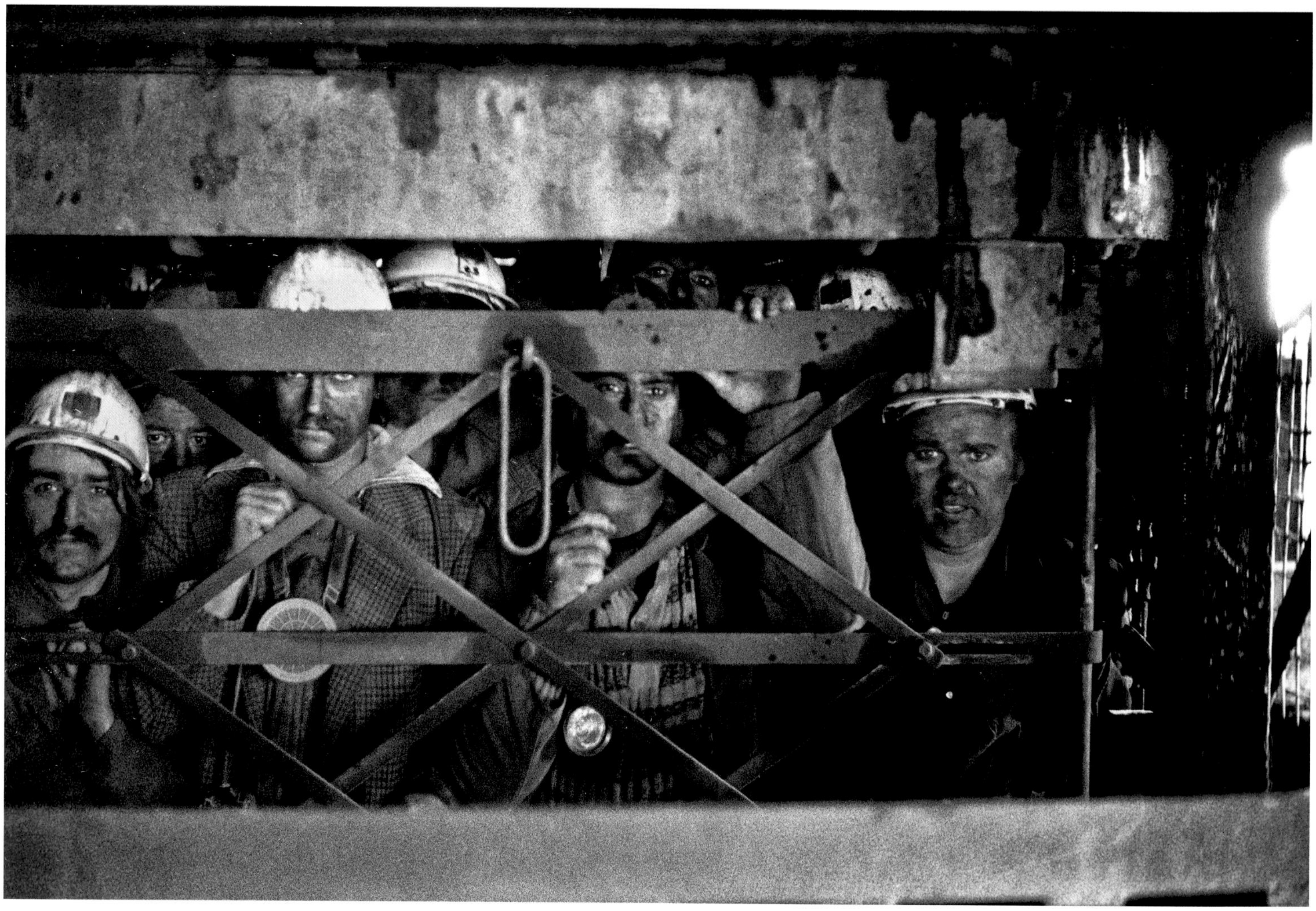

South Kirkby, Yorkshire. 1979

At the end of a seven hour fifteen minute shift, plus forty five minutes 'riding time', South Kirkby Colliery miners return to the surface in 'the cage'. As a rule, the closer that miners worked to the coalface the more they were paid. An experienced miner who was an electrician working at the coalface could receive a daily wage of 84 old shillings a shift. Equivalent to approximately £250 per week in 2018. The pit closed in 1988.

Snowdown, Kent. 1976

The Snowdown Colliery pithead gear. Miners, some with their lamps still on, make their way to the lamp room where they would drop off their 'pit checks' and recharge their lamps. There was a great camaraderie amongst the men; they were miners first and then their specific trade, never the other way around.

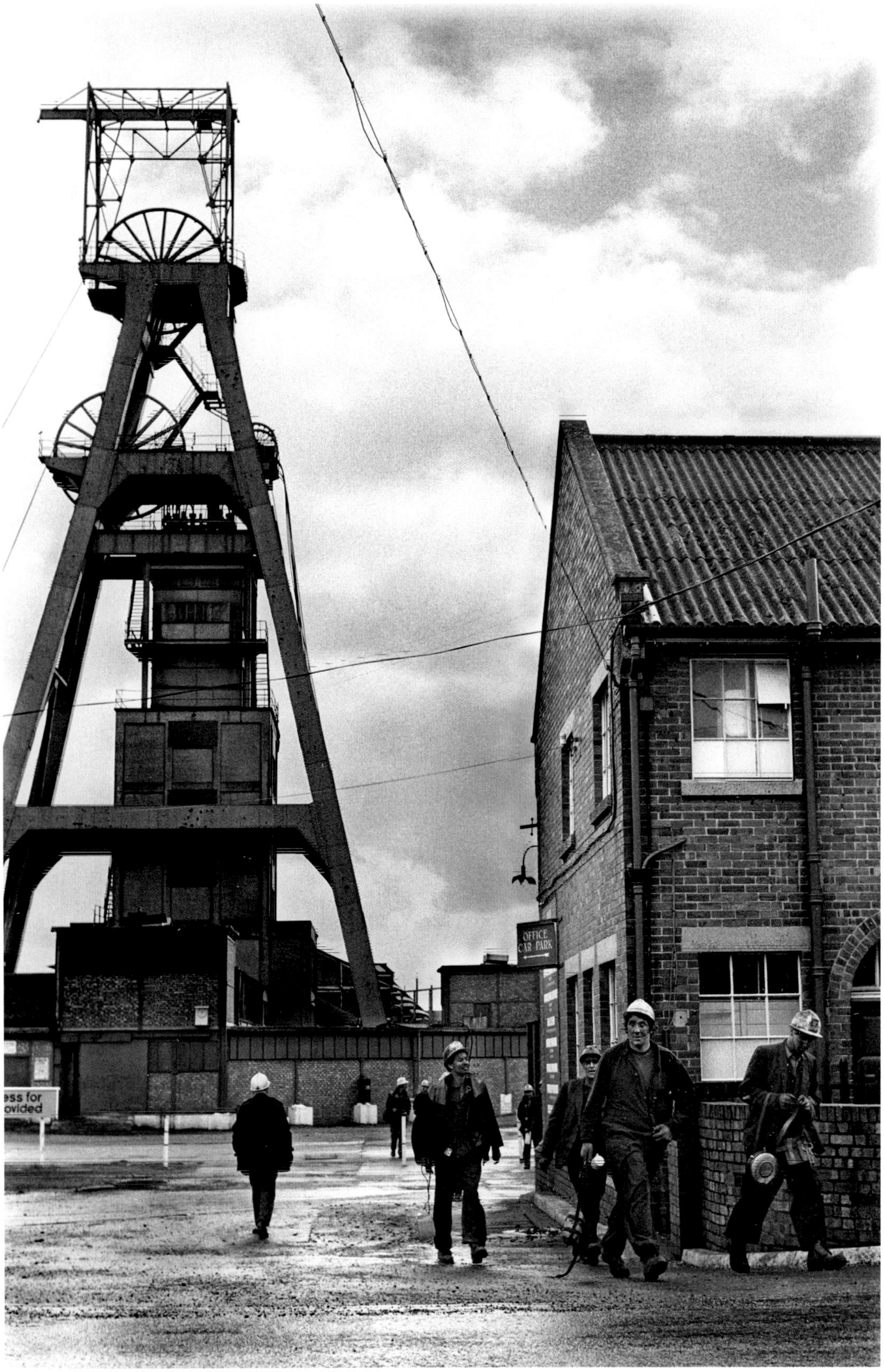

Snowdown, Kent. 1976

Albert Christian and workmate smoking in the pithead baths. There were two sides, the clean and dirty side, a miner had a locker in each, and on the dirty side he hung his Pit Black working clothes. Nicknamed Dante's Inferno, Snowdown was the deepest and hottest colliery in the entire Kent coalfield; it closed in 1987.

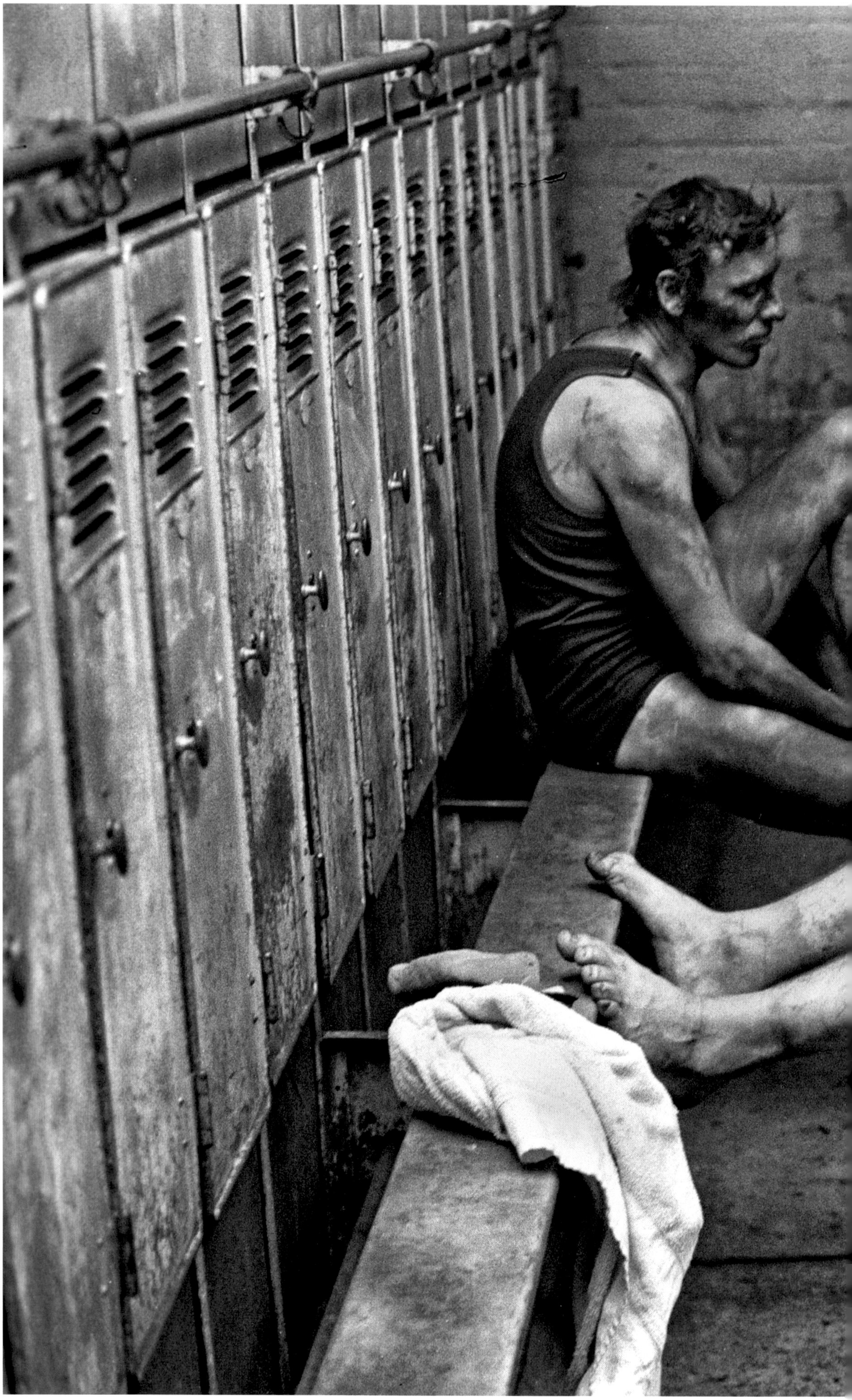

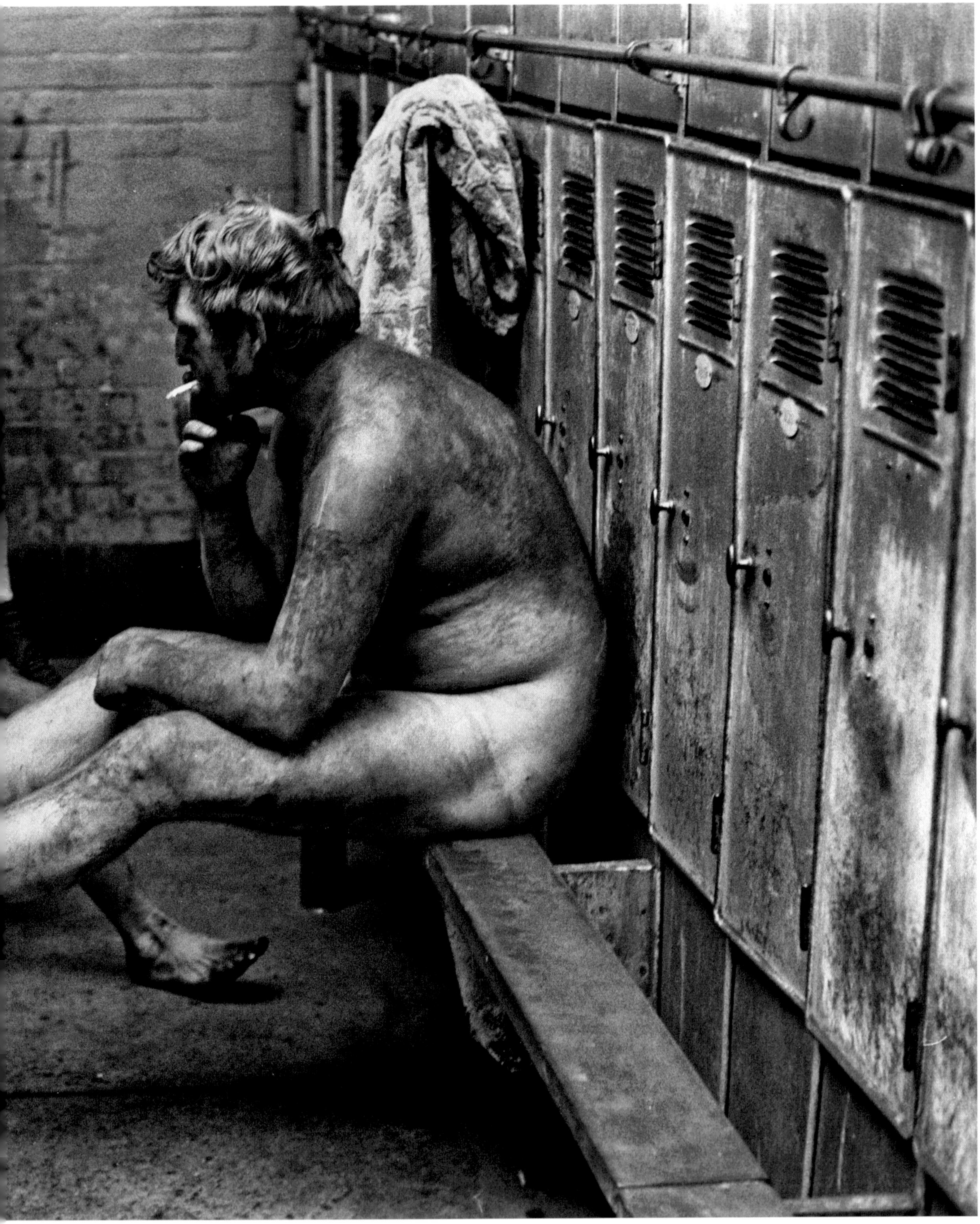

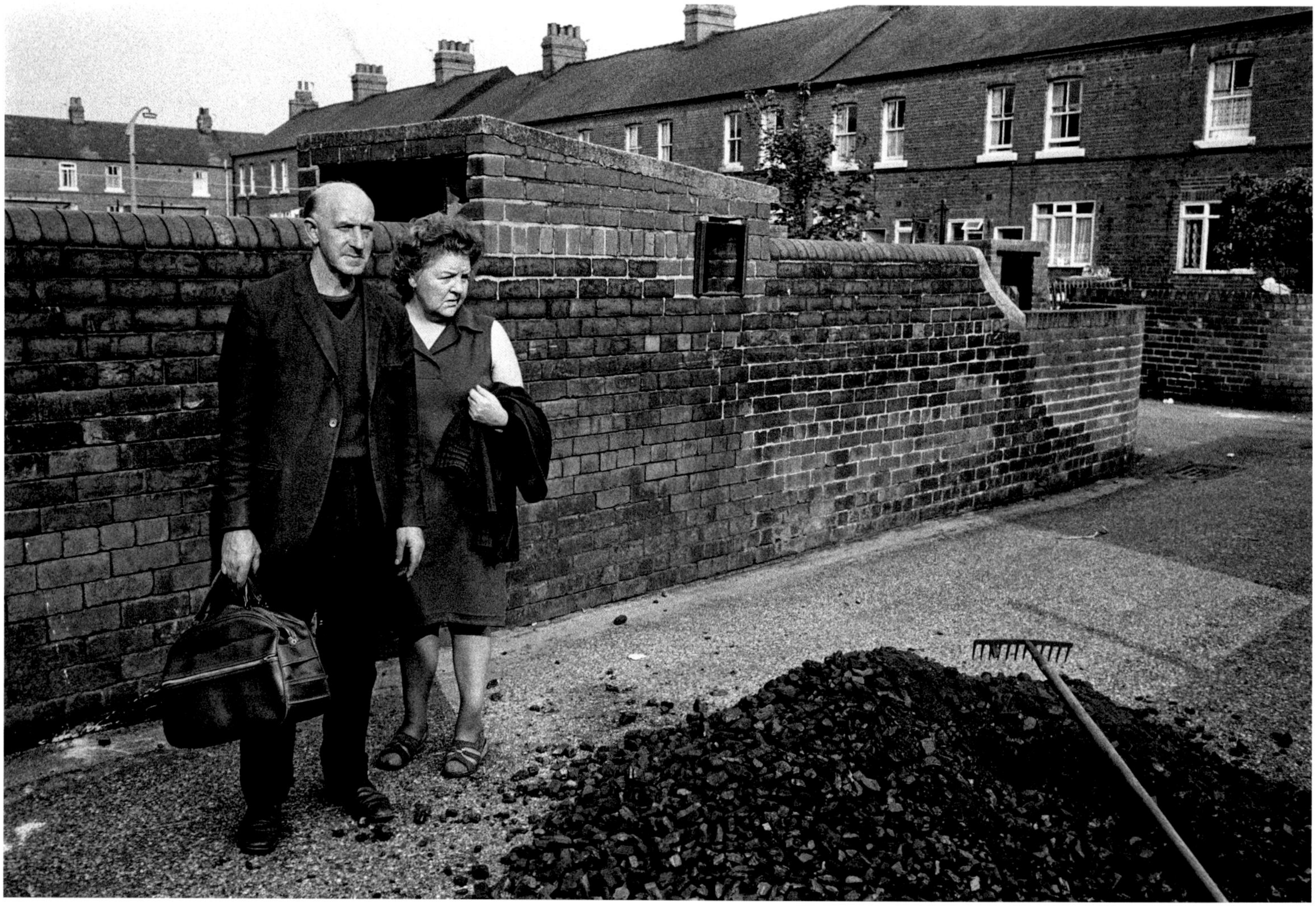

South Kirkby, Yorkshire. 1979

A free coal delivery, tipped at the 'back entry'. Each household that burnt solid fuel received one ton of loose load every month. It was left for householders to transport it into their own coal-house. This led to the local youths making a bob or two by barrowing the coal into storage areas. Pit houses, as they were always known, were built in the 1900s by the pit owners and later taken over by the National Coal Board. At the bottom of the garden were coalhouses also containing an outside toilet. By the 1970s these were being converted into bathrooms with an extension for a new coal house.

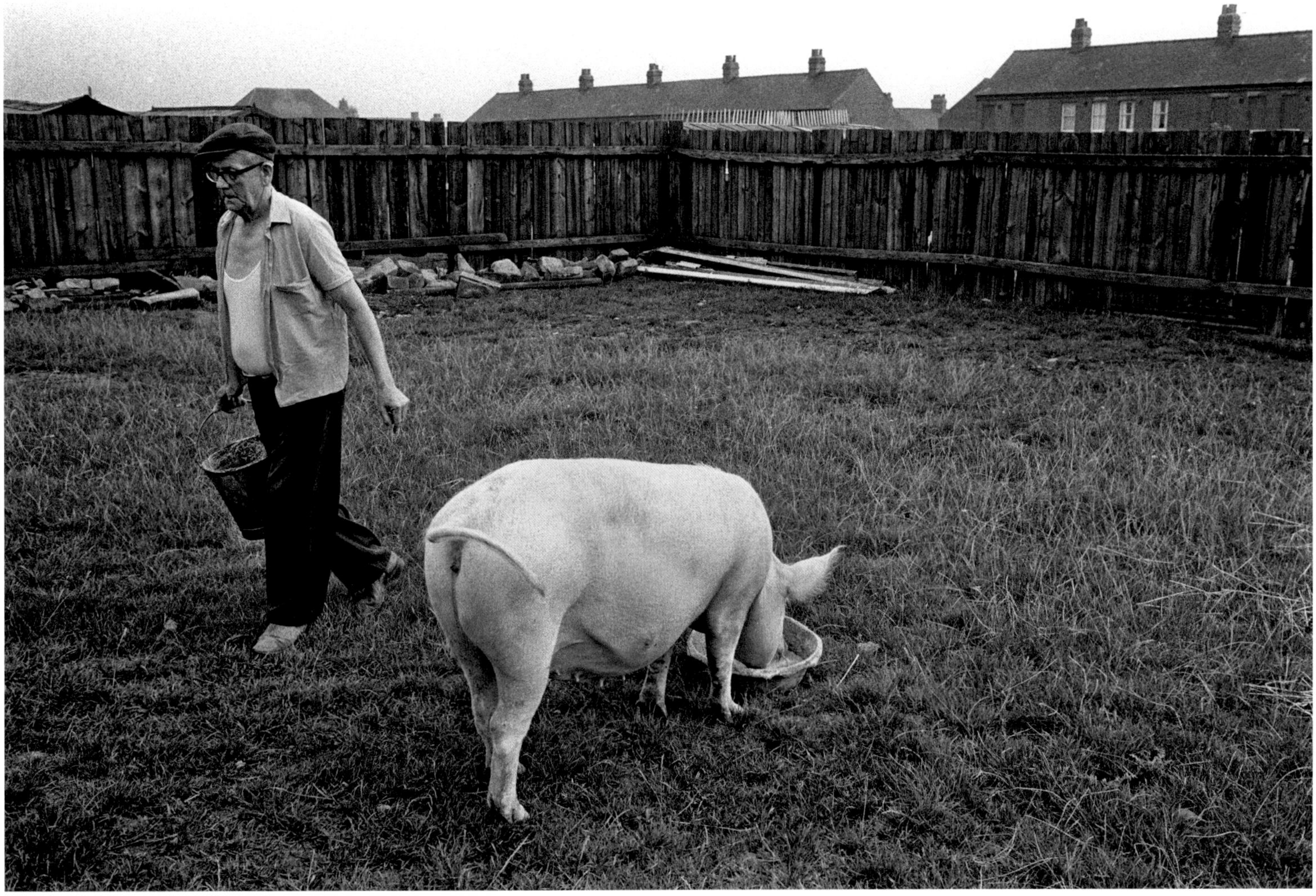

South Kirkby, Yorkshire. 1979

Retired miner Tommy was a bandsman at Hemsworth Colliery. On his smallholding he kept several pigs, on land that he rented from the National Union of Miners.

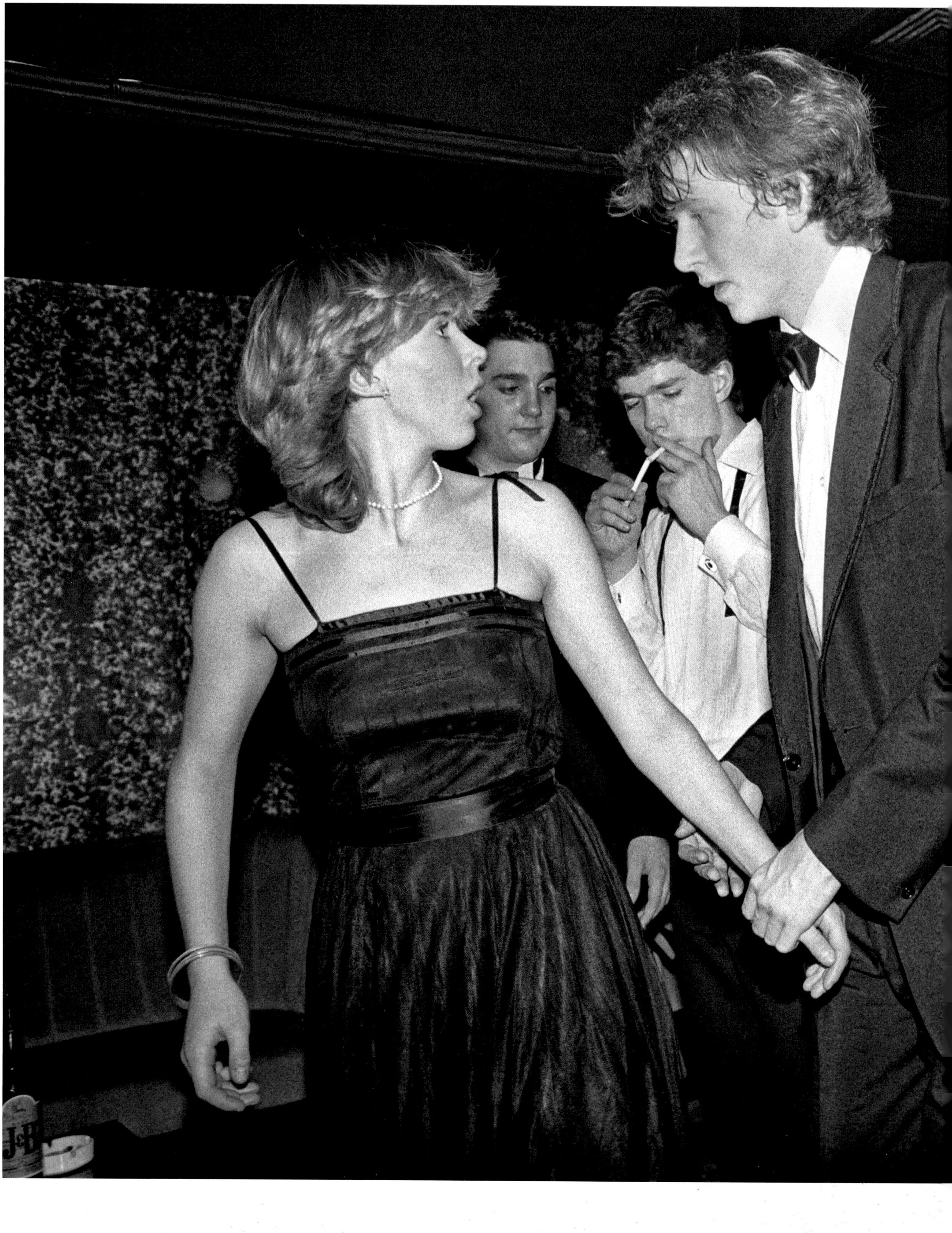

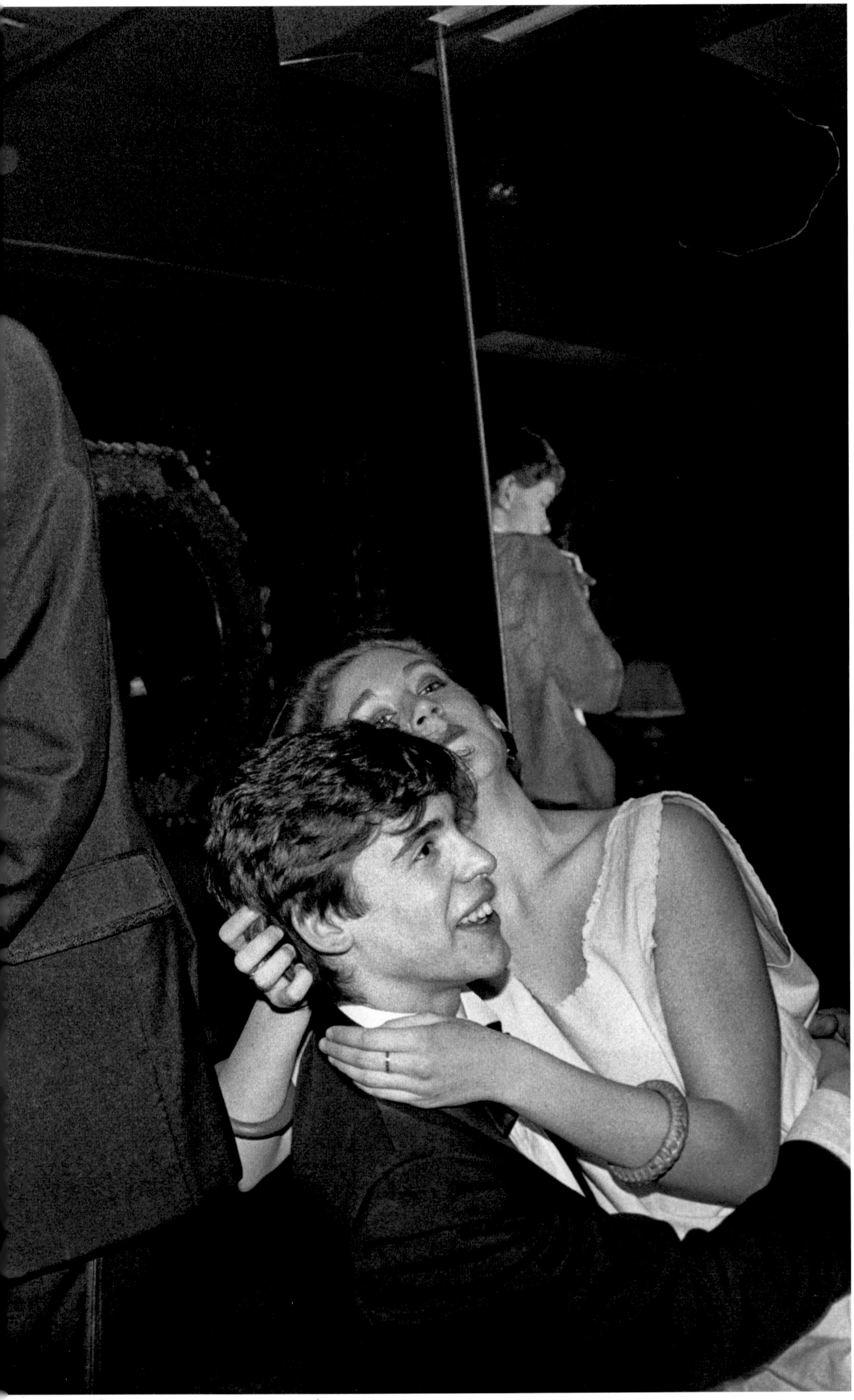

Chelsea, London. 1982

Teenage Sloane Rangers at Wedgies nightclub on the King's Road. It was managed by playboy and bon viveur Sir Dai Llewellyn.

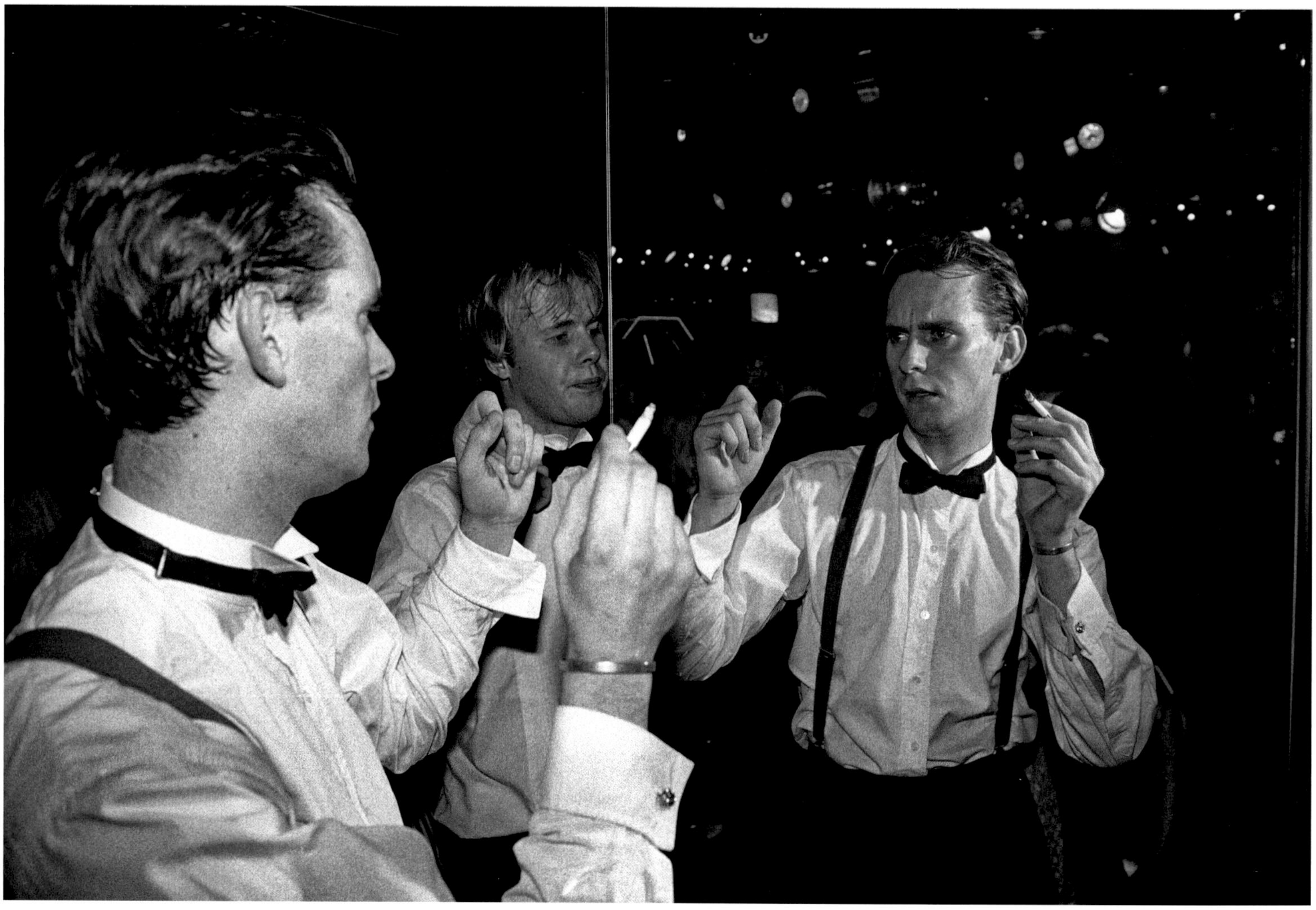

Chelsea, London. 1982

Bow-tied and looking cool, this Narcissus gazes upon his own reflection in a mirrored pillar in the basement at Wedgies.

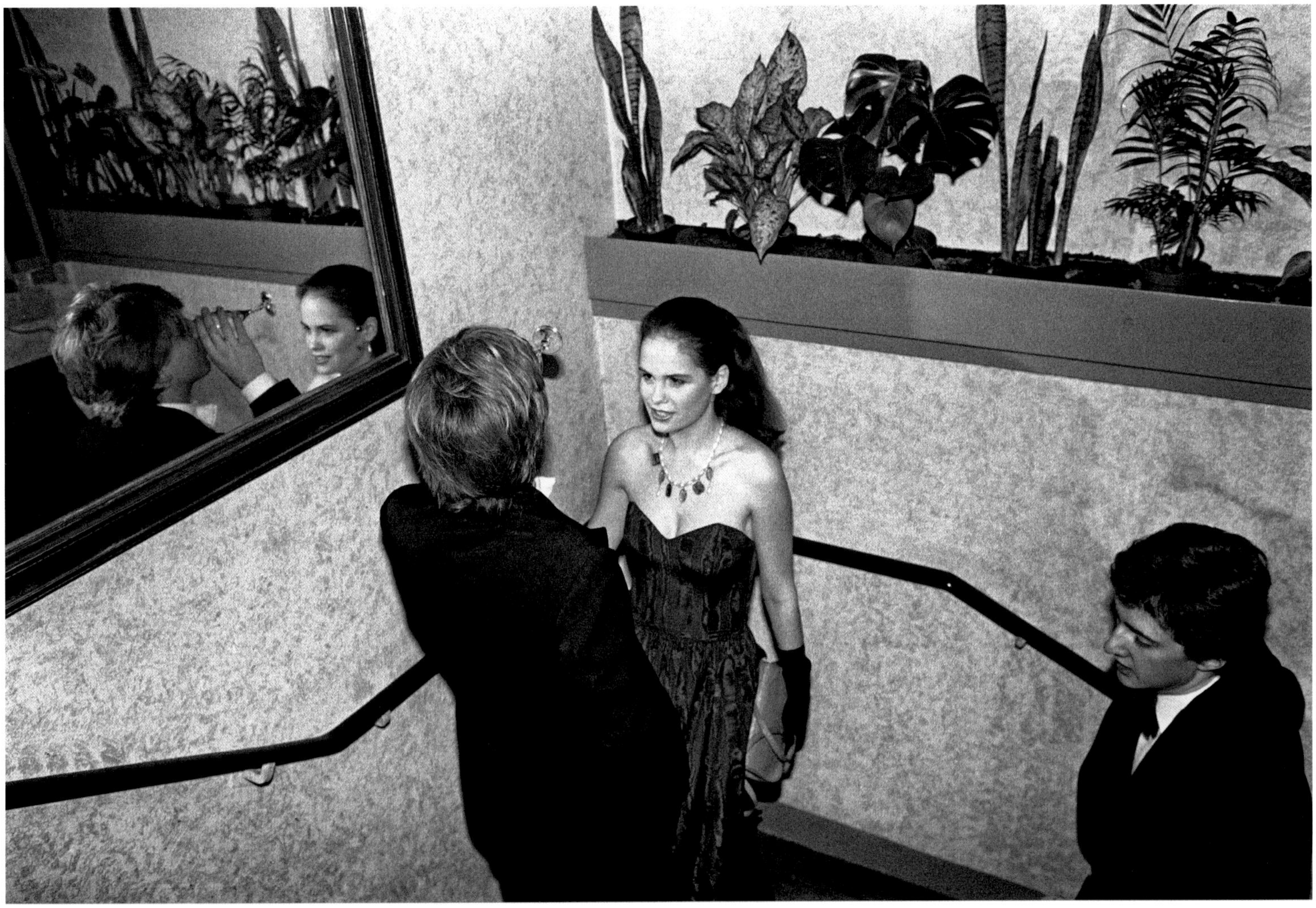

Chelsea, London. 1982

Quaffing champagne at Wedgies, with his Chelsea girl in a strapless off the shoulder cocktail dress and long black gloves.

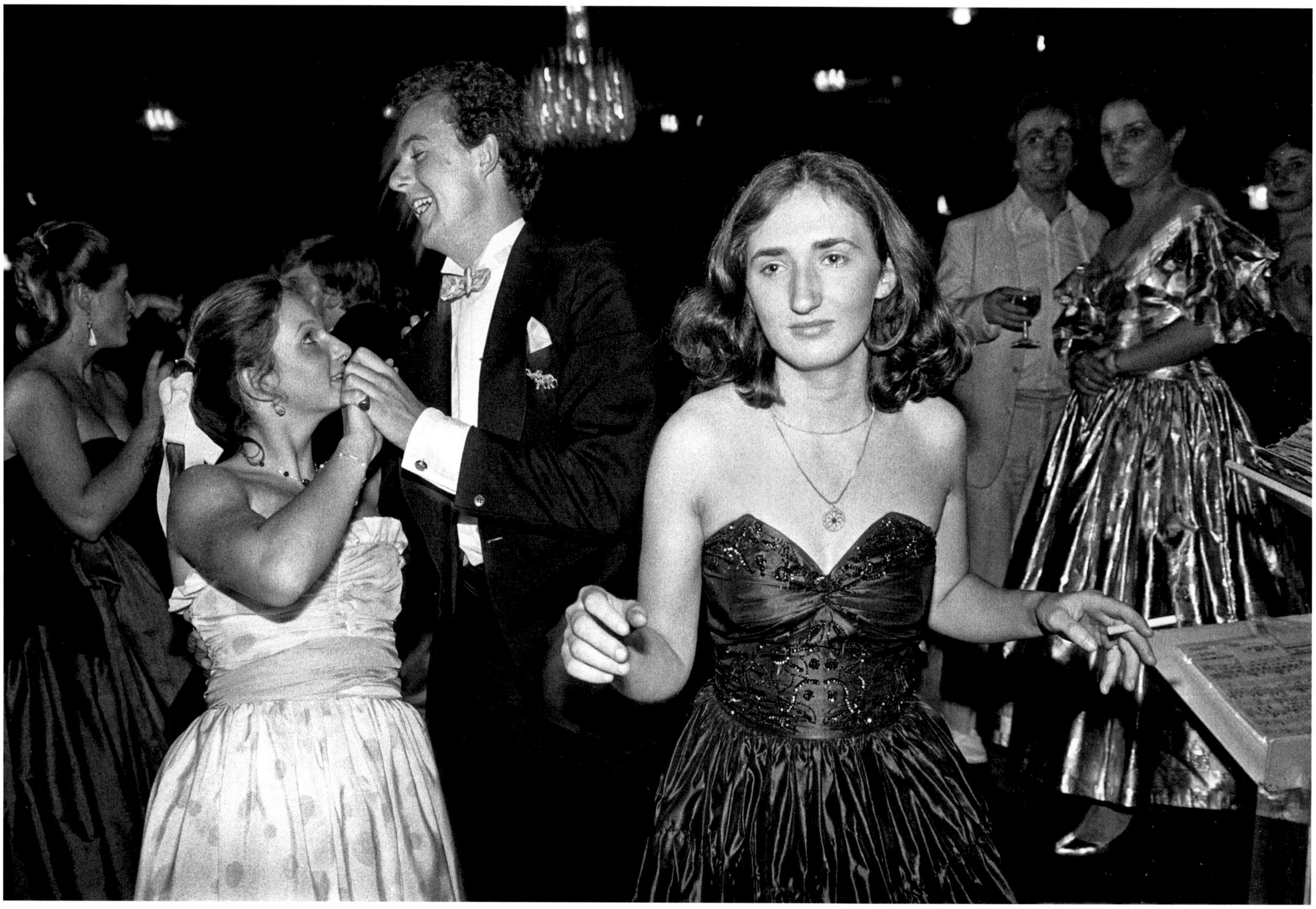

Westminster, London. 1982

With the ubiquitous cigarette in hand, a lone Sloane Ranger takes to the dance floor to sashay the night away at the annual charity Rose Ball; held in the Grosvenor House Hotel, Park Lane.

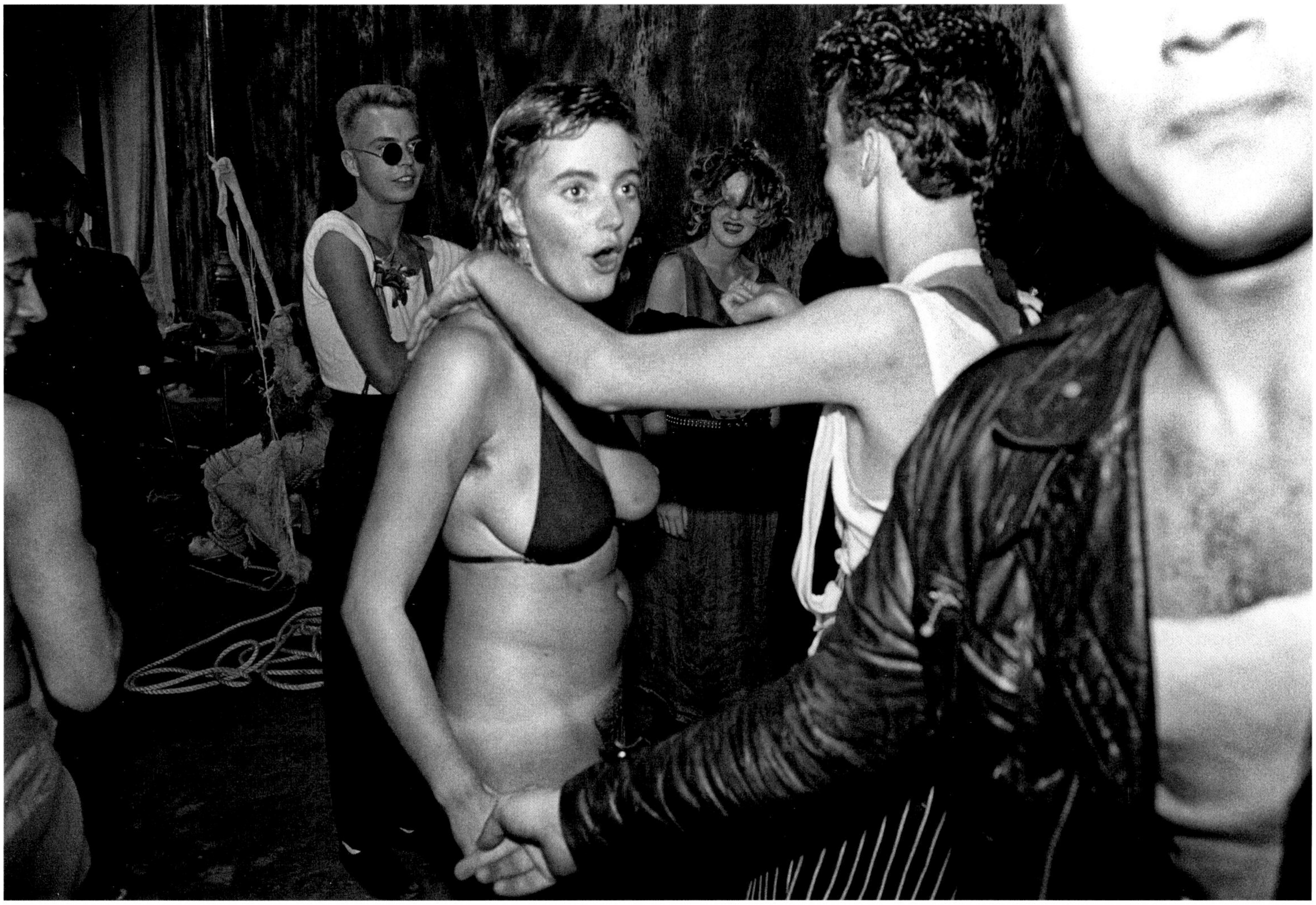

Olympia, London. 1981

Artist Andrew Logan started the Alternative Miss World beauty pageant in 1972. The 1981 theme, held in the Grand Hall at Olympia, was 'The Royal Imperial'. Backstage, Wilma Johnson, a founder member of the Neo Naturists performance art movement, prepares to take to the stage as Miss Windsurf.

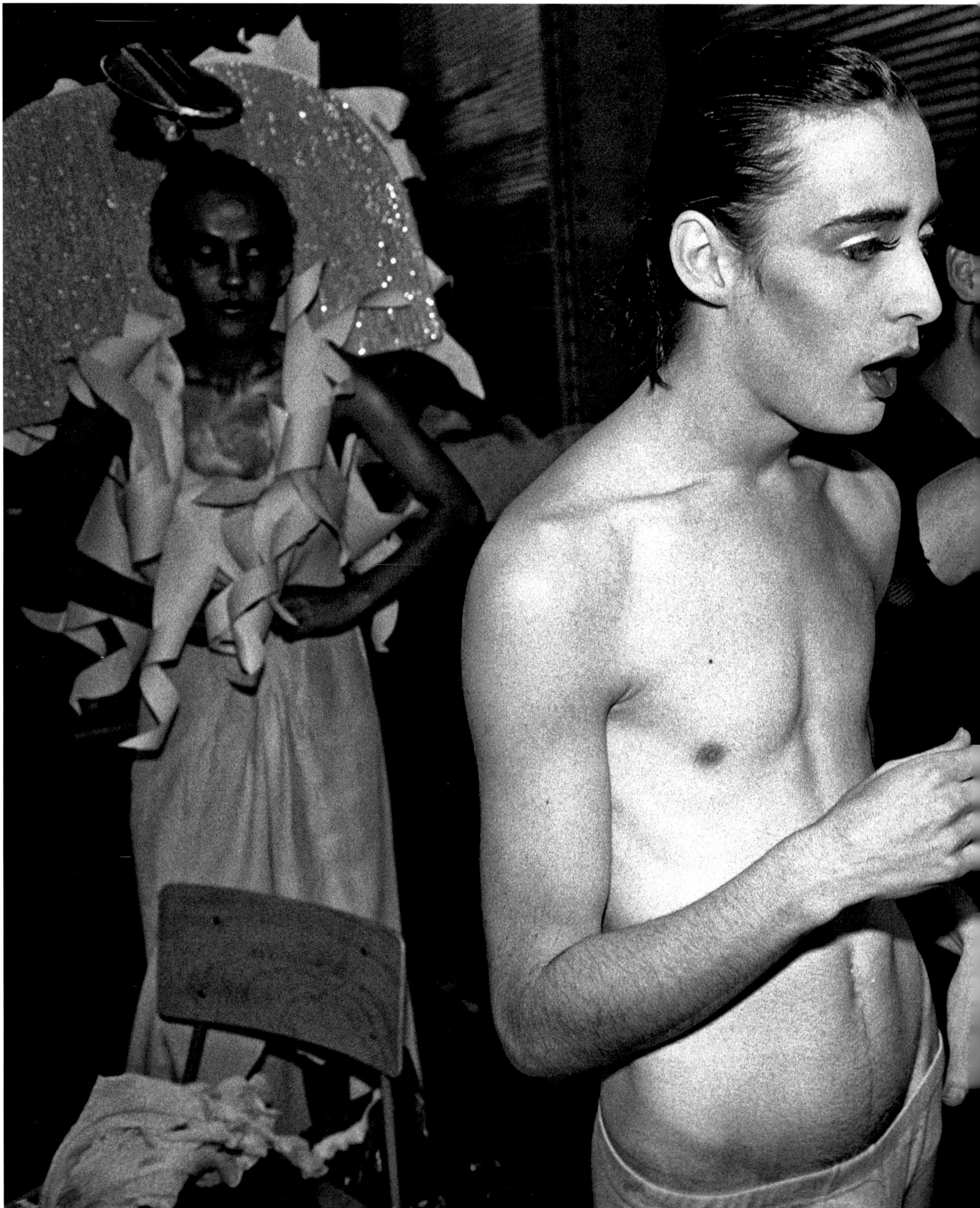

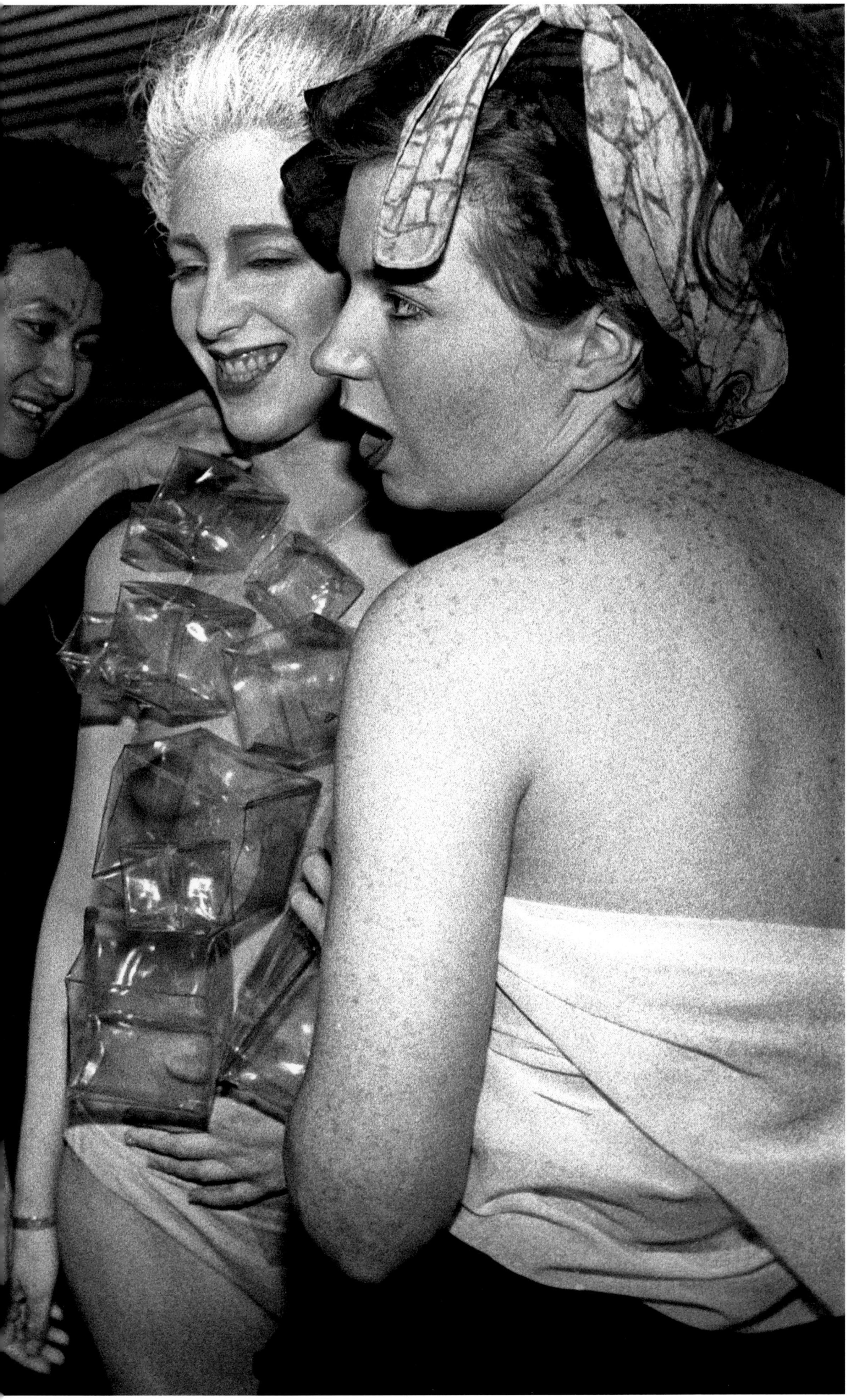

Olympia, London. 1981

Back stage at The Alternative Miss World beauty pageant.

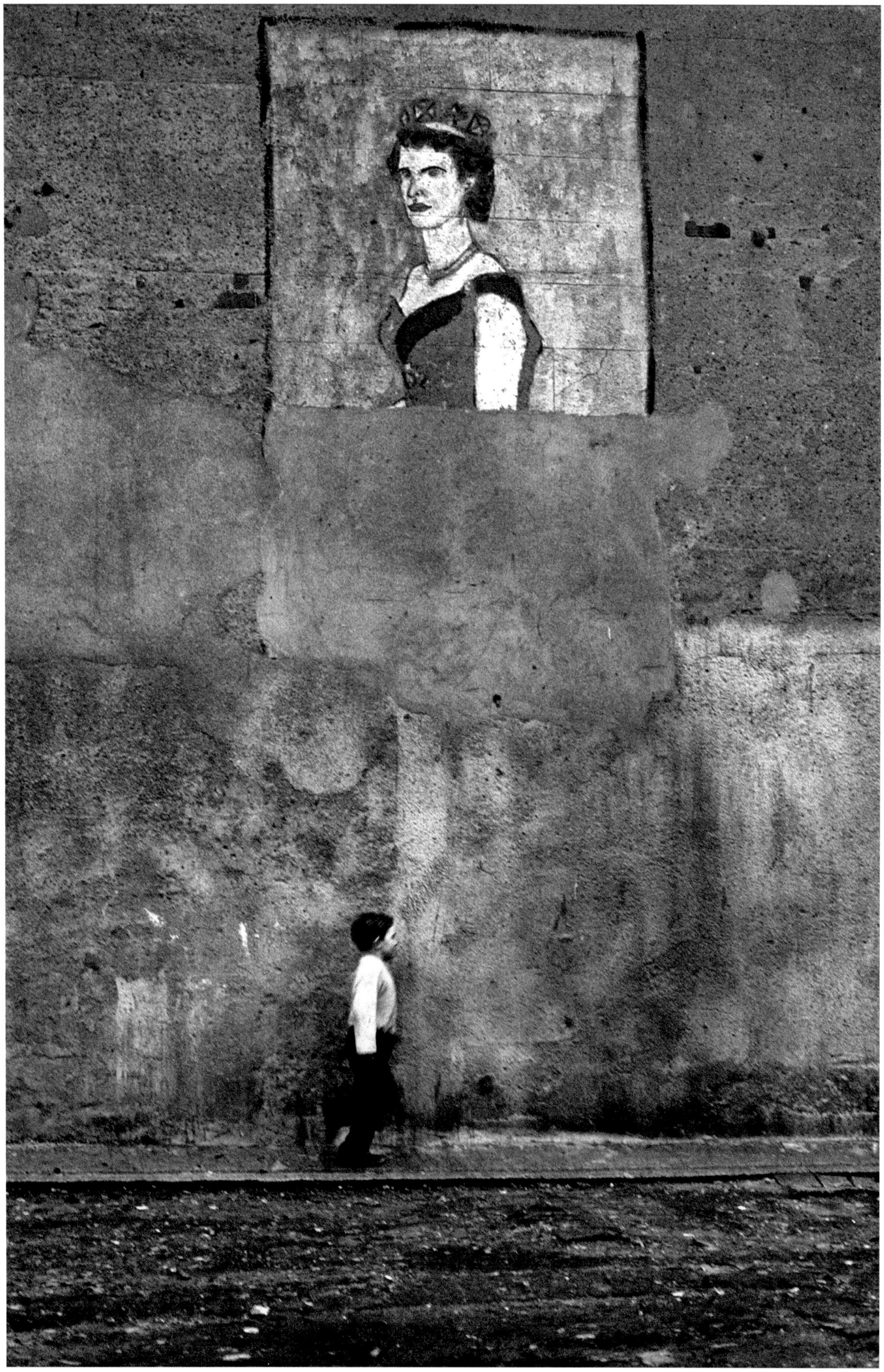

Belfast, Northern Ireland. 1970

A partially destroyed mural of Queen Elizabeth II in a Protestant inner city enclave. Ulster Protestants and Unionists were predominantly working class loyalists attached to the British monarchy. They supported the continued existence of Northern Ireland and were opposed to a united Ireland.

Belfast, Northern Ireland. 1981

The Troubles. On the Falls Road, a predominantly working class nationalist ghetto, two young Catholic men hold empty glass bottles ready to be made into petrol bombs.

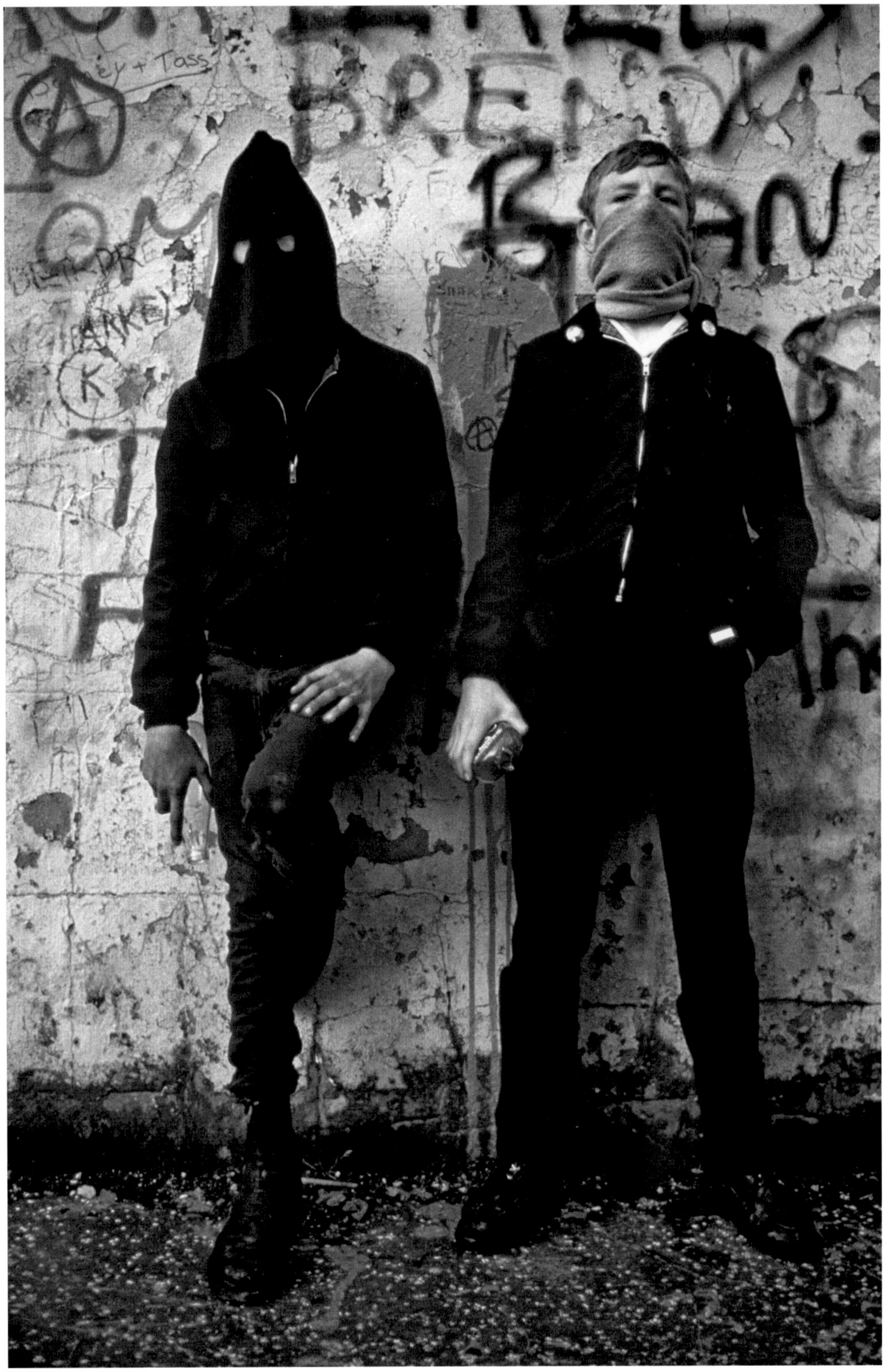

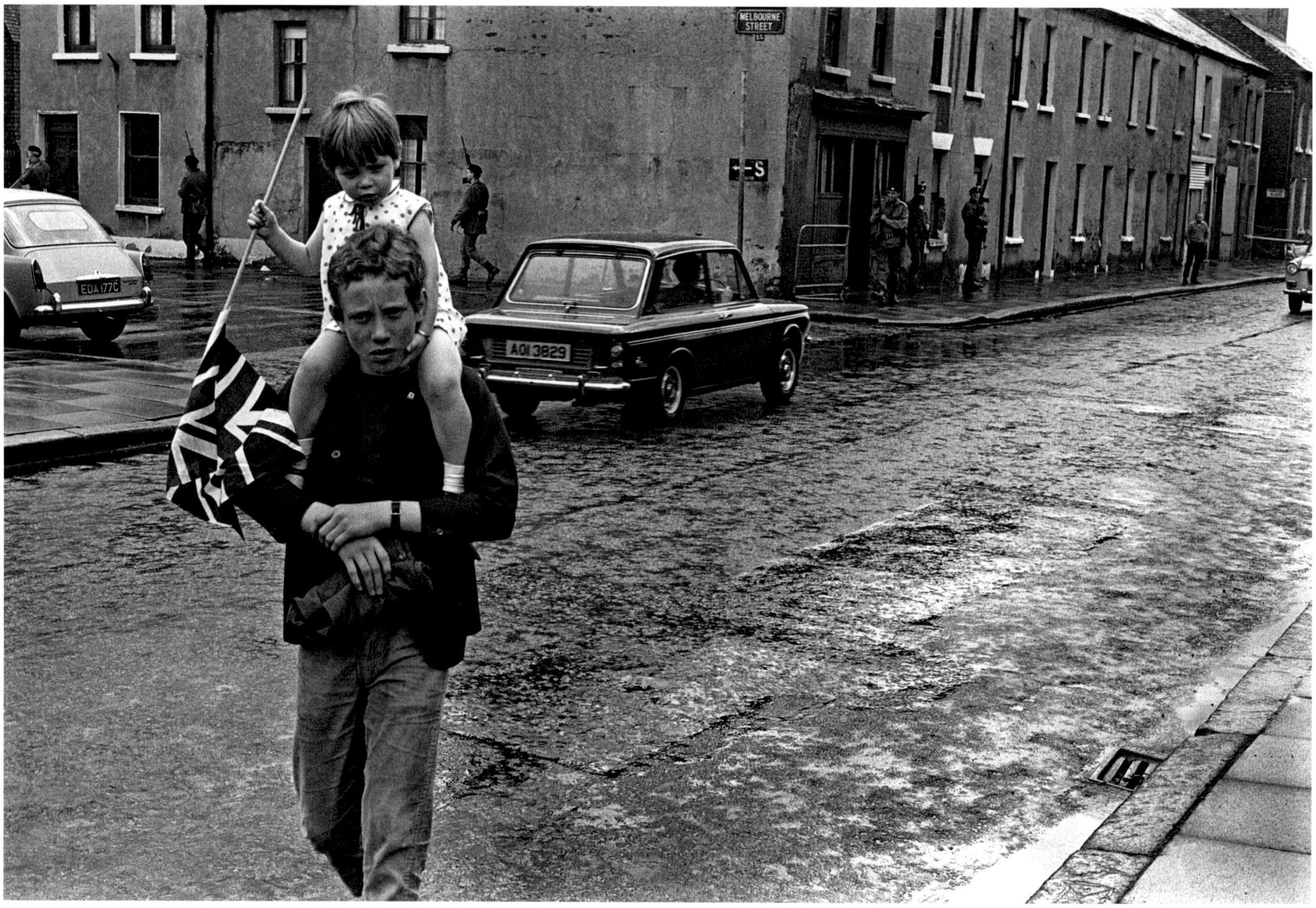

Belfast, Northern Ireland. 1970

British soldiers patrol an inner city working class area as a young loyalist carries his sister shoulder high through the depressed rain-dampened streets.

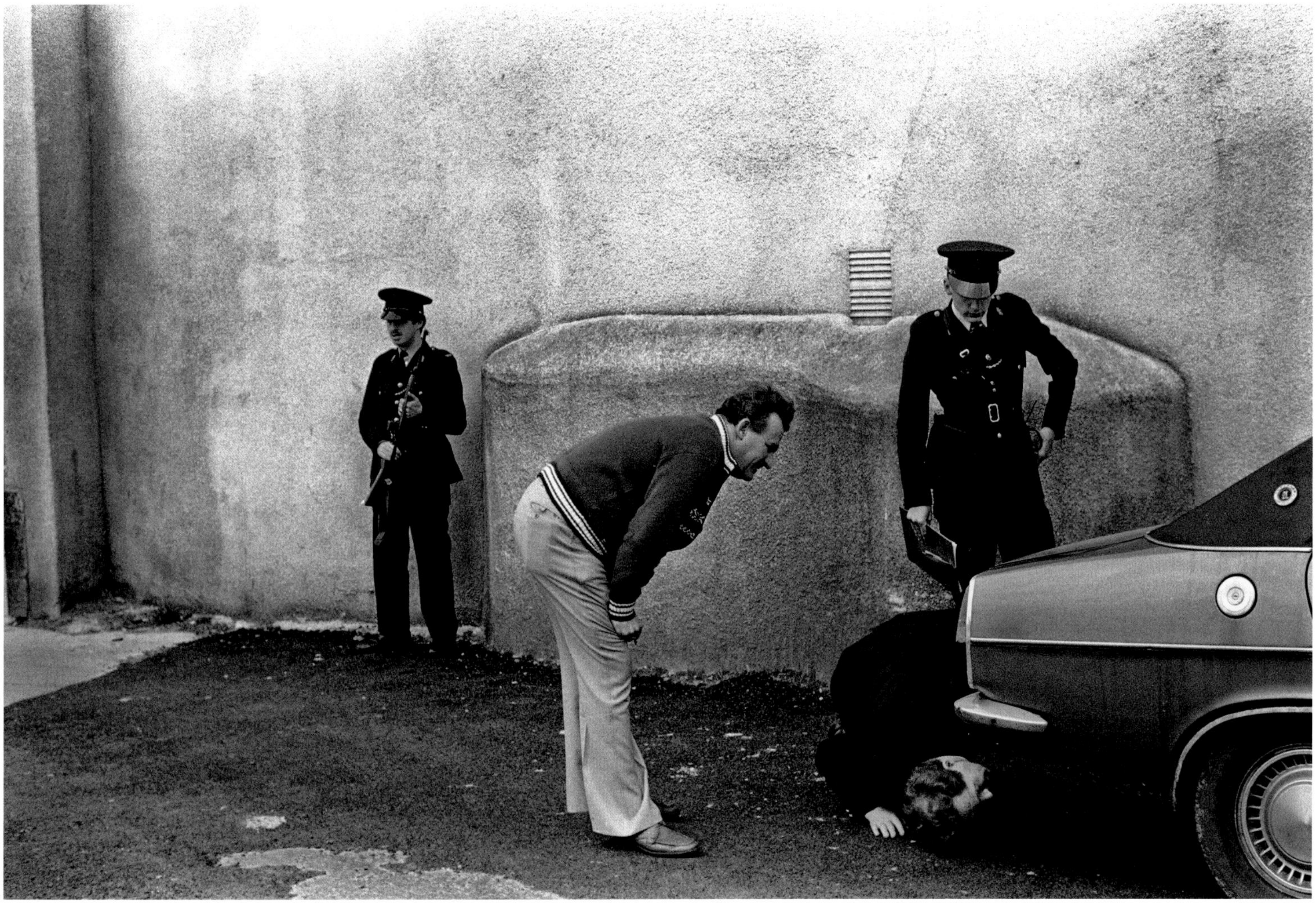

Derry, Northern Ireland. 1979

An armed Royal Ulster Constabulary officer stands guard, while colleagues check for a car bomb, and the owner looks on.

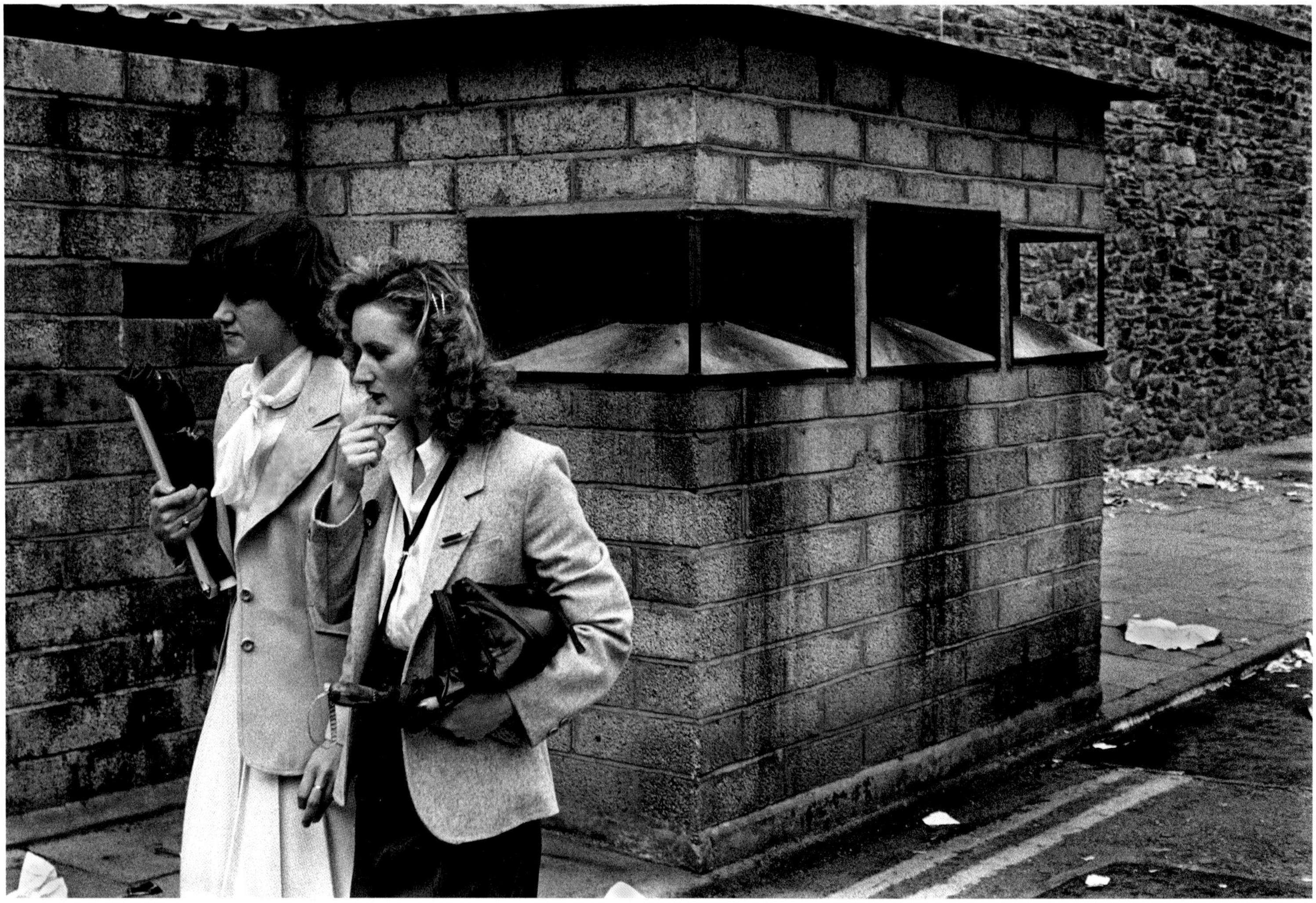

Derry, Northern Ireland. 1979

Two smartly dressed women walk past a burnt-out British Army checkpoint at Butchers Gate, a gateway through the old city wall and into the commercial centre of Derry.

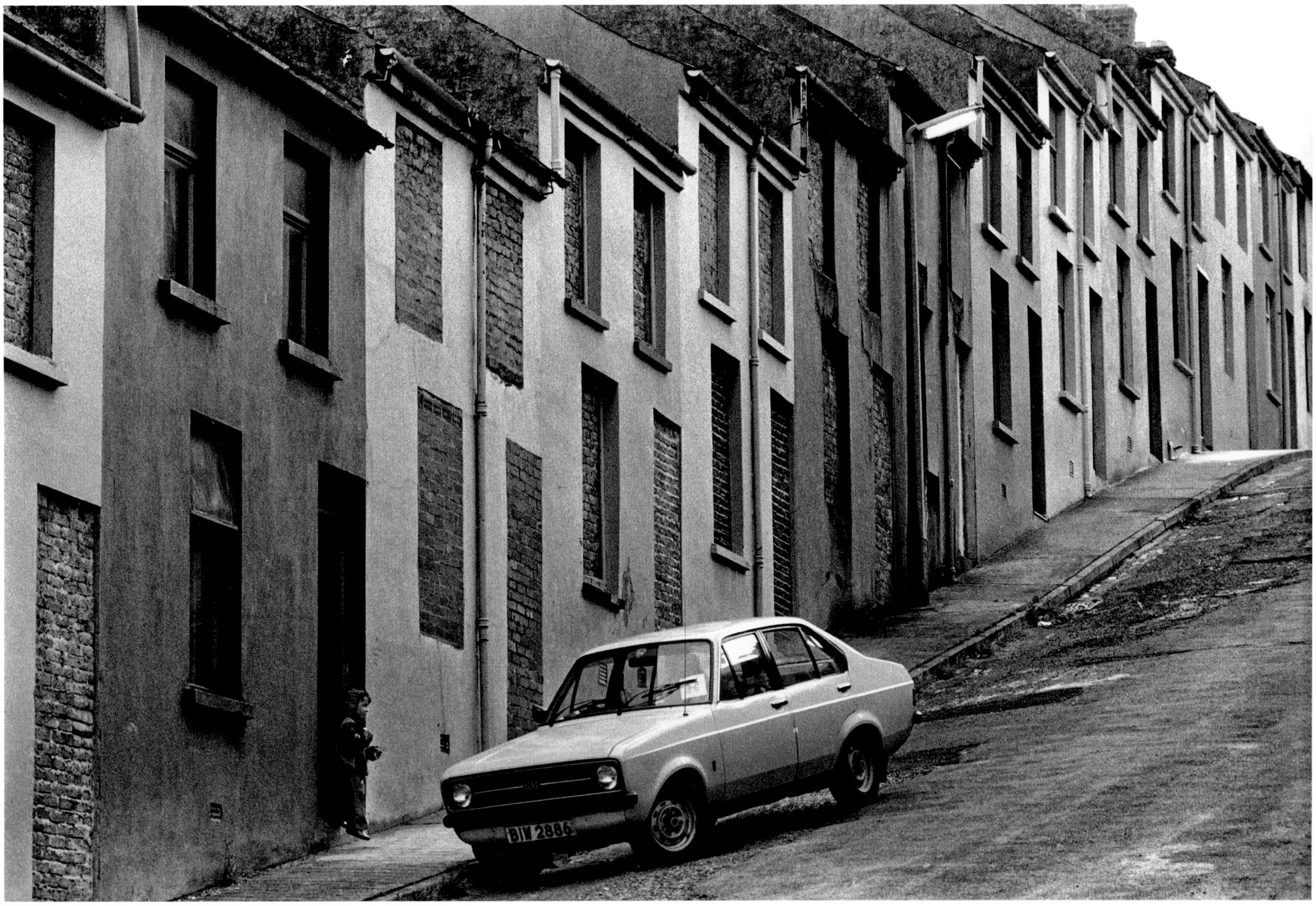

Derry, Northern Ireland. 1979

Only one family remains in this Waterside street. The houses are abandoned and boarded up as residents have moved away due to sectarian violence.

Belfast, Northern Ireland. 1981

The Troubles. Disguised in balaclavas, rioting catholic youths hurl petrol bombs and missiles at British soldiers in Etna Drive, Ardoyne, north Belfast.

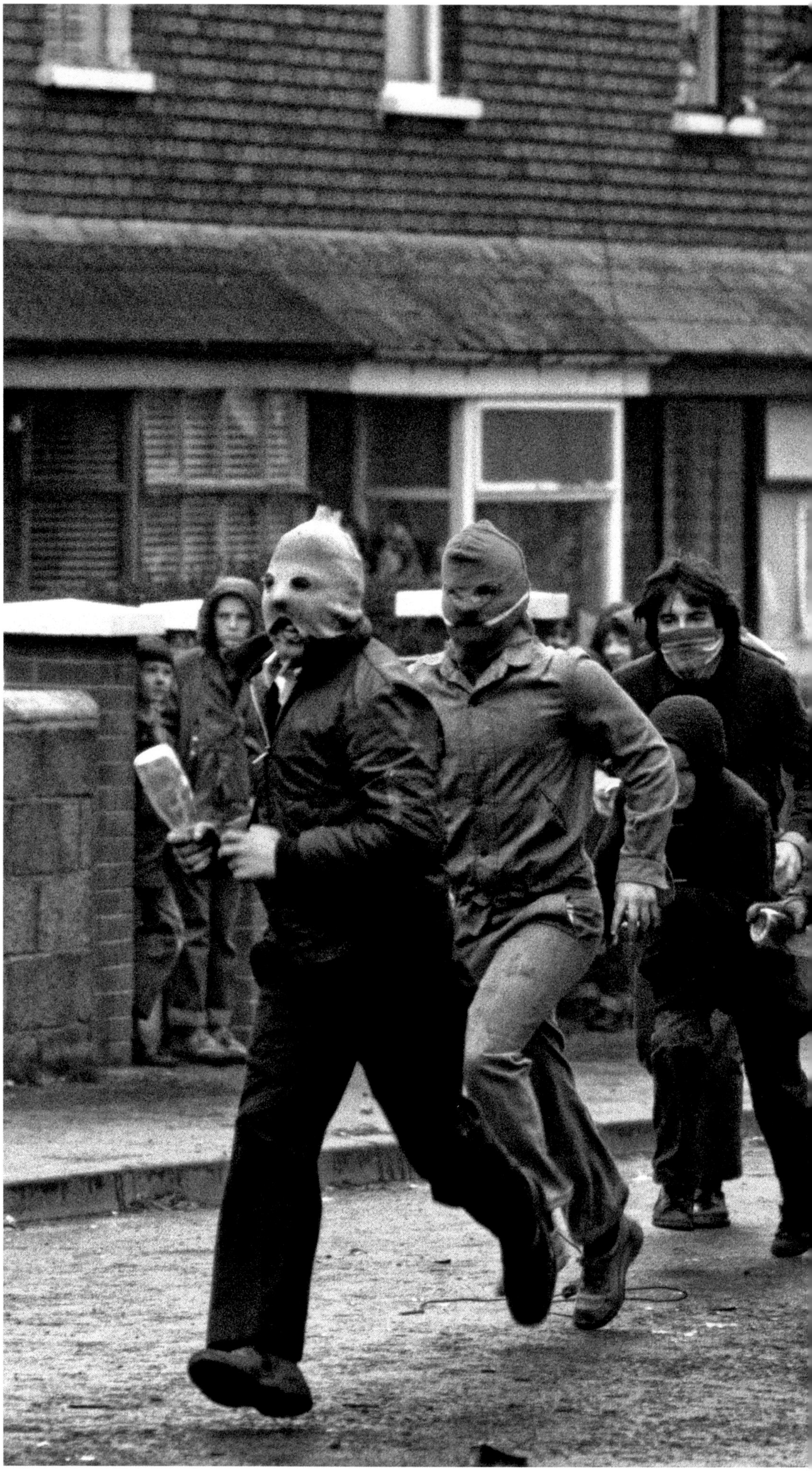

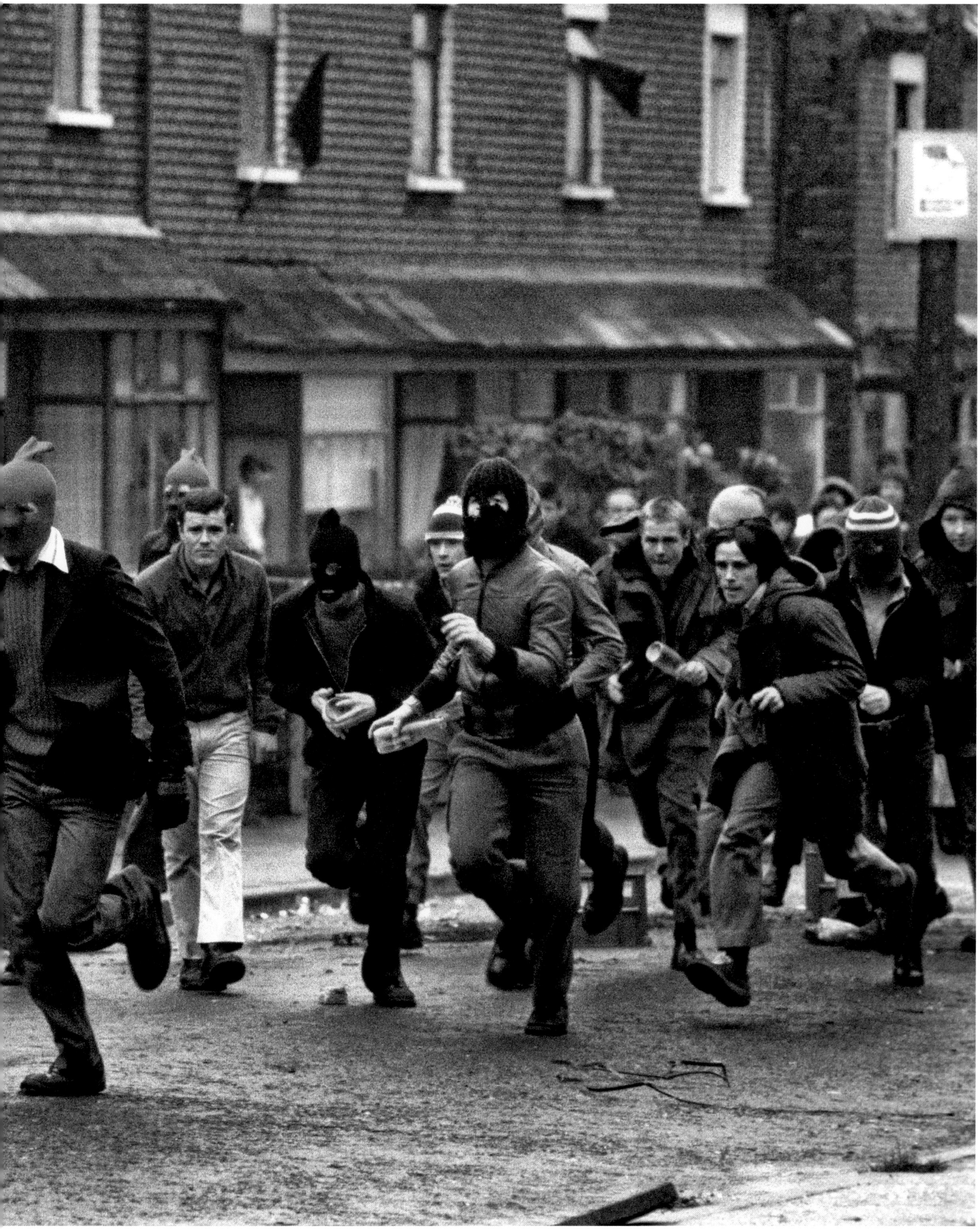

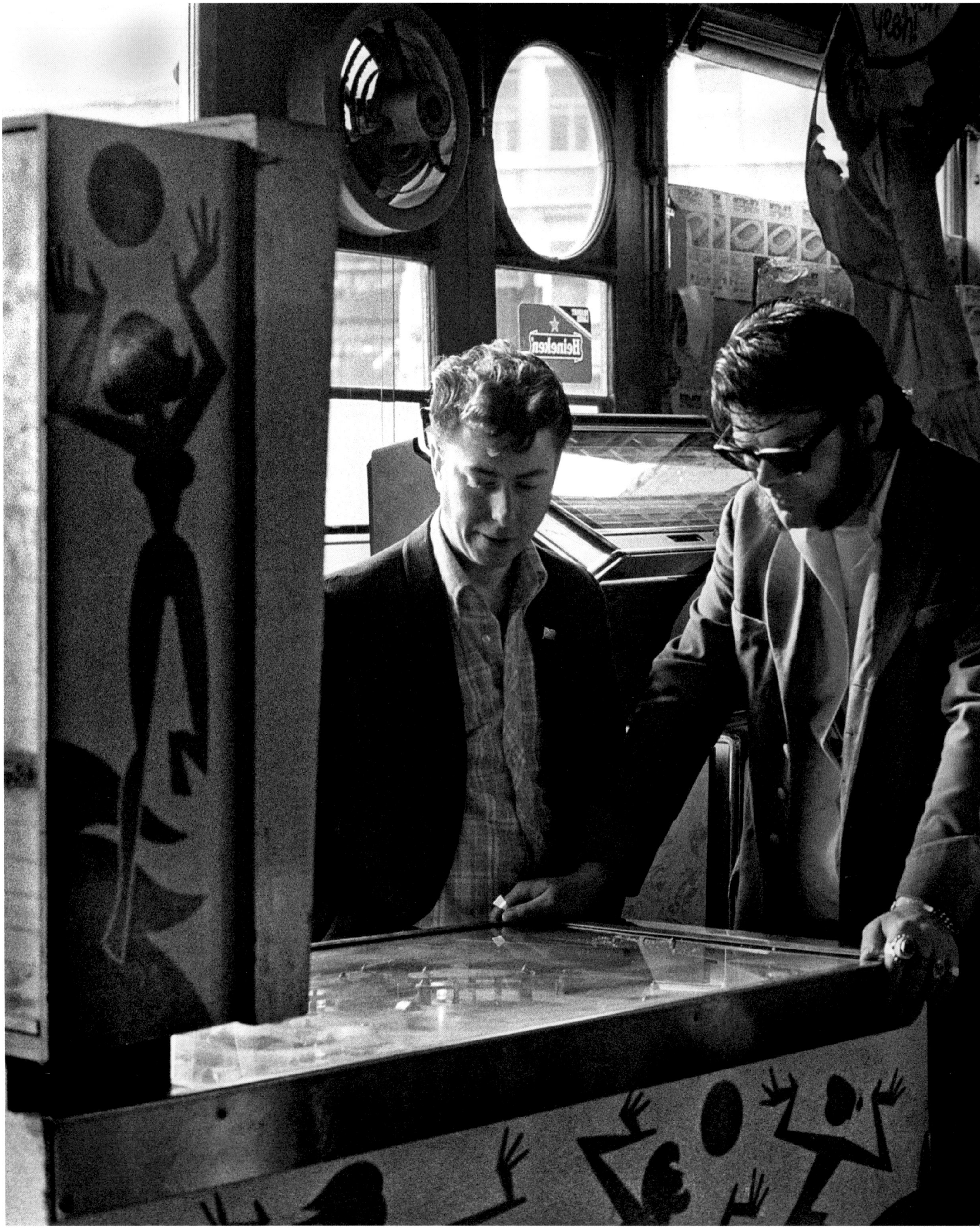

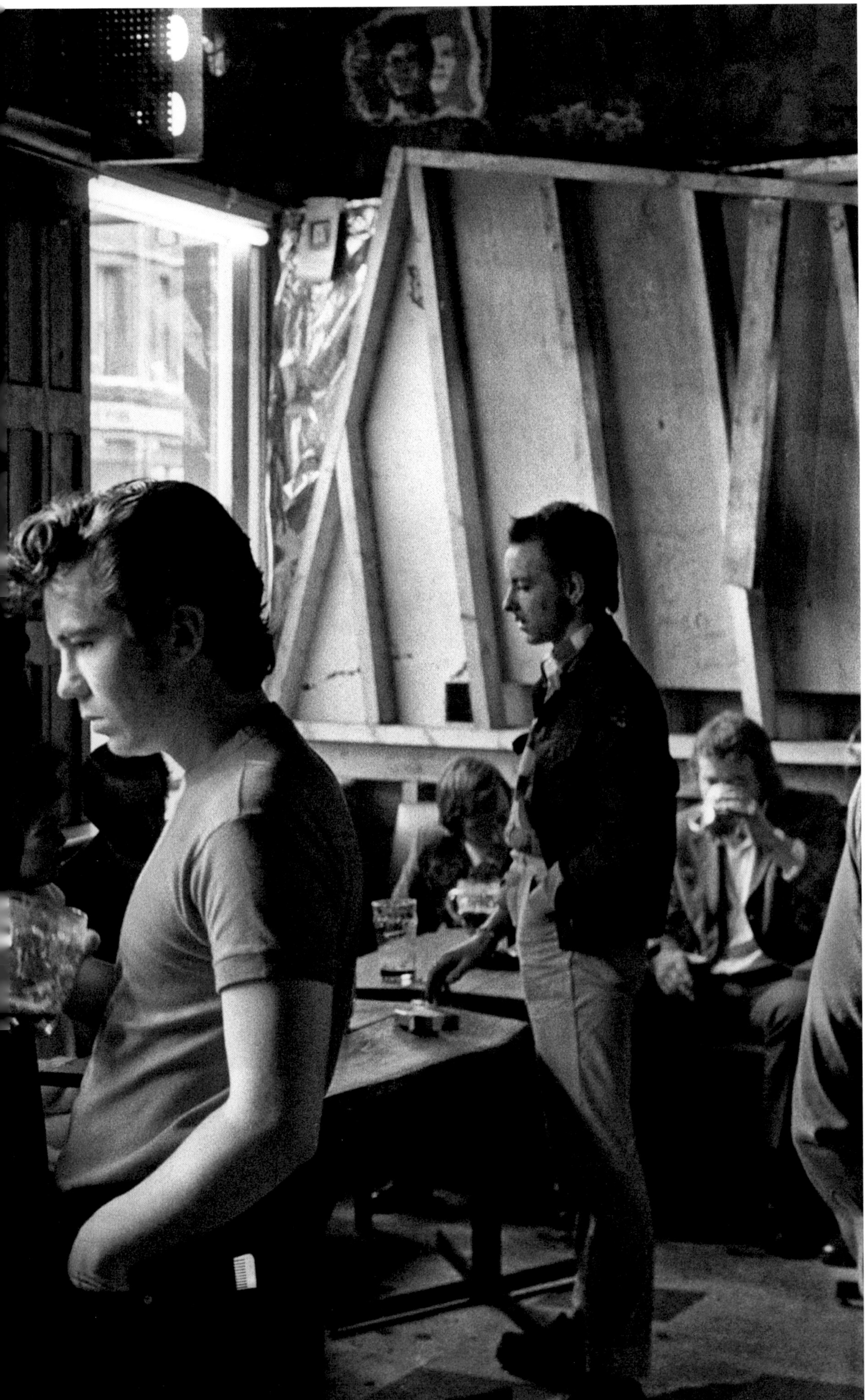

Moorgate, London. 1975

Playing a pinball machine at The Black Raven in Bishopgate Street, Sunglasses Ron Staples styled himself the King of the Teds, the Edwardian Teddy Boy.

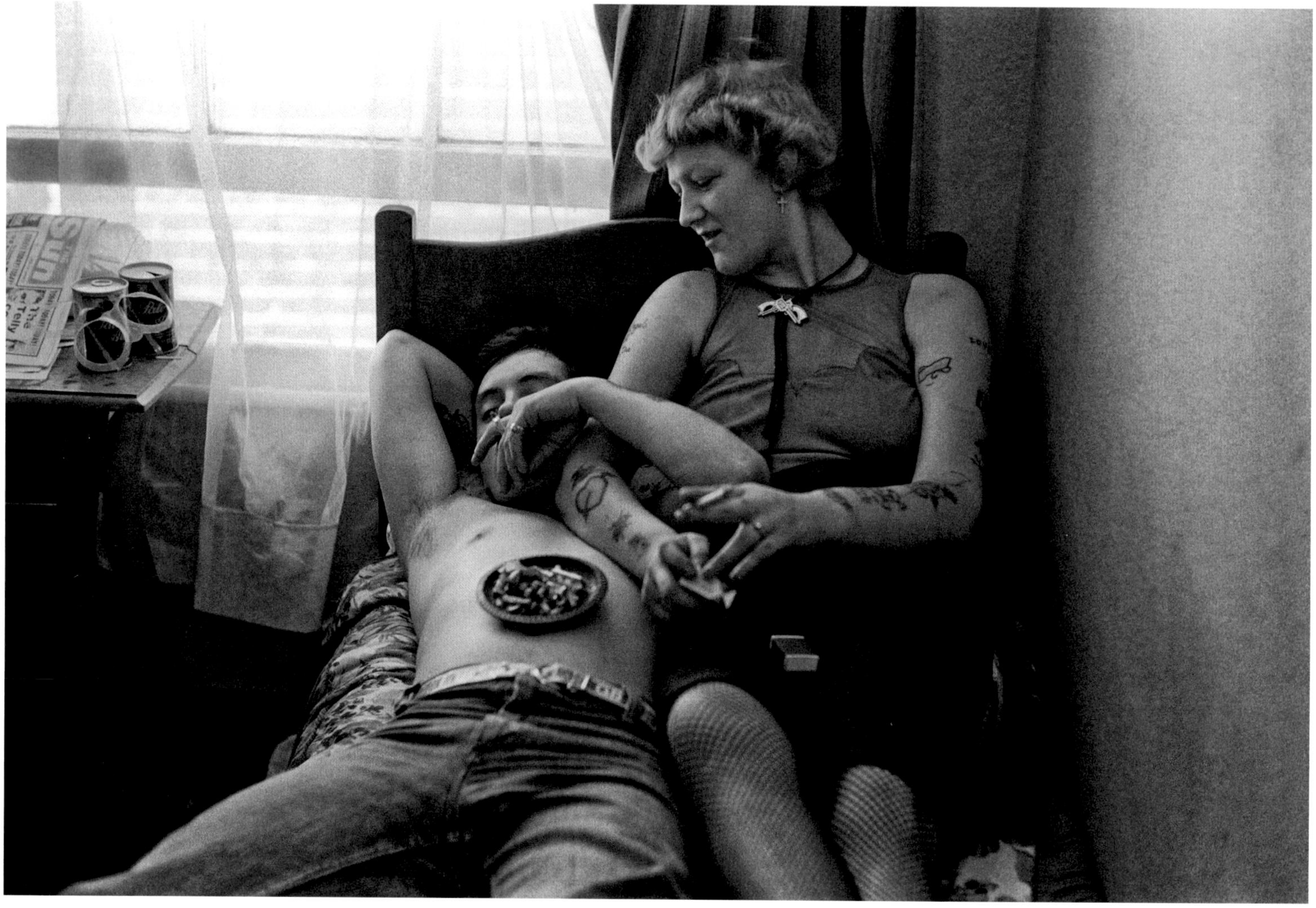

Earls Court, London. 1977

Absent Without Official Leave and on the run, an army deserter in his bedsit enjoys a quite smoke and a tinny or two, and contemplates life with his doodle-decorated, tattooed girlfriend.

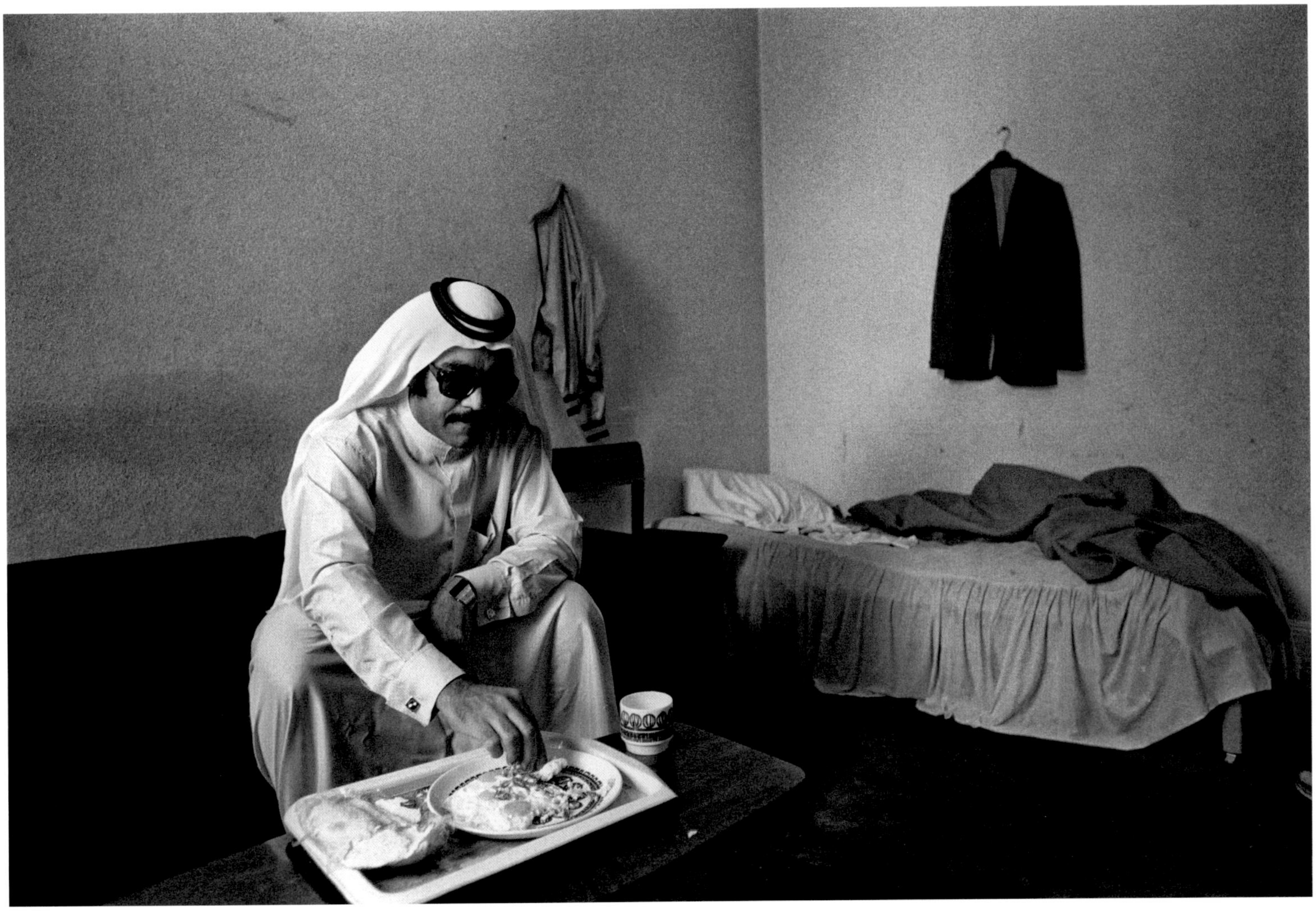

Earls Court, London. 1977

During the late 1970s some Middle Eastern governments provided healthcare for their nationals in London, many of whom stayed in cheap bedsits in the Earls Court area.

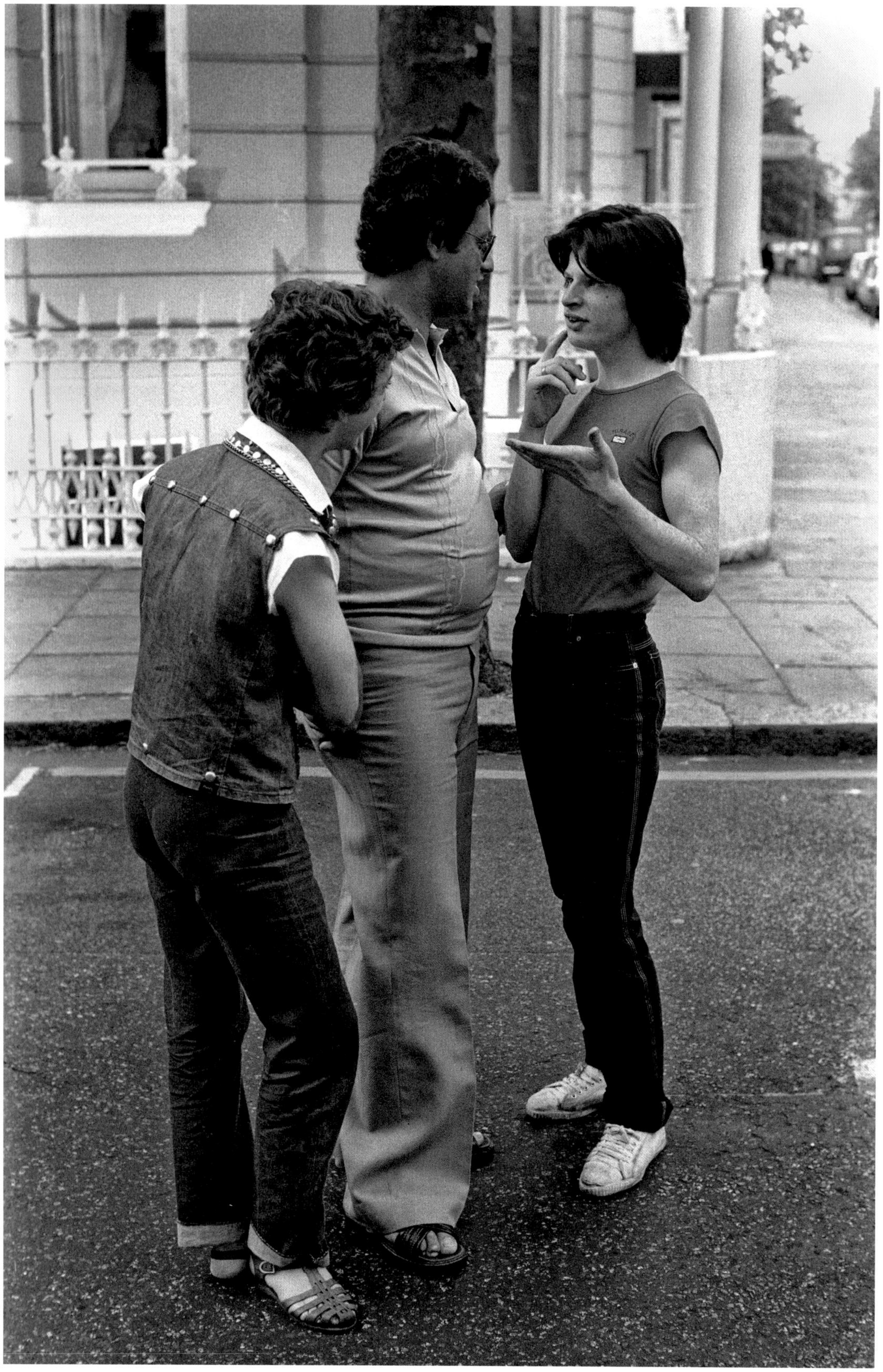

Earls Court, London. 1977

Two rent boys use sign and body language to ask a male Arab healthcare tourist if he would like to join them.

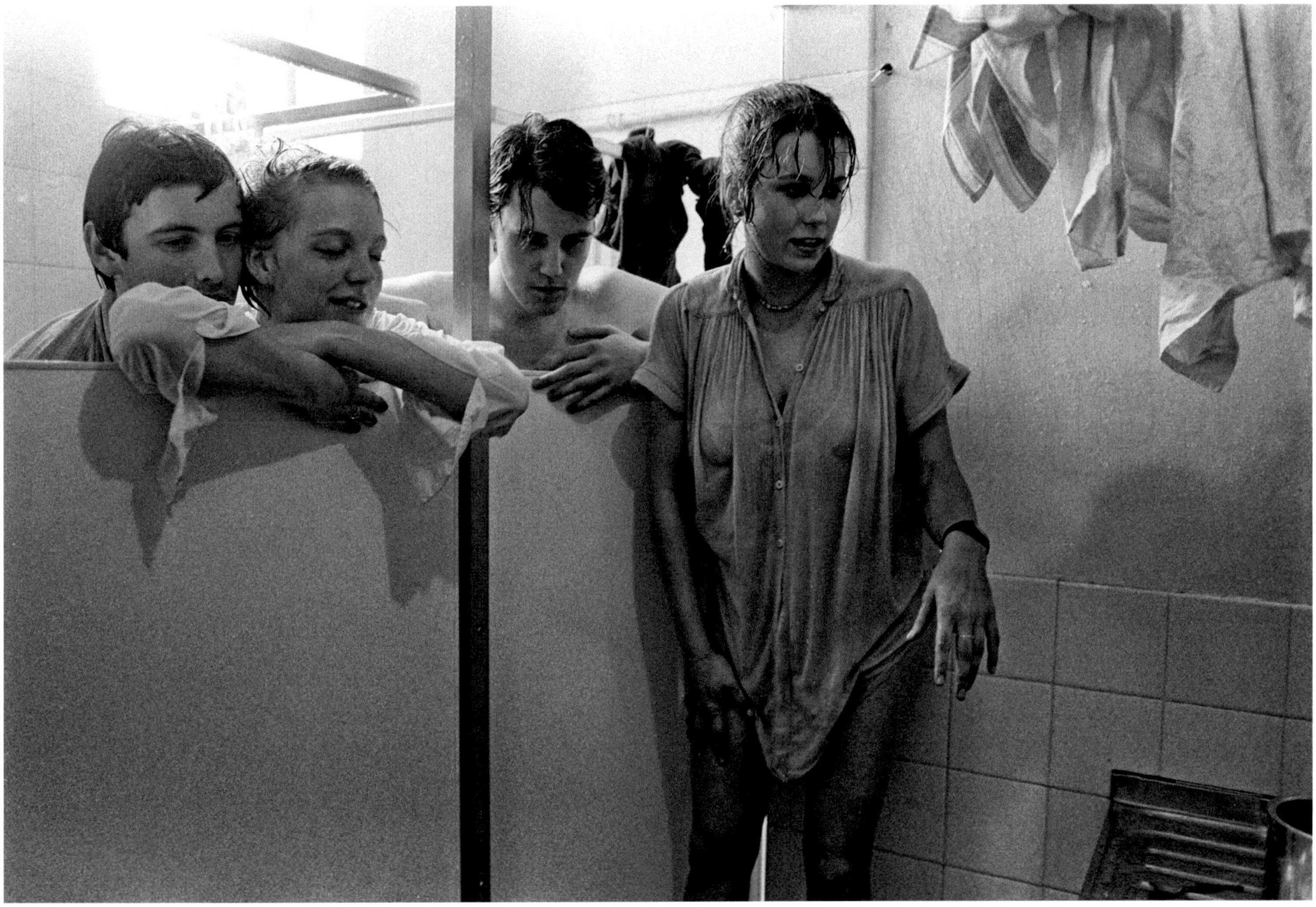

Cambridge, Cambridgeshire. 1983

Shower foreplay at The College of Corpus Christi and the Blessed Virgin Mary, to give this ancient college its full name. Often shortened to Corpus or The Body, it was founded in 1352 by local townspeople and has a reputation as being one of the more academically successful Cambridge colleges.

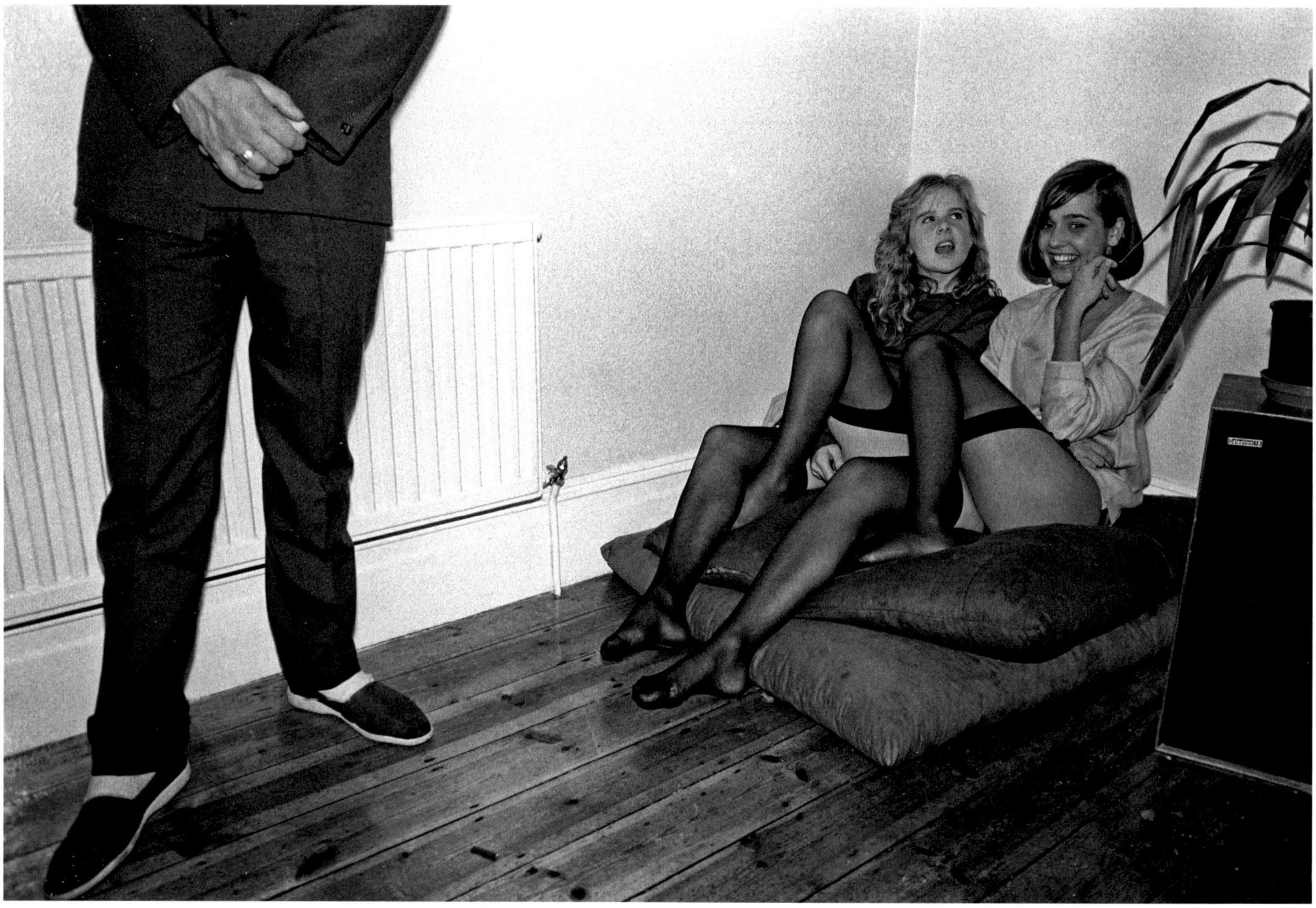

Wimbledon, London. 1983

A suburban middle class Christmas fancy dress party, themed after the 1970's and 80's pop group Hot Chocolate. 'You Sexy Thing' was one of their numerous hits.

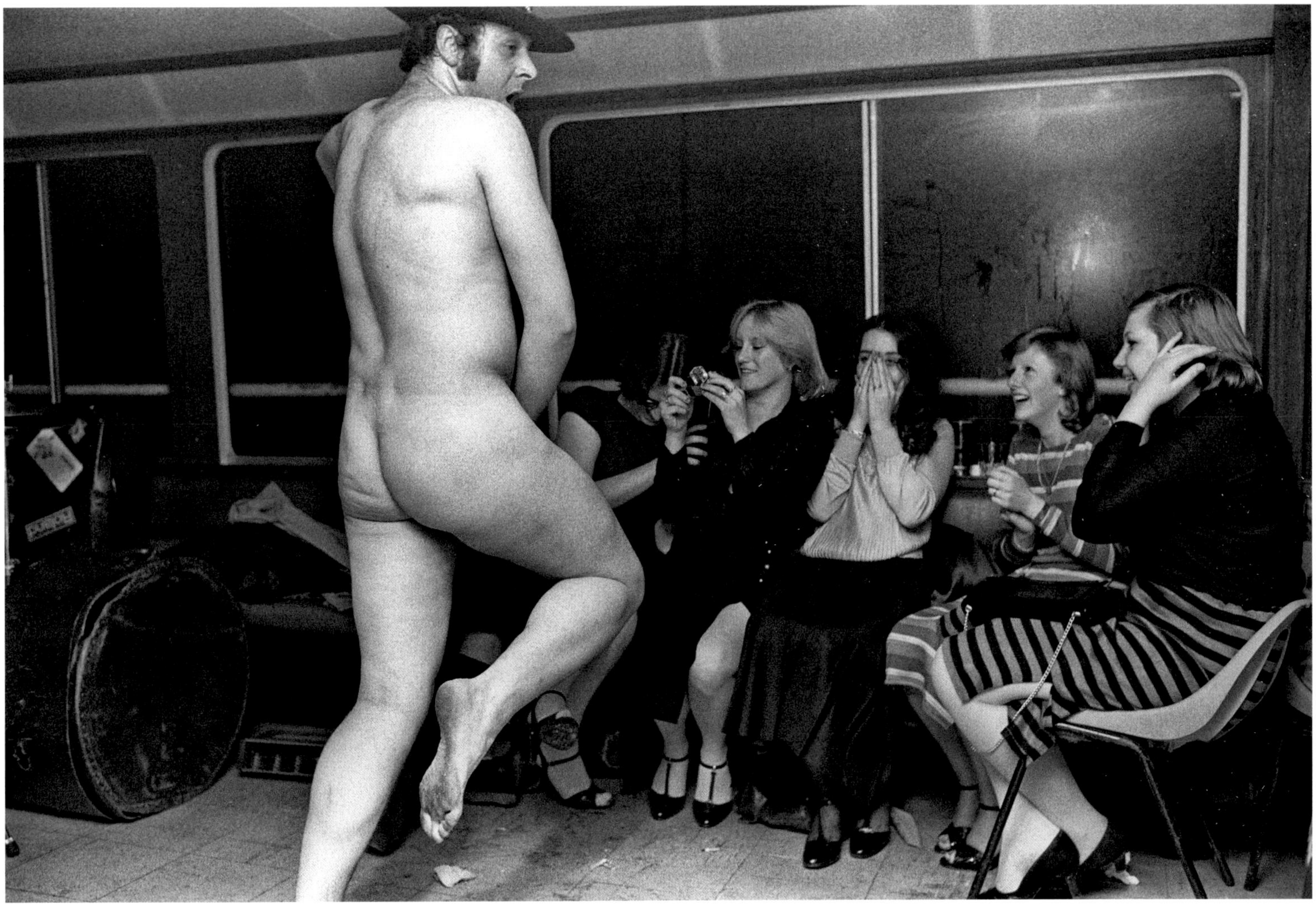

River Thames, London. 1979

The Rhinestone Cowboy, a male stripper, surprises, shocks and entertains, teenage hen party guests on a private riverboat cruise.

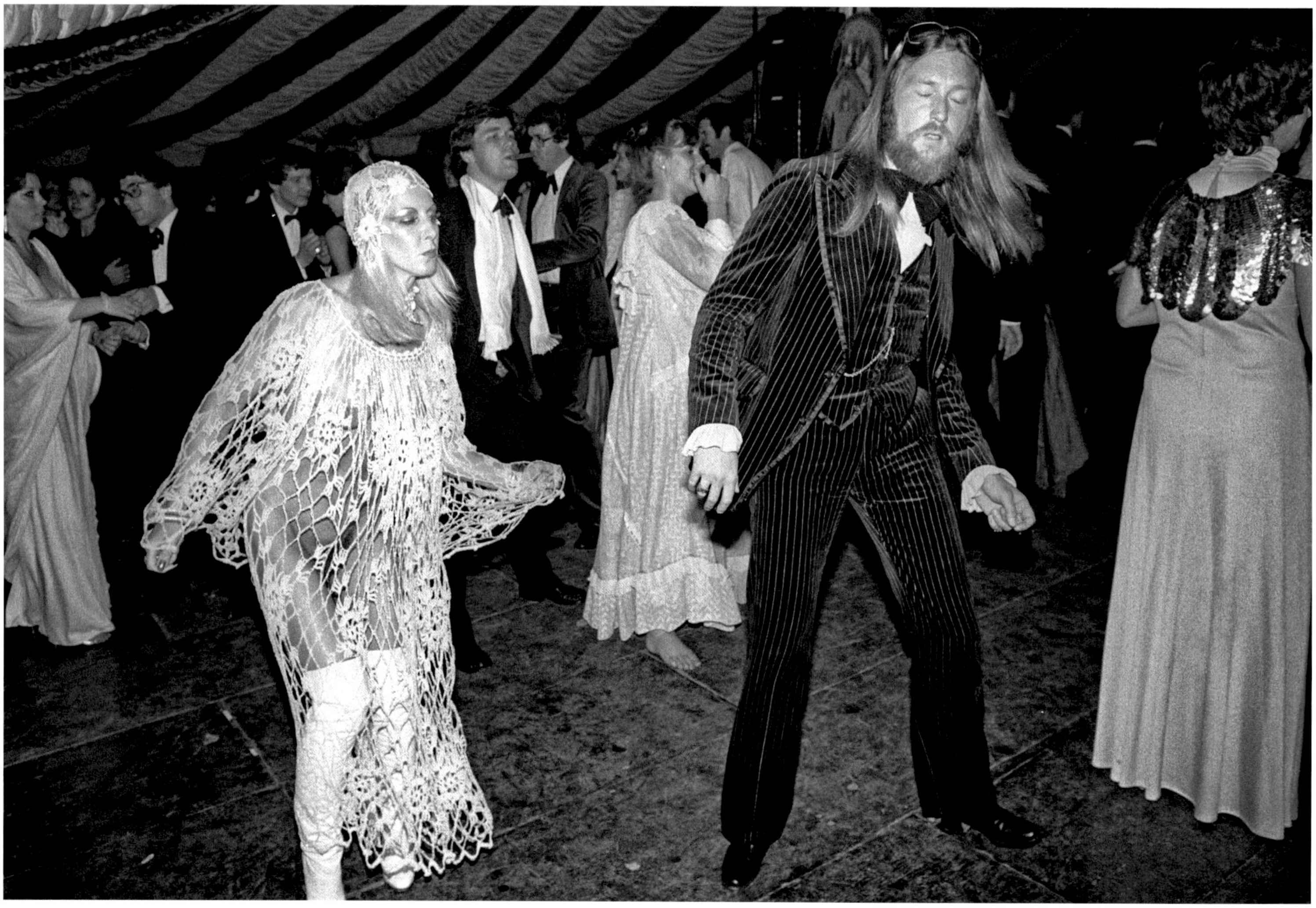

Westminster, London. 1981

Bopping the night away at the annual Berkeley Square Ball. A reveller in a see-through maxi bohemian crochet dress, designed to be worn with a white bikini that she must have forgotten to put on! A matching 1920's style cloche cap and white overknee boots set off her ensemble. With her longhaired bearded beau, they swish their hair in time to the live tribute band.

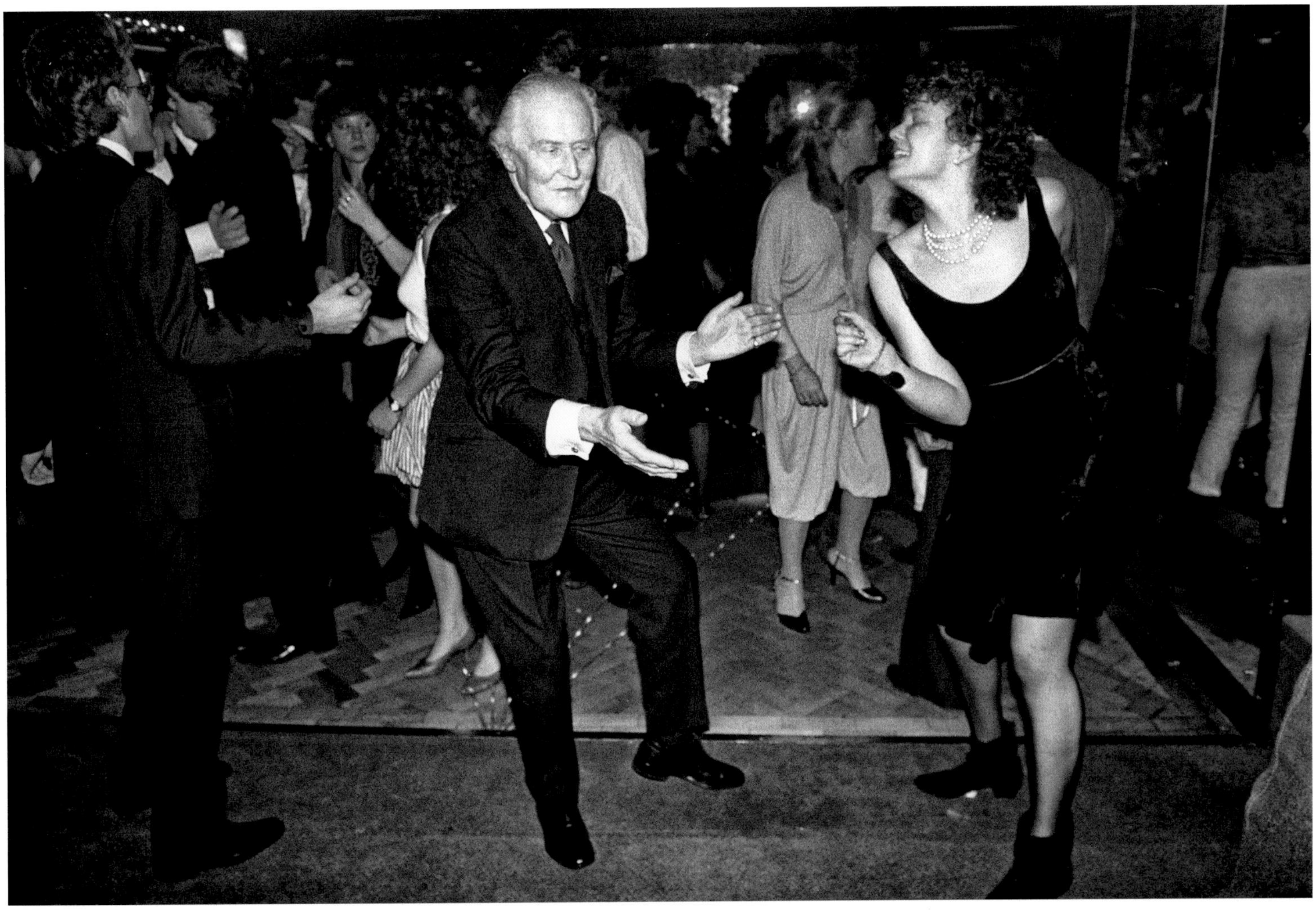

Chelsea, London. 1982

Dancing to the pounding beat of the basement disco at Wedgies on the King's Road.

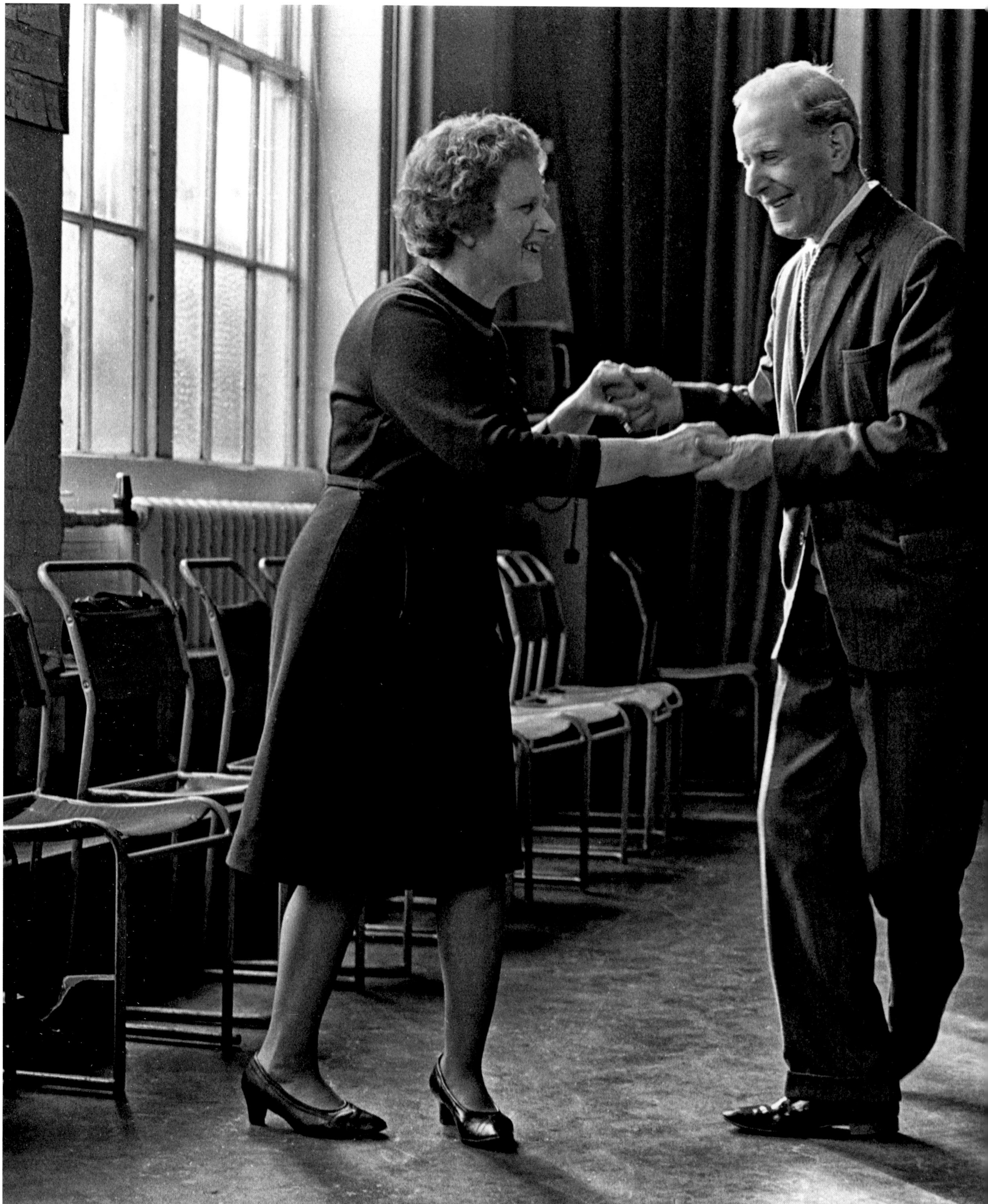

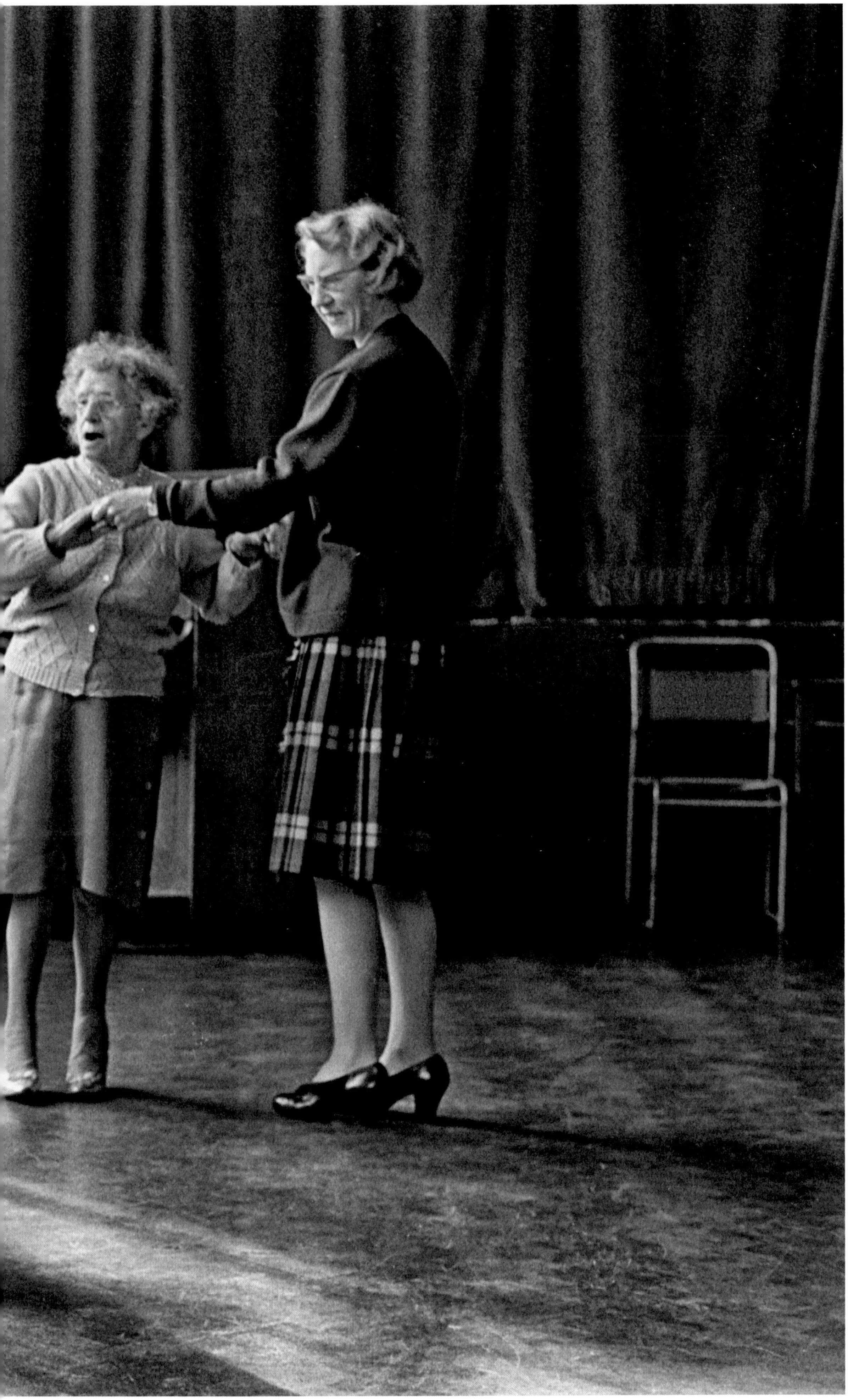

Battersea, London. 1970

At the Battersea Institute, the Darby and Joan Club, a blind and partially sighted afternoon dance class is underway. John Darby and his wife Joan were first mentioned in a 1735 poem published in *The Gentleman's Magazine* by Henry Woodfall. They became synonymous with the idea of the happily married couple celebrating an even and uneventful life together, always side by side.

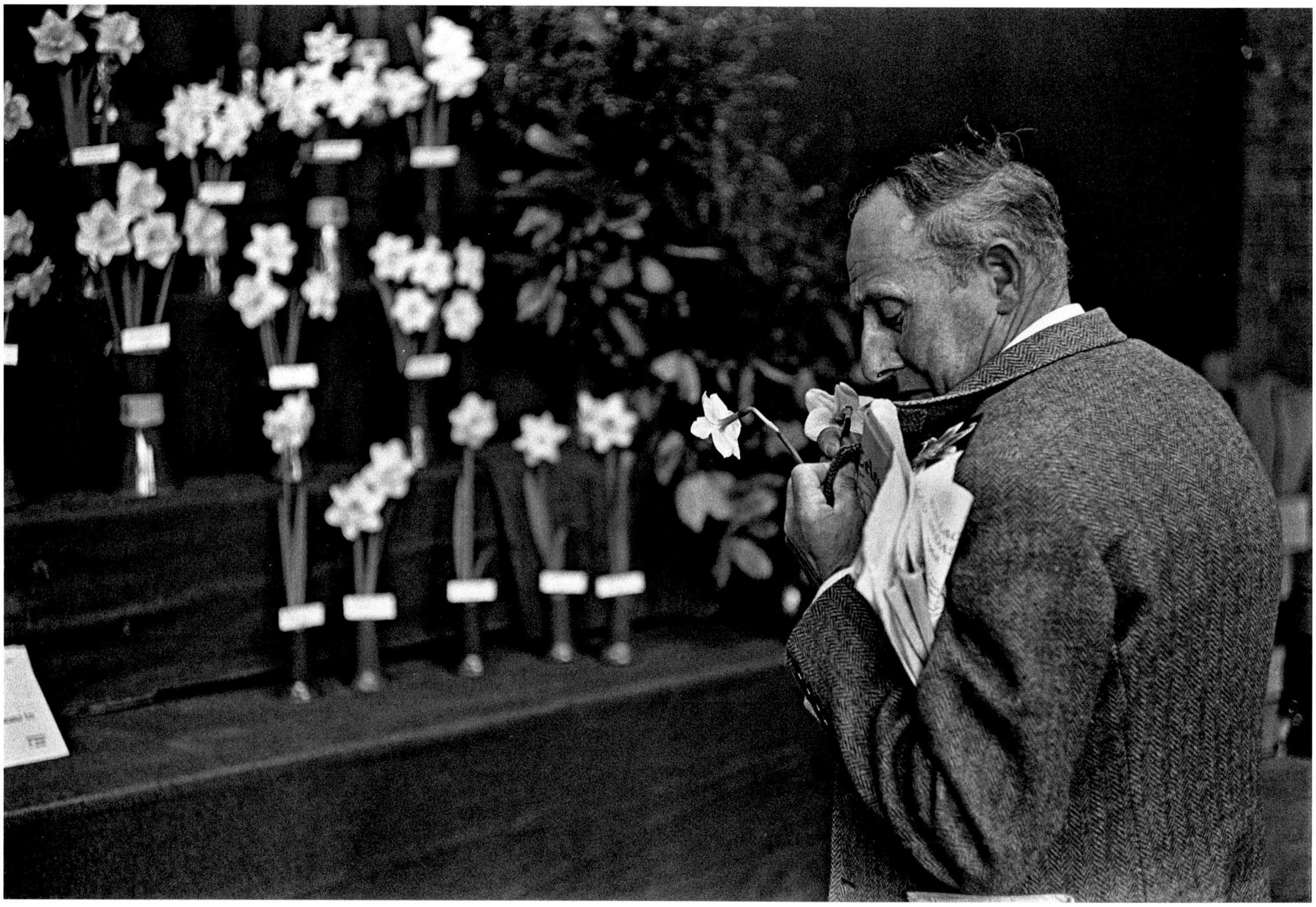

Victoria, London. 1969

The Royal Horticultural Society flower show; a member of the public makes himself a buttonhole with some competition narcissi.

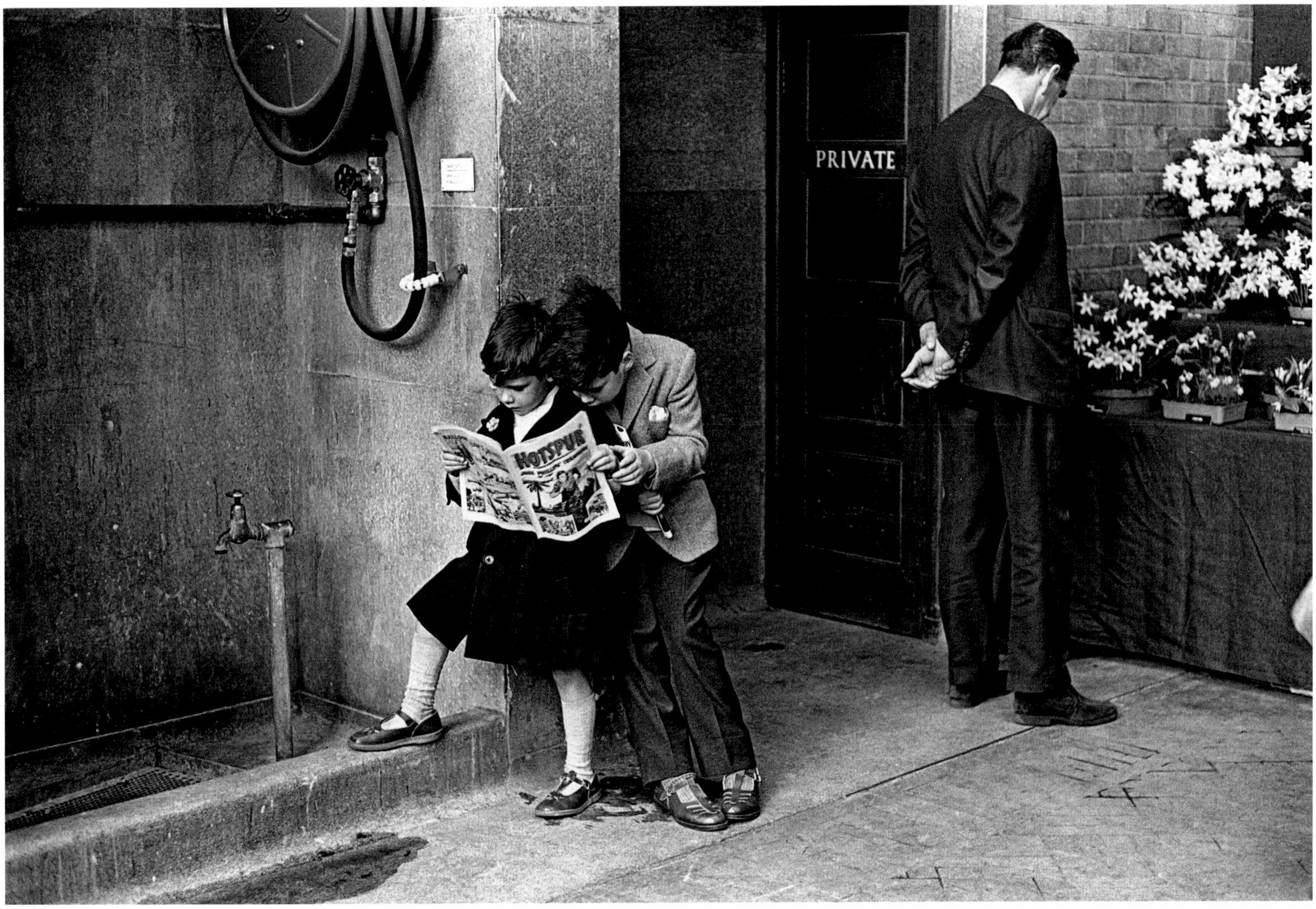

Victoria, London. 1968

Engrossed in *The Hotspur* comic, sibling brothers in their best weekend prep school clothes. They show no interest in the flower display that their father admires at the Royal Horticultural Society Annual Flower Show.

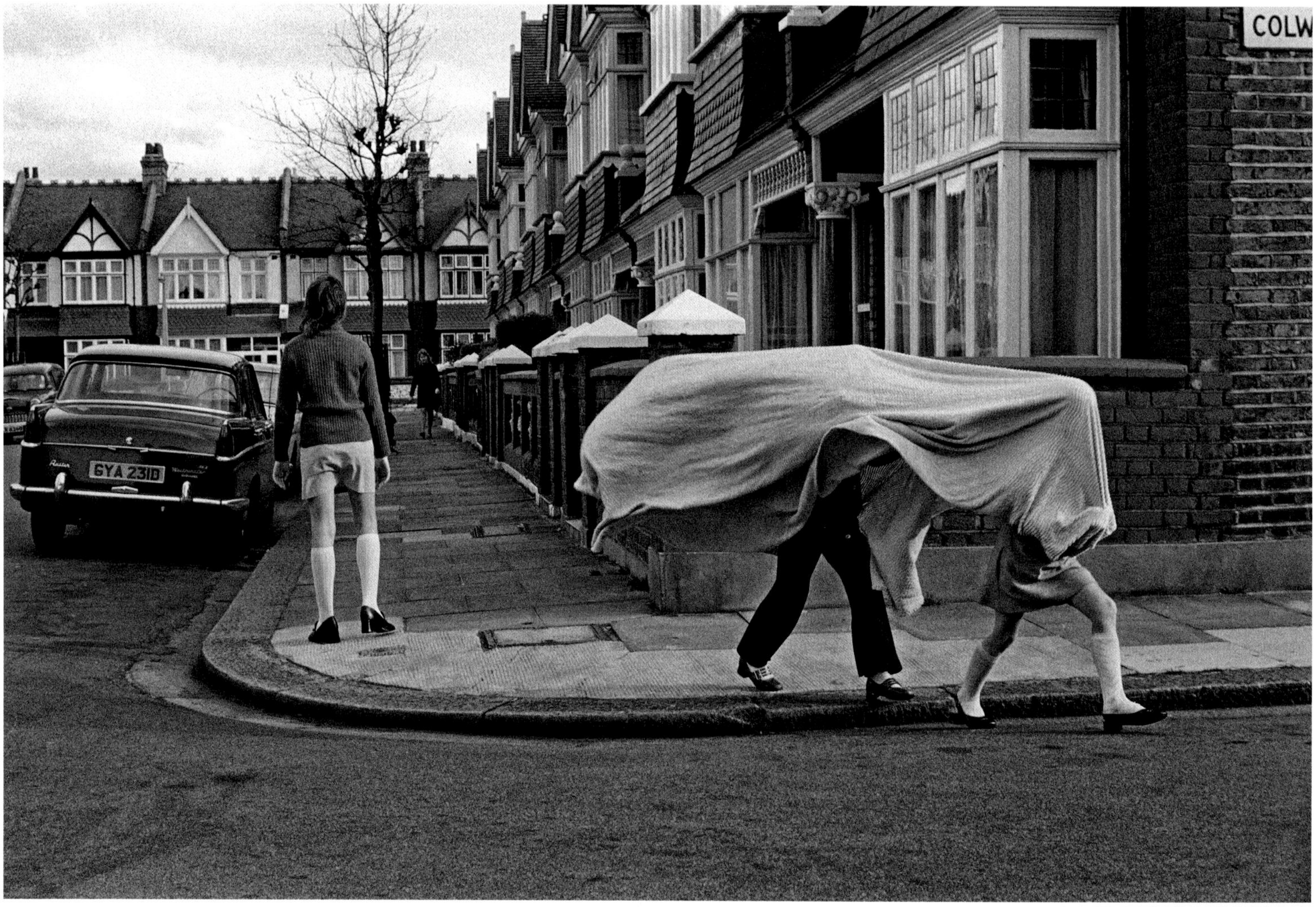

Wandsworth, London. 1970

Children playing in the street.

Elephant and Castle, London. 1975

Shoeless and in their underclothes, two young girls play outside their prefab home. After the Second World War it was estimated that 750,000 new homes needed to be built in England and Wales, both cheaply and quickly. Prefabs were intended to be temporary and had a 10 year life span.

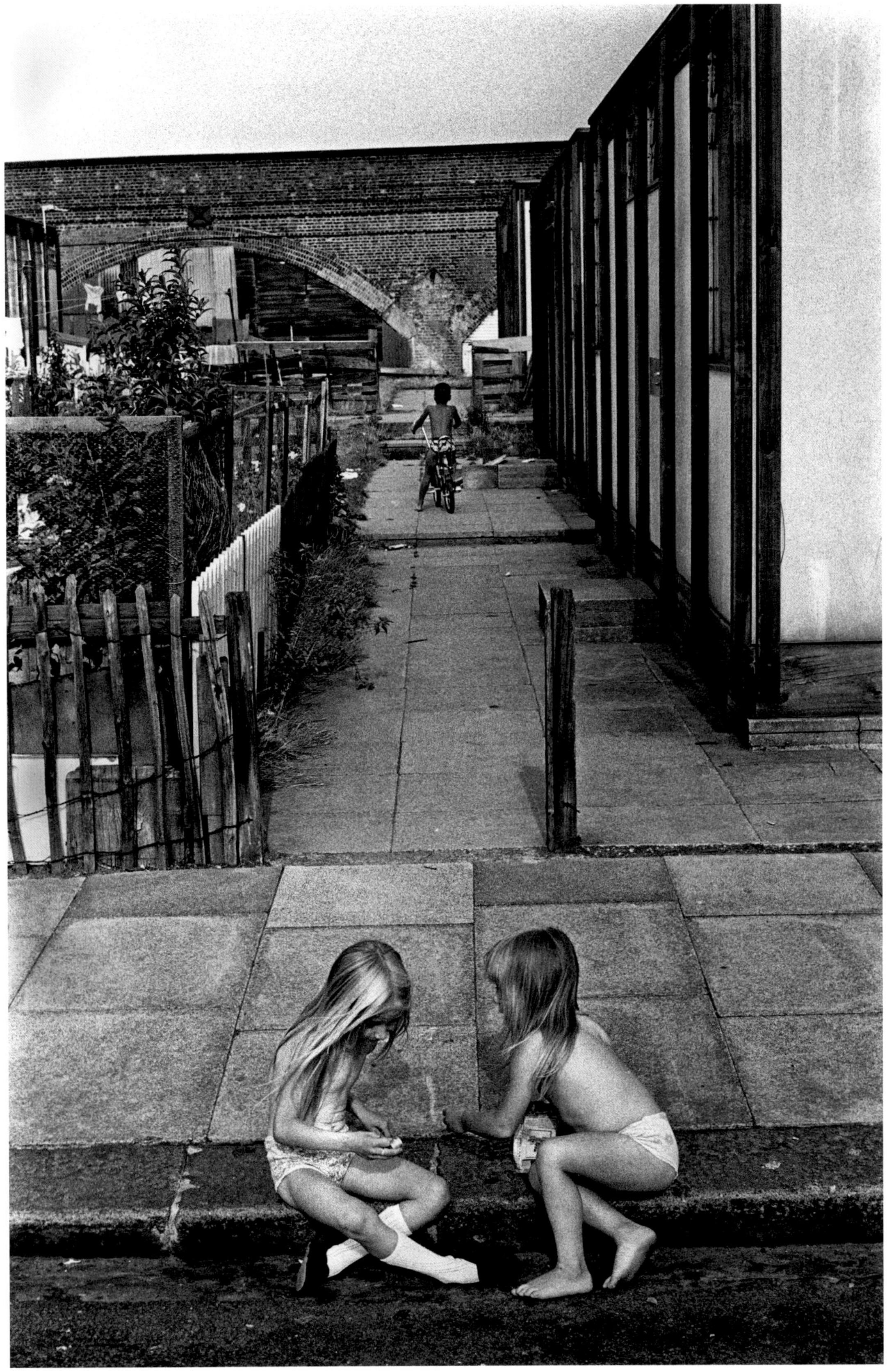

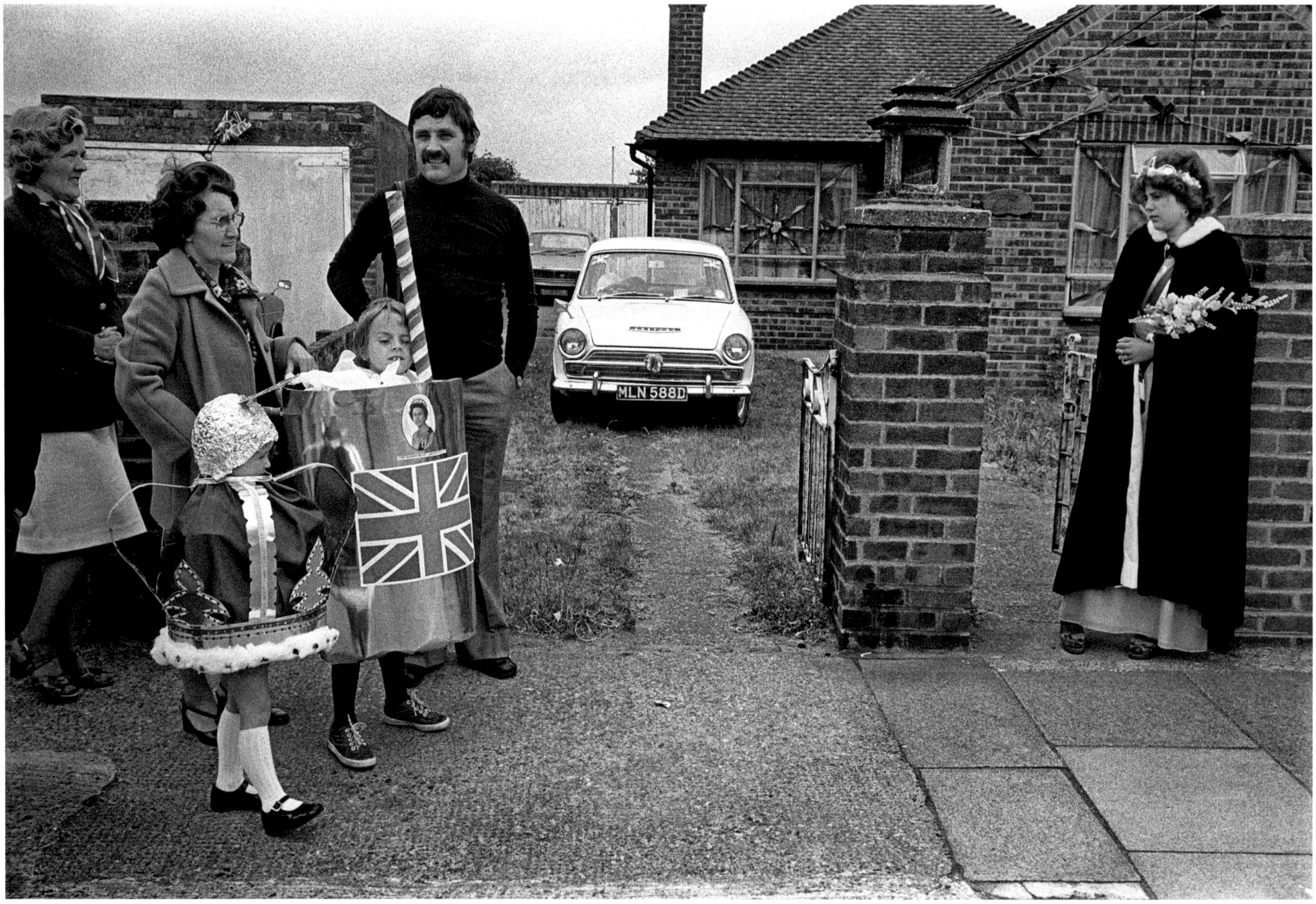

Rainham, Essex. 1977

Spring Bank Holiday Monday, 6th June. Betterton Road residents hold a celebratory street party and elect a Silver Jubilee Queen.

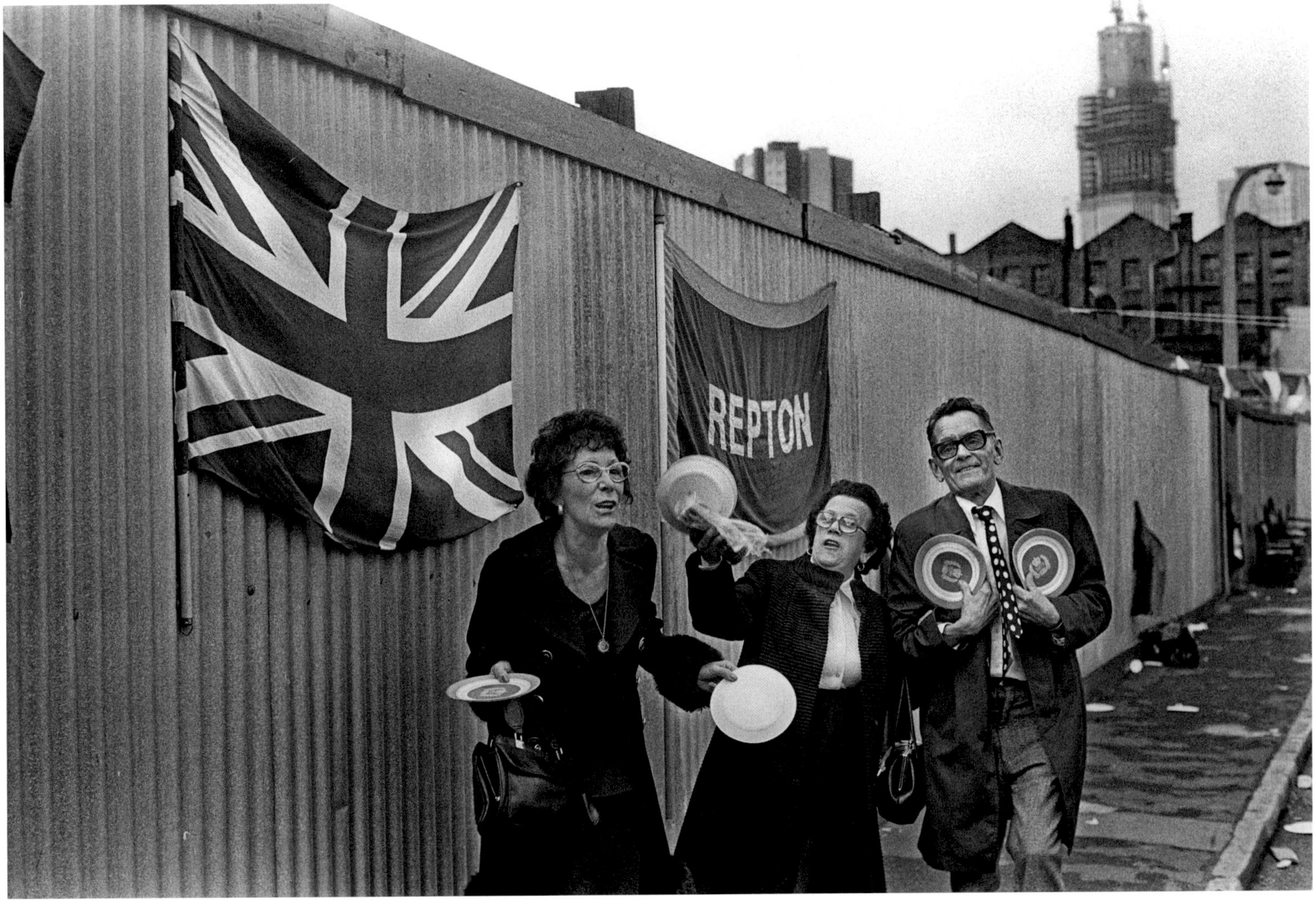

Whitechapel, London. 1977

Repton Street, Tower Hamlets. Residents sing along at the end of their Silver Jubilee street party.

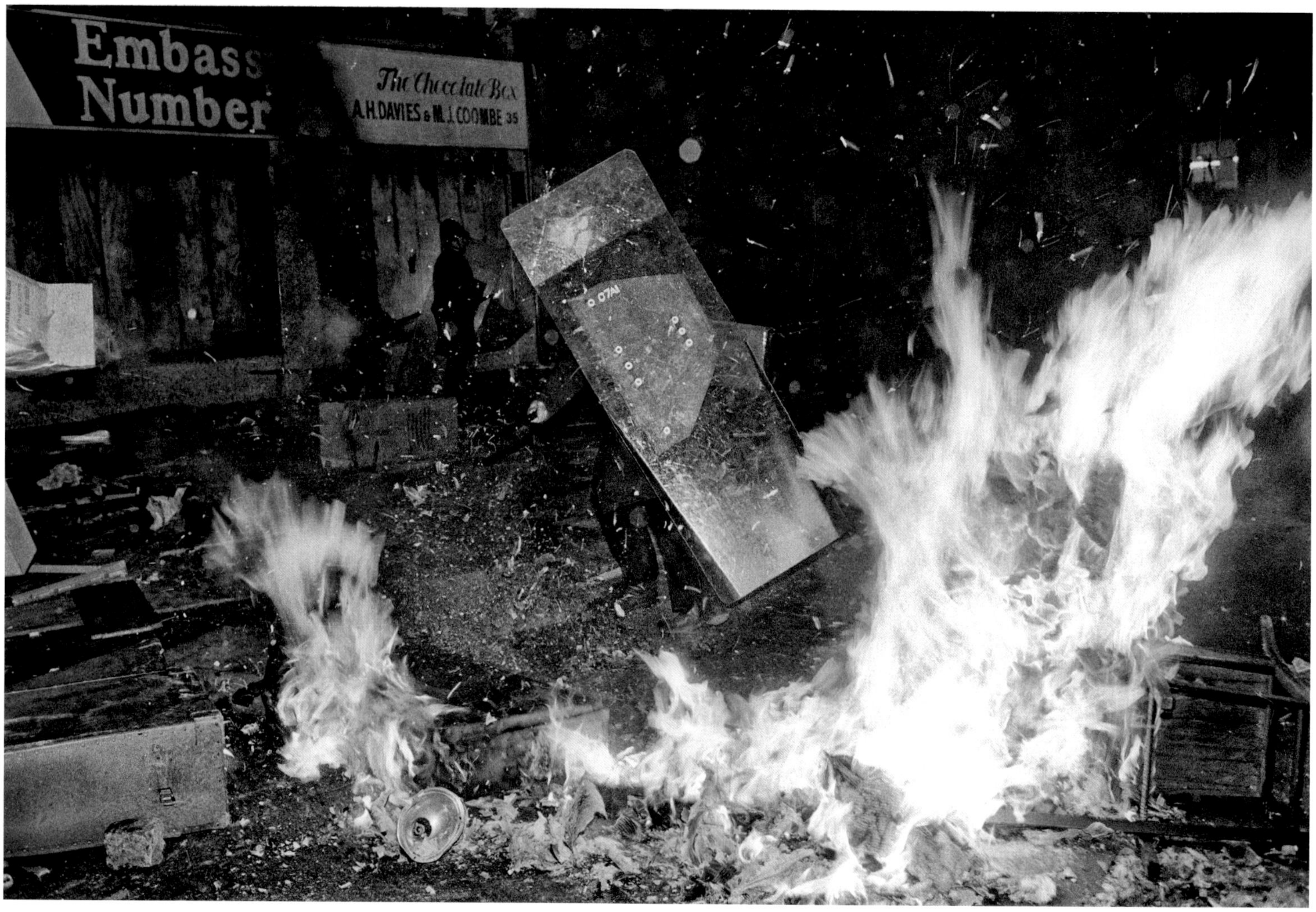

Toxteth, Liverpool. 1981

A petrol bomb explodes as police charge rioters. Also known as Liverpool 8, Toxteth is an inner-city neighbourhood. The Toxteth riots were the result of long-standing tensions between the police and the black community: Merseyside police being frequently accused of discriminatory and racist attitudes, including the misuse of the hated sus laws, which allowed police to stop and search anyone deemed suspicious.

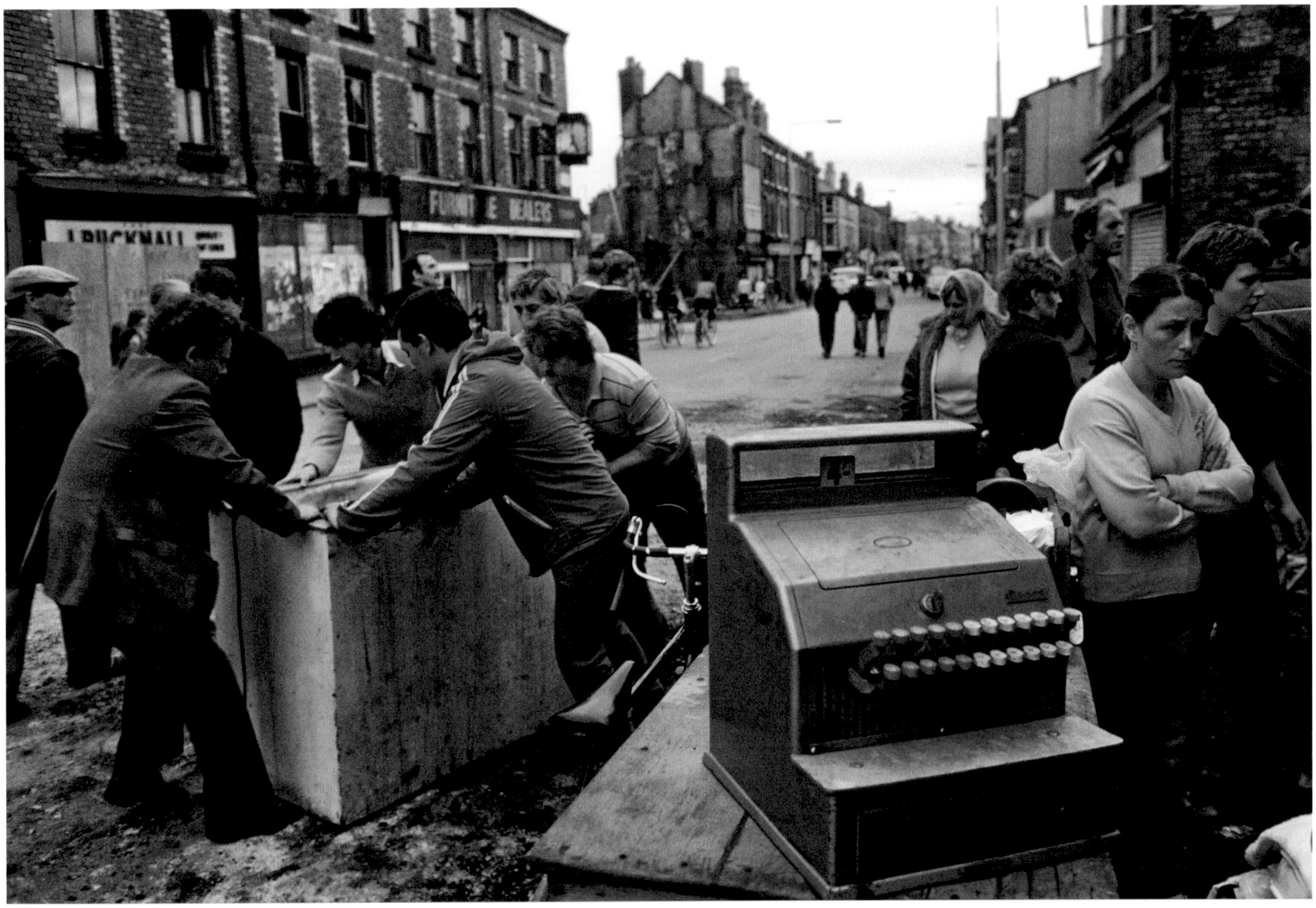

Toxteth, Liverpool. 1981

The cash till shows four shillings, but no doubt everything has been stolen. Local men help themselves from a burnt-out shop, attacked by rioters during the night.

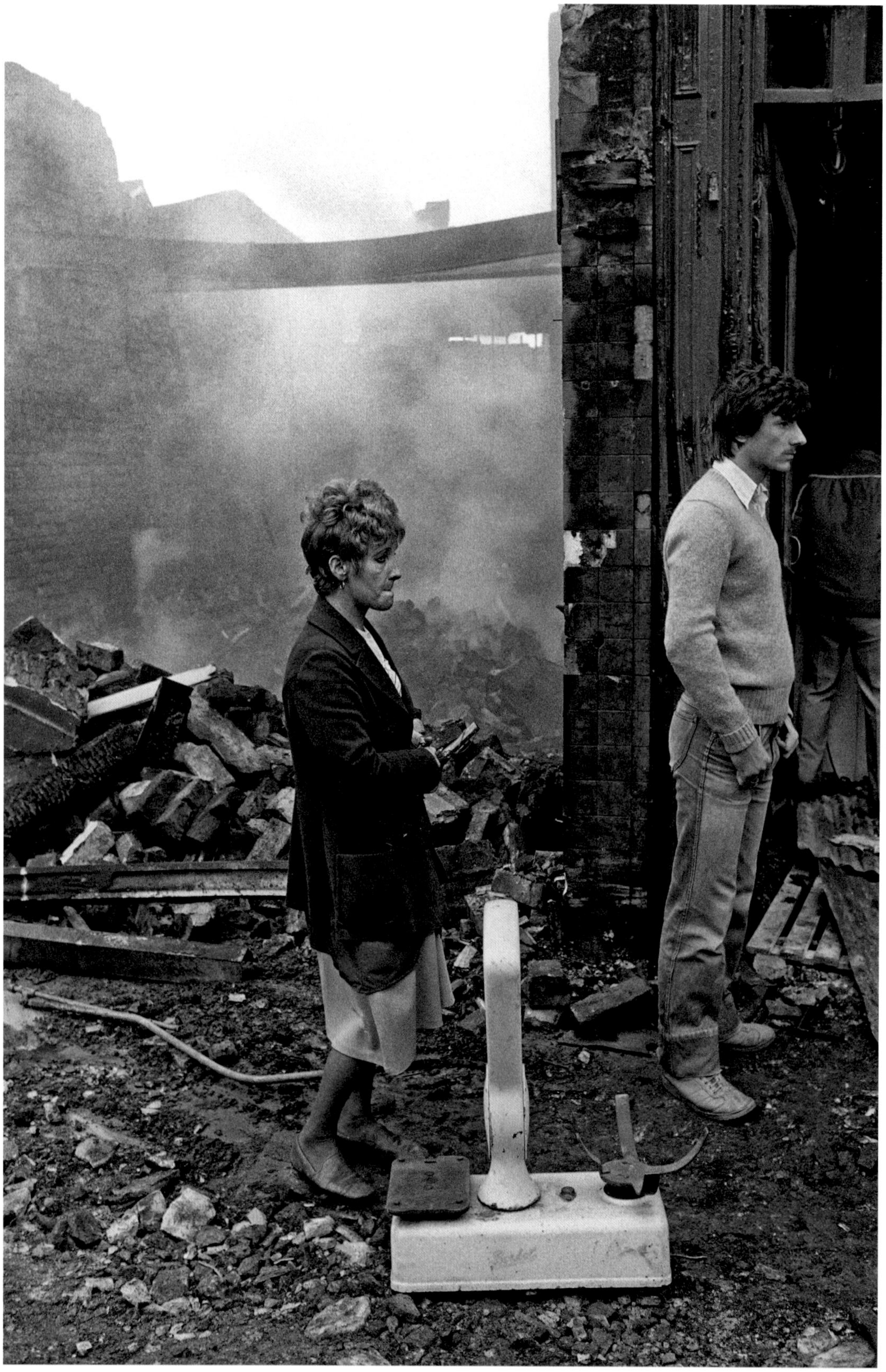

Toxteth, Liverpool. 1981

Greengrocer's scales lie abandoned outside a burnt-out shop, as residents look on in disbelief at what has happened to their neighbourhood.

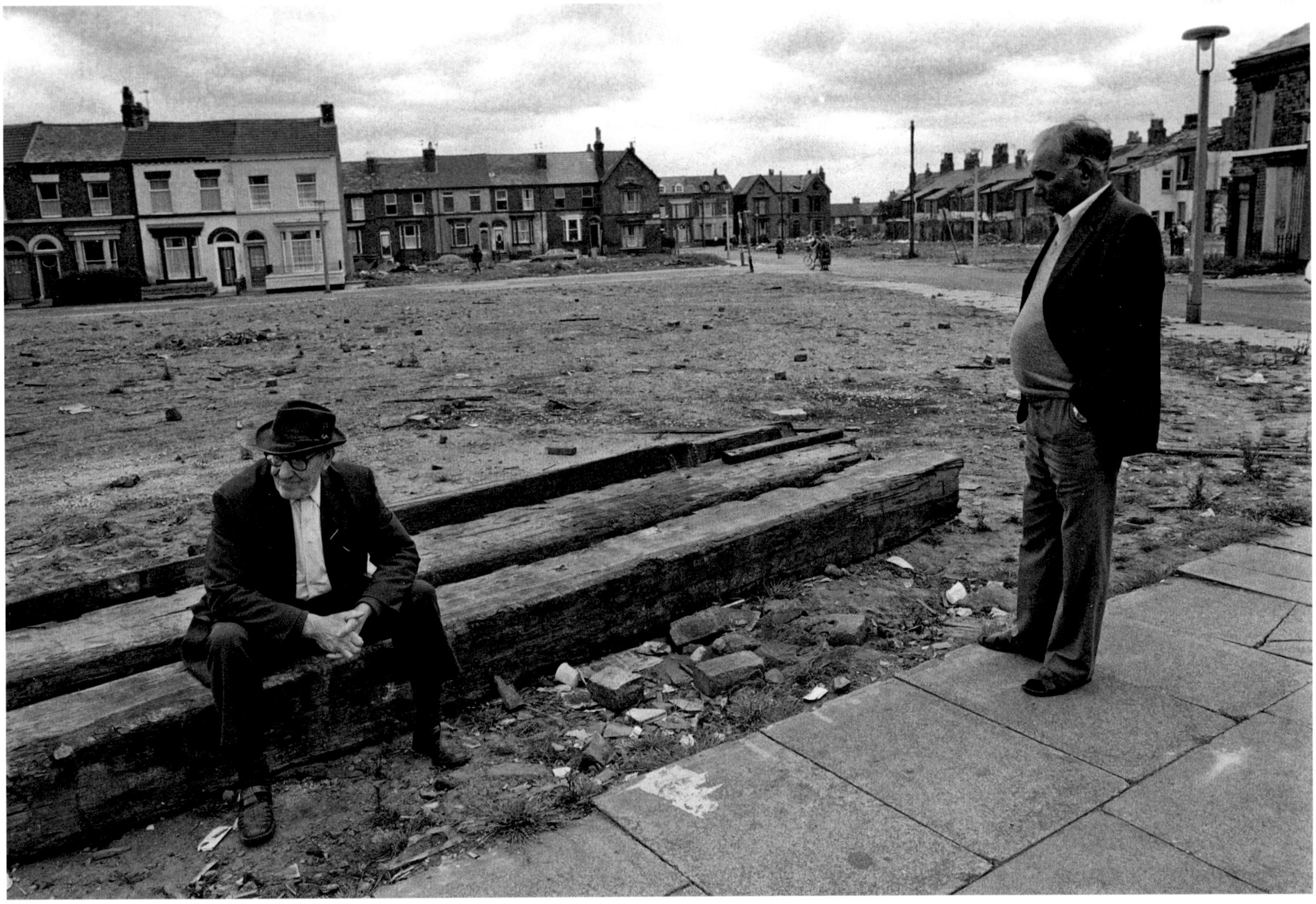

Toxteth, Liverpool. 1981

Local resident John Hopkins and his friend pass the time of day. Poverty, deprivation and bad housing were common features of Liverpool 8.

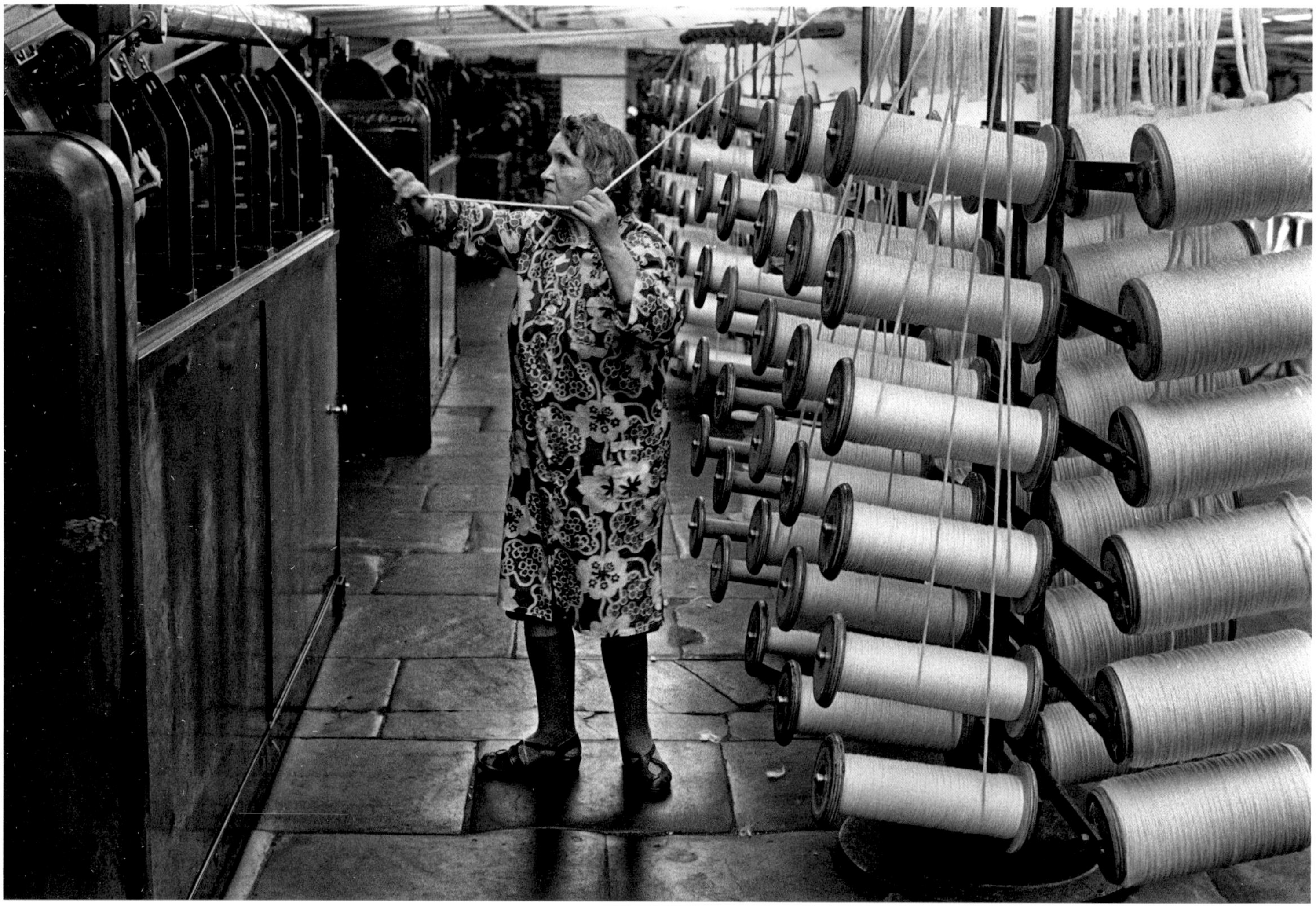

Saltaire, Bradford. 1981

Sir Titus Salt built Salt's Mill in the 1850s, creating a mill large enough to consolidate his textile manufacturing business in one place. It closed in February 1986.

Saltaire, Bradford. 1981

At the end of their lunchbreak two young women return to work at Salt's Mill along the still cobbled Albert Terrace, named after Prince Albert, Queen Victoria's consort. This model village was built by Sir Titus Salt who died in 1876. It is estimated that as many 100,000 people lined the streets to watch his funeral cortege.

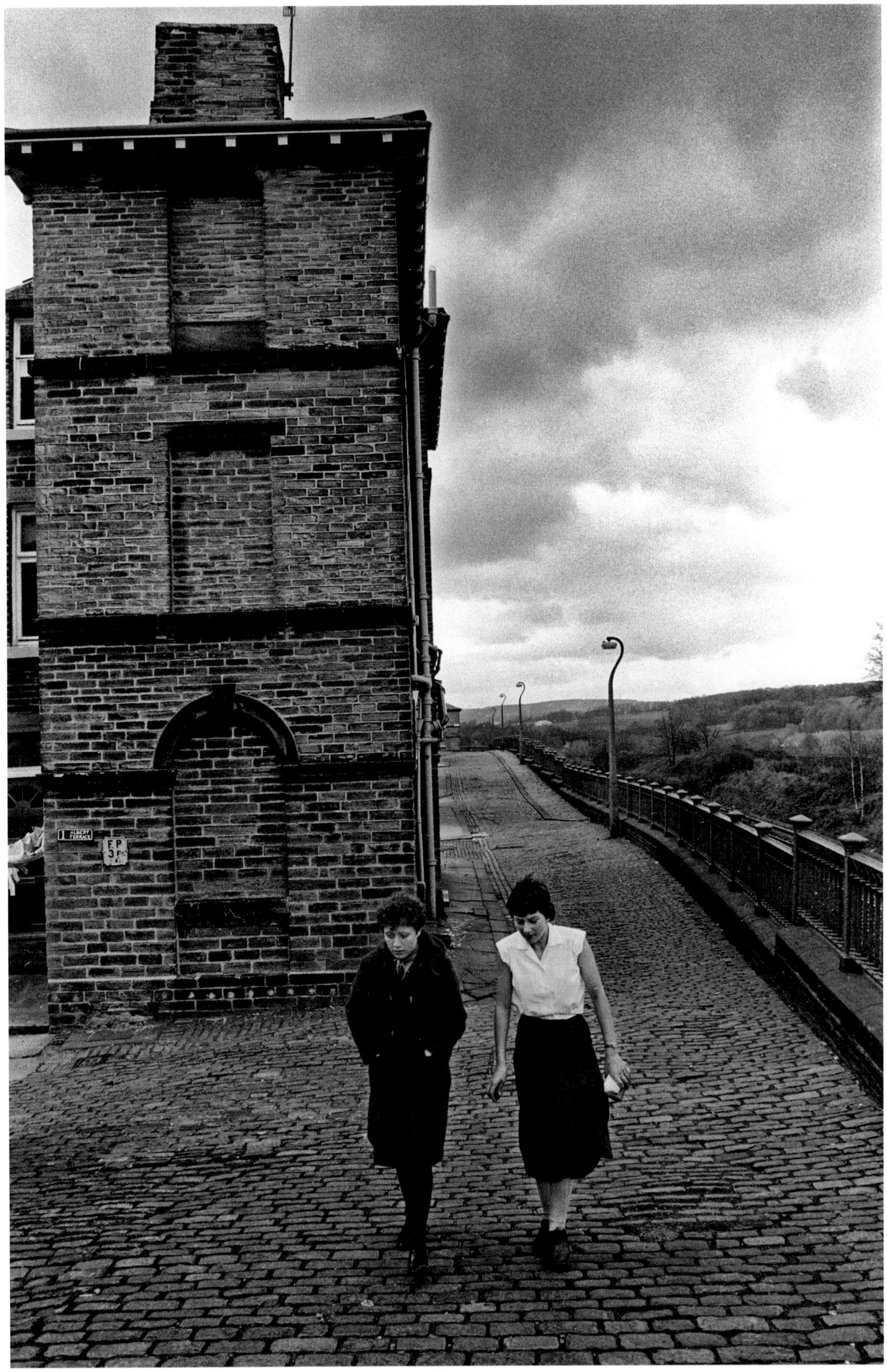

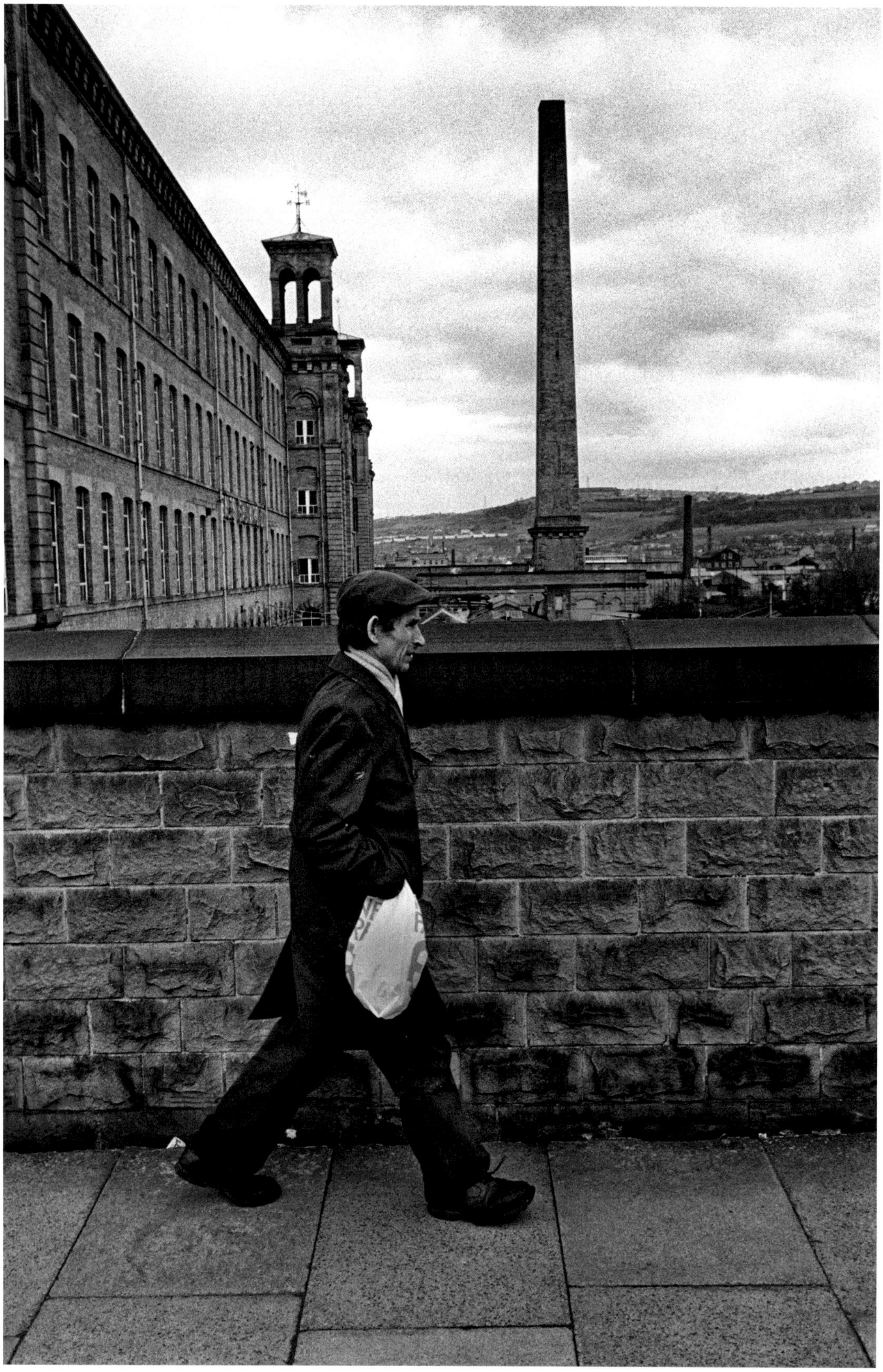

Saltaire, Bradford. 1981

A factory worker walks home after a day's shift in Salt's Mill.

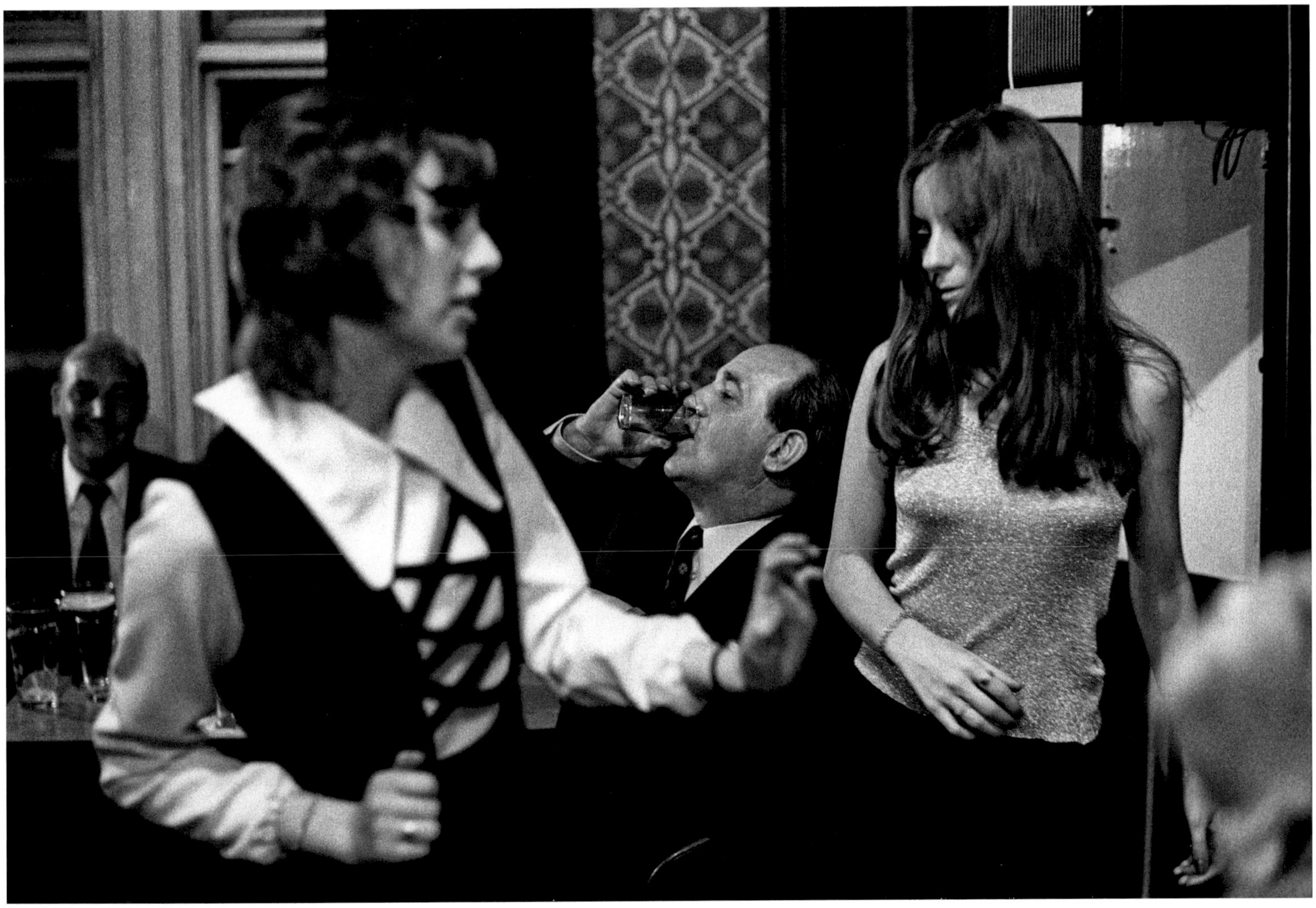

Byker, Newcastle upon Tyne. 1973

Dancing to the live band, Saturday night at Byker & St. Peters Working Men's Social Club.

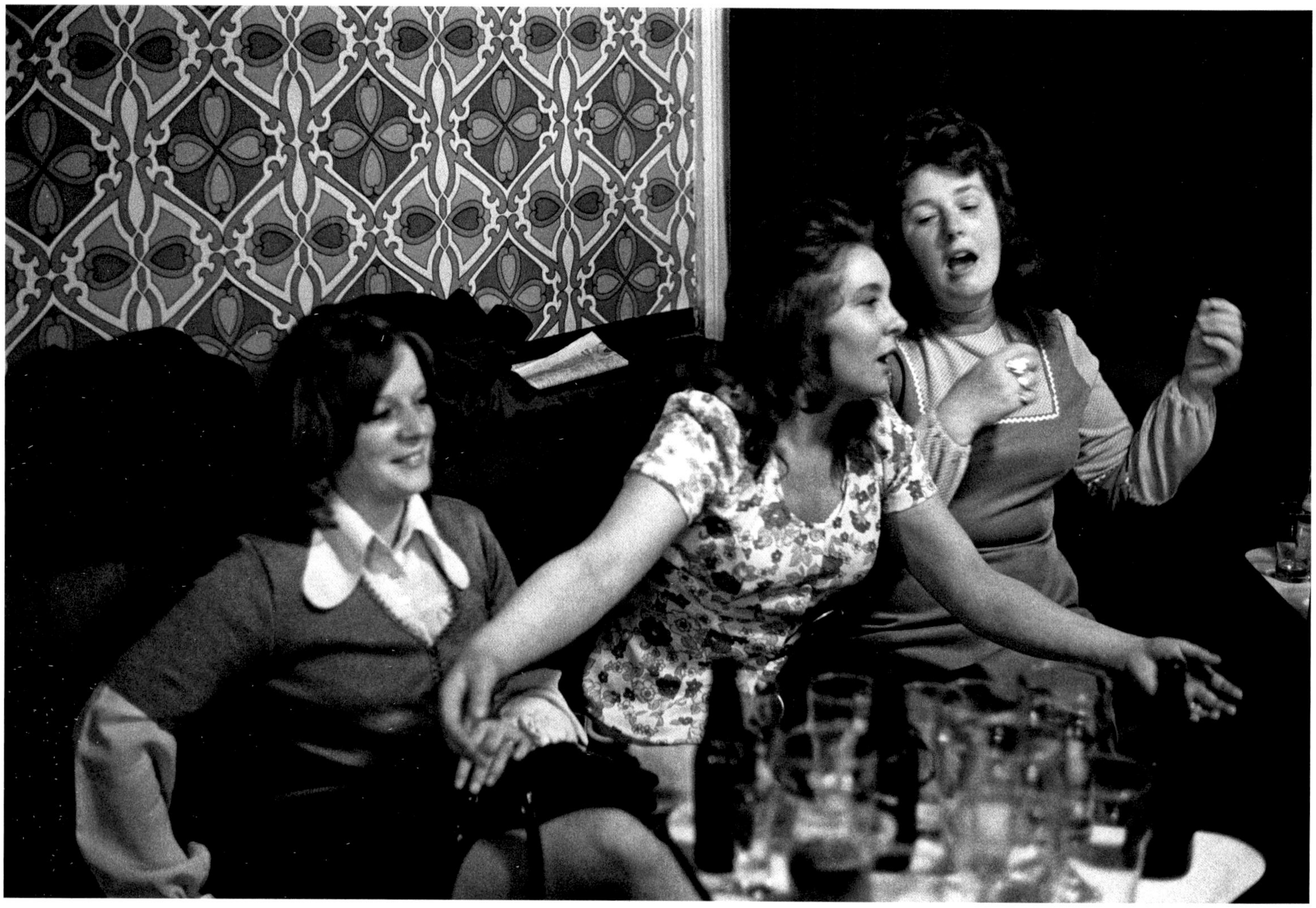

Byker, Newcastle upon Tyne. 1973

A group of friends enjoy a singsong; it's Saturday night at the Byker & St.Peters Working Men's Social Club.

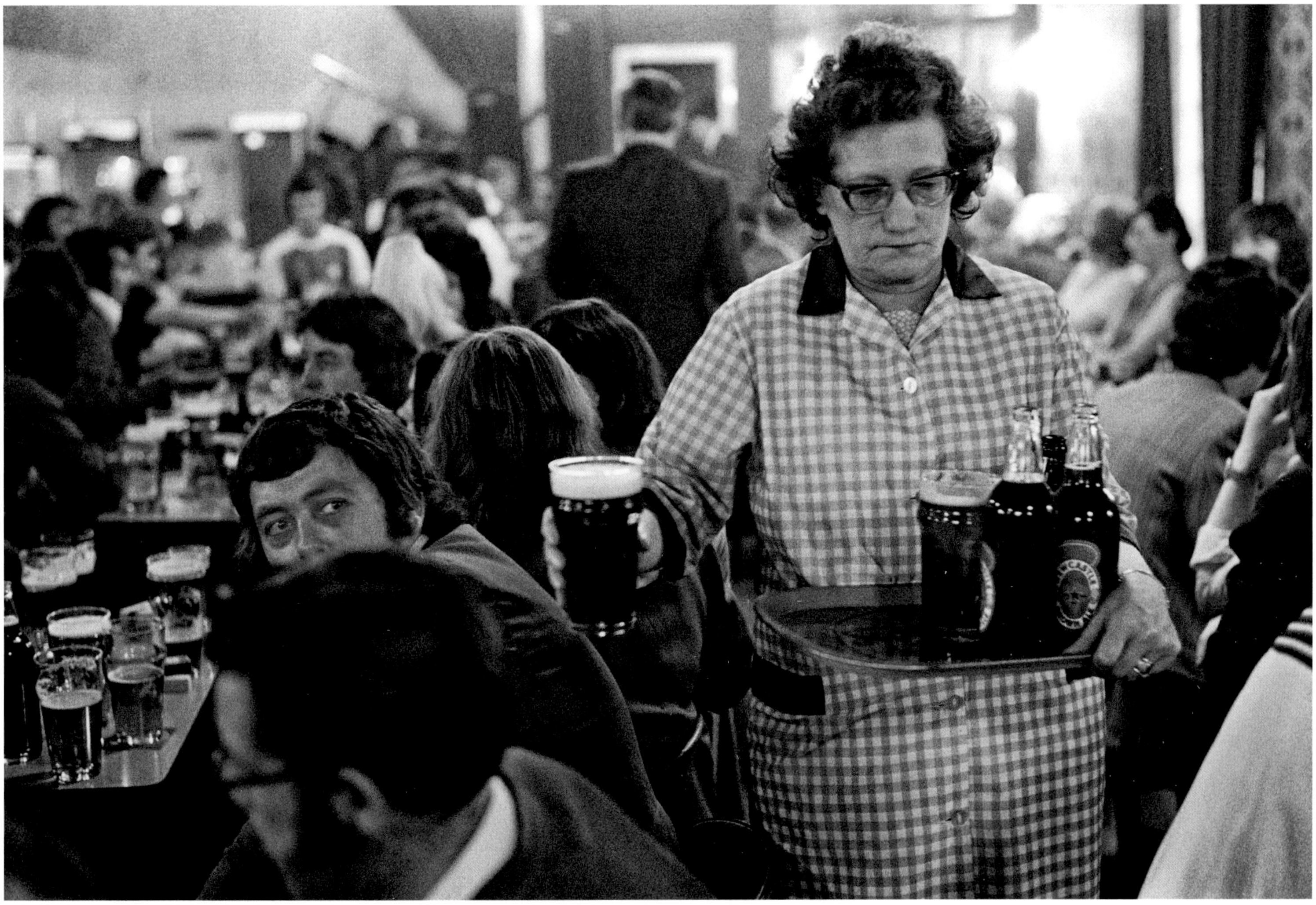

Byker, Newcastle upon Tyne. 1973

A barmaid serves members their pints of beer and bottles of Newcastle Brown Ale. Newcastle Brown was a working man's beer, associated with the North East and heavy industry, a staple on a night out at the working men's club.

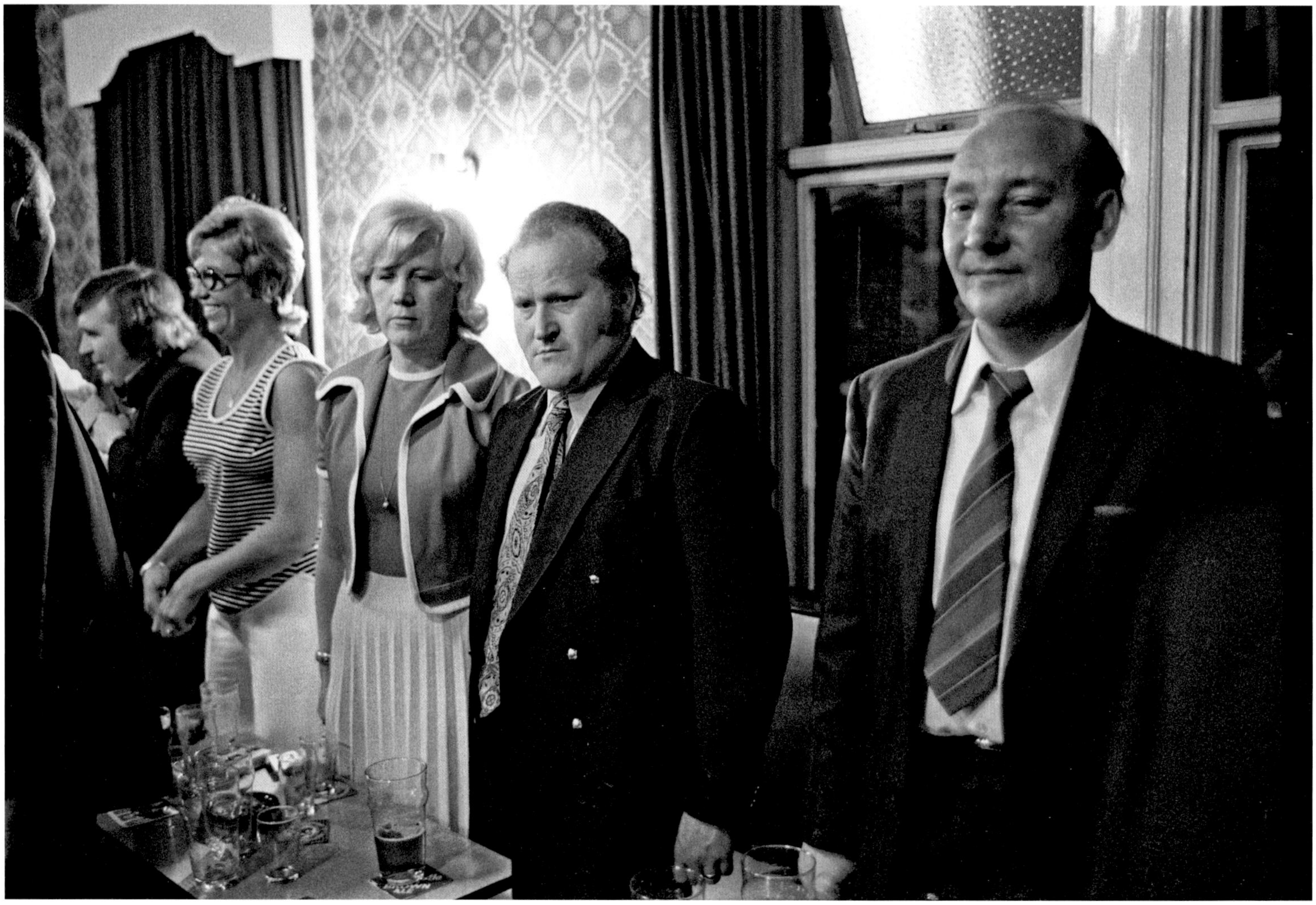

Byker, Newcastle upon Tyne. 1973

Saturday night and wearing their best clothes, members and their wives stand to attention at the end of the evening while the National Anthem, God Save the Queen, is played at Byker & St.Peters Working Men's Social Club.

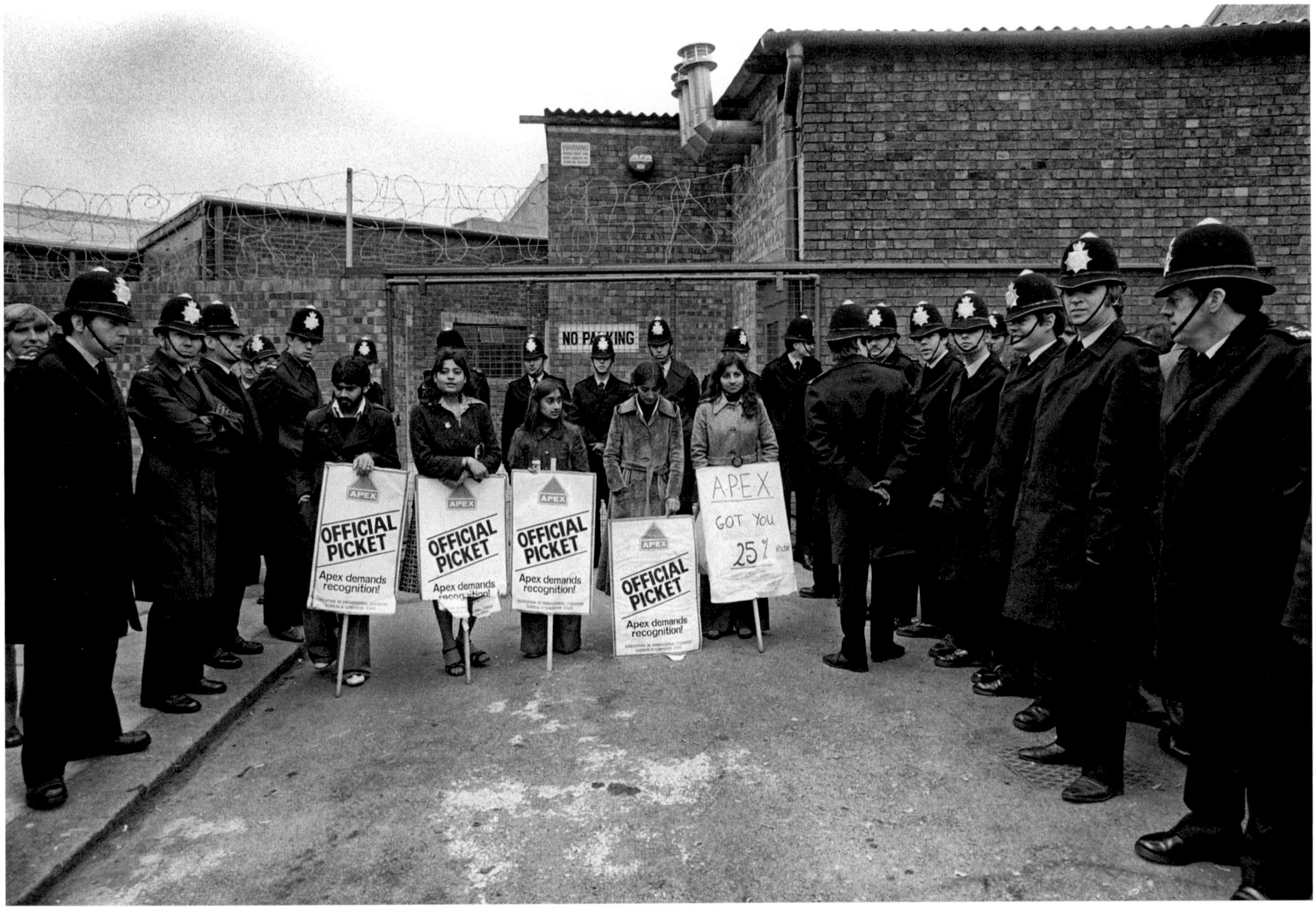

Willesden, London. 1977

The Grunwick film processing plant dispute was over the sacking of 100 mainly south Asian women workers who wanted to join a union. The strike became a cause célèbre involving thousands of demonstrators; over 500 arrests were made during two years of often violent clashes.

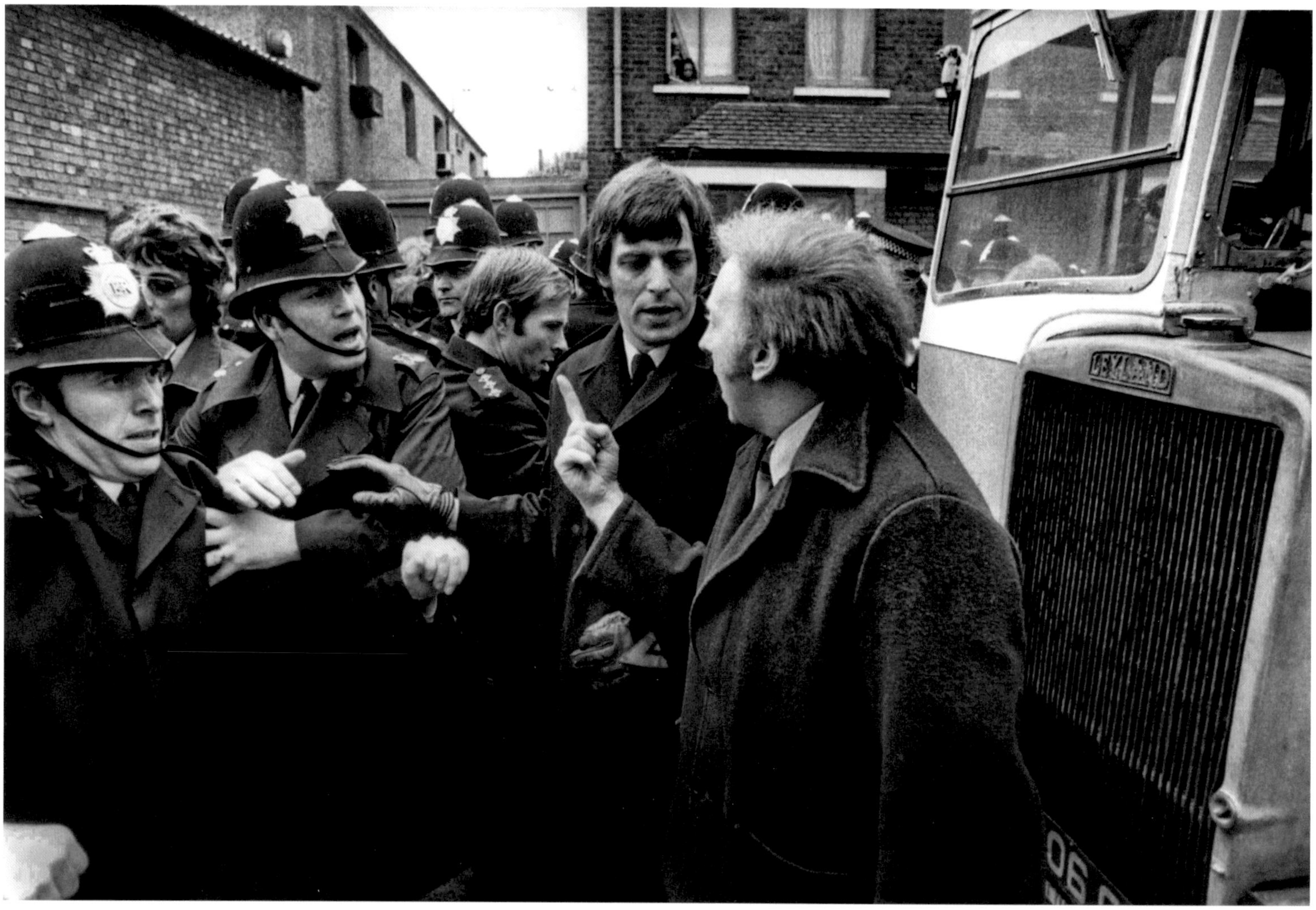

Willesden, London. 1977

Arthur Scargill, president of the National Union of Miners, Yorkshire branch, having words with the police. He attended the mass picket with a delegation of miners from Yorkshire, South Wales and Kent, in a show of solidarity.

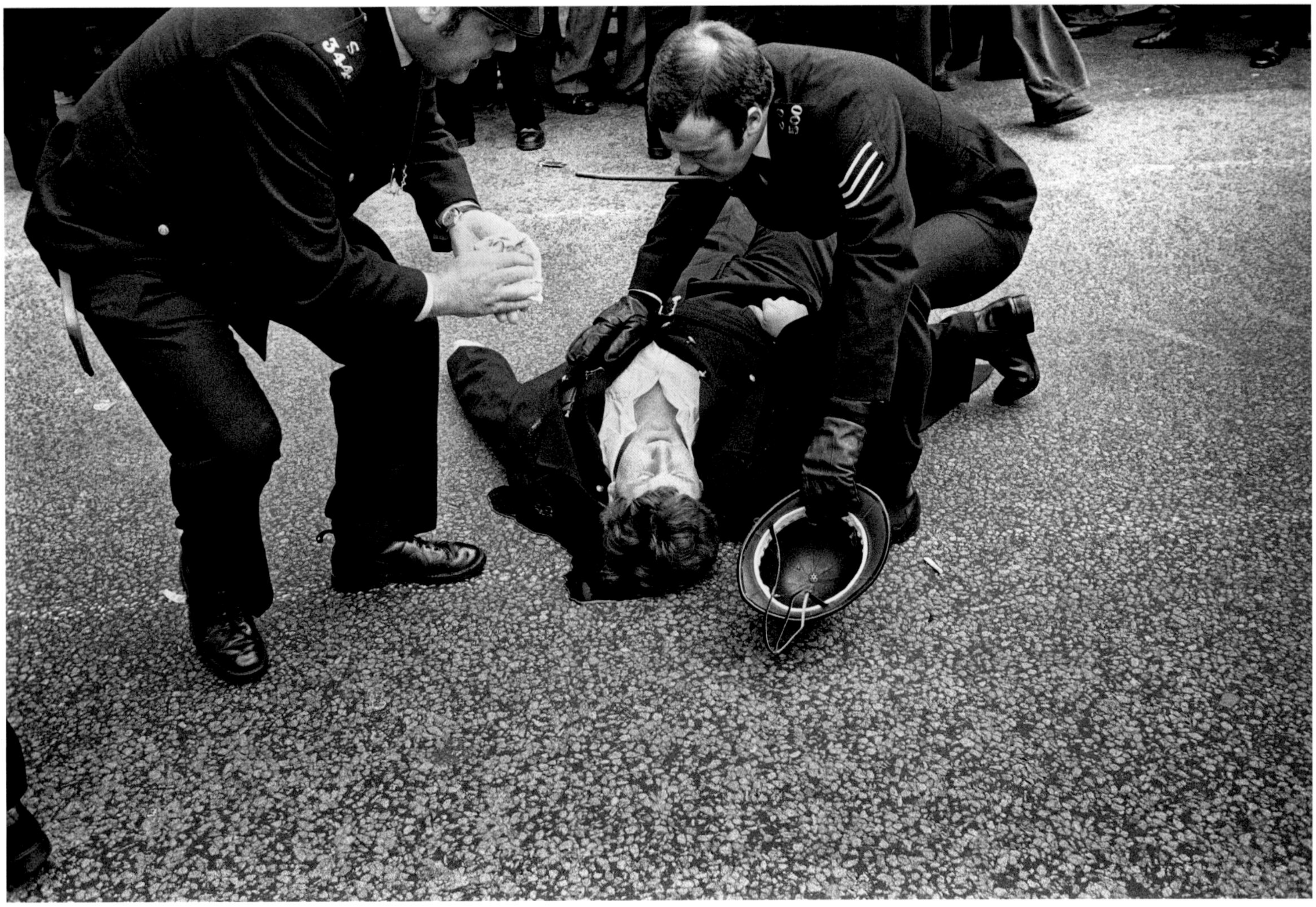

Willesden, London. 1977

PC Trevor Wilson lies in a pool of his own blood during violent clashes between demonstrators and police outside the Grunwick film processing plant.

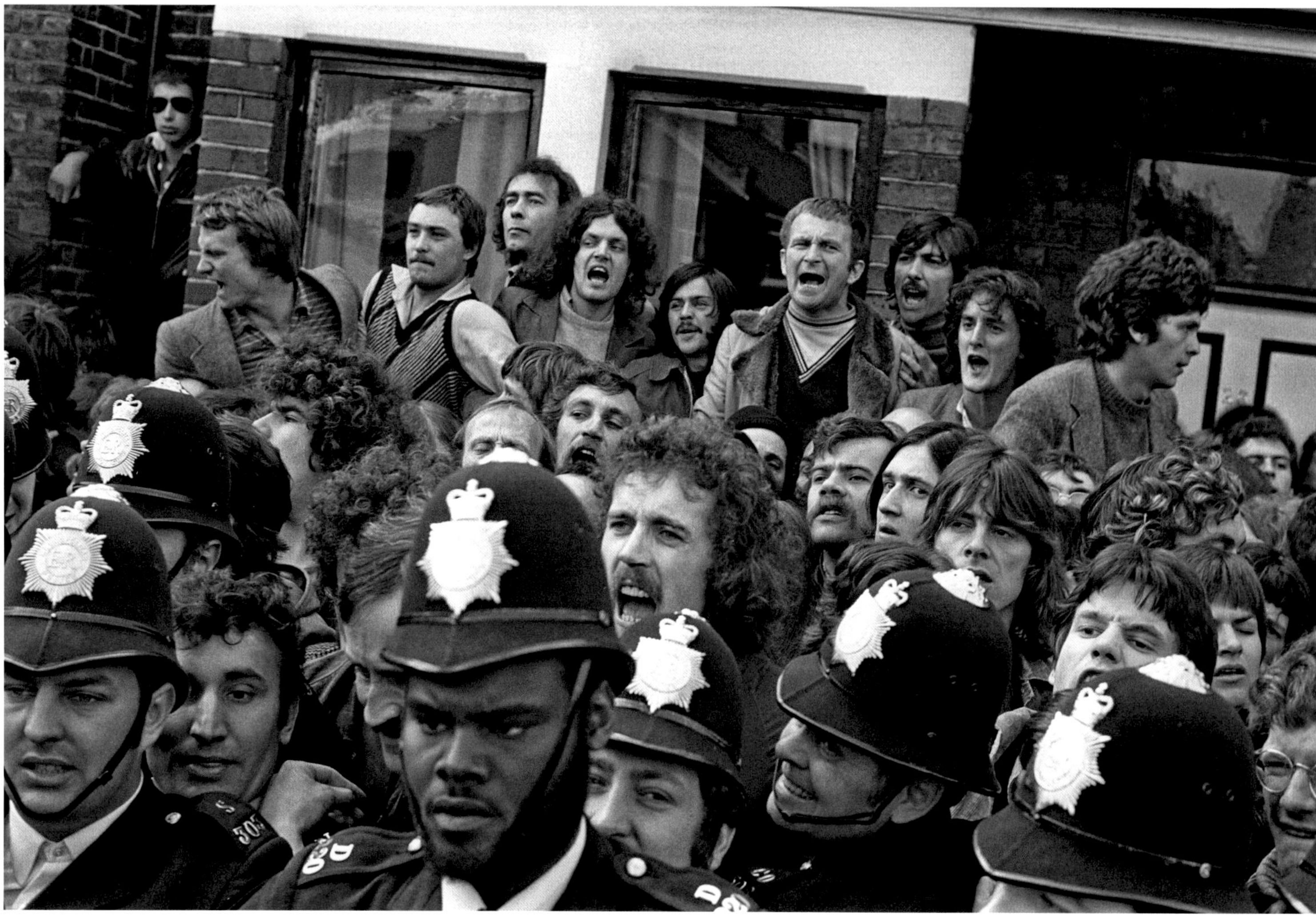

Willesden, London. 1977

The police line holding back demonstrators who are shouting at the scabs, those workers refusing to join the strike. Every day non-strikers were bussed into the factory owned by George Ward, an Anglo-Indian businessman.

Willesden, London. 1977

Mrs Jayaben Desai leader of the Asian women's strike at the Grunwick film processing factory. In protest over working conditions and not being allowed to join a union, Mrs Desai confronted the management. She is reputed to have said: 'What you are running here is not a factory, it is a zoo. In a zoo there are many types of animals. Some are monkeys who dance on your finger tips; others are lions who can bite you... We are the lions Mr Manager.'

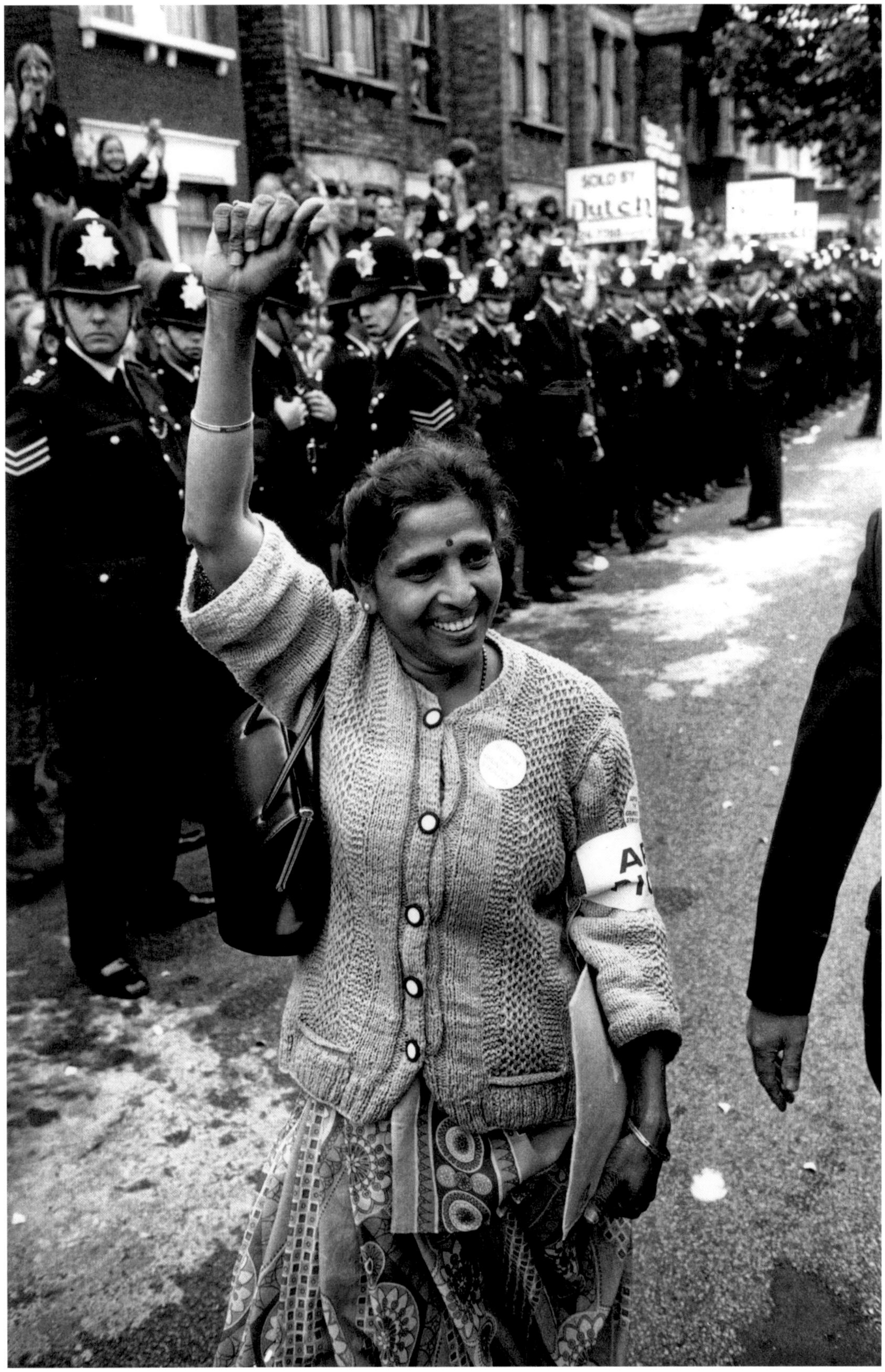

Balsall Heath, Birmingham. 1968

An Irish Travellers' encampment and temporary scrap car dump on waste ground in Balsall Heath, an inner city slum and red light district.

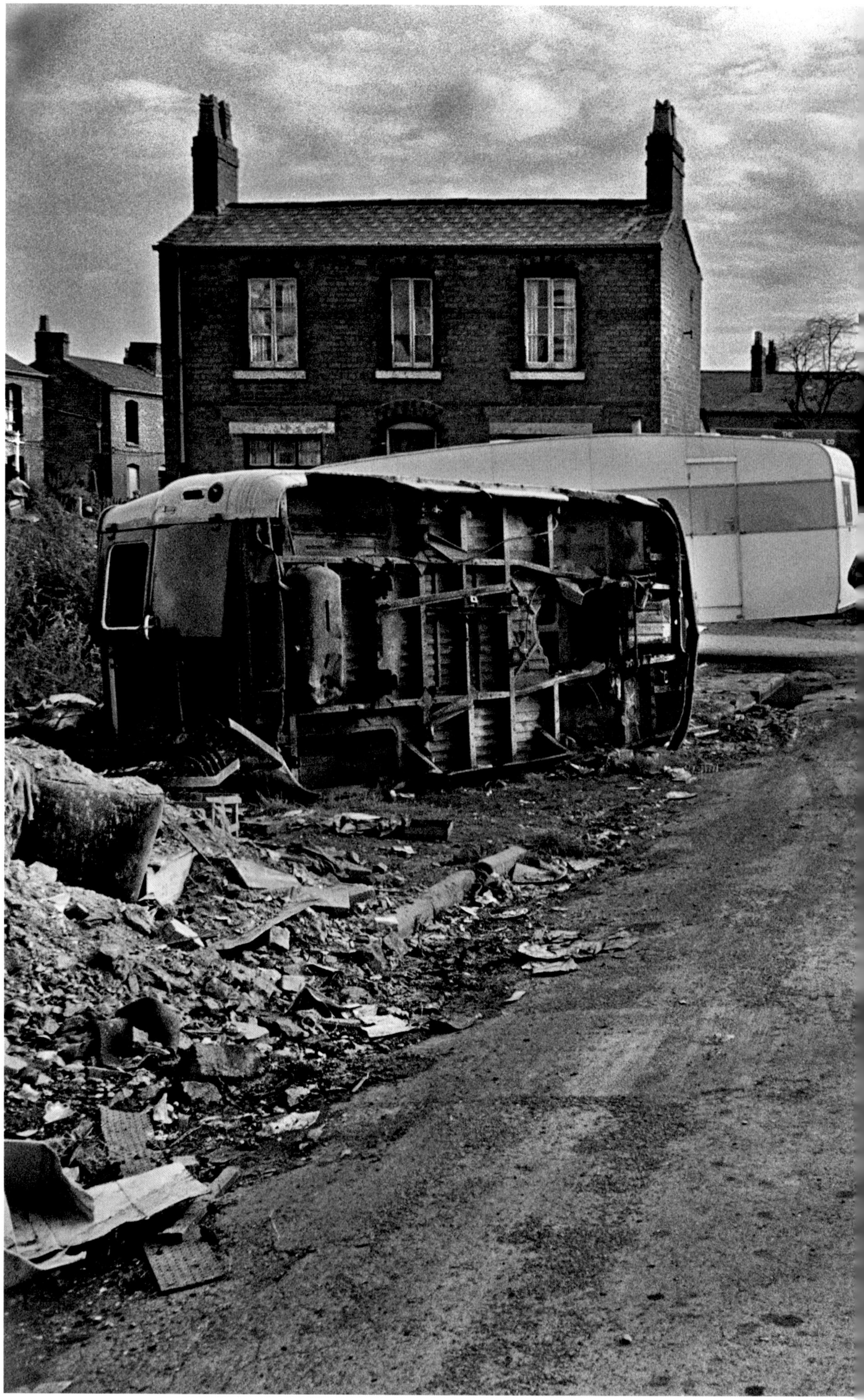

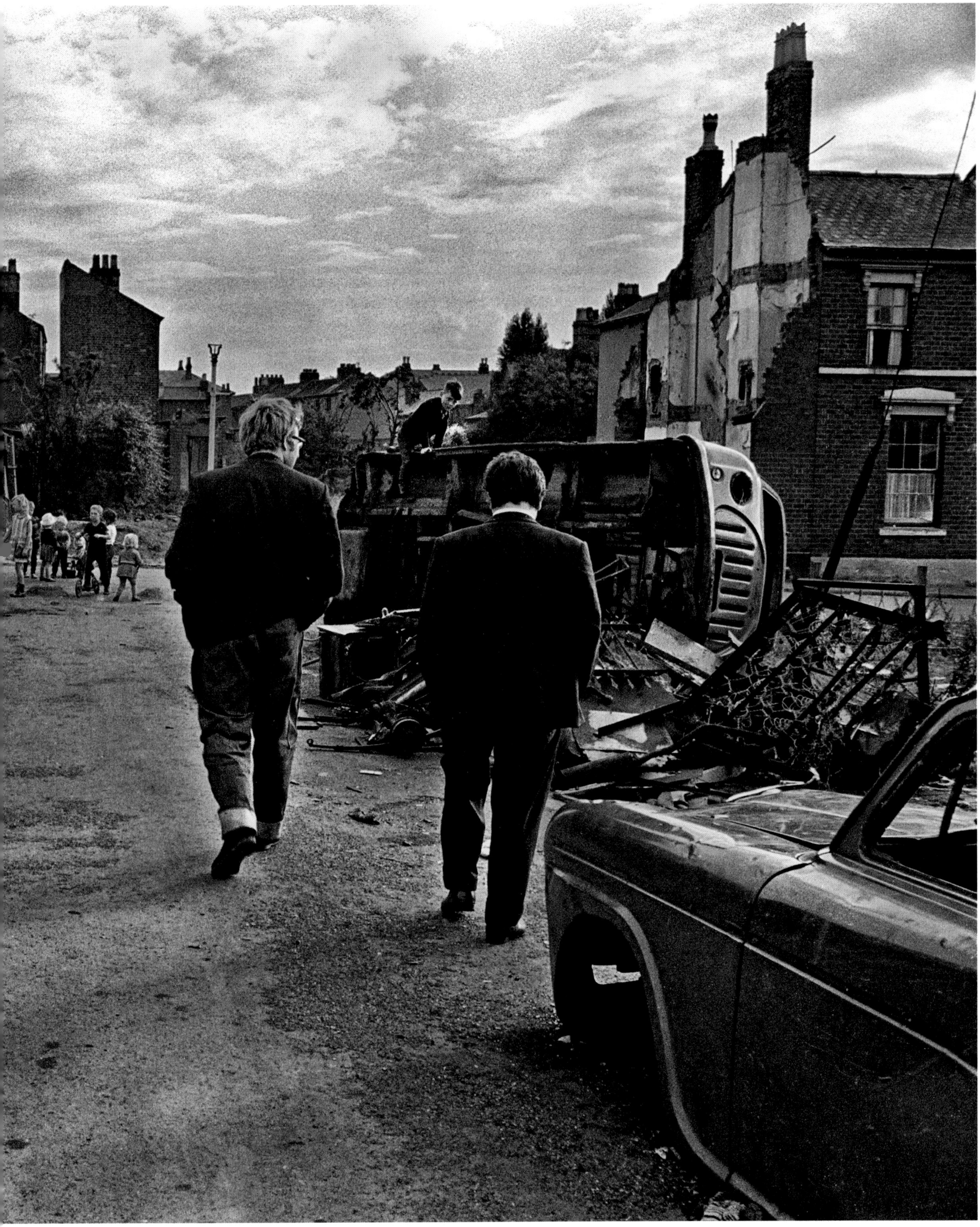

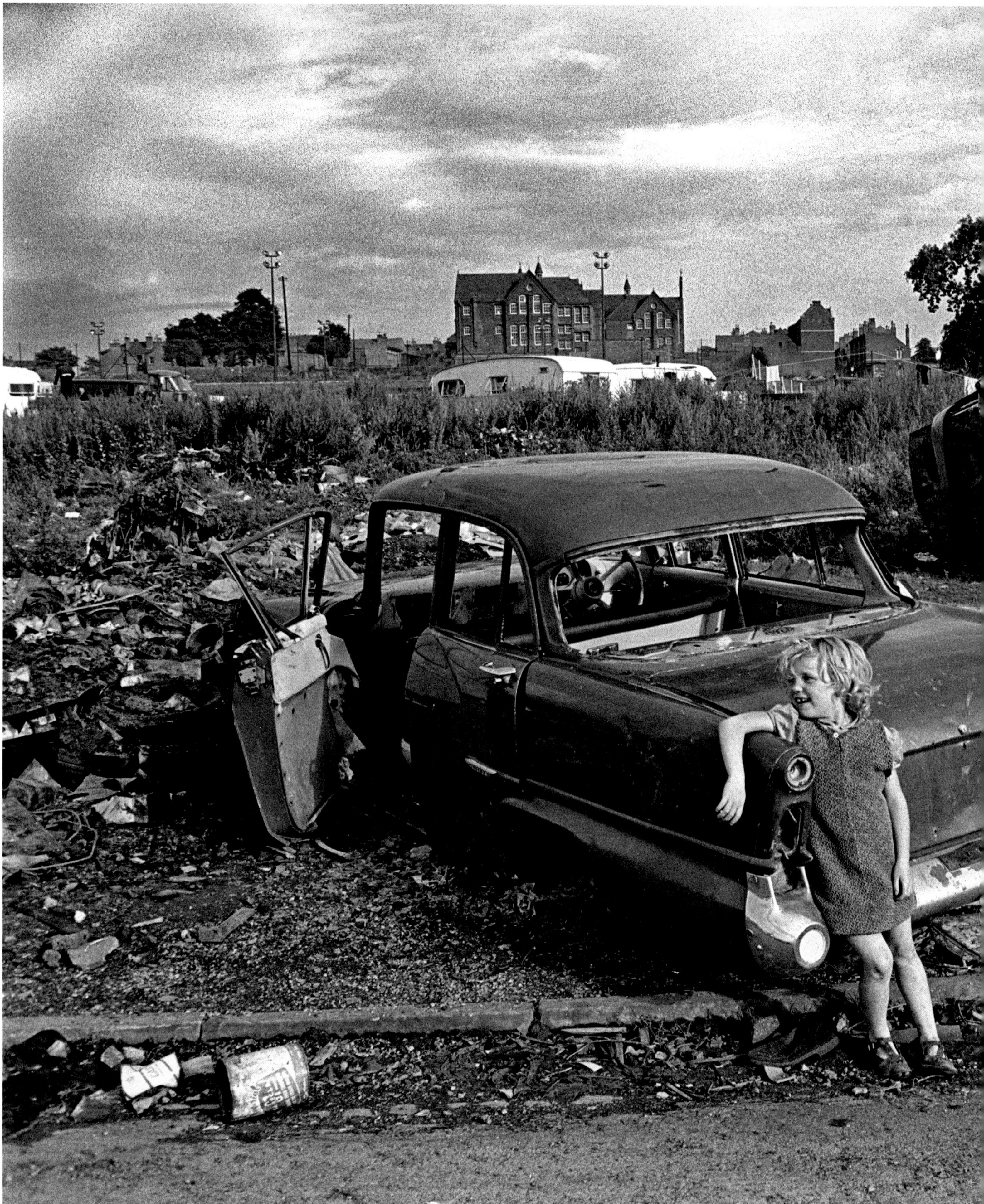

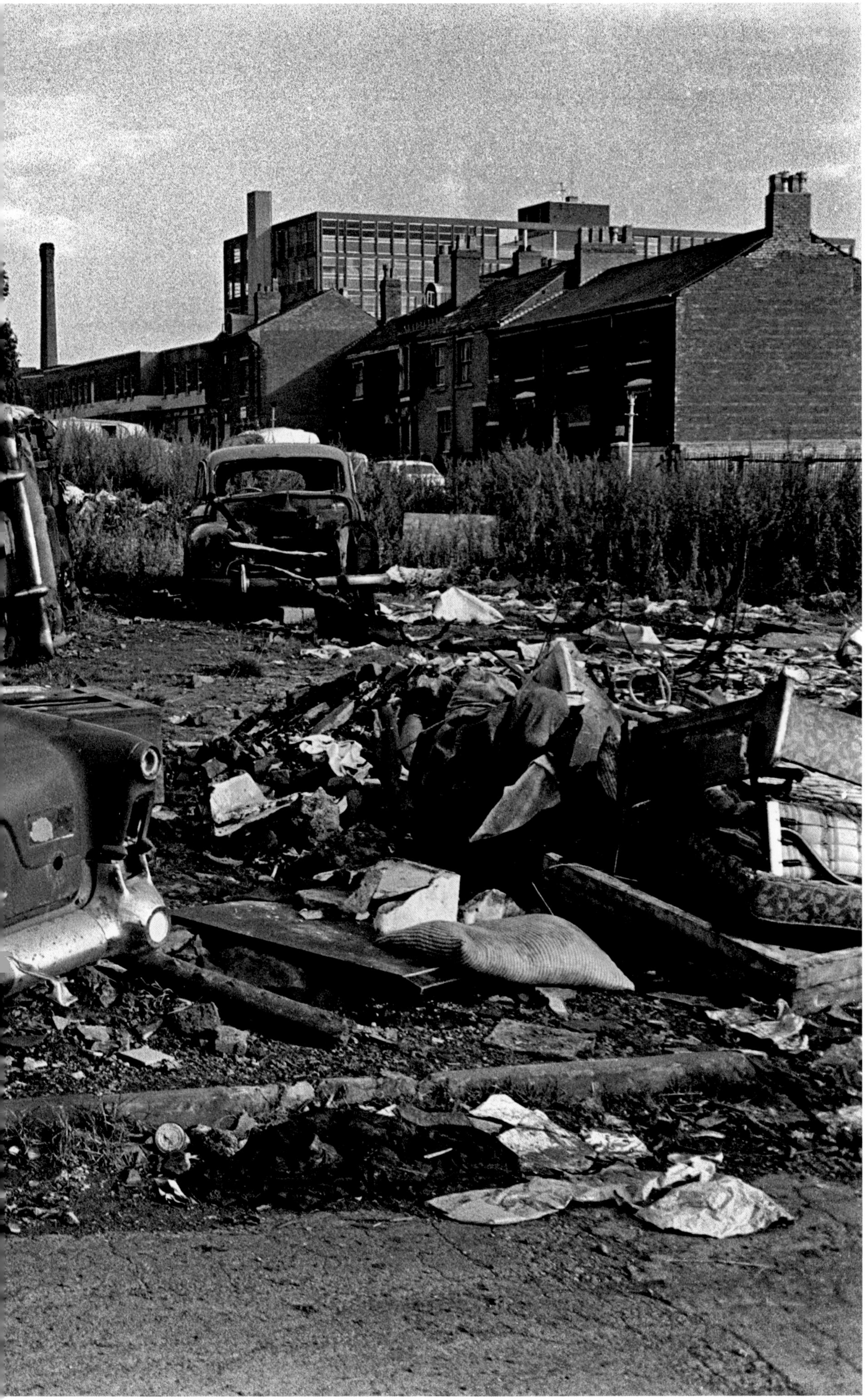

Balsall Heath, Birmingham. 1968

A young Irish gypsy girl. About twenty traveller families lived on waste ground, and made a living from scrap metal dealing.

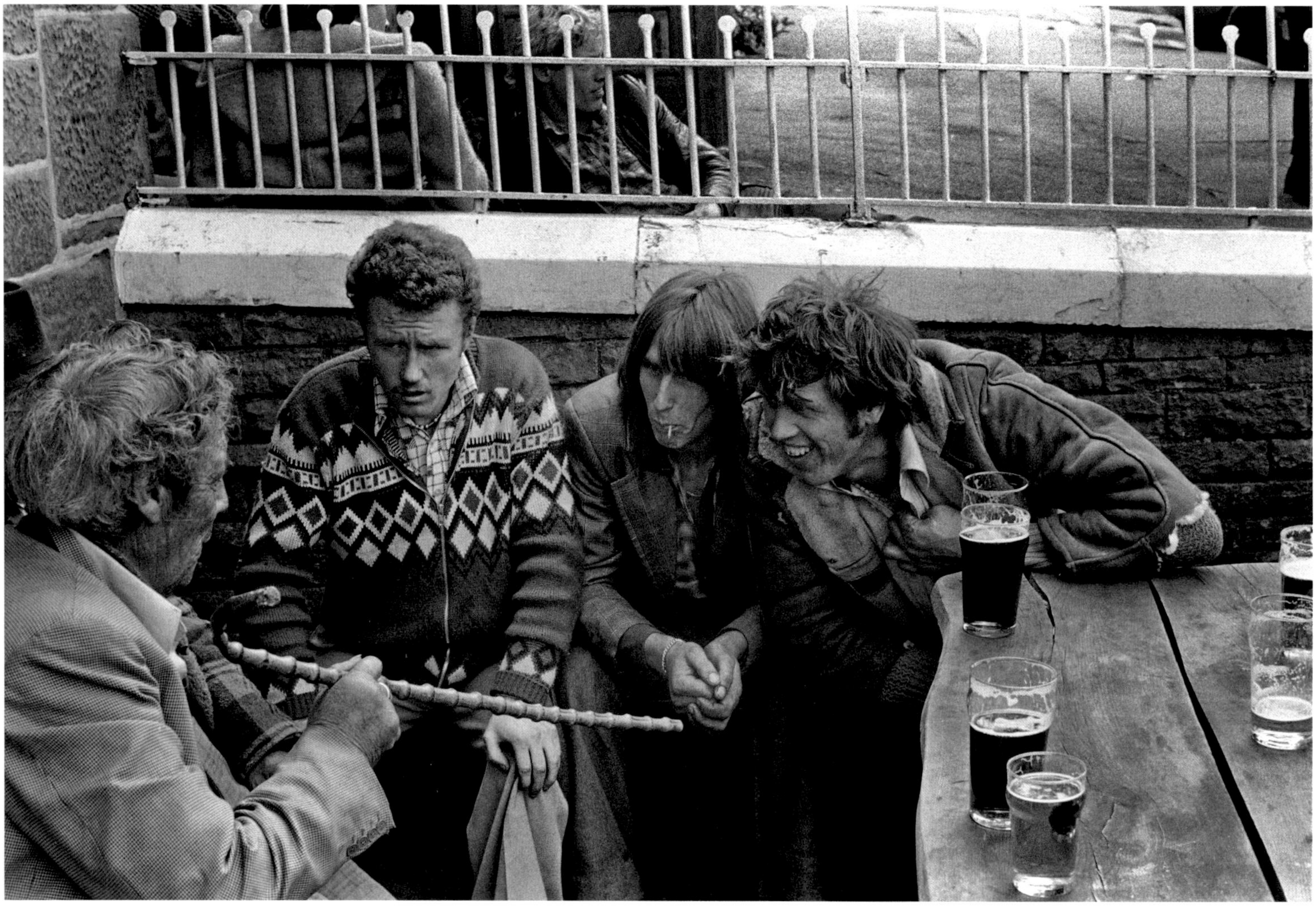

Appleby-in-Westmorland, Cumbria. 1981

At the annual Appleby Horse Fair, gypsies Joe Ewbank, George Coffee Lowther and Big Joe Big Foot Ewbank, listen in awe, to gypsy tales as told by Aries, over a pint or two.

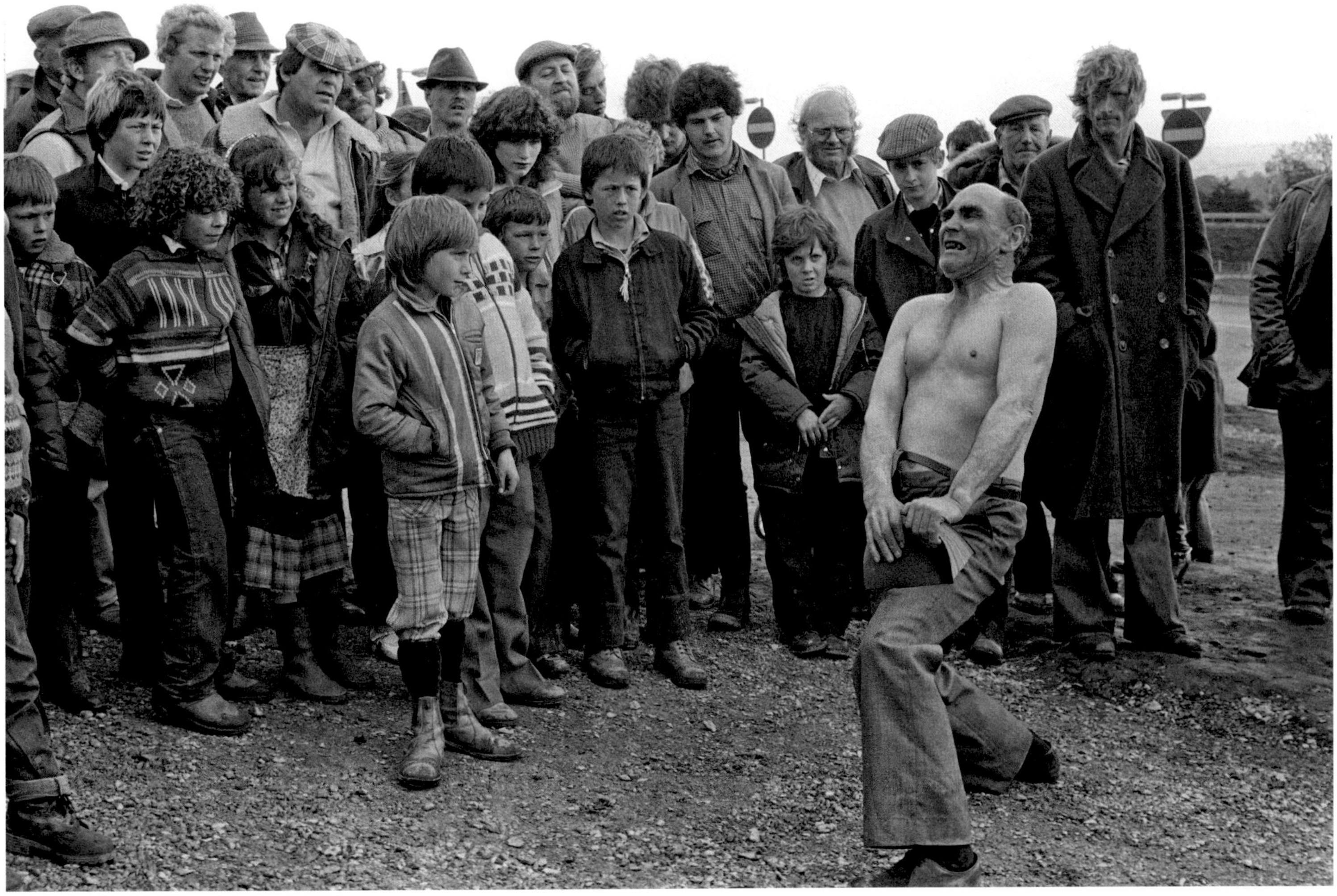

Appleby-in-Westmorland, Cumbria. 1981

Johnny Eagle, a well-known gypsy strongman, puts on a show for a crowd of travellers.

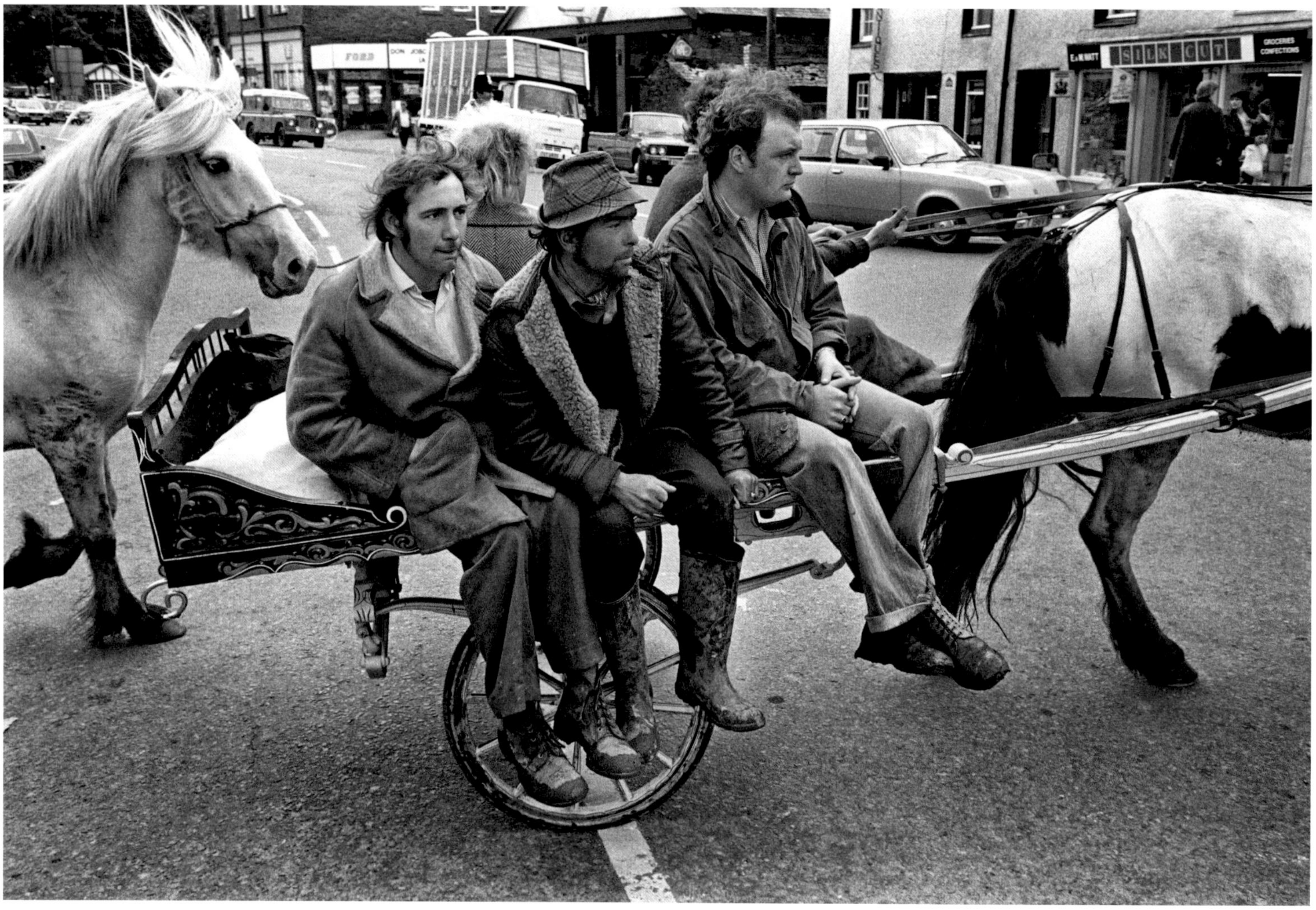

Appleby-in-Westmorland, Cumbria. 1981

Travellers arrive in Appleby town, for the annual Horse Fair.

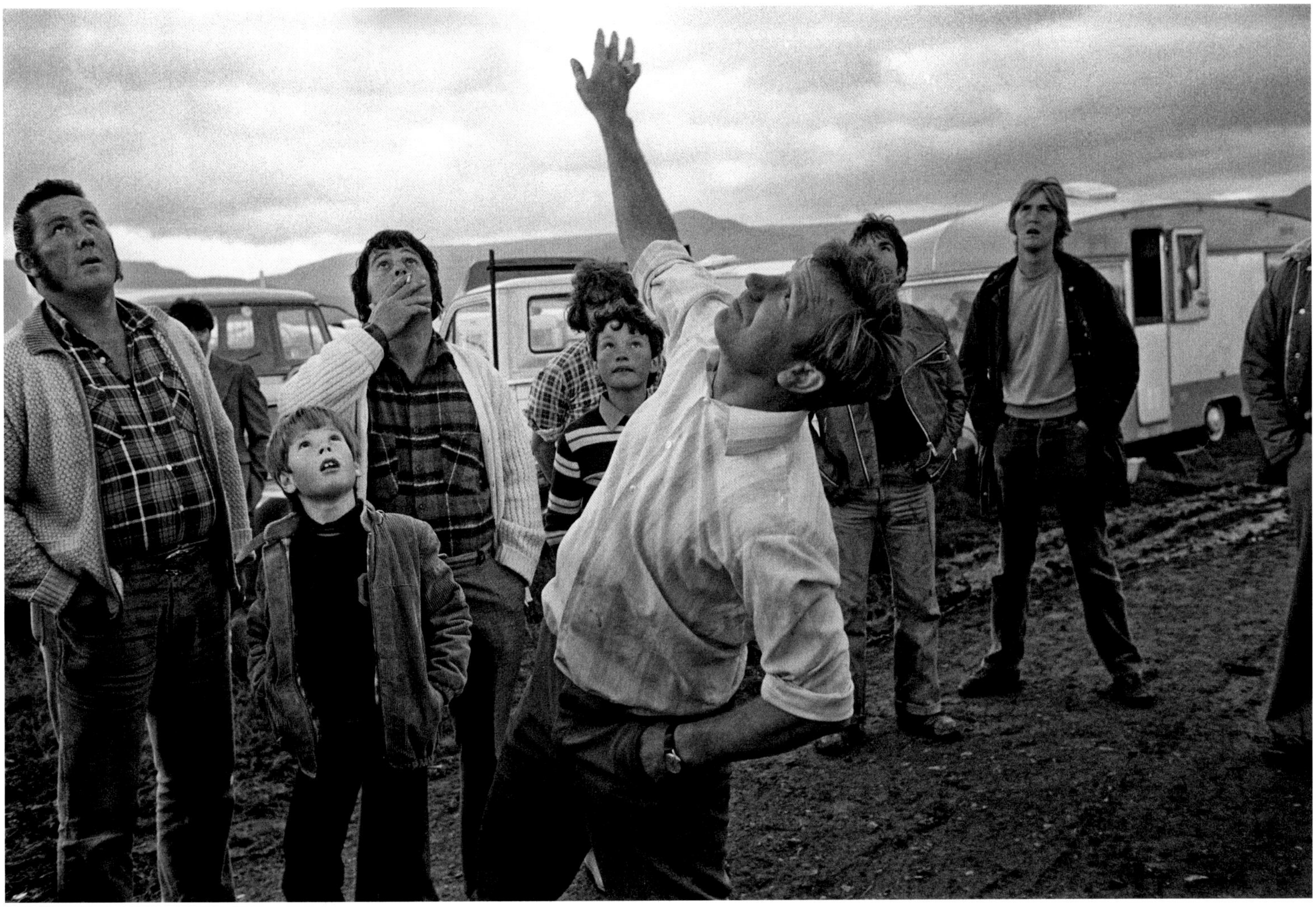

Appleby-in-Westmorland, Cumbria. 1981

Spinning pennies. A traveller throws two pennies up in the air in a game of chance. If both coins land heads up or tails up, you win depending on your call. If one is heads and the other tails then everyone loses apart from the thrower-upper of the coins.

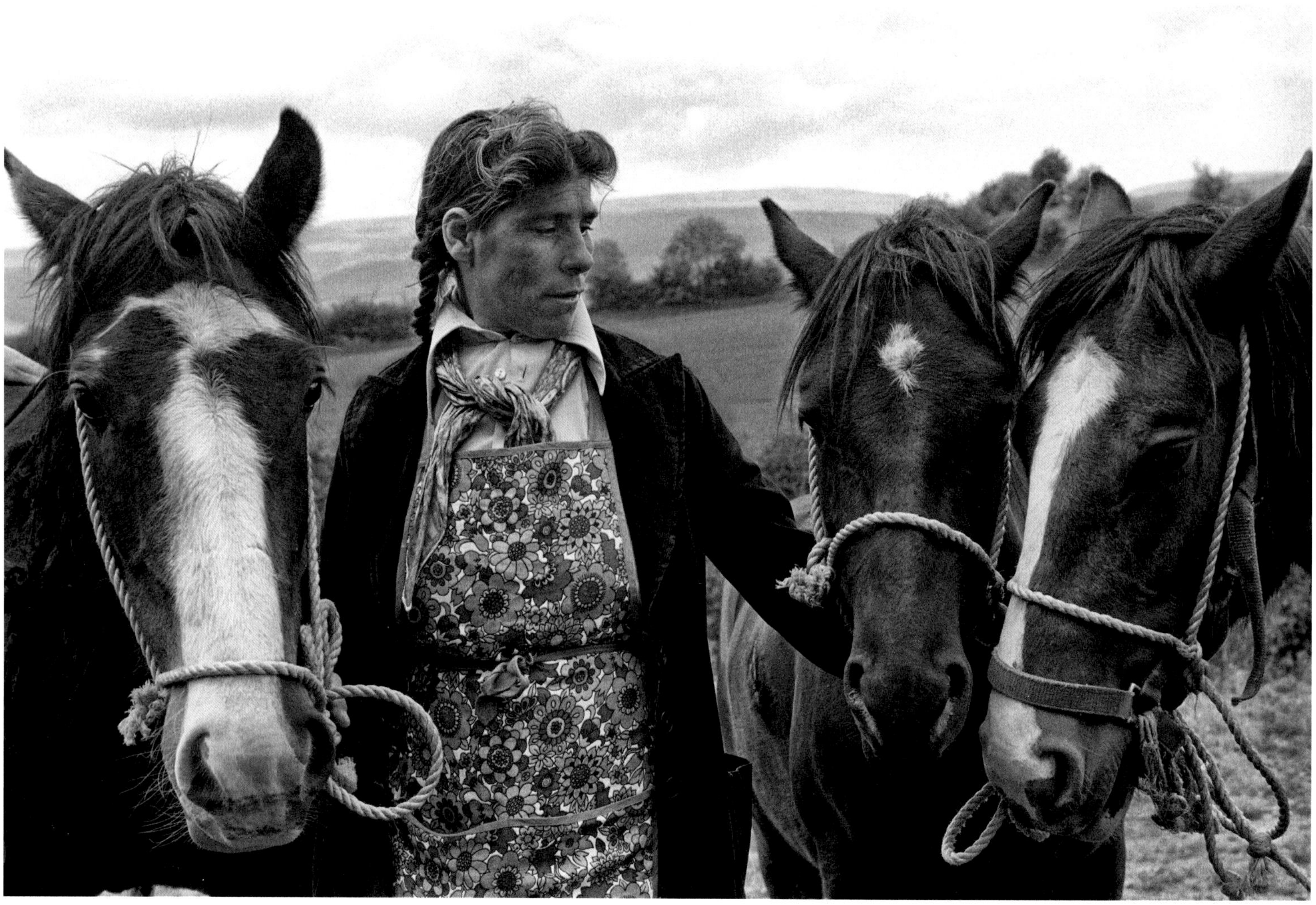

Appleby-in-Westmorland, Cumbria. 1981

A Roma woman in apron and traditional loosely tied neck scarf showing horses that are for sale.

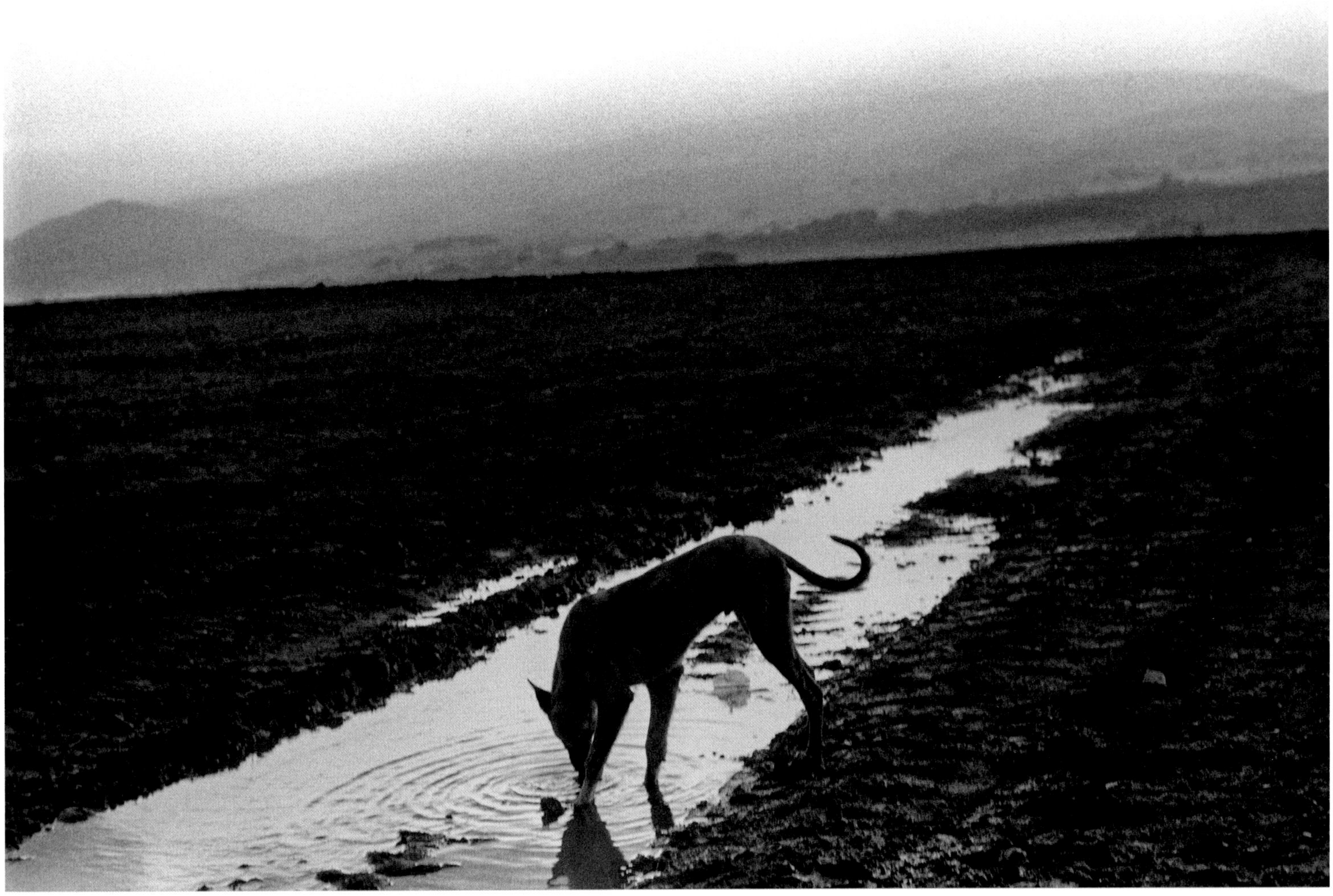

Appleby-in-Westmorland, Cumbria. 1981

Dawn at Appleby Horse Fair, with mist on the hills. The dog is a lurcher, known as a poacher's dog, and traditionally a cross between a sighthound and another working dog breed.

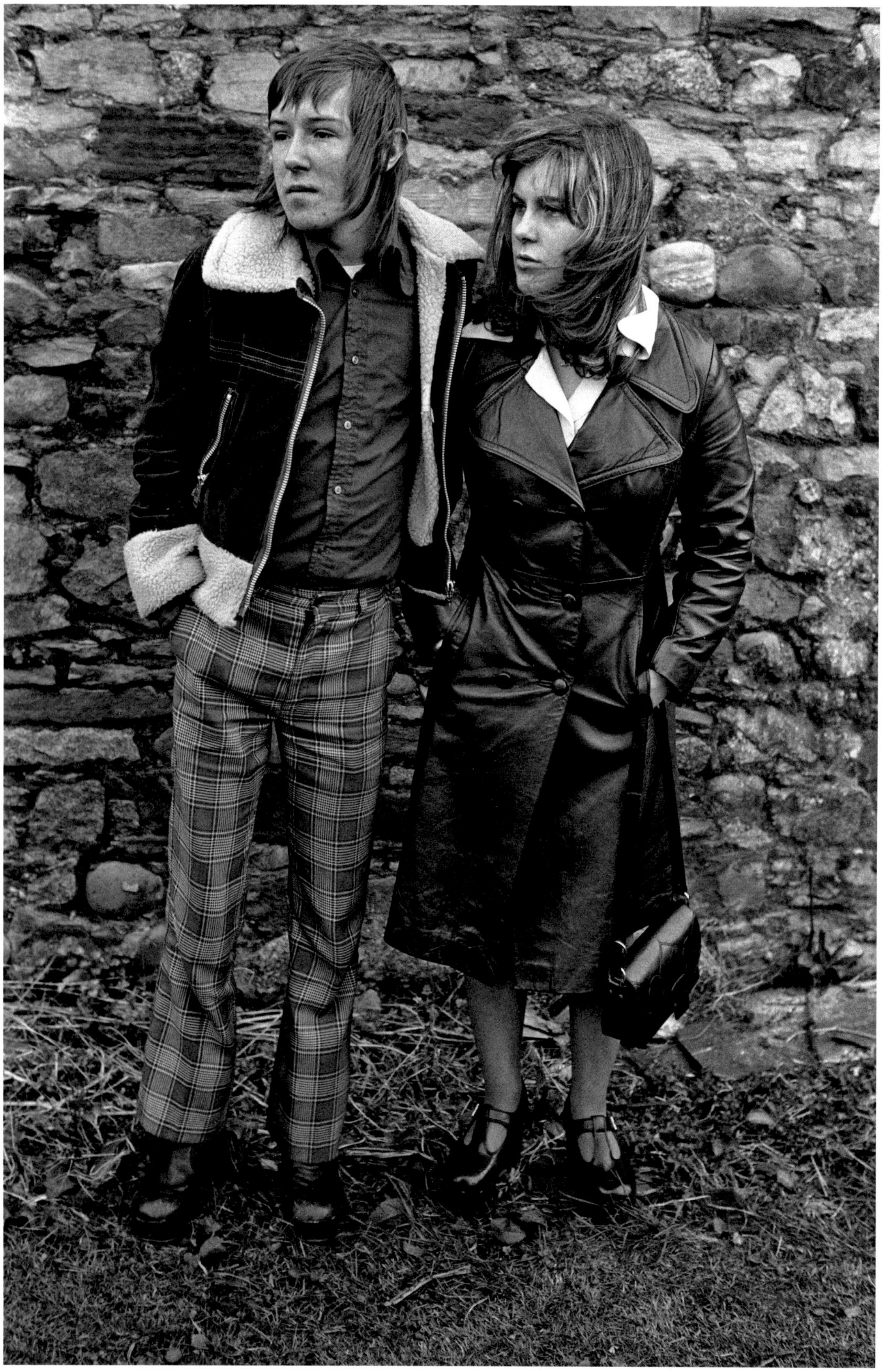

Workington, Cumbria. 1975

Margaret and Barry Kirkbride. He's fashionably dressed in tartan trousers that were made popular by boy band, the Bay City Rollers. Long hair, long leather trench coats and bomber jackets were all the rage.

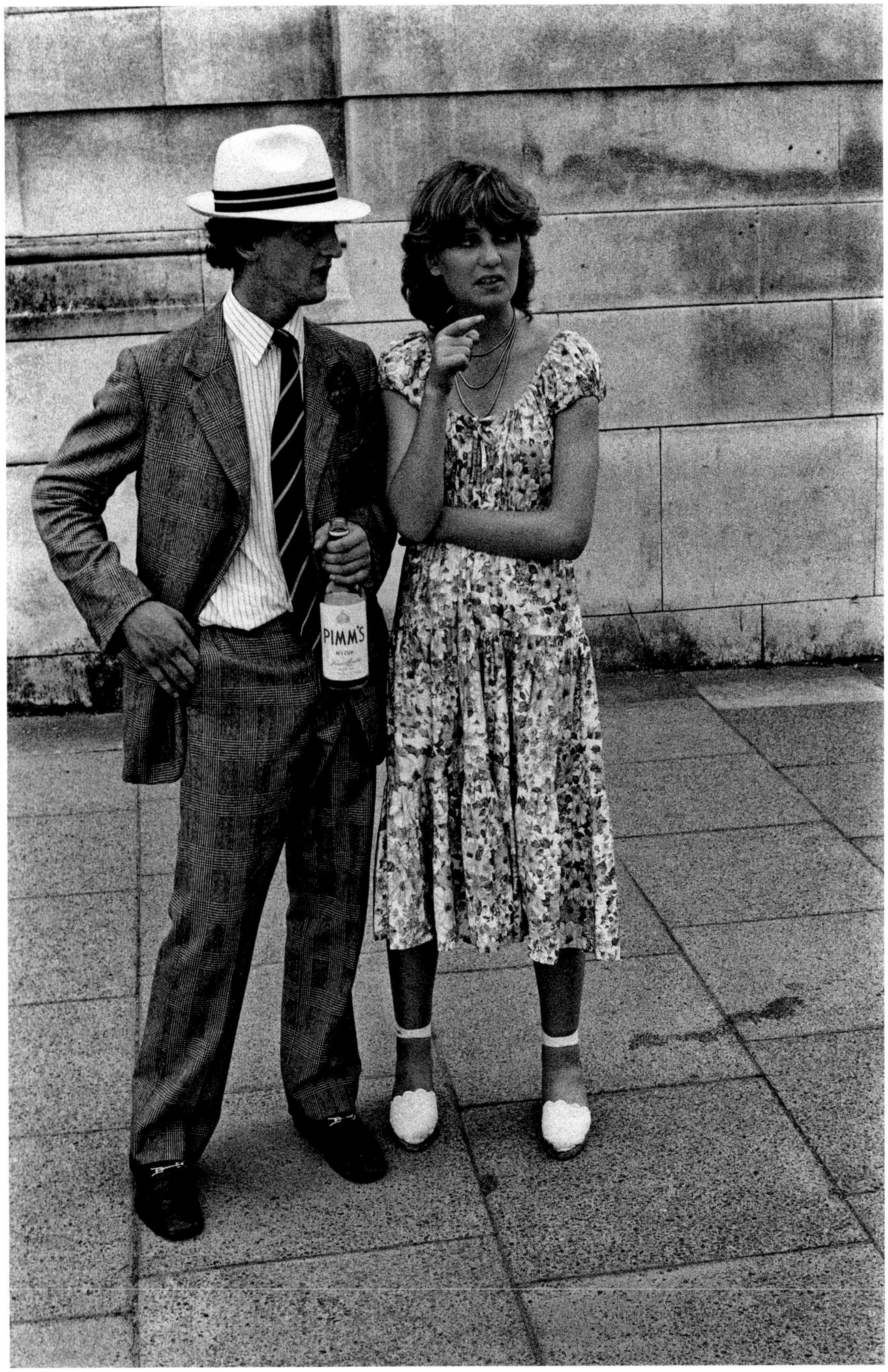

St Johns Wood, London. 1978

With a bottle of Pimm's No 1 in hand, an old Harrovian and his girlfriend make their way to the annual Eton v Harrow cricket match at Lords. He's looking posh in a Panama straw hat, and Prince of Wales Check suit and loafers. She's wearing a Laura Ashleyesque floral dress and espadrilles.

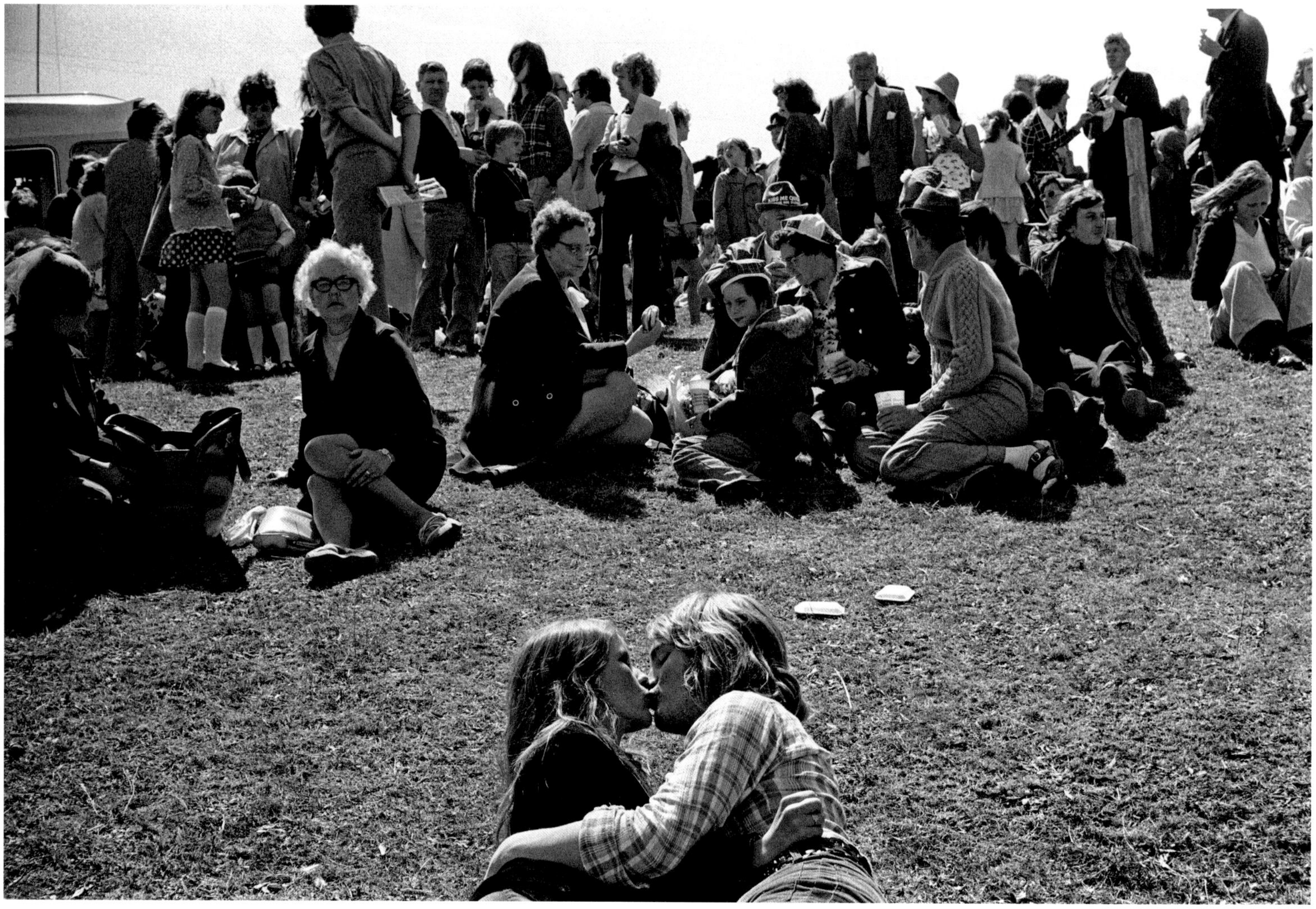

Durham, County Durham. 1974

A young couple share a kiss at the annual Durham Miners Gala. Started in 1871 it was the largest unofficial gathering in the country of miners and trade unionists. At its peak as many as 300,000 attended.

St Johns Wood, London. 1975

In his dark grey school suit and cricket jumper she places a wedding band on his ring finger. Young lovers at the Eton v Harrow cricket match.

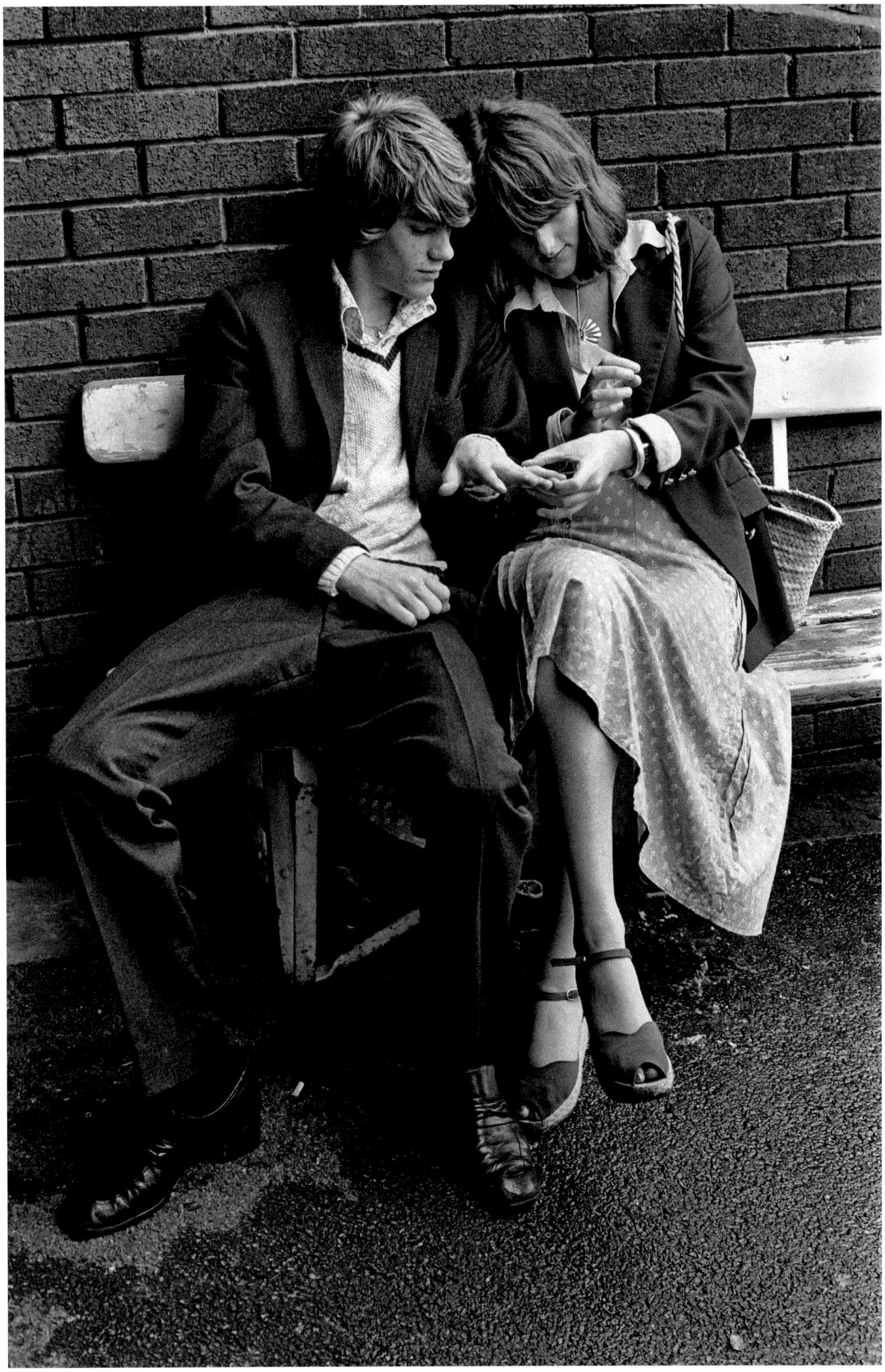

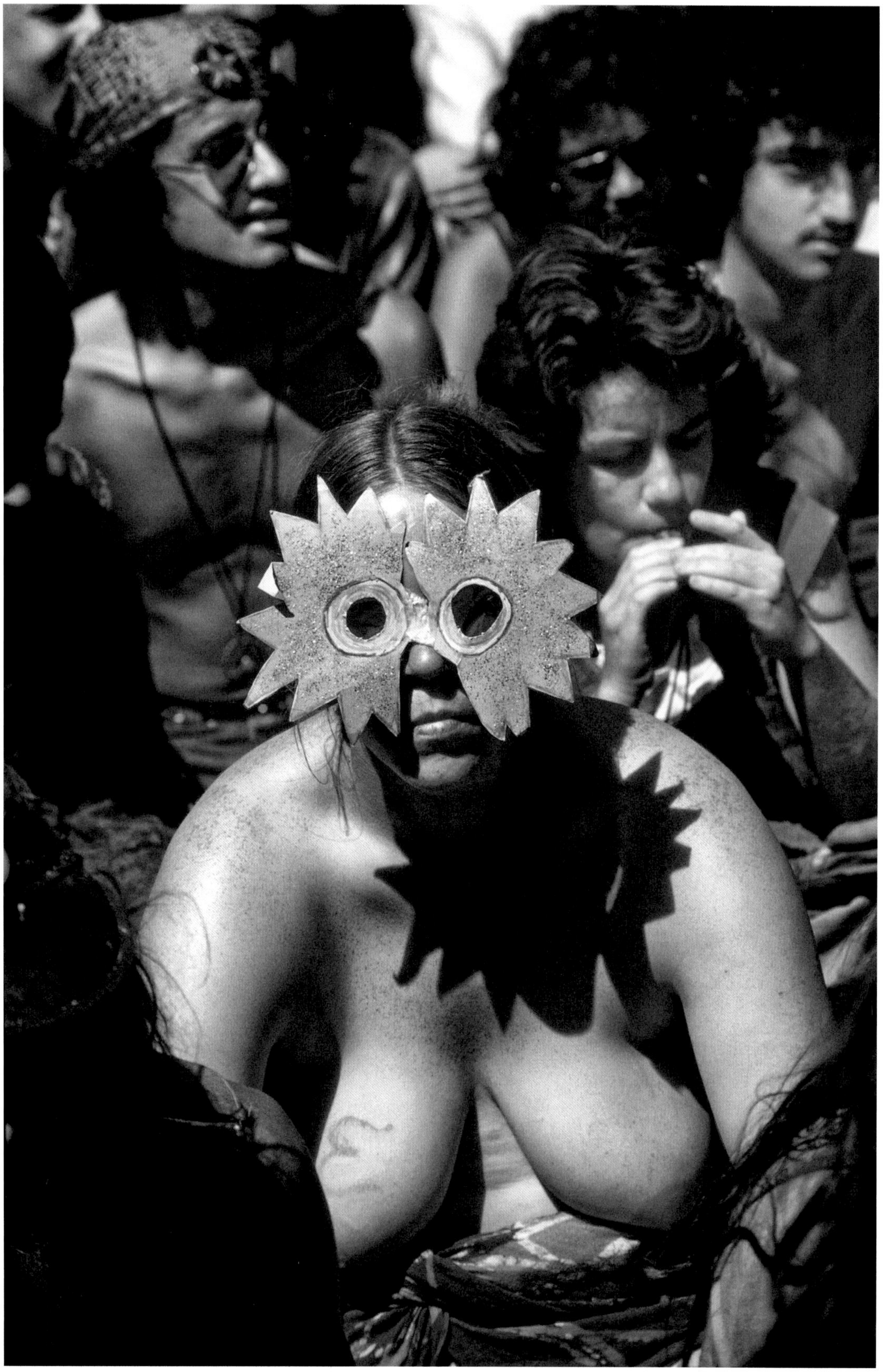

Stonehenge, Wiltshire. 1979

A bare-breasted hippy celebrates the Celtic mythological Sun god Belenus during the summer solstice on 21st June.

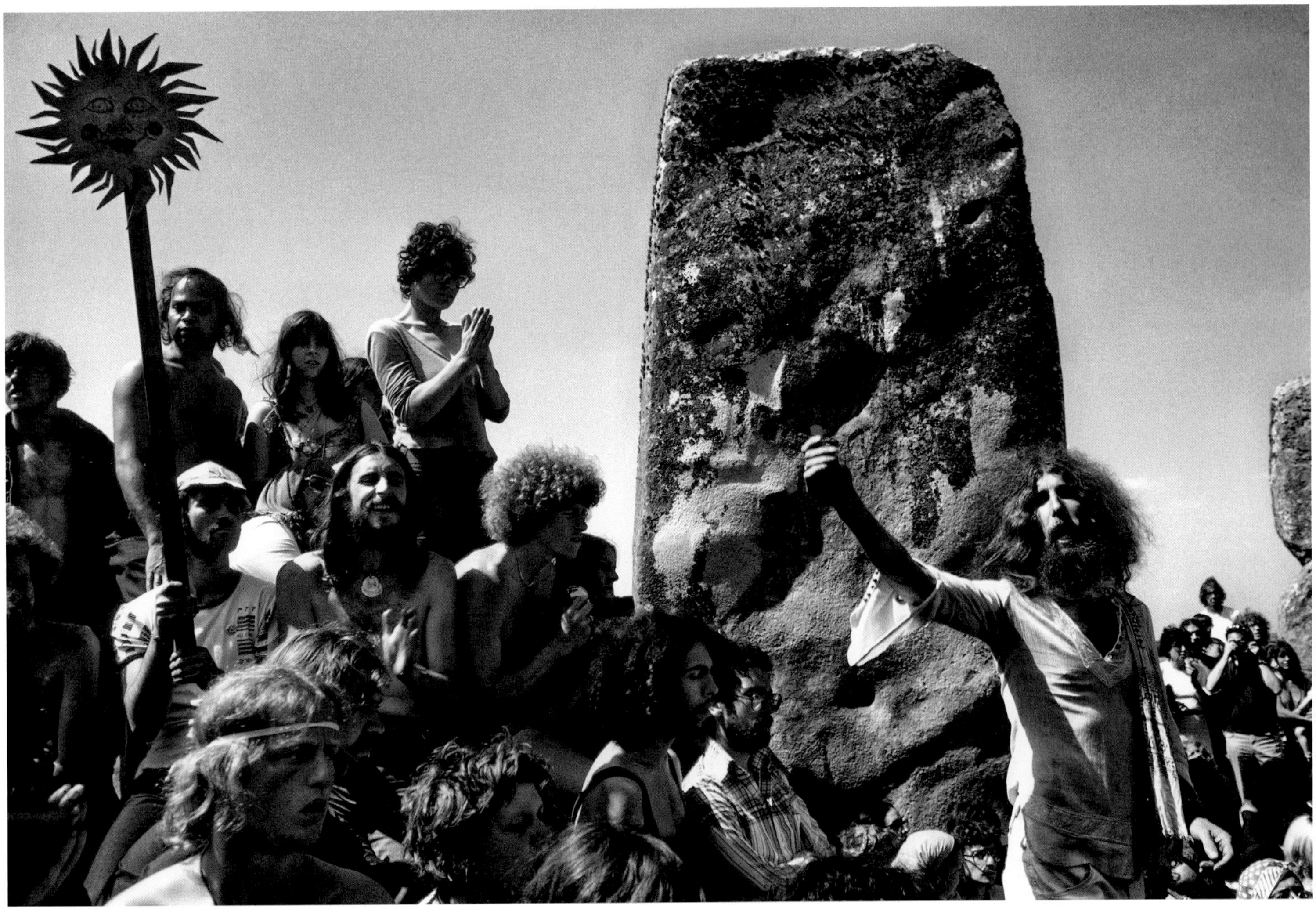

Stonehenge, Wiltshire. 1979

Hippies gather at Stonehenge to celebrate the summer solstice with John Pendragon, a much revered poet, songsmith and editor of *Tribal Messenger* magazine, which extolled the virtues of an alternative life style. He died in 1998 aged 59.

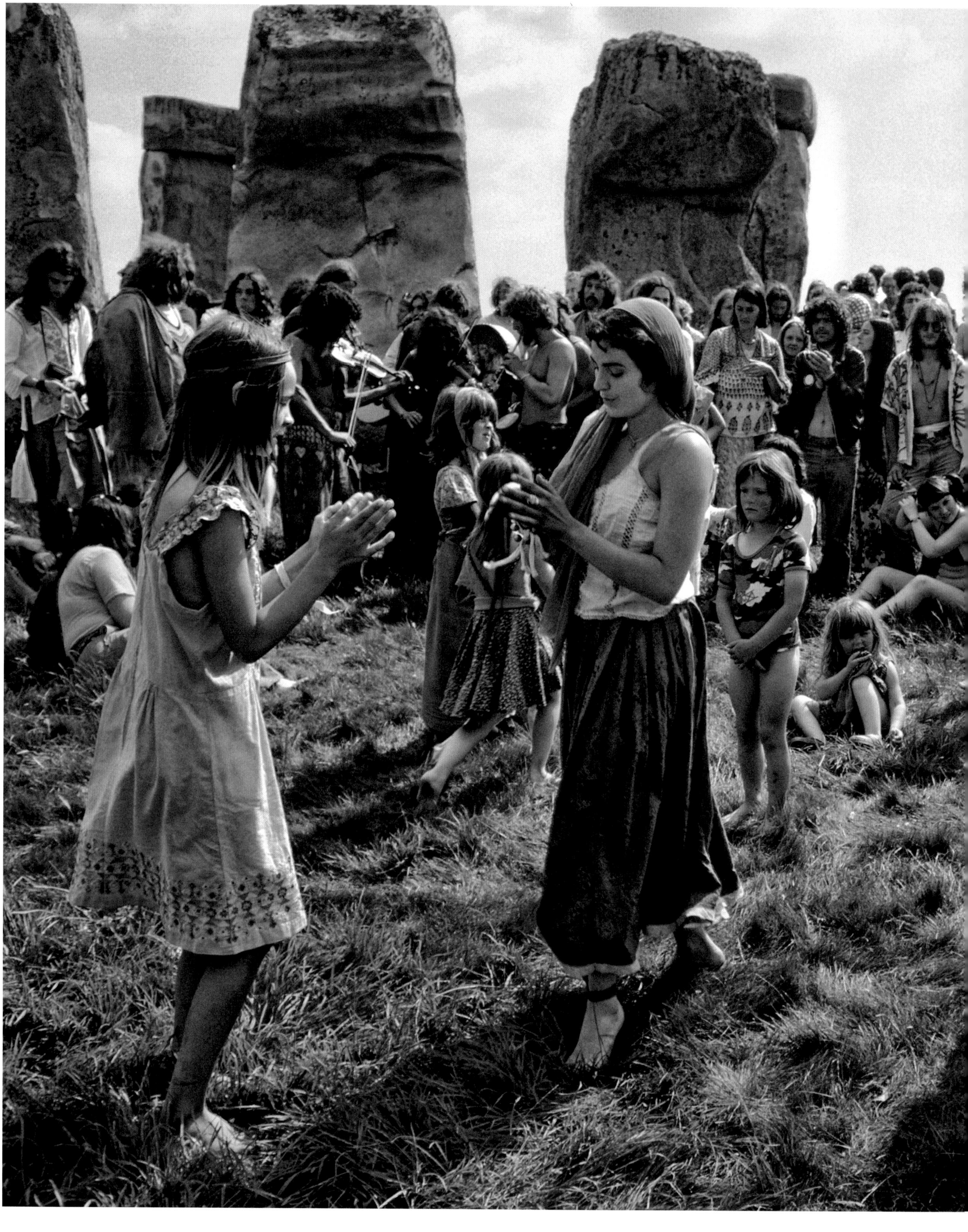

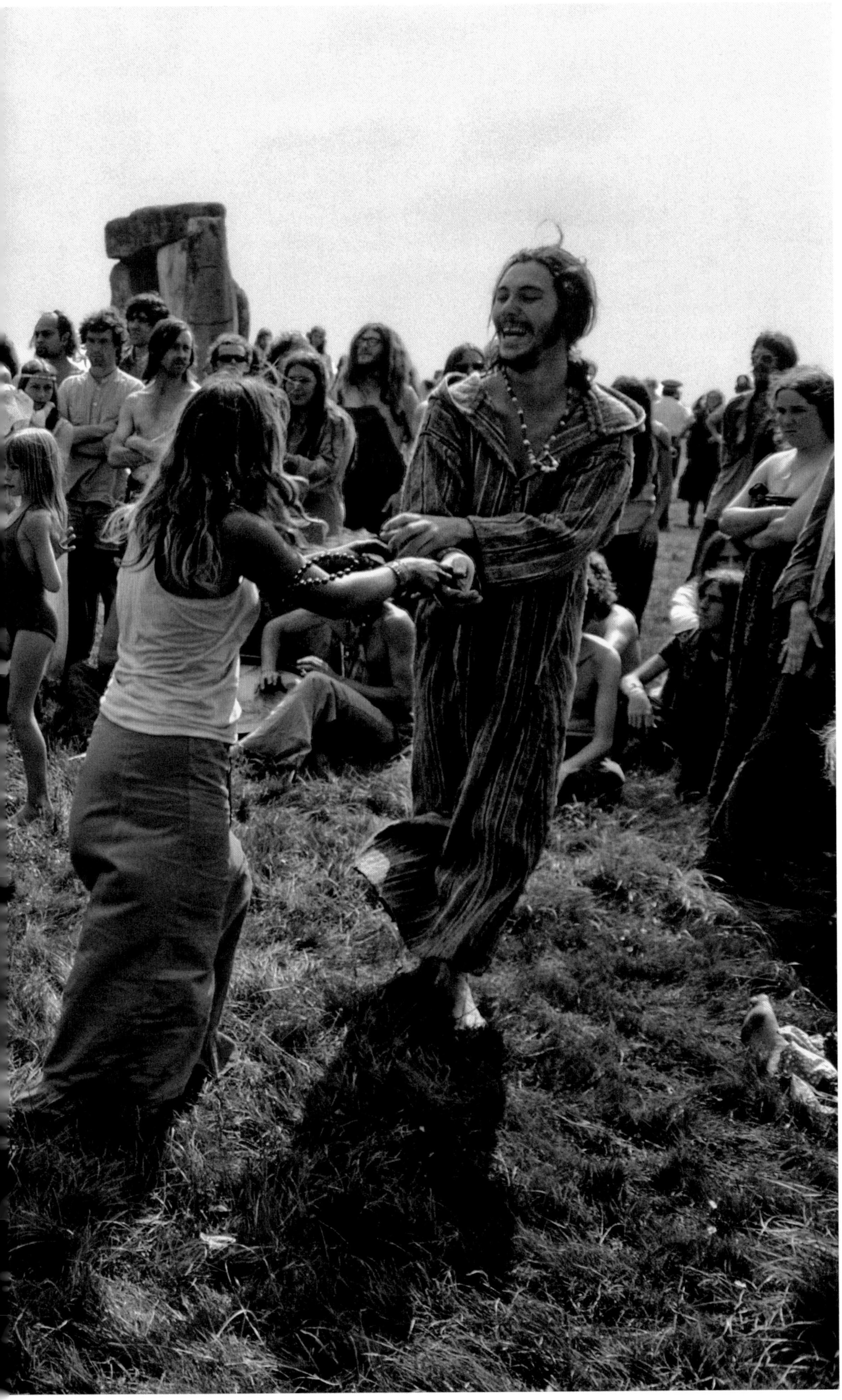

Stonehenge, Wiltshire. 1979

From 1974 to 1984, Stonehenge free festival was held over three days. It was a celebration of the summer solstice and the spirit of alternative lifestyles. By 1984 as many as 30,000 revellers attended.

Stonehenge, Wiltshire. 1979

Tourists, revellers and police attend the three-day free festival.

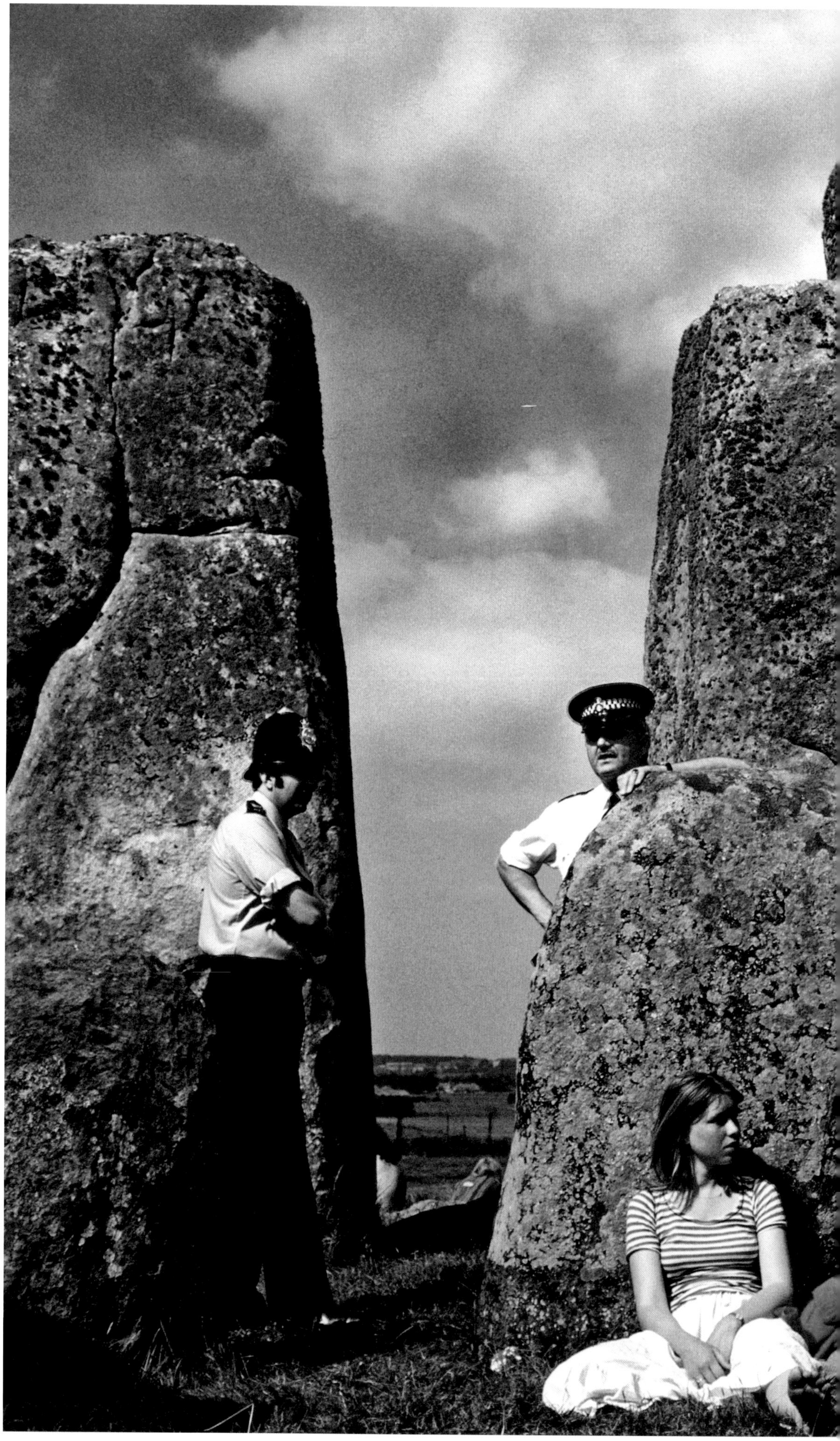

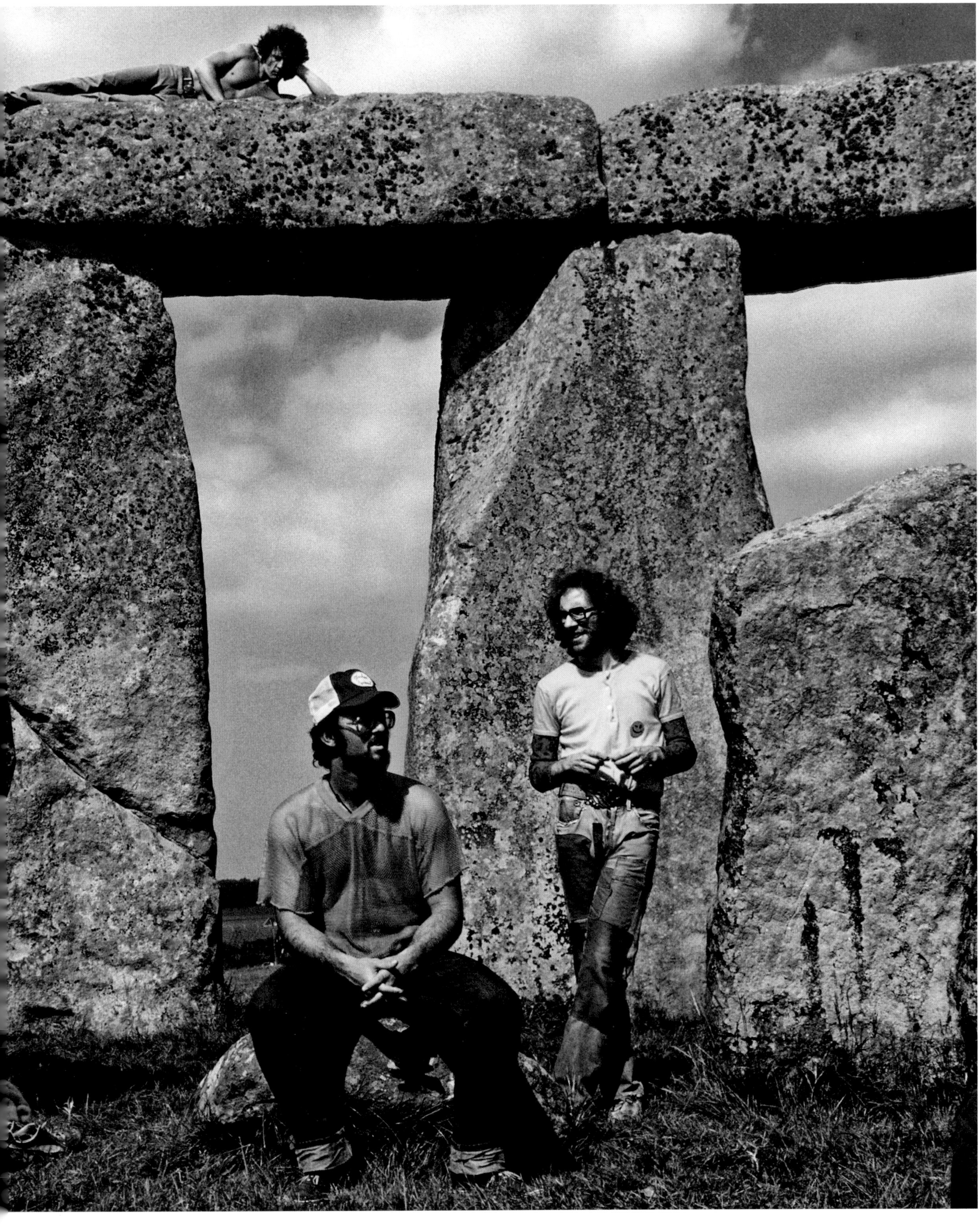

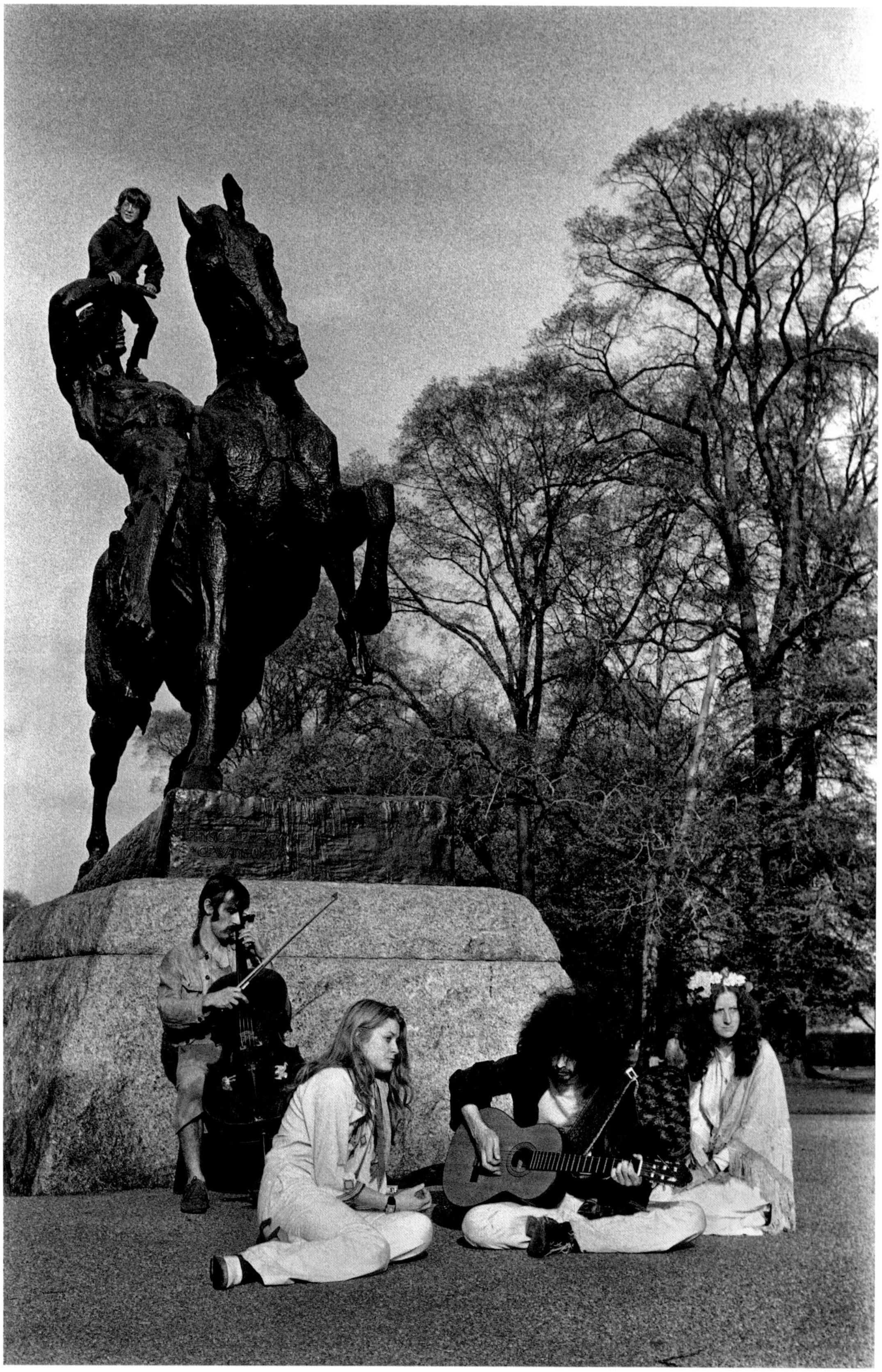

Kensington, London. 1971

Flower power; hippies in Kensington Gardens make music under the Physical Energy statue, by George Frederick Watts, who said that it was, 'a symbol of that restless physical impulse to seek the still unachieved in the domain of material things.' Flower power was a term coined in America by the Beat poet Allen Ginsberg as a peaceful alternative to the Vietnam War. 'Be Sure to Wear Flowers in Your Hair', became the unofficial anthem of the 1960s counter culture movement.

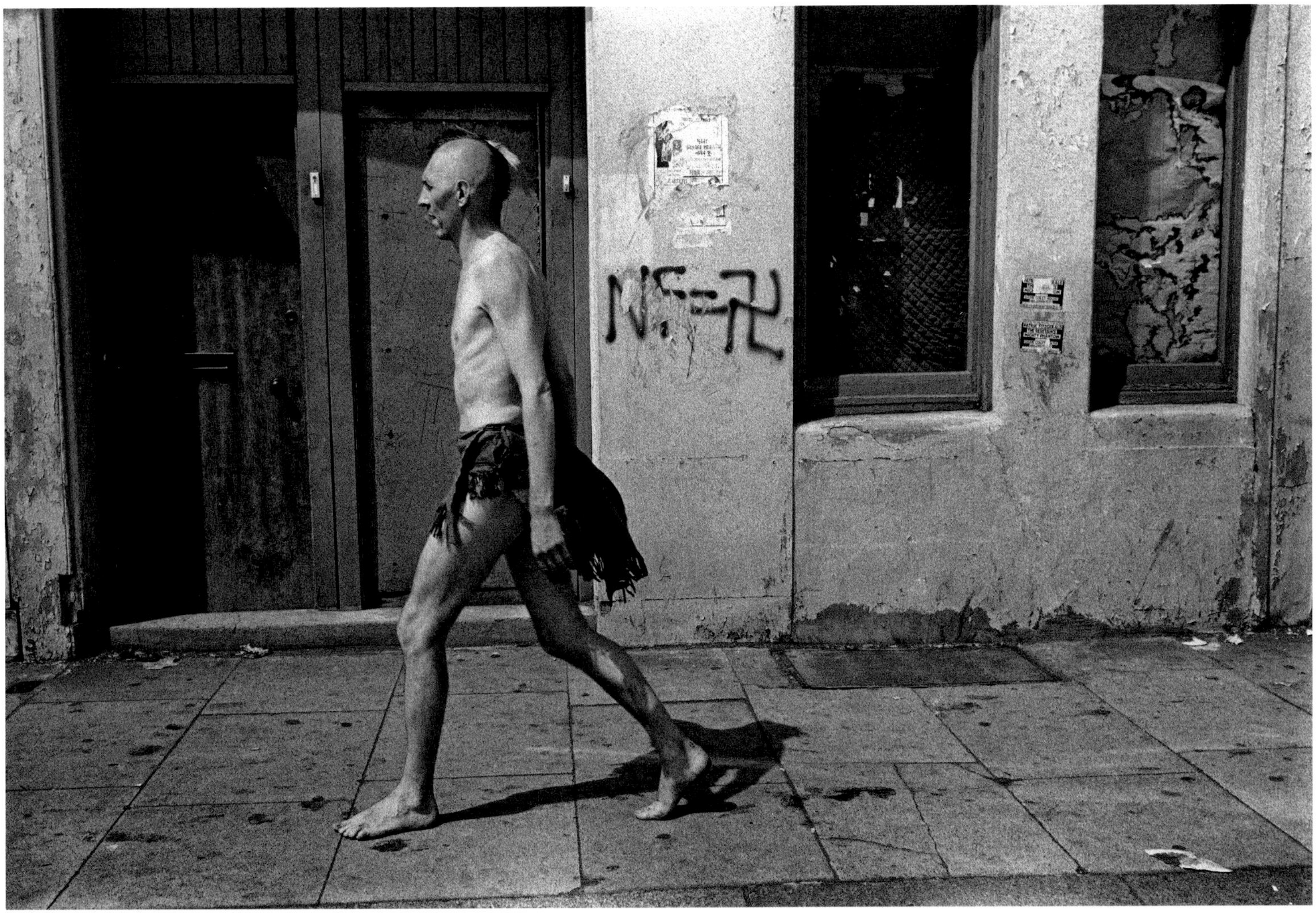

Whitechapel, London. 1978

An urban Red Indian in Bethnal Green Road. Graffitied on the wall is a 'NF' the initials of the National Front, an extreme right wing racist party and a swastika. Not, however, the Nazi swastika it was intended to be, instead the ancient religious icon, a sacred symbol of the spiritual principles in Hinduism, Buddhism and Jainism.

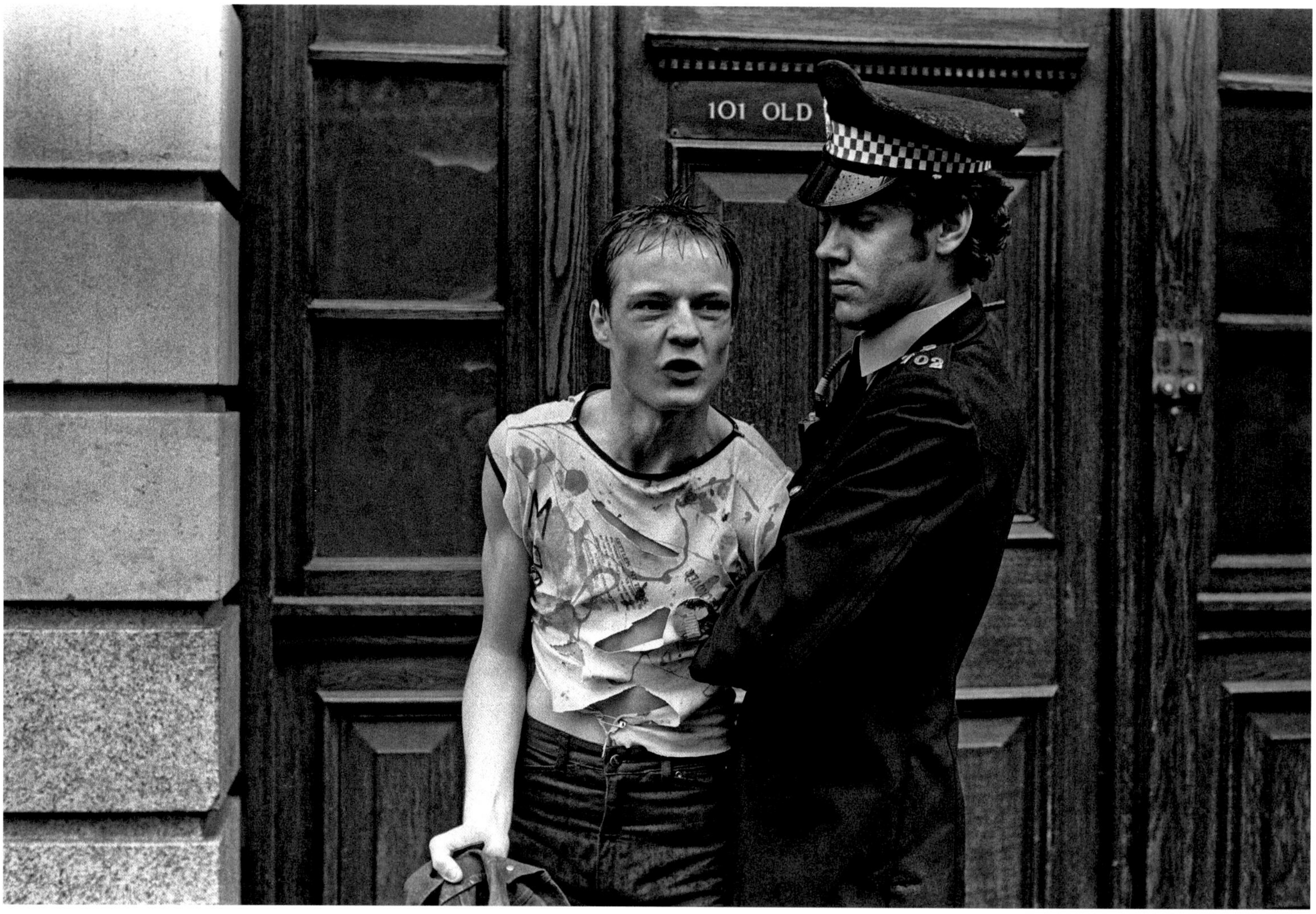

Chelsea, London. 1977

During the summer of 1977 Punk Rockers gathered each Saturday by the tube station in Sloane Square to walk down the King's Road, handing out flowers and blocking the free flow of traffic. There were occasional skirmishes with Mods who also turned up, and of course the police were there too. He is wearing a fashionably torn, and neatly pinned together, t-shirt from Smutz, which was upstairs in Beaufort Market at 374 King's Road.

Chelsea, London. 1977

A Punk Rocker waits thoughtfully at the bus stop in the King's Road. 'There is no future and England's dreaming ... God Save the Queen...' His pin button badges proclaim his allegiance to the Sex Pistols and The Roxy Punks Rule OK! and adorn a God Save the Queen Seditionaries boutique t-shirt designed by Malcolm McLaren and Vivienne Westwood based on a graphic by Jamie Reid.

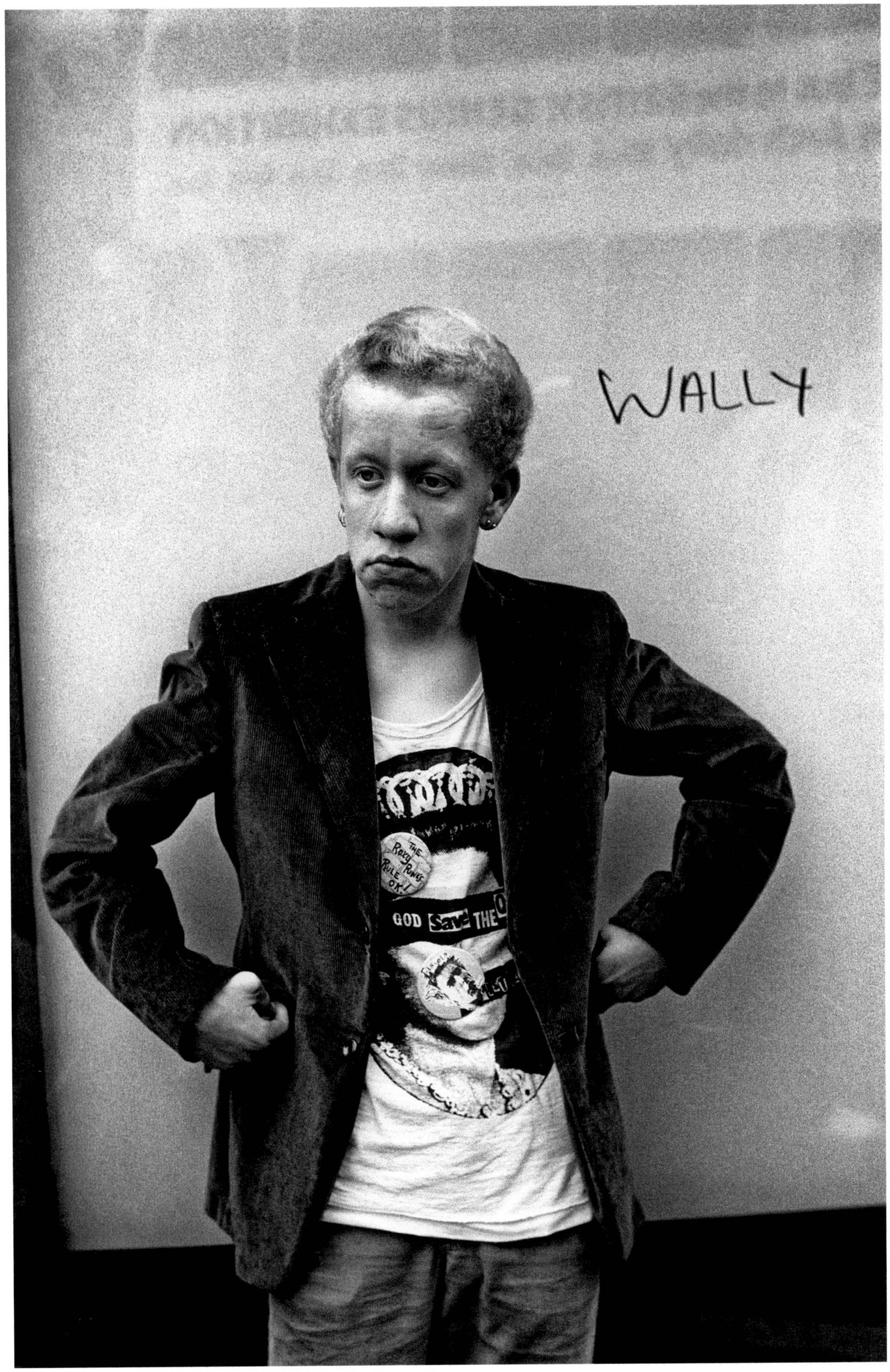

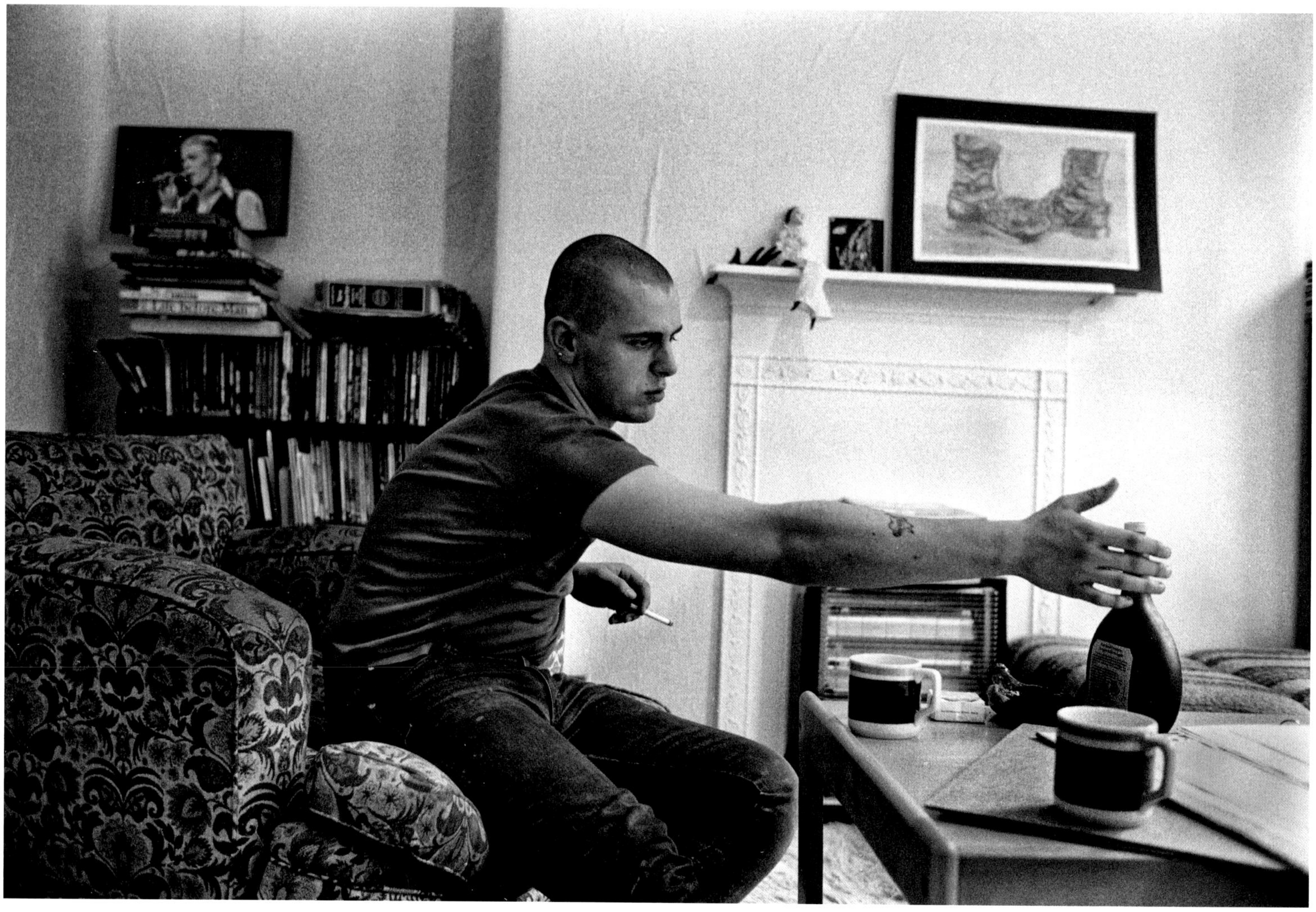

Tower Hamlets, London. 1980

Skinhead Jimmy John was a hospital refuse porter at the Royal London Hospital, Whitechapel. He liked to look tough and smiled when he told me that people walking towards him often crossed the street to avoid his glare. At home he drank Mateus Rosé wine, a medium sweet Portuguese staple of the 1970's dinner party circuit, introduced into his milieu by his French girlfriend who thought of him as her Gift of God.

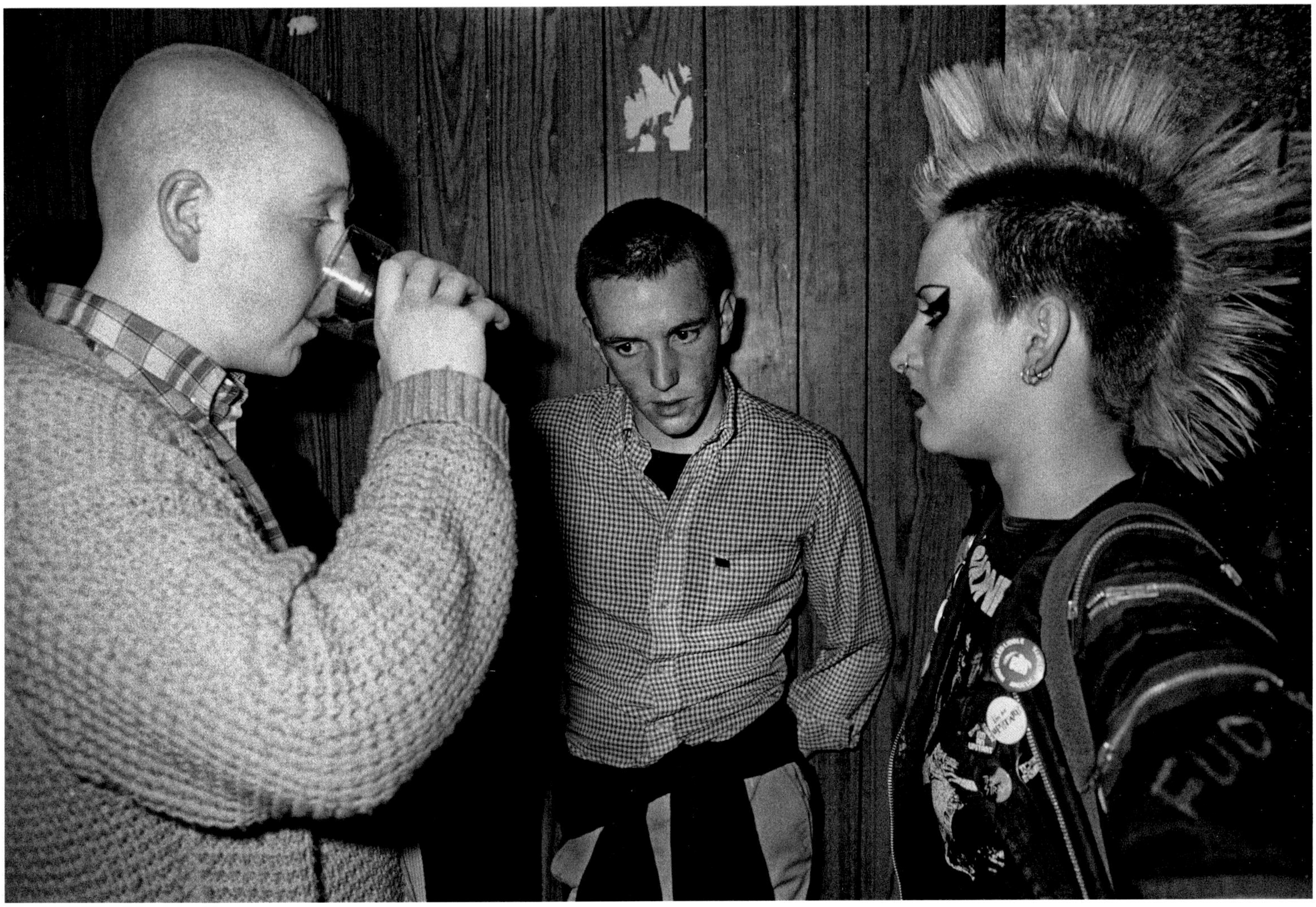

Camden Town, London. 1980

A skinhead, a suedehead and a punk, in the bar above the Electric Ballroom. In the late 1970s and early 1980s, at least three youth subculture groups were defined by hairstyle. Skinheads wore their heads shaven and were often considered tough and hostile; they wore tight short jeans and Doc Martens boots that were good for kicking people. Suedeheads were early Mods, but without the scooter and parka. They wore their hair a little longer and had an interest in fashion. And, of course, punks who wore their hair dyed and extravagantly styled.

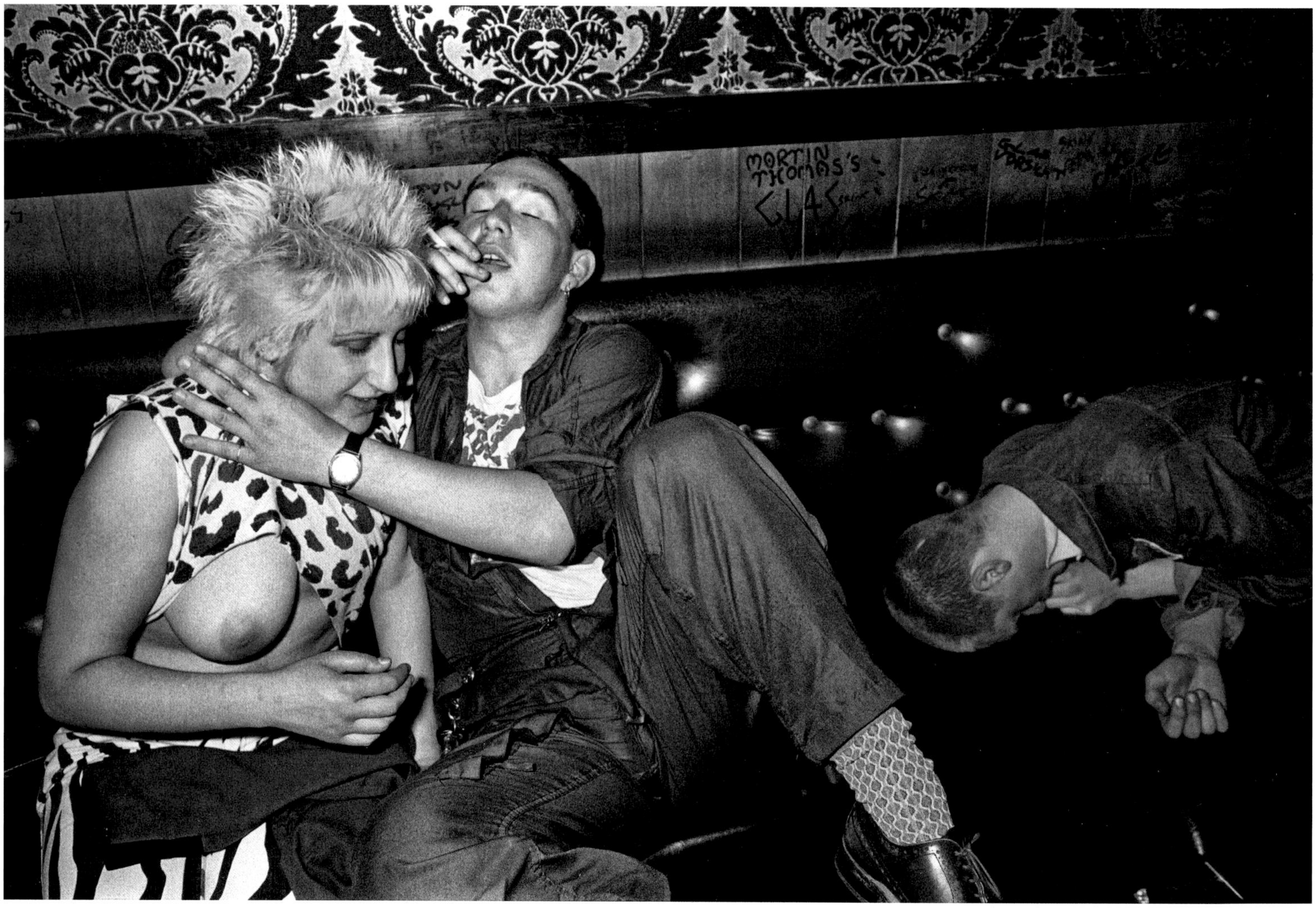

Camden Town, London. 1980

Three friends, drunk and high on dope in the bar above the Electric Ballroom after a UB40 gig. The British reggae pop band took their name from the Unemployment Benefit Form 40 that no longer exists.

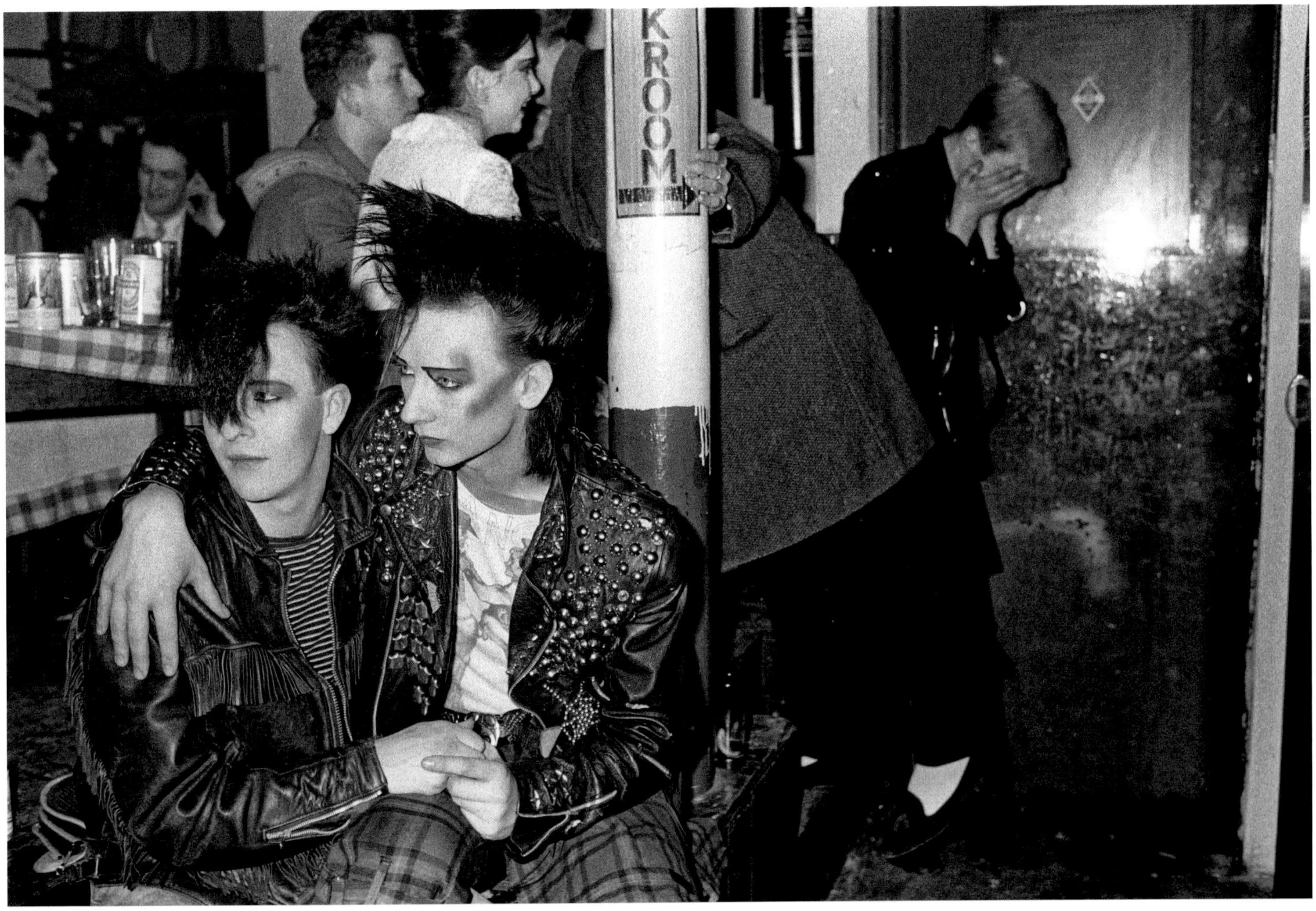

Covent Garden, London. 1980

George O'Dowd, later known as Boy George, with friend Wilf Rogers at the Blitz Club, where George was working as a cloakroom attendant. He is wearing a Malcolm McLaren cowboy t-shirt based on a Jim French drawing, from Seditionaries, a Vivienne Westwood boutique at 340 King's Road, Chelsea.

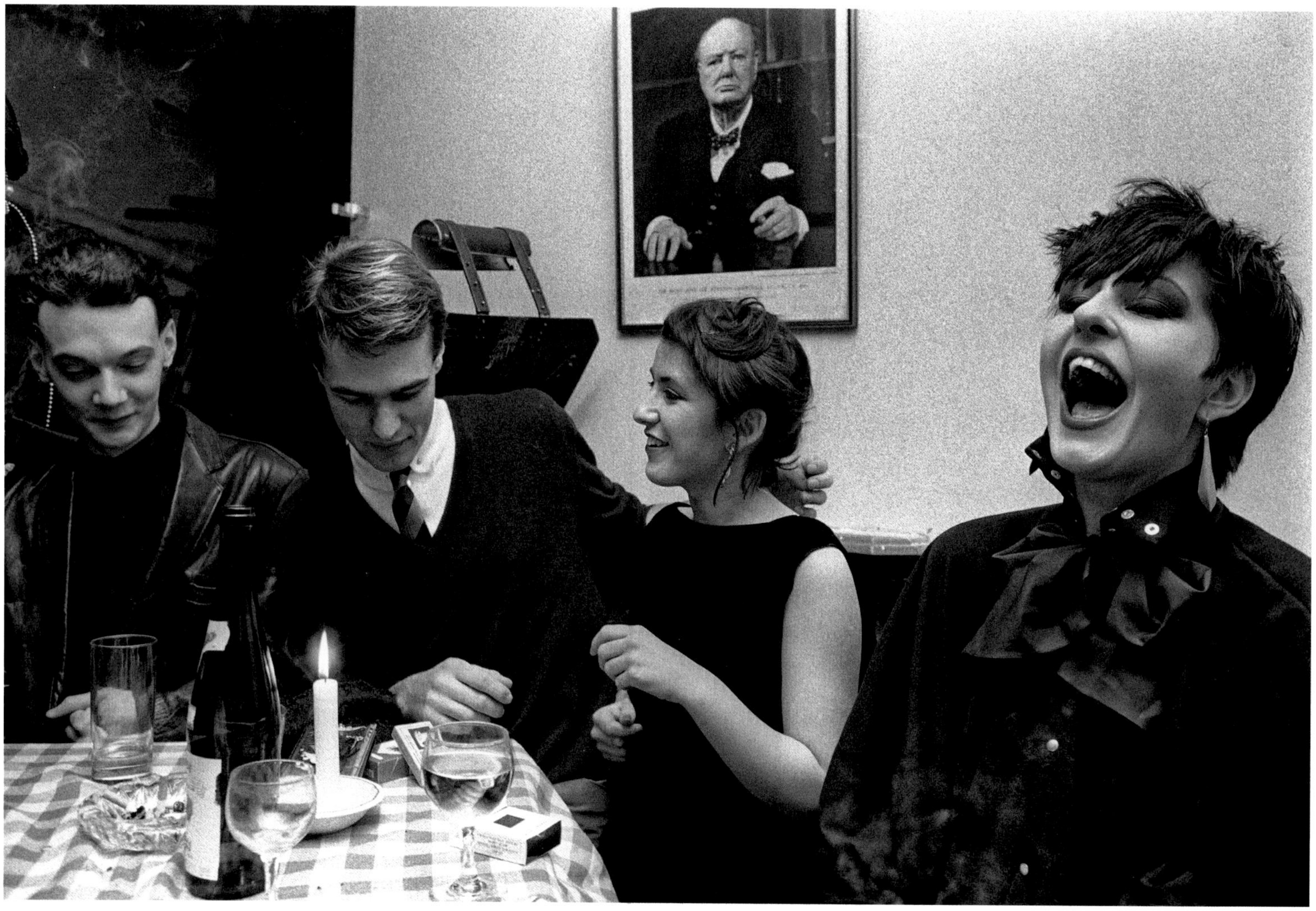

Covent Garden, London. 1980

By 1980 the Blitz Club had relocated from Soho, to a down-at-heel wine bar in Great Queen Street, which was decked out in Second World War posters and a photograph of Prime Minister, Winston Churchill.

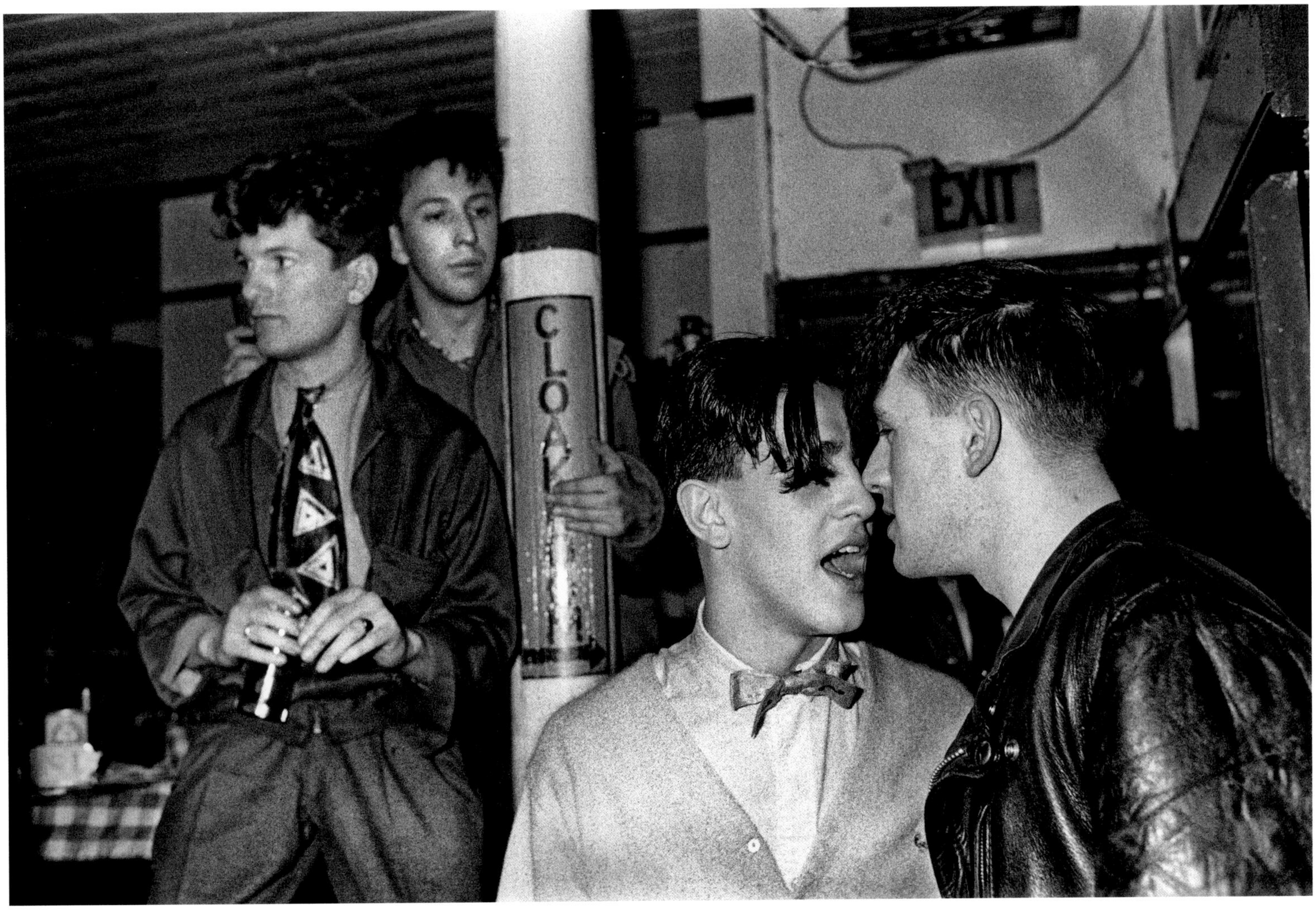

Covent Garden, London. 1980

Friends and onlookers at the Blitz Club.

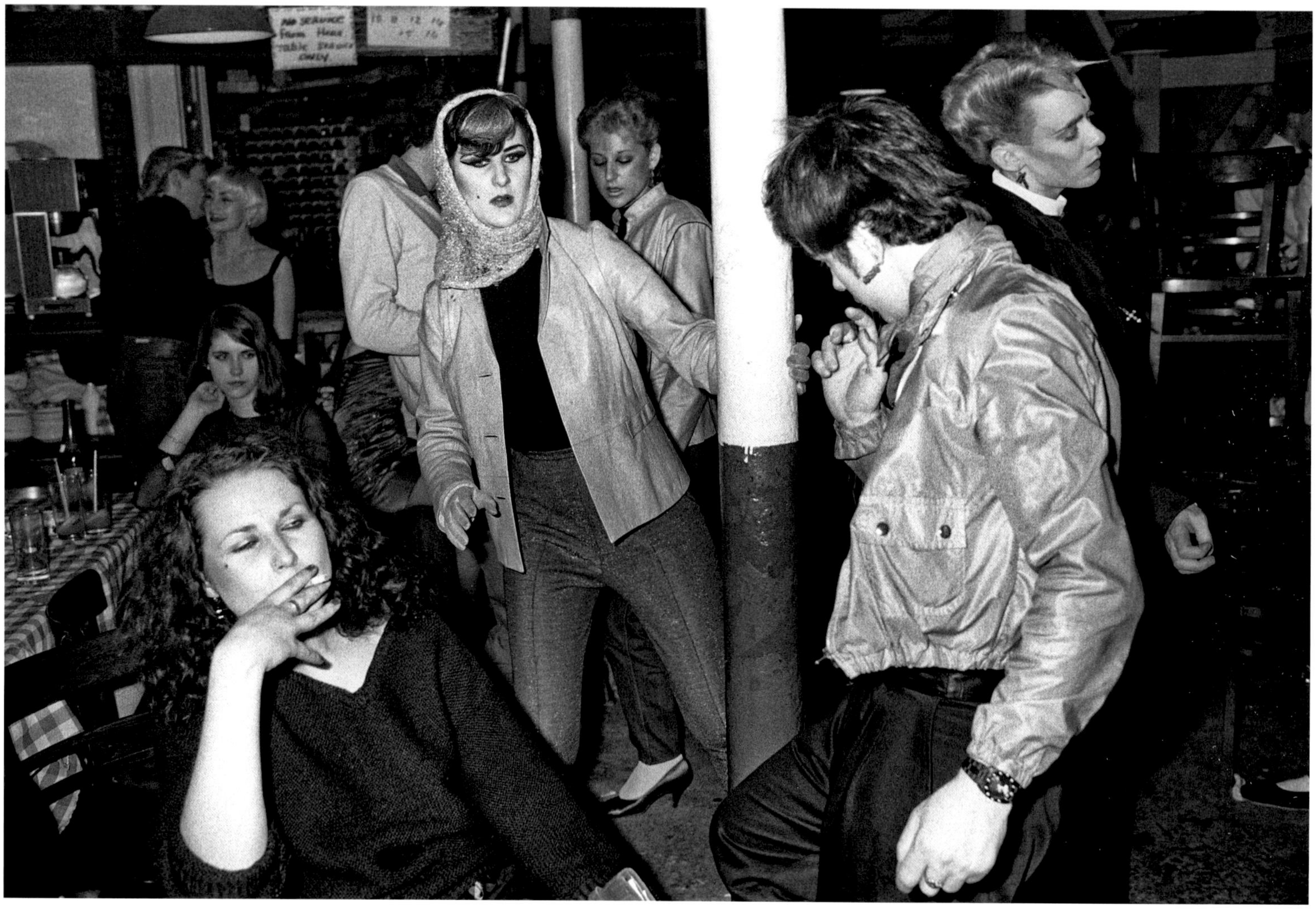

Covent Garden, London. 1980

The Blitz Club was a once a week club situated between two of London's most important art schools, St Martins and the Central School. Many fashion students, who had become fed up with the punk genre, frequented it. They wanted to express themselves differently; many in a more androgynous way. The Blitz Club was a test bed for their fashion ideas. This new look later became known as the New Romantic movement.

Covent Garden, London. 1980

Seen here strutting her stuff at the Blitz Club, fashion student and rock angel Wendy TigerPearson worked at Granny Takes a Trip in the King's Road, Chelsea. She was also a dancer at the Embassy nightclub in Bond Street.

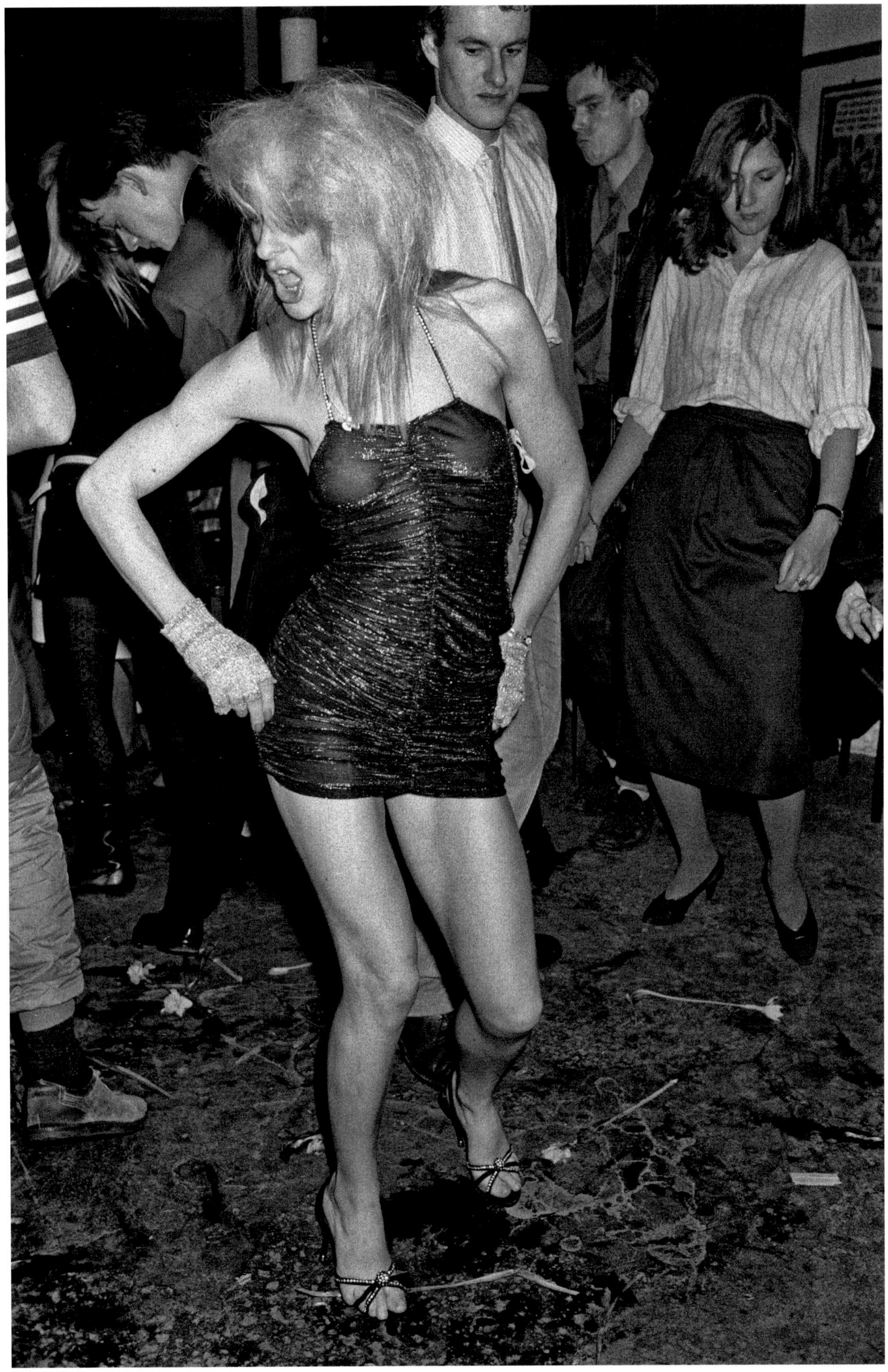

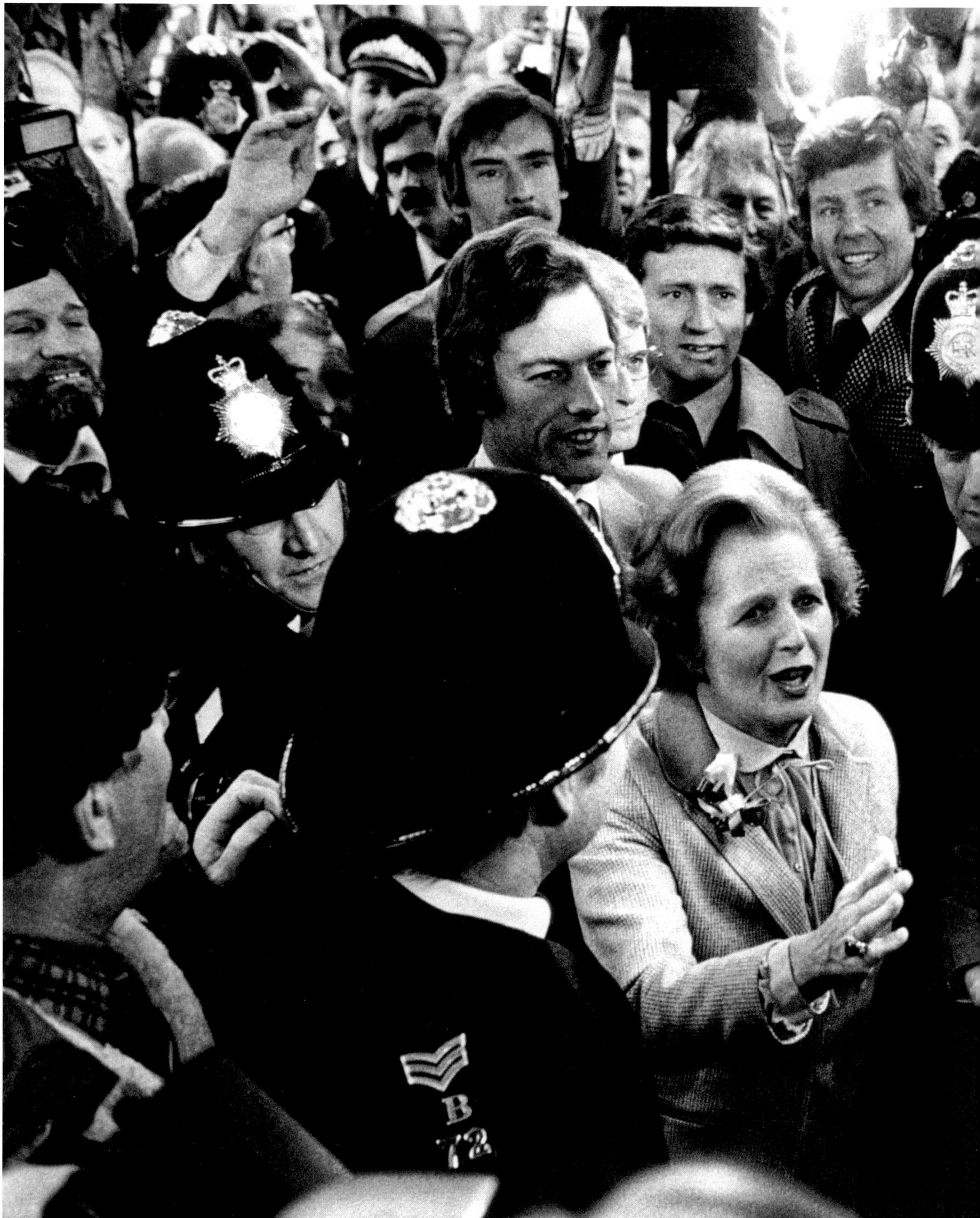
B
72

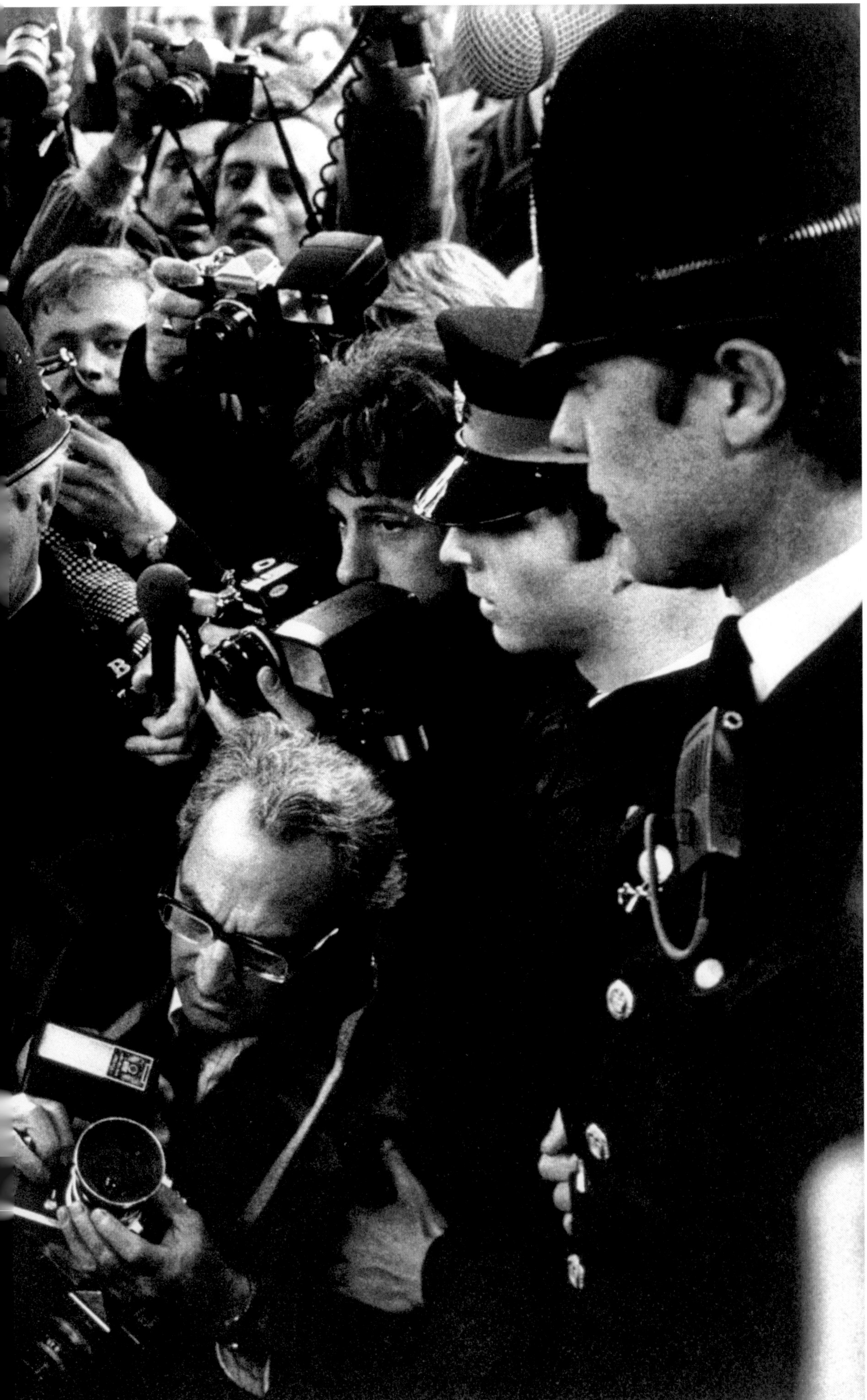

Chelsea, London. 1979

The 3rd May, Mrs Margaret Thatcher followed by her son Mark, meets the press as she goes to cast her vote in the General Election at Chelsea Town Hall. The next day the Conservative Party victory was announced making the Iron Lady, Britain's first female Prime Minister.

ACKNOWLEDGEMENTS

I would like to thank everyone who appears in this book. Of course, most of my subjects didn't know that I had taken their photograph and still don't. However, from time to time, I get emails saying: that's me, that's my mum and dad. She's my nan, sadly she's recently died ... can I have a print or scan please? Yes, of course, you can.

I would like to thank Juliet Sykes, who put up with me constantly travelling and working on a wing and a prayer, while she in the main brought up our young family. While going through my diaries of the time, checking dates and information, I found an entry for 27th December 1976 which she had written, and which I had not seen before, 'Your 2nd child is expected'.

Most of these photographs were self-assigned, but I would like to thank in particular my great friend, commissioning editor and art director Peter Baistow (1941-2013) who at *New Society* magazine, assigned stories, bought stock and generally encouraged me. And, of course, the many editors and agents who I worked with and who kept me very busy on assignments throughout those first fifteen years.

Michael Houlette of Maison de la Photographie Robert Doisneau, Paris. His interest in my early documentary work, and the 2014 retrospective that he gave me, reawakened a determination to make my various bodies of work, that had largely been forgotten, more accessible to a new and younger audience.

Geoff Howard, a fine photographer, a loyal friend for over half a century.

I would also like to thank everyone who has made contact; helping me with the names of some people I photographed, as well as providing additional caption information.

Christine Binnie, Ishmahil Blagrove, Jill Clapham, Maryjane Coleman, Darran Cowd, Leah Elsey, Bernadette Foulkes, Mike Golding, Paul Gorman, Steven Harris, Robert Johnson, Wilma Johnson, Gabe Mcauley, David Papadopoulos, Karen Peacock, Wendy Pearson, Erin Pissey, Rick Smallman, Caroline Swan, Bryan Thomas, Vanessa Toulmin, Wendy Waller and the many contributors to the invaluable Wikipedia website.

Once again I am grateful to Caroline Warhurst and Dewi Lewis who in 2016 published *Once a Year, Some Traditional British Customs*, a body of work that I created while working on this slow evolving project.